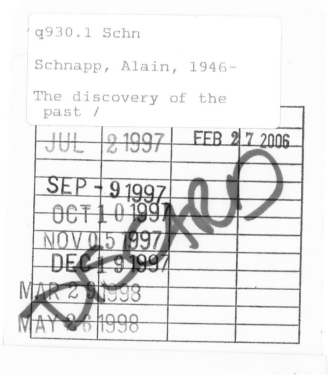

THE

DISCOVERY

OF THE PAST

THE

DISCOVERY

OF THE PAST

ALAIN SCHNAPP

HARRY N. ABRAMS, INC., PUBLISHERS

IN MEMORY OF BOHUMIL SOUDSKY

AND CARL-AXEL MOBERG

Translated from the French by Ian Kinnes and Gillian Varndell

Library of Congress Cataloging-in-Publication Data

Schnapp, Alain, 1946–
　　[Conquête du passé. English]
　　The discovery of the past / Alain Schnapp.
　　　　p.　　cm.
　　Includes bibliographical references.
　　ISBN 0–8109–3233–4 (clothbound)
　　1. Archaeology—History.　2. Antiquarians.　I. Title.
　CC100.S3613　1997
　930. 1—dc20　　　　　　　　　　　　　　96–29269

Published in 1997 by Harry N. Abrams, Incorporated, New York

A Times Mirror Company

First published in 1993 by Éditions Carré, Paris

Printed and bound in Spain

CONTENTS

ACKNOWLEDGEMENTS

The idea for this book was suggested by Henri de Saint-Blanquat. I began work on it at Churchill College, Cambridge, but without the help of Irène Aghion, Jean-Paul Demoule, François Lissarrague and Krzysztof Pomian, it would never have been written. Viviane Regnot, Guy Gagnon and Jean-Paul Desroches were unstinting in sharing with me their knowledge of the Chinese world, Sylvie Lackenbacher in that of Mesopotamia, and Dominique Valbelle and Jean Yoyotte advised me on the Egyptian world. Jean-Claude Schmitt and Michel Pastoureau were both tireless interlocutors in the exploration of the Medieval period.

At the Cabinet of Medals, in the various departments of the Bibliothèque nationale, at Cambridge University Library, at the Warburg Institute, I was continuously given help and the use of diverse facilities. It would be impossible to list all those institutions which have enabled me to complete this work, but I would like to record my debt to the Vatican Library, the university libraries of Heidelberg, Munich and Göttingen, the library at Wolfenbüttel, the Museum für Kunst und Gewerbe in Hamburg and the National Library of Copenhagen.

I would like to thank the following individuals for their help: Michel Amandry, Jean-Pierre Aniel, Daniel Arnaud, François Avril, Ida Baldassare, Ursula Baurmeister, Laure Beaumont-Maillet, Claude Bérard, Laurence Bobis, Mathilde Broustet, Monique Cohen, Marie-Hélène Colom, Richard Cooper, Monique Crick, Pierrette Crouzet-Daurat, Michel Dhénin, François Dupuigrenet-Desroussilles, Yves Duroux, Andreas Furtwängler, Pascale Galey, Jean-Baptiste Giard,

Michel Gras, Pier-Giovanni Guzzo, François Hartog, Francis Haskell, Jean-Louis Huot, Ian Jenkins, Athanasios Kalpaxis, Kristian Kristiansen, Max Kunze, Christian Landes, Annie-France Laurens, Emmanuel Le Roy Ladurie, Karin Lundbeck-Culot, Jean-Michel Massin, Cécile Morrisson, Tim Murray, Laurent Olivier, Ricardo Olmos, Pierre Pinon, Florence de Polignac, François de Polignac, Martine Prosper, Giuseppe Pucci, Joselita Raspi-Serra, Francis Richard, Jhon Scheid, Nathan Schlanger, Jean-Pierre Sodini, Alessandra Themelly, François Thierry, Gustav Trotzig, Sander Van der Leeuw, Jean-Claude Vaysse, Andreas Wittenburg, Richard Whitaker.

The English translation of this book was revised during my stay at the Getty Center for the History of Art and the Humanities at Santa Monica. I am indebted to Louise Hitchcock for her tireless support in reading the translation and to all the Getty staff for their continuous attention. I also wish to express my gratitude to the translators, Gillian Varndell and Ian Kinnes, and to Joanna Champness, the editor at British Museum Press.

PREFACE TO
THE FRENCH EDITION

The discovery of the past is not just the historian's definition of his own territory. Even the term discovery invites us to reflect on the motivation which, since the dawn of human consciousness and history, has led mankind to recognise, preserve and at times study the traces of his predecessors.

Alain Schnapp's book is a long voyage in time, a statement which on the surface may seem trivial. It is not sacrificed to the cult of discovery, the excitement of excavation, or the admiration of monuments; it seeks to understand rather than to recount. In a work which, in its time (1952), was a considerable publishing success, *Gods, Graves and Scholars*, C.W. Ceram (Kurt Marek) conquered a wide public in revealing the secrets of archaeological adventure. Alain Schnapp has chosen a different role. His book is not a history of discoveries but of their reception. Throughout his investigation he seeks to penetrate the mystery of the continuity of mankind in its pursuit of the past. Georges Dumézil coined the phrase 'ultra-history' for a particular method (his own), which revealed the structure of Indo-European myths from the most varied Eurasian narratives. In its turn the present work sees itself as 'a sort of ultra-archaeology'. What is the connection between Khaemwaset, son of Rameses II, Nabonidus, king of Babylon in the sixth century BC, Cicero, Saint Augustine, Petrarch, Rabelais and Boucher de Perthes, the founder of prehistory? Each, in his concern for the past, wished at some point to take a variety of information from the earth with a view to extracting – from the rough results of digging – a name, a date, a sign; in short, the material aspect of Clio.

History, such as it is still practised today, is a product (amongst others) of the Renaissance and the Enlightenment. Alain Schnapp, as a good archaeologist, rebuilds (or rather dismantles) the layers one by one and reveals so much the better the origins of archaeology, which are as old as humanity itself. A humanity which is not confined by the limits of the Graeco-Roman world. It embraces, in fact, the Egyptians, the Assyrians and the Chinese, those empires which had need of the past to ensure the present. This book is a sounding-board for debates, ideas and discoveries drawn from scholarship and historiography; it tries to reconstruct the often tortuous paths taken by men towards a better understanding of the infinite space of 'times gone by'. Ever since antiquity observers, thinkers and philosophers in China and in Greece, just as in the East, have had an intuition of the very long history of the world and of humanity. For over a millennium in Europe (from Saint Augustine until Darwin), specialists, learned societies and the ruling powers in particular, refused to allow that human history ran to hundreds of thousands of years, and that it was the heterogeneous prolongation of a still older venture: the history of nature. At the heart of this book the reader will discover the 'handful' of creative minds who, over the centuries, championed and finally established the idea of the great antiquity of mankind. So it is that the history of archaeology is a part of the history of humankind confronted by nature, or by the ideal which we create for ourselves.

The illustrations in this book owe much to the collections of the Bibliothèque nationale in Paris. The Departments of Prints, Manuscripts, Coins, Medals and Antiquities have been drawn on extensively. What could be more natural, especially for the Cabinet of Medals, the 'King's Cabinet', which can be taken for the oldest museum in France? Closely linked to it are the famous figures of the Comte de Caylus and the Abbé Jean-Jacques Barthélemy. Both (nobility and clergy) played in their time a decisive role in changing the perspectives of archaeology. They thus deserve to be cited as illustrious 'links in the chain' from the Bibliothèque nationale to the present work.

EMMANUEL LE ROY LADURIE
Professor of the Collège de France,
Director of the Bibliothèque nationale.

Piero di Cosimo, *Vulcan and Aeolus, the Teachers of Humanity*, c.1495–1500.
The invention of the arts which distinguish humans from animals was one of the
fundamental themes of Graeco-Roman anthropology and was strongly echoed during
the Renaissance. Piero di Cosimo, inspired by his reading of Vitruvius and Boccaccio,
devoted an entire cycle of paintings to these inventions. Here, Vulcan is shown at his forge
as the 'arch-craftsman and first teacher of human civilisation' (E. Panofsky). Piero di Cosimo
was an ardent advocate of a return to nature and led 'a life more bestial than human',
according to the portrait given of him by Giorgio Vasari.

ARCHAEOLOGY AND THE PRESENCE OF THE PAST

THE COLLECTOR OF ANTIQUITIES
In these decadent times we fall in love with antiquities and allow ourselves
– willingly – to be duped. We spend thousands on manuscripts and
paintings and hundreds more on authenticating them. Chipped jade
insignia, bronze seals decorated with turtles and dragons, bronze tiles from
the Bird-Tower made into ink-stones, all displayed on lacquered shelves;
golden incense-burners in the shape of a lion on ivory stands, a cup, a
goblet, any kind of antique vessel – and we comb the ancient texts in order
to verify the inscriptions. As if obsessed we search near and far, into our old
age. Blood relatives drag each other in front of the courts, close friends
mistrust each other. These things are bought for a fortune by the rich, but a
poor man would not part with a rice cake for any of them.

ZHENG XIE, 1693–1765, YANGZHOU, CHINA.

By what authority does archaeology exist, and how is it justified? Who benefits from its practice, and what is its purpose? Here are sites, monuments, statues, jewels – all kinds of artefacts – but also, we are told, much less spectacular remains, from tiny pieces of flint down to concentrations of phosphates in the soil, visible only in a laboratory.

In a recent and provocative book the philosopher and historian Krzysztof Pomian (1987) remarked that archaeology is no more than a presumptuous branch of collecting, and that collecting, in so far as its history can be traced, is part of being human. Human beings, from the moment of their emergence as a cultural and biological entity, have in one way or another collected, preserved and hoarded items which have no other significance than as carriers of messages from a more or less remote past. However, that which connects archaeology to collecting is not the actual or perceived antiquity of the object, for one may collect contemporary items, nor is it the act of collection itself, for archaeology may be purely descriptive and need not involve the physical extraction of an object from the ground. The vital link between the two is the status accorded to an object which has been isolated, conserved, displayed, associated with or distinguished from others as a result of certain traits observed through its analysis. When an object is treated as a signifier (Pomian's *sémiophore*), it may be collected and then subjected to various processes, of which archaeological enquiry is only one. Archaeology is, in my view, the little bastard sister of collecting. Little, because restricted in the ways in which she can proceed and deliver; bastard, because since the nineteenth century at least she has been operating from a position of denial (an archaeologist, as everyone knows, is not a collector, and archaeologists themselves are at pains to point this out).

Merlin raises the stones of Stonehenge, shown in a fourteenth-century English manuscript. In this astonishing illustration Merlin erects Stonehenge. He was regarded by many medieval authors as the founder of the arts and the supreme magician.

Yuri Dombrowski, an expert on the subject,[1] said that the archaeologist would rather be taken for a policeman than for a collector (despite the fact that the police did not have a good reputation at Alma-Ata during the 1930s!). How low the self-esteem of any archaeologist would be who saw himself or herself as a successor to the tomb-robbers of Egypt, or to the traffickers in medieval relics, or to the Renaissance *Wunderkammer* mentality. However, when subjected to scrutiny the resemblance becomes clear: Dombrowski's archaeologist harries the pillagers of the tombs of an obscure Central Asian kolkhoz while the NKVD [Soviet secret police agency which was later absorbed by the KGB] looks on, knowing that both the pillaging and the harrying are less innocent than they might seem. Chadi Abdessalam in the film *The Night of Counting the Years*[2] is more accurate in his depiction of the archaeologist as the legitimate rival of the traffickers in antiquities. One can say that the archaeologist is a collector, but of a particular kind, more meticulous than the others, and accountable to various institutions, to the state and the public.

MEMORY NEEDS THE EARTH
The sands of Larsa, the mound of Xi'an, the site of Retoka

Pierre Nora, in his writings, reminds us that there are places where memory is stored, places which carry the mark of time;[3] from Lascaux to Beaubourg, these are the secretions of history itself. The megaliths of Britain and of Brittany alike have stood for millennia as living question marks in the landscape.

Merlin is depicted building Stonehenge in a fourteenth-century manuscript;[4] Johan Picardt shows giants building their enormous 'beds',[5] and witches appear comfortably installed in tumuli furnished with wooden staircases and windows, dispensing blessings. These are strange and marvellous things, even in the erudite work of a scholar such as William Stukeley.[6] Other minds of a more rationally antiquarian persuasion were to document megalithic monuments carefully. A sixteenth-century engraving shows an entire expedition of learned men carving their names on the *pierre levée* near Poitiers,[7] and a plate in William Camden's *Britannia* of 1600[8] gives us what is probably one of the earliest known illustrations of an excavation: two figures are digging in front of the ring of Stonehenge and beside them appear a skull and some femurs.

However far back we look, the monument as an object of interest has appealed just as much to the imagination as to reason. The history of archaeology cannot be divorced from this dichotomy which, in a way, is part and parcel of the subject. But before attempting to trace the long route by which the curious became first antiquarians, then archaeologists, we must stop and look at what is, in a way, the first historical evidence of the practice of archaeology. This is a brick with a cuneiform inscription found at Larsa in Iraq, which dates to the sixth century BC. It is a difficult document, since it refers constantly to an historical tradition and to a world far removed from our own. But if we can get past our initial alienation and accept this text, we shall see that it demonstrates the Babylonians' desire for historical legitimacy and for dynastic continuity.

I am Nabonidus, king of Babylon, shepherd, named by Marduk, provider

The *pierre levée* near Poitiers. This sixteenth-century engraving from Braun and Hogenberg's atlas, *Civitates orbis terrarum*, shows the famous Poitiers megalith, already well-known from Rabelais. Interpreted as a man-made post-diluvial construction, it is here shown covered with the carved names of the most noted geographers of the period.

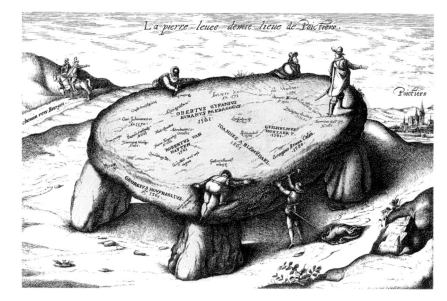

La pierre-leuee demie lieue de Poictiers.

Scenes of primitive life, engraved by Johan Picardt in 1660. Picardt, a Dutch pastor, drew on medieval superstitions in his dramatised scenes of 'primitives'.

for Esagil and Ezida, who multiplies the offerings, who restores the cities of the great gods, with providing hands, sumptuous with the temples, provider of the sanctuaries, who increases the gifts, unflagging emissary, conqueror of the high mountains, thoughtful shepherd, leader of the people, he who the lord of the gods, Marduk, has firmly pronounced as the one to provide the cities and restore the sanctuaries [...].

When the great lord of heaven and earth, Shamash, shepherd of the Black-headed people[9], lord of humanity[10] – Larsa, his resident town, the E-babbar, his house of dilection, which had long been a desert and become ruins, beneath dust and rubble, a great heap of earth, was covered to the point where its setting was no longer recognisable, its plan no longer visible[11] – under the reign of my predecessor king Nebuchadnezzar, son of Nabopolassar, the dust was lifted and the mound of earth which covered the town and temple, disclosing the temenos of the E-babbar of an old king, Burnaburiash, a predecessor, but the search was made, without discovery, for the temenos of a more ancient king. He rebuilt the E-babbar on the observed temenos of Burnaburiash to house the great lord Shamash [...].

It was thus that in the year 10, on a favourable day for my reign, during my eternal royalty beloved by Shamash, Shamash remembered his former dwelling; he happily decided from his chapel on the ziggurat to re-establish, better than before, and it is to me, king Nabonidus, his provider, to whom he entrusted the task of restoring the E-babbar and remaking his house of dilection.

By order of the great lord Marduk, the winds of the four quarters arose,

great storms: the dust which covered town and temple was lifted; the E-babbar, the mighty sanctuary, could be seen [...]. From the seat of Shamash and Aya, from the raised chapel of the ziggurat, the eternal holy place, the eternal chamber appeared the temenos; their plan became visible. I read there the inscription of the ancient king Hammurabi, who had built for Shamash, seven hundred years before Burnaburiash, the E-babbar on the ancient temenos and I understood its meaning. I adored with trembling; I worried, I thought, 'The wise king Burnaburiash rebuilt the temple and had the great lord, Shamash, live there. For me, [...] this temple and its restoration' [...]. I swore myself to the word of my greatest lord Marduk, and to those of the lords of the universe, Shamash and Adad; also my heart exulted, my liver enflamed; my tasks became clear and I set about mobilising workers for Shamash and Marduk, holding the pick, carrying the shovel, moving the basket. I sent them en masse *to rebuild the E-babbar, the mighty temple, my exalted sanctuary. Specialists examined the setting where the temenos had been found to understand its decoration.*

In a favourable month, on a propitious day, from the E-babbar, the temple of dilection of Shamash and Aya, the sanctuary, their divine dwelling, the room of their delights following the ancient décor of Ham-

The site of Stonehenge in an engraving from William Camden's *Britannia* (1600). This plate, one of the earliest known illustrations of an excavation, presents a relatively realistic view of the site, even if the *ossa humana* unearthed by the diggers in the lower left seem to be the bones of a giant.

murabi, I placed bricks upon the temenos of the ancient king Hammurabi. I rebuilt this temple in the ancient style and I decorated its structure. For the link of heaven and earth,[12] *his house of dilection, I raised the roof beam. I finished the construction of the E-babbar for Shamash and Aya and built the access [...].*

That which was not accorded to any king, my great lord, Shamash, accorded to me, for me, his devotee, and entrusted it to me. I finely rebuilt the E-babbar properly in the ancient style, for my lords, Shamash and Aya, and I restored it. I place, on a tablet of alabaster, the inscription of the ancient king Hammurabi that I have read there with my own and I replace it there for ever.

Foundation tablet of the temple of Larsa in Iraq, dating to the sixth century BC. This cuneiform inscription is the first written evidence of the awareness and practice of archaeological excavation.

The sands of Larsa have given us an astonishing document, perhaps the first written testament to the awareness and practice of archaeology. Nabonidus (556–539 BC) was clearly not the first to carry out excavations to recover the traces of a distant predecessor – he tells us himself that Nebuchadnezzar II (605–562 BC) found the temple of Burnaburiash (1359–1333 BC) – but what is extraordinary in this account is that he is acting consciously and methodically. The Babylonian king shows no desire simply to locate a place loaded with symbolic meaning, or to uncover a monument which demonstrates the continuity of power. He explicitly wishes to establish his place in the *longue durée*, and the expression of time here assumes a material dimension. Excavation is necessary not only to reveal the abode of memory, but also – and above all – to activate it. Archaeologists know (and Nabonidus knew better than any) that all excavation is destruction. The earth is a book whose pages are obliterated as we leaf through them, and only conservation allows us to slow down the ravages of time. Nabonidus, his workmen, scribes and architects would not have disagreed. To conclude their enterprise successfully it was not enough to find and symbolically confirm a prestigious place, a symbol of power; it had to be identified and restored. In doing this, writing played a vital part. The scribe who deciphered Hammurabi's (1792–1750 BC) inscription established the authenticity of the site and confirmed the length of the monarchy. (Nabonidus, unlike Nebuchadnezzar, was not content with the Burnaburiash inscription; he found and deciphered Hammurabi's inscription which was seven hundred years older.) In so doing the scribe endowed the reign of Nabonidus with hopes of a longevity equal to that of his predecessor, and to make the point absolutely clear, he added a new inscription to the old, signalling across the years that Nabonidus was a new Hammurabi. However, the excavation and the inscription (old and new) were still not enough. In restoring the temple the architects added something more: they installed a tangible sign of ancient time in the landscape, which was to be perceived and identified with a revisited past, a living past; we speak today of a past museologised.

Such a process may seem surprising but, as we shall see, it is not too far removed from what we today call archaeology. The tablet from Larsa affirms explicitly that the material world is not just a space for men to occupy and use, but a territory to be characterised symbolically, to be marked. It is in this marking of the earth, however fragile and temporary, that the power of archaeology lies. We have to engage with the idea that other human beings, maybe tomorrow, maybe in a few hours' time, maybe a few years or centuries from now, will look upon our traces. Understood in this way, the archaeological consciousness is born more of confrontation with the future than with the past. The hunter-gatherers who covered their traces knew that they must leave as few signs as possible, and in removing the evidence of their passing showed that they were conscious of the possibility of being located and identified. Some nascent awareness of a relationship between space and time which might be termed 'minimalist archaeology' can be seen here.

A significant boundary separates the slight traces of the Palaeolithic hunter-gatherers from the sumptuous monuments of the Eastern empires, and this cannot be crossed without risk. Yet any mark left upon sand, clay or wood presupposes the existence of, and the awareness of, such traces, however subtle or faint. The rulers of Egypt, the Fertile Crescent or China knew this well: their monumental and funerary art was a challenge to time. They set out to leave an immutable stamp upon the earth, one which would resist the depredations of the seasons, natural disasters and potential destroyers. The pyramids demonstrated the power of the pharaohs and hid from view (and from thieves) the wealth which accompanied the deceased. The monument is displayed whilst the objects are safely hidden within it, but their presence is evident. What is more, they can be described; the tomb can be read as a scale map of the entire country: invisible certainly, but in such a perfect state that the accounts could not fail to bear witness to it. The text which follows was written by Sima Qian and dates to the end of the second century BC; it describes the tomb of Qin Shi Huangdi, the first emperor of unified China during the second half of the third century BC:

In the ninth month the First Emperor was interred at Mt. Li. When the emperor first came to the throne he began digging and shaping Mt. Li. Later, when he unified the empire, he had over 700,000 men from all over the empire transported to the spot. They dug down to the third layer of underground springs and poured in bronze to make the outer coffin. Replicas of palaces, scenic towers, and the hundred officials, as well as rare utensils and wonderful objects, were brought to fill up the tomb. Craftsmen were ordered to set up crossbows and arrows, rigged so they would immediately shoot down anyone attempting to break in. Mercury was used to fashion imitations of the hundred rivers, the Yellow River and the Yangtze, and the seas, constructed in such a way that they seemed to flow. Above were representations of all the heavenly bodies, below, the features of the earth. 'Man-fish' oil was used for lamps, which were calculated to burn for a long time without going out. [13]

The Second Emperor said, 'Of the women in the harem of the former ruler, it would be unfitting to have those who bore no sons sent elsewhere.' All were accordingly ordered to accompany the dead man, which resulted in the death of many women.

After the interment had been completed, someone pointed out that the arti-sans and craftsmen who had built the tomb knew what was buried there, and if they should leak word of the treasures, it would be a serious affair. Therefore, after the articles had been placed in the tomb, the inner gate was closed off and the outer gate lowered, so that all the artisans and craftsmen were shut in the tomb and were unable to get out. Trees and bushes were planted to give the appearance of a mountain.[14]

General view of the burial mound of Emperor Qin Shi Huangdi at Xi'an in China.

Visitors to Xi'an today can still see the mound (which remains unexcavated) covering the first emperor. Excavations at the periphery of the mound carried out by contemporary Chinese archaeologists[15] have revealed the largest terracotta army ever found beneath the earth, armed with bows and crossbows. The rows of horsemen and infantry accompanied by their officers correspond perfectly to the symbolic world in microcosm described in the text of Sima Qian. And while the Chinese archaeologists have yet to begin excavation of the imperial tomb itself, initial surveys[16] indicate a large concentration of mercury in the area of the mound ...

In just the same way as Nabonidus, the emperor and his counsellors set out to mark their territory with an indelible sign of their sovereignty, and in so doing they went even further in exploring a path outlined two thousand years later by the Argentinian writer Jorge Luis Borges: they drew a map of the empire, a map of imperial dimensions which overlay the empire itself.[17] Just as the map recreates the territory, so the world of the dead fossilises that of the living. It is not difficult to imagine those leaders, engaged to the point of obsession with such a paradox. To draw attention to the tomb they had to collect the most splendid of masterpieces and commission the most sophisticated architecture, whilst simultaneously ensuring protection against thieves (who might even be the king's successors). The death of labourers and architects was as necessary a part of the process as the depth of the trenches or the strength of the walls.

The terracotta army of the Emperor Qin Shi Huangdi, third century BC. This is one of the most fabulous archaeological discoveries made in China. Buried more than a kilometre from the imperial tumulus, soldiers, officers and cavalrymen were arranged in lines as in the plan opposite.

The Babylonian king and the Chinese emperor did not have quite the same vision of time, because the nature of their power was different. Nabonidus was asserting continuity of succession with the most august of his ancestors. Shi Huangdi wished to be the first, the founder, so must have no predecessors but only successors: He

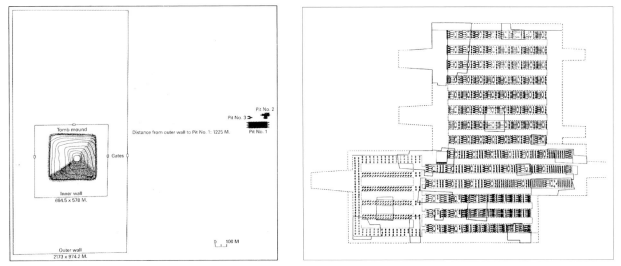

dreamed of founding an immortal dynasty; he decreed that his heirs should be called Second Emperor, Third Emperor, Fourth Emperor, and so on to infinity.[18] Yet whatever their separate visions, the king of Babylon and the Chinese ruler were intent on marking the earth with a permanent symbol of their sovereignty.

Brick, stone, marble – are these really the best bastions of memory? In Greece of the fifth century BC, one voice was raised in defence of the living memory of men against the inertia and fragility of monuments. In a famous poem Pindar puts the case for words versus marble:[19]

> *Listen! It is the field of Aphrodite*
> *with the fluttering eyes or the Graces*
> *we labor now. We approach the templed*
> *centerstone of the thunderous earth.*
> *There stands builded for the glory of Emmenos' children*
> *and Akragas of the river, and for Xenokrates,*
> *a treasure house of song*
> *for victory at Pytho in Apollo's*
> *glen, with its burden of gold.*
>
> *Neither rain driven from afar on the storm,*
> *not the merciless armies*
> *of the crying cloud, no wind shall sweep it, caught*
> *and stricken with the blown debris into the corners*
> *of the sea. The front shines in the clear air,*
> *Thrasyboulos, on your father announcing*
> *for you and yours the pride*
> *of a chariot victory in the folds of Krisa –*
> *a tale to run on the lips of men.*[20]

The monument which Pindar dedicated to Xenocrates of Agrigento (Akragas), champion of the Delphic chariot races, is not built in stone. It is a poem – fragile stuff, but for all that more enduring than stone or bronze. Intangible, incapable of subversion and sounder than an inscription, the poem is an original work, entrusted to memory. In the face of all the apparatus of the great empires, their hierarchies and their riches, Pindar proclaims the pre-eminence of memory; and because Greek culture also embraces the plastic arts, he sets the incorruptible nature of the poem against the greatest of these arts. The revenge of the humble upon the mighty? Of the poor upon the rich? Do poems and songs represent an alternative to monuments? Are they able to commemorate humanity down the centuries? In a way Pindar was right, and the archaeolgoist José Garanger has given us at least some evidence of this. Let us follow him to Melanesia, to the New Hebrides, where the archaeologist has to play the ethnographer in order to link the archaeological remains to the unwritten history of the modern population. He depends on the techniques of stratigraphy and radiocarbon (C14) dating to form the bases of a chronology.

In his research into the colonisation of the New Hebrides, Garanger[21] drew upon the main foundation narrative of native oral tradition. According to this, Roy Mata, the legendary first settler, established a chiefdom on the principal island of Efate which quickly embraced the whole group. On his death an important ceremony took place on the coral islet of Retoka, north-west of Efate, and representatives of the principal clans were buried alive at his side. Retoka was clearly an area of potential archaeological importance and excavations there soon revealed a major funerary complex with features corresponding exactly to the legend of Roy Mata. Let us look at Garanger's comparative analysis of narrative and excavation:

View of the Athenian Treasury at Delphi. It was to this type of monument, built to last for centuries, that Pindar (fifth century BC) compared his poems, proclaiming their even more enduring qualities.

The information gathered from oral tradition is confirmed and enhanced by the results obtained via the methods of prehistoric archaeology.

'Roy Mata lived long before the days of Ti Tongoa Liseiriki.'[22] *A date of AD 1265 ±140 years obtained from bone collagen is correct within two or three hundred years.*

'He was a very important chief.' *His tomb is by far the grandest of any studied in the South Pacific, as much for the number of individuals collectively buried there as for the richness of the grave goods.*

'He was buried on Retoka at the foot of two standing stones.' *Confirmed exactly.*

'Representatives of every clan owing him allegiance were buried alive.' *Excavation was unable to verify this, apart from the young woman buried at the feet of Roy Mata. Were the men just drugged with kava, or poisoned? Were the women stunned or strangled before being buried? All we know is that live burial was still being practised when the first missionaries arrived [...]. Roy Mata's importance would be sufficient to explain the observance of this custom at the time of his departure to the land of the dead [...].*

'Others were sacrificed too.' *This is certainly the case with the offering placed in the centre of the tomb. The bones of these individuals are virtually articulated (the limbs were bent in order to fit them in), and some still wear items of dance costume. There are also individuals, sometimes mutilated, scattered within the northern zone of the site.*

'Members of Roy Mata's entourage were buried close to him.' *These were the young woman, the man and the couple found in the deep grave.*[23]

The rest of Garanger's excursus is just as fascinating, but it is sufficient here (and after consideration of a few of the extraordinary

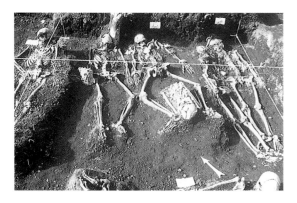

The Roy Mata burial, discovered by José Garanger in 1964.

pieces of evidence revealed by the excavation) to observe that a very precise funerary ritual has reached us intact from a point in time seven hundred years distant, not just through the testimony of the soil, but through the memories of the native storytellers, whose work has never ceased. Confirmation indeed of Pindar's bold assertion that memory is tougher than marble, but also a victory of words over matter. The companions of Roy Mata would not, like Nabonidus, entrust their memory to the bricks of the palace, or to the surfaces of tablets; they would not, like the emperor of China, build a tomb to the dimensions of the inhabited world. However, they would bequeath to future generations the memory of an exceptional ritual celebration made the more memorable by the practice of human sacrifice. No need for monumental elaboration: on the small island of Retoka, just two standing stones testify to the truth of the narrative.

Memory needs the earth in order to survive. Whether inscribed in stone, brick or parchment, or flowing in human memory by the agency of bard or poet, a foundation narrative must root itself in the land, invest itself with that reality which is sealed within the soil. It matters little if that seal is never broken, as long as there is some corner of the land which bears witness to its existence. This is the essence of the thin line which separates archaeology from collection; for the archaeologist it is not enough that the objects make sense, they must be linked to a place, to an area, to practices which allow them to be viewed as assignable, interpretable entities. In the nineteenth century Jacques Boucher de Perthes strove to see the artificer behind the artefact.[24]

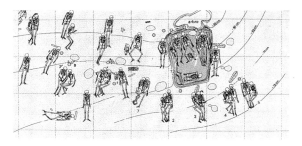

From the Egyptians to the Babylonians, the Chinese and the navigators of the Pacific, a brief investigation demonstrates the existence in very different societies of a spontaneous archaeology, of a monumentalisation of space able to face the erosion of time. We see perhaps why, in the West, the Greeks were the first to attempt to explain the past not in terms of dynastic continuity or the heroic, but by the discovery of objects.

Plan of the Retoka cemetery, near Efate island in the New Hebrides. In the centre is the burial of Roy Mata, who is accompanied by his 'assistant' (to his right), a couple (to his left), a young woman (stretched out at his feet) and a pig, intended as a guardian in the after-life (to the left). Between his legs is a secondary burial.

A SCIENCE OF OBJECTS
The interpretation of the past

Plato gives a summary of Greek anthropology which it is worth recalling:

Since man thus shared in a divine gift, first of all through his kinship with the gods he was the only creature to worship them, and he began to erect altars and images of the gods. Then he soon developed the use of articulate speech and of words, and discovered how to make houses and clothes and shoes and bedding and how to till the soil. Thus equipped, men lived at the beginning in scattered units, and there were no cities.[25]

The concept of evolutionary development, in some ways so alien to practices such as foundation burial, is an affront to time, neither defiant nor threatening, but necessary. Plato, in *The Laws*, tells us that after the castastrophe which swallowed up the first civilisations:

Human affairs were in a state of infinite and dreadful solitude; that a prodigious part of the earth was unprolific; and other animals having perished, some herds of oxen, and a few goats, which were rarely found, supplied those men with food that escaped the devastation.[26]

These herdsmen, the survivors of the deluge, had to exist as best they might in a hostile world:

I do not therefore think it would be very possible for them to mingle with each other. For iron and brass and all metals would have perished, confused together; so that it would be impossible to separate and bring them into light.

Hence trees would be but rarely cut down. For, if any instrument should happen to be left on the mountains, these rapidly wearing away would vanish; and no other could be made, till the metallic art should again be discovered by men.[27]

The concept of evolutionary development in this sense implies that of archaeology: the consciousness that the earth can reveal objects made long ago. This might seem obvious, but it is an idea rarely expressed so clearly in an ancient text. If there were human beings before ourselves, and if they left, whether by accident or design, some of their artefacts buried in the earth, it follows that we might find them. Furthermore, if we examine these carefully, we can

The building of primitive dwellings, in an engraving from the *Treaty on Architecture* (1460–64) by Antonio di Petro Averlino, called 'Il Filarete'. Averlino gives a good example of the primitivist theme in a view of the discovery of architecture derived from the Graeco-Roman tradition.

compare them to others and so date and attribute them to these antecedants of ours. Thucydides was one of the first to articulate this basic rule of archaeology when he wrote:

Piracy was just as prevalent in the islands among the Carians and Phoenicians, who in fact colonized most of them. This was proved during this present war, when Delos was officially purified by the Athenians and all the graves in the island were opened up. More than half of these graves were Carian, as could be seen from the type of weapons buried with the bodies and from the method of burial, which was the same as that still used in Caria.[28]

We now know that these tombs were of the Geometric period (ninth to eighth century BC). Thucydides' contemporaries were unable to establish the exact date and origin, but this is of little importance in view of the historian's reasoning, which is here truly archaeological. The method employed to analyse the tombs was both typological and comparative: the material found was observed to be different from the weaponry in use during the fifth century BC, and the burial practice was similar to that of a people well known to the Greeks at that time, the Carians, placed by ancient sources in the Cyclades. From the moment an object or monument is perceived not just as a symbol of power but as an element of history, archaeology begins. And from that moment in Greece when history became a discipline, archaeology began to play along with it: a supporting voice destined to accompany it down the centuries.

I do not wish to suggest that archaeology as we recognise it today sprang fully armed from the Greek science of history, but I would like to draw attention to that shift in thinking which alters the significance of an object such that it becomes an historical source and not just an element in the structure of history. Another text dating from the first century BC (so almost contemporary with Sima Qian) demonstrates the Greek historian's desire to proceed from object to fact. This is Strabo's account of Caesar's founding of a Roman colony on the site of ancient Corinth:

Now after Corinth had remained deserted for a long time, it was restored again, because of its favourable position, by the deified Caesar, who colonised it with people that belonged for the most part to the freedmen class. And when these were removing the ruins and at the same time digging open the graves, they found numbers of terracotta reliefs, and also many bronze vessels. And since they admired the workmanship they left no grave unransacked; so that, well supplied with such things and disposing of them at a high price, they filled Rome with Corinthian 'mortuaries', for thus they called the things taken from the graves, and in particular the earthenware. Now at the outset the earthenware was very highly prized, like the bronzes of Corinthian workmanship, but later they ceased to care much for them, since the supply of earthen vessels failed and most of them were not even well executed.[29]

Caesar's soldiers are more like Pomian's ancient collectors than modern archaeologists, but they demonstrate the existence of a taste for things past and a market for antique objects which is as old as the custom of placing offerings with the dead. The soldiers' interest in the tombs is linked to the prestige of the site, but also to the rarity and exotic nature of the objects. Corinth's ancient pottery vessels, dating from the end of the seventh and the sixth centuries BC, seem to have appealed to first-century Romans just as much as the famous statuettes and bronze vessels also found there; the rediscovery of a lost technique confers further distinction.

Despite all the shortcomings of the evidence, we can pick out several ways in which monuments and objects were deployed. They were used as symbols of power (Nabonidus, Qin Shi Huangdi, Roy Mata), as the building blocks of history (Thucydides), and as antiquities to be collected and exchanged (Strabo). This set of differing practices is much like a complex piece of stratigraphy, which can be interpreted as best suits the observer. From Nabonidus to the Greeks the awareness of the antiquity of objects and the mastery of time have marched hand in hand.

However, the aim of archaeology, in the West at least, is to frame a science of objects, of their discovery as well as their interpretation. Faced with the rudimentary knowledge of contemporary archaeologists, Borges suggested a method not altogether unlike that of Nabonidus and his predecessors. His short story *Tlön, Uqbar, Orbis Tertius* describes a world in which objects exist only in so far as they are used or imagined. Tlön is an imaginary world called into being by a group of scholars anxious to demonstrate that transformation of the spirit can be as effective as that of matter. Here, nothing exists which has not been thought up individually by each inhabitant; the language does not recognise nouns, and the philosophy of Tlön does not acknowledge the concept of time:

Example of a vase from the Archaic cemeteries of Corinth, of the type which aroused the enthusiasm of the Romans.

> One of the schools in Tlön has reached the point of denying time. It reasons that the present is undefined, that the future has no other reality than as present hope, that the past is no more than present memory.[30]

Here is a definition of time which the Assyrian kings shared with the emperors of China, and probably with all those who, like the intrepid navigators of the Pacific, believed that funerary art (of which poetry is a branch) must testify to the mystery and majesty of power. Tlön is not just a fascinating world where things are transformed into ideas; it also gives us the chance to submit archaeology to a test of truth. If objects only exist in the minds of those who desire them, use or experience them, how can archaeology be possible? Borges tells us that the sciences of Tlön are not like ours, except as a mirror image. If we look behind the mirror at the archaeologists of that planet we can see what modern archaeologists hide from us and probably from themselves:

> In the very oldest regions of Tlön, it is not an uncommon occurrence for lost objects to be duplicated. Two people are looking for a pencil; the first one

Illustration from Paracelsus' *Prognosticatio* (1536 edition). This is an image of erosion: like human life, human works are subject to progressive destruction.

finds it and says nothing; the second finds a second pencil, no less real, but more in keeping with his expectation. These secondary objects are called hrönir *and, even though awkward in form, are a little larger than the originals. Until recently, the* hrönir *were the accidental children of absent-mindedness and forgetfulness. It seems improbable that the methodical production of them has been going on for almost a hundred years, but so it is stated in the eleventh volume.*[31] *The first attempts were fruitless. Nevertheless, the* modus operandi *is worthy of note. The director of one of the state prisons announced to the convicts that in an ancient river-bed certain tombs were to be found, and promised freedom to any prisoner who made an important discovery. In the months preceding the excavation, printed photographs of what was to be found were shown the prisoners. The first attempt proved that hope and zeal could be inhibiting; a week of work with shovel and pick succeeded in unearthing no* hrön *other than a rusty wheel, postdating the experiment. This was kept a secret, and the experiment was later repeated in four colleges. In three of them the failure was almost complete; in the fourth (the director of which died by chance during the initial excavation), the students dug up — or produced — a gold mask, an archaic sword, two or three earthenware urns, and the moldered mutilated torso of a king with an inscription on his breast which has so far not been deciphered. Thus was discovered the unfitness of witnesses who were aware of the experimental nature of the search.*[32]

This is an important lesson in archaeology which reminds us that the desire for objects may prejudice the chances of their discovery. Things which are anticipated in too much detail slip out of one's grasp and, above all, all excavation is fabrication. The object or monument is only brought to light through the act of seeking it, and whilst observing a certain number of rules of study and interpretation. Isn't the archaeologist often taken for a *discoverer*? The 'discoverer' must not compel the reality of the past but imagine it:

The methodical development of hrönir *[...] has been of enormous service to archaeologists. It has allowed them to question and even to modify the past, which nowadays is no less malleable or obedient than the future.*[33]

In bringing his reasoning to its logical conclusion Borges hits upon an idea of archaeology very close to that of the Mesopotamians. In the middle of the ninth century BC the Babylonian king Nabu-apla-iddina decided to restore the temple of the Shamash in the town of Sippar:

Shamash, the great lord, who dwells in Ebabbara [the E-babbar], which is in Sippar, which during the troubles and disorders in Akkad the Sutû, the evil foe, had overthrown, and they had destroyed the sculptured reliefs, – his law was forgotten, his figure and his insignia had disappeared, and none beheld them. [...] At a later time Nabû-aplu-iddina, the king of Babylon, [...] who overthrew the evil foe, the Sutû, [under his reign] Shamash, the great lord, who for many days with Akkad had been angry and had averted his neck, [...] had mercy and turned again his countenance. A model of his image, fashioned in clay, his figure and his insignia, on the opposite side of the Euphrates, on the western bank, were found, and Nabû-nadin-shum, the priest of Sippar, [...] that model of the image to Nabû-aplu-iddina, the king, his lord, showed, and Nabû-aplu-iddina, [...] who the fashioning of such an image had given him as a command and had entrusted to him, beheld that image and his countenance was glad and joyful was his spirit.[34]

The gods, not content with having revealed to the Babylonian ruler the site of the ancient temples, also showed him buried figures in their image, sculpted by remote ancestors. For the Babylonians, the discovery of the past was a religious necessity intended to reestablish a cult or to restore a temple. Digging into the earth allowed for the discovery of monuments or objects necessary to the present. This fascination with the past goes hand in hand with a remarkable concept of time. The Sumerians and the Assyrians/Babylonians seem to have viewed time with their eyes turned back upon the past:

The term used to designate the future is warkatu, *which means, in fact, that which is found behind one's back. On the other hand the word which means 'in the past', 'formerly', pananu, derives from a root which means 'facing', 'in front of'. So the future was that which was behind one, while the past was that which was in front of one's eyes.*[35]

Such a concept may seem strange to us, but it makes it clear that the intelligence of the time demanded the knowledge of the succession of kings and events which the scribes recorded so minutely on their tablets. If to understand the past is to see it, then this attitude is more easily understood, since the future is not delineated and the past can be viewed as a long sequence of inventions, rulers and victories. In order to see the future we must turn the other way and stop contemplating history as a way of discovering that which is to come. At the dawn of the Enlightenment Francis Bacon was to take up this image to challenge the principle of authority: if we look at the long chain of human history, we must admit that the men of the present are older (and so more experienced) than those of the past. This idea would doubtless have appalled the Mesopotamians, who saw in the continuity and even the repetition of the past a gauge of the stability of the present. In a world where writing played such a decisive role, it

Statue of a king of Mari, last quarter of the third millennium BC, discovered in the 'museum' at Babylon.

was logical for the scribes to be interested in the most ancient tablets and inscriptions. During the reign of Nabonidus a scribe named Nabu-zer-lishir copied an inscription dating to the reign of Kurigalzu II (1332–1308 BC) at Akkad. The same scribe recovered an inscription on stone of Shar-kali-sharri, king of Akkad (2140–2124 BC). He not only copied the text, but indicated precisely where he had found it. This antiquarian oddity of the neo-Babylonians is not an isolated case. In the British Museum there is a tablet on to which an anonymous scribe has copied the inscription from the base of a statue which a merchant of Mari had dedicated to the god Shamash during the pre-Sargonic period (second half of the third millennium BC). The archaic script is perfectly reproduced, and the tablet ends with a commentary which tells us that the statue was set up in the E-babbar (of Sippar).[36]

To the enthusiasm for collecting must be added a reverence for sacred objects. It was a Mesopotamian tradition for the conqueror to haul away the cult statues of the conquered and to erect them in his own temples. In the palace of King Nebuchadnezzar in Babylon, considered by its builder to be a truly great marvel of architecture, German archaeologists discovered what they called the 'museum'. This was an assortment of statues and tablets ranging from the middle of the third millennium to the end of the seventh century BC. Here Eckard Unger believed that he was looking at the first museum in antiquity.[37] His interpretation should of course be qualified, since the idea of a museum open to the public seems oddly anachronistic in the Mesopotamian world. It is more likely that such an accumulation of cult objects and tablets of varying origin was preserved because, for religious reasons, it would have been difficult to destroy them. Like inscriptions, cult objects have their own power and must therefore be kept in a place where they would not be dangerous. At Nippur, in a level of the same period, a jar was found containing a series of objects dating back to more ancient times: a tablet bearing a plan of the town, bricks and tablets of the Sumerian period, contracts dating to the end of the second millennium BC. These documents had been deliberately selected[38] and show that the scribes were interested in antiquities.

Tablet bearing on one side an impression of a Sumerian inscription from the end of the third millennium BC, and on the other a commentary by an antiquarian scribe of the sixth century BC.

The Mesopotamians were the first to discover that nothing is immune to the destructive hand of time, except – to a certain extent – that which is buried in the soil. To guard against the effacement of memory, what better way than to leave a foundation text buried beneath a temple or palace, or inscribed on the reverse of its bas-reliefs. Addressed to future generations, it is for them to find, decipher and re-bury with a fresh inscription,[39] a link in the continuous chain of memory. As Borges suggested, the soil is ready to speak of the remotest past, and it matters little whether a king or an archaeologist poses the questions. Such was the conclusion arrived at by the Norfolk antiquary Sir Thomas Browne, and it is not surprising that Borges, in the last line of his text, announces that he is in the process of translating Browne's own work on funerary urns.[40]

GLORY, LOVE AND MEMORY IN MEDIEVAL PERSIA

The fabric of history is a fragile thing, but archaeology will always preserve some of the threads. However, for memory to persist mankind must observe, interpret and create the narrative upon the bedrock of material things. One of the most fascinating traditions uniting memory and monument comes to us from the Iranian plateau.[41] There, some kilometres from the present town of Kirman-shah, the Sasanian king Khusrau erected some extraordinary reliefs in the caves of Taq-i-Bustan. Dating to the beginning of the sixth century AD, these dominated the landscape in a place situated on the route between northern Mesopotamia and the Iranian plateau. The façade of the cave is carved with pilasters bearing ornate floral motifs supporting an arch; in the centre is a diadem and two winged figures. Within the arch are two groups of sculptures, one above the other; the lower depicts a horseman in armour identified as Khusrau II, king of Persia from 590 to 628 AD, the upper depicts two men and a woman, identified as the god Ahura-Mazda crowning the sovereign while the goddess Anahita (left) holds a crown and a vessel.

This relief, one of the best known within the Sasanian tradition, was described many times by Muslim authors from the tenth century onwards. At first they associated the two male figures in the upper relief with the king Khusrau and his general and architect, Farhad. The female was said to be Shirin, the Christian wife of the monarch. During the eleventh century the poet Nizami of Ganjah based a hugely successful poem upon this scenario. *Khusrau and Shirin* is a sort of saga in the Arthurian genre which tells of the love of the architect for the king's wife. Farhad, hopelessly in love with Shirin, seduces her by means of his fabulous talents as a sculptor and an architect. He creates wonderful monuments and works of art for the king and his consort. This Merlin of the East thus became the builder of the monument at Taq-i-Bustan. The romance of the architect and the queen is illustrated in a series of Persian illuminated manuscripts of the fifteenth and sixteenth centuries. Strange indeed that these reliefs, which were originally created to celebrate the glory of the monarch, should have come to signify his supposed misfortune.

THE DISCOVERY OF ARCHAEOLOGY
A stormy sea

For archaeology to have a real existence it is not enough to observe the stamp of time upon the soil in the shape of a monument or a series of objects. It has to be acknowledged that any discovery is not wholly accidental, and that objects and monuments become part of the landscape by means of demonstrable, observable processes. It is not that Nabonidus and Strabo and many other minds were unaware of this, but received wisdom in antiquity and during the Middle Ages preferred to see flint artefacts as 'thunderbolts' or 'elf-shot', rather

Above: A 'thunderbolt' striking Ensisheim in the Lower Rhine region, fifteenth-century engraving. For a long time the origin of 'ceraunites' was attributed to thunder and lightning.

than as objects shaped by the hand of man. History of the knowledge of the past is suffused with paradox. While some individuals enquired rigorously into the origins of objects and monuments, most of their contemporaries preferred to see these same objects as the product of the magical powers of mysterious beings, or of strange natural phenomena. The discovery of stratigraphy – the chronological study of the deposits laid down upon the earth's surface – is usually associated with the invention of prehistory during the nineteenth century; some Scandinavian archaeologists, however, had already evolved a stratigraphic interpretation of tumuli in the seventeenth century.[42]

The history of archaeology, from antiquity to the present day, is

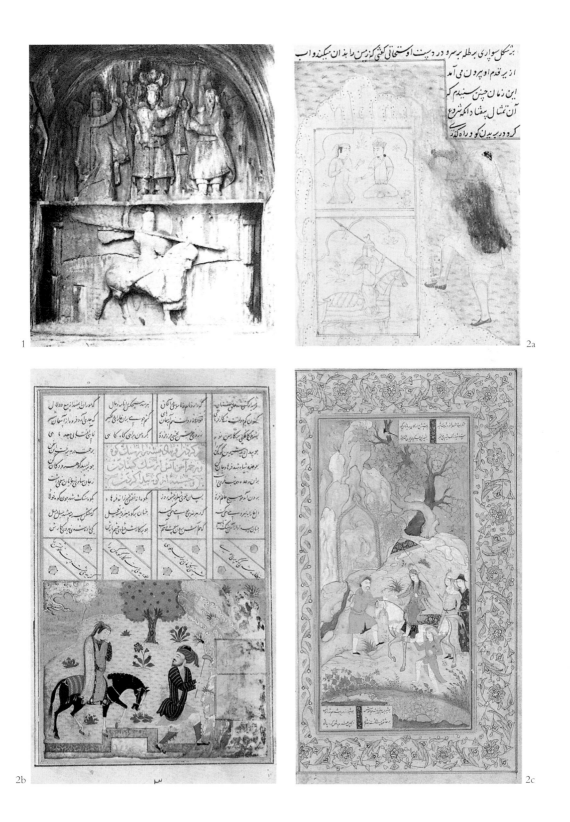

1

2a

2b

2c

not a loose history of the progress of knowledge. It is much more like an account of a sea troubled by violent waves, which cast up shells on the shore that are then washed away by other waves.

The first wave, in a challenge to written tradition, established the importance of objects over texts in matters of historical proof.[43] For the antiquaries of the sixteenth and seventeenth centuries the object was a direct, tangible and indisputable source; in fact, all but a time machine. In 1638, Ole Worm, Antiquary-Royal of Denmark and Norway, addressed the following letter to the bishop of Stavanger:

> It will be a light task for you if you get some young man (preferably a student with some ability in painting) to go the rounds of the deans and pastors with a letter of recommendation from yourself. [...] He should take a note of (1) the site, what county and parish it is in, (2) the orientation, eastwards, westwards, and so on, (3) the dimensions of the monument, its length, breadth, and thickness, (4) he should make a drawing showing the external appearance and structure of the monument, (5) he should add the interpretation he decides on, (6) local stories about the monument, even if fanciful, (7) noteworthy events in the vicinity, together with any other particulars that may be material to our investigations.[44]

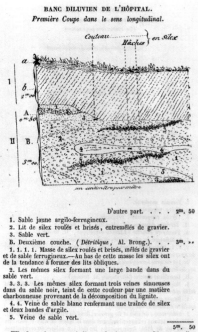

BANC DILUVIEN DE L'HÔPITAL.
Première Coupe dans le sens longitudinal.

D'autre part . . . 2ᵐ. 50
1. Sable jaune argilo-ferrugineux.
2. Lit de silex roulés et brisés, entremêlés de gravier.
3. Sable vert.
B. Deuxième couche. (*Détritique*, Al. Brong.). . . 3ᵐ. »
  1. 1. 1. 1. Masse de silex roulés et brisés, mêlés de gravier et de sable ferrugineux.—Au bas de cette masse les silex ont de la tendance à former des lits obliques.
  2. Les mêmes silex formant une large bande dans du sable vert.
  3. 3. 3. Les mêmes silex formant trois veines sinueuses dans du sable noir, teint de cette couleur par une matière charbonneuse provenant de la décomposition du lignite.
  4. 4. Veine de sable blanc renfermant une traînée de silex et deux bandes d'argile.
  5. Veine de sable vert.

5ᵐ. 50
☰ Ces trois marques indiquent des instrumens celtiques en silex qui ont été trouvés dans la masse diluvienne.

Longitudinal section of an alluvial bank, drawn by Boucher de Perthes in 1847. Taken from his *Antiquités celtiques et antédiluviennes* (1847), this drawing of a stratigraphic section made it possible to establish a geological chronology.

Ole Worm's programme was the same as that of any modern archaeological cartographic survey. He aimed to establish a precise inventory of each monument, and to assign to each a definite and detectable place in a greater order. The description depended upon a visual assessment carried out on the site, an analytical drawing, measurements, and a survey of local opinion – the entire range of expertise. The second wave confirms a theory of archaeological evolution defined most clearly by the Comte de Caylus:

> I should like us to seek less to dazzle than to instruct, and to join the Ancients more frequently in their method of comparison which is to the antiquary what observation and experiment are to the physicist. The inspection of several monuments, carefully compared, may reveal their purpose, in the same way that the ordered consideration of several effects of nature may reveal their principle; so excellent is this method that the best way to convince the antiquary and the physicist is to confront the first with new documents and the

second with new experiments. The difference lies in the fact that the physicist, so to speak, always has nature at his disposal and his instruments to hand, and is always in a position to check and repeat his experiments, whereas the antiquary is often obliged to seek far afield for the fragments he needs for comparison.[45]

What was begun by the first hunter-gatherers was completed by the scholars of the Enlightenment – the encoding of a rigorous and exact science of archaeological remains. To rid archaeology of the dross of antiquarianism a third wave was necessary, that of comparative stratigraphy, still a century away. In order to bring it about, Boucher de Perthes had to contend with the principal scholars of his day.

It was a long, slow march which led to the emergence of archaeology – not its status nor its object, but its method, constructed upon its trinity of principles: typology, technology and stratigraphy.

1 Dombrovski 1979
2 Abdessalam 1970.
3 Nora 1984.
4 Michell 1982, p. 24.
5 Michell 1982, p. 25.
6 Michell 1982, p. 10ff.
7 Michell 1982, p. 41.
8 Michell 1982, p. 122.
9 Humanity. Excerpt taken from the French translation of D. Arnold.
10 Break in the text.
11 Break in the text.
12 Name of the ziggurat of Larsa.
13 The *renyu* or 'man-fish' appears to be a type of aquatic mammal; some kind of seal or whale have been suggested as possibilities.
14 *Records of the Grand Historian: Qin Dynasty* by Sima Qian, trans. Burton Watson, Hong Kong, New York, 1993, pp. 63–4.
15 See Cheng Yong and Li Tong 1983.
16 Ibid.
17 Borges 1981, p. 31.
18 Borges 1964, p. 4.
19 Svenbro 1976.
20 Pindar, *Pythia 6*, lines 1–18, trans. R. Lattimore, Chicago, 1976.
21 Garanger 1980.
22 The legendary coloniser of the Shepherd Islands.
23 Garanger 1980, pp. 196–7.
24 Boucher de Perthes 1847, p. 16.
25 Plato, *Protagoras*, 322 a–b, trans. C.C.W. Taylor, Oxford, 1976.
26 Plato, *The Laws III*, 677e–678a, trans. T. Taylor, New York and London, 1984.
27 Ibid. 678c.
28 Thucydides, *History of the Peloponnesian War*, I.viii, trans. R. Warner, Harmondsworth, 1972.
29 Strabo, *Geography*, VIII.6.23, trans. H.L. Jones, London, 1917.
30 Borges 1985, p. 25. Compare Borges' definition with St Augustine, *Confessions*, XIV, 17, see Pomian 1984, pp. 246–50.
31 Borges 1985, p. 28.
32 Ibid., pp. 28–9.
33 Ibid., p. 29.
34 King 1912, pp. 121–3. See also Cassin 1969, p. 243, and Glassner 1993, p. 24.
35 Cassin 1969, p. 243; see also Glassner 1993, p. 24.
36 Sollberger 1967.
37 Unger 1931.
38 Hilprecht 1903.
39 Lackenbacher 1990, chap. V, pp. 151–73.
40 Borges 1985.
41 Soucek 1974.
42 Klindt–Jensen 1975, pp. 30–31.
43 Momigliano 1983.
44 Klindt–Jensen 1975, p. 20.
45 Caylus 1752, III–IV.

CHAPTER 1

ANTIQUE AND
MEDIEVAL
SOURCES

A single letter shines between two points and this single sign,
.L., marks the forename. Next is engraved what I believe to be an M
but which is incomplete: A\. A part has gone missing where a piece of stone
has broken off. Is it a Marius, a Marcius or a Metellus who lies here?
No one can know for certain. The broken letters rest here, their lines
mutilated, and in the confusion of characters the meaning has been lost.
Should we be surprised that men should die? Monuments crumble;
death comes even to stones and names.

·

AUSONIUS, *ON THE NAME, ENGRAVED IN MARBLE, OF A CERTAIN LUCIAN*

We have always known, and the hunter-gatherers of the most distant periods knew, that there were people before us. Perhaps the cynegetic beginnings of humanity might explain man's deep-rooted attention to the traces left by the other individuals of his species. For to move around, to find food, to shelter within nature, one must identify the fleeting signs without which life is not possible. In our industrial societies archaeologists follow (or precede, when they can) the machines which dig up the soil. They believe themselves, through their knowledge, delegated to observe the men of the past, and with their minute and comical attention to detail they recover remains which are often so difficult to observe that all the resources of the laboratory are required in order to record them. In the West, the archaeologist was slowly distinguished from the antiquary through seeking to recover and to analyse in the most objective fashion the material traces of ancient times. The antiquary's aim was to gather and present uncommon

Christians excavating the mountain in search of the bones of St Etienne, evangelist of Echternach, eleventh-century manuscript illumination. The search for relics required the exploration of the soil.

objects, chosen for their individual qualities, which distinguished them from current objects because they symbolised a lost, invisible world. Carefully described, methodically displayed, these objects thus acquired new properties which made them different, precious, moving, material witnesses of time's physical depth. The archaeologist was more ambitious; he sought (so he said) neither emotion, nor quality, nor exemplar. He was no longer even in search of his close or distant ancestors, but looked for the ancestors of all mankind. His enquiry was not restricted to particular works or styles; his appetite

Polidoro da Caravaggio, *The Discovery of the Books of the Sabine King, Numa Pompilius*, 1525. The discovery of Numa's grave was one of the most celebrated archaeological episodes in the history of Rome. According to Titus Livius the burial was found in 181 BC. It contained philosophical treatises composed by Numa (seventh century BC).

for knowledge made every trace worthy of recording and, if possible, of analysis.

Our vision of the past has evolved alongside our experience of the world. However, it would be quite presumptuous to believe that we are the only ones to make an art of memory. Very different people, in the most distant latitudes, were conscious, as we have seen, that there had been people before themselves. In using their capacity for observation, in exercising their memory, in inventing scripts which their successors would know how to decipher, groups of men have wittingly, from earliest antiquity, attempted to read the past, to record the present, even to transmit to the future traces of their activities. In Egypt, in Mesopotamia, in China, writing was the privileged means of an extraordinary, silent contact between generations.

EMPIRES AND ARCHAEOLOGY

CONTINUITY

The evidence of past empires legitimates the new

Nabonidus, conscious of being the contested inheritor of a long tradition, was undoubtedly the most resolute of the ancient antiquaries. On another tablet, discovered at Ur in Mesopotamia, he expressed the near-archaeological dimension of his sense of the past:

Because for a very long time the office of high priestess had
*   been forgotten*
and her characteristic features were nowhere indicated, I
*   bethought myself day after day.*
The appointed time having arrived, the doors were opened
*   for me;*
indeed I set eyes on an ancient stele of Nebuchadnezzar,
son of Ninurta-nadin-šumi, an early king of the past,
on which was depicted the image of the high priestess;
moreover, they had listed and deposited in the Egipar
her appurtenances, her clothing, and her jewelry.
I carefully looked into the old clay and wooden tablets
and did exactly as in the olden days.
A stele, her appurtenances, and her household equipment
I fashioned anew, respectively inscribed on it,
and deposited it before my lord and lady Sin and Ningal.

At that time Egipar, the holy precinct, wherein the rites of the high priestess
*   used to be carried out,*
was an abandoned place, and had become a heap of ruins,
palm trees and orchard fruit were growing in its midst.
I cut down the trees, removed the rubble of its ruins,
I set eyes on the temple and its foundation terrace became visible.
Inside it I set eyes on inscriptions of old earlier kings,
I also set eyes on an old inscription of En-ane-du, high priestess of Ur,
daughter of Kudur-Mabuk, sister of Rim-Sin, king of Ur,
who renovated Egipar and restored it ...[1]

Nabonidus was not only curious about the more ancient past; he was not satisfied in this dedication simply to take his place within a

Copper plaque of the Neo-Assyrian period. This plaque was discovered in a stone casket containing five other plaques of copper, silver or gold, placed in the foundations of the town of Dur Sharrukin, built by Sargon II of Assyria (706 BC). In the text the king relates the circumstances of the town's construction and the splendour of its monuments.

long line of royal predecessors; he drew on his knowledge and that of his scribes to restore a forgotten cult. In this sense archaeology, as is excellently suggested by Borges, was a necessary and effective practice, a science of the sacred which gave the king as much power over the present as the future.

In Chinese tradition, as in the Mesopotamian, the examination of the earth and digging were the means of establishing a calm relationship between past and present. But the interest of dignitaries and kings was not just cultural. Often it was the search for treasure which led them on:

> King Chu of Guangchuan loved to surround himself with wastrels, sporting with them and hunting energetically with nets and arrows. He had all the tombs in his kingdom opened. One of my friends by the name of Yuan Meng remembers that his grandfather, who was commander of the capital in the service of the king, had repeatedly warned him not to do this, but he did not want to stop.[2]

We shall see later how organised looting was also an art of collecting which presupposed a knowledge and interpretation of the objects found. But these examples suffice to show that observation of the ruins and the analysis of the remains of antiquity played a not inconsiderable role in the great kingdoms of the East. For the Asian sovereigns mastery of the present indicated to a certain degree the mastery of the past. The annals of the ancient rulers allowed those of the present to win legitimacy and recognition, to realise the same reinvention of cults or rituals which helped to establish the throne, to magnify their grandeur and to make visible the invisible aspect of power. From this the role of the various inscriptions which, placed in temple or palace foundations, or set on their walls, made possible the necessary communication between the people of the past and those of the present. For the actual administrators, the scribes and archivists, were also the only ones who could read and write the messages sent by the kings to their distant successors. Like government or administration, history could only be practised by the king or his dependants, and this essentially dynastic history assumed a perfect knowledge and mastery of sacred areas: temples, royal palaces, tombs. 'Oriental despotism' also controlled burial. All of these monuments were naturally symbolic. Also the scribes, royal architects and other functionaries had, to some extent, to act as antiquaries able to identify, date and interpret the ancient monuments which contemporary needs found useful or in some cases indispensable. However, history does not just require competence (which was not lacking in the scribes) but also a certain freedom for collection, comparison and criticism. This did not lend itself well to dynastic eulogy. Throughout the sixth century BC, when the first travellers from the Greek cities discovered the splendour and antiquity of the great eastern civilisations – those of the Egyptians, Assyrians and the Persians – they were all as much impressed by the grandeur of the palaces and the power of the monarchs as by the knowledge of the scribes.

THE INVENTION OF HISTORY
Herodotus

The discovery of what the great historian Arnaldo Momigliano called 'alien wisdom' was critical to the development of Greek civilisation. Whilst aware of their originality and their singular status as citizens of tiny city-states of uncertain origin, when faced with the wealth and antiquity of the great empires the Greeks rapidly discovered that their freedom of trade was also the freedom to think, enquire and question:

Letter from Michaux addressed to members of the Institute and curators of the cabinet of antiquities, written in 1800. In this letter Michaux announces the government's intention to purchase his discovery: a pebble covered with inscriptions, dating to the eleventh century BC.

> *These are the researches of Herodotus of Halicarnassus, which he publishes, in the hope of thereby preserving from decay the remembrance of what men have done, and of preventing the great and wonderful actions of the Greeks and the Barbarians from losing their due meed of glory ...*[3]

This foundation text for Western history was also the first to declare a new way of looking at the past. This was a past no longer the property of a dynasty or even of an ethnic group, but the common heritage of humanity – Greeks and barbarians – a history to be studied, not for what it revealed about the superiority of some over others, but because it recorded the 'great and marvellous' achievements of all mankind. Herodotus did not commemorate on stone or mud-brick the story of a conquest or a victory; he presented the results of an enquiry (*historia*) and this created a new genre of writing, which was not to be confused with the dedicatory, annalistic or foundation inscriptions, but which from then on took the name history. It was a setting out of what was intended to be a balanced overview. Up until that point memory had been the privilege of the royal courts and, without doubt to a significant degree, of the priests, story-tellers and minstrels. But from then on men's curiosity was opened to a new method of discovering and telling the past. Inscribed on stone, mud-brick, ivory or wood, the inscription spoke for itself and imposed itself on all those able to read it; the scribe effaced himself from the system, from the event which had engendered the text. Thus it retained its legitimacy by speaking for

itself. By contrast, Herodotus offered his reader a text which claimed its authorship, a written discourse (*apodexis*) which was the result of his own work, of his research: here was the lever to transform the art of memory into history. Naming himself, speaking in his own voice, not that of a past king or a legendary hero, but that of a man of Thurii (an Athenian colony in southern Italy), he invited the reader to examine a story born of reflection and experience. Herodotus was no better informed than the scribes of Nabonidus and tells us himself that he knew less than those of the Pharaoh, but he had other curiosities and customs to relate and, above all, to investigate. At the end of the day there are only two ways of collecting information, by eye and by ear. Herodotus set out to see all that he

Bust of Herodotus (484–425 BC). In proposing an 'enquiry' into the past, Herodotus invented history.

could of customs, practices and peoples, and whenever that proved impossible he made every effort to understand what other persons had heard before him.

For centuries scholars have investigated Herodotus' methods by comparing them with those of his successors, especially the greatest of these, Thucydides, and in reconciling these with those of the explorers and ethnographers of the sixteenth century in their discoveries beyond Europe. But Herodotus' work, in a particular way, resists all of these classifications. Herodotus was not as preoccupied with method as Thucydides, and he did not have Polybius' taste for realism. In a previously unattested leap of curiosity he makes us penetrate places and societies both exotic and familiar to the curious Greek travellers of the sixth and fifth centuries BC. Perhaps he is difficult to classify precisely because he gave free rein to his desire to see and to hear, to describe and to write. Whatever it was, his successors,

and foremost among them Thucydides, could not wholly free themselves from the tradition of a man who established a new and original pathway for the art of memory, one which linked the experience
of the past to the present – what we would today call ethnohistory
and geohistory.

As here defined, history sought method and discipline; under the
influence of the philosophers it had to be explanatory. The founder,
Herodotus, appeared to be above the fray, neither the prophet of
writing nor the flatterer of orality, hardly encumbered by explanatory
categories but happily mixing all the descriptive disciplines.

Modern historians have wished to see Herodotus as the precursor
of our Renaissance geographers and explorers. But Herodotus was
no Marco Polo or Jean de Léry. He never learnt Egyptian or Ara-
maic, as his successors learnt Mongolian or Tupi-Guarani, because,
whilst the Greeks were curious about 'alien wisdom', they saw no
reason to learn the languages of the ancient east. Did they not write
as Greeks, for Greeks? And is not the only barbarian book ever completely translated into Greek the Bible, at the end of the second century BC? The Greeks visiting the great kingdoms of the east were
certainly conscious of their own originality but did not perceive
themselves as carriers of a superior civilisation. Or at least their superiority was in no way felt as technical: in matters of architecture,
astronomy and medicine the Greeks were fascinated by what they
found in the east. The aim of their ethnographic and historical
curiosity was more comparative than speculative. The Barbarians
allowed them to think about differences, to relativise the singularity
of the hundred or so micro-states from which they came by observing what separated them from the peoples which surrounded them.

OBSERVATION OF THE RUINS
Pausanias and Thucydides

The Greeks did not have (or as some among them said, no longer
had) monarchs capable of building gigantic cities. They had no
knowledge like that of the oriental scribes adept at preserving and
exalting the memories of their monarchs. But like us, they knew how
to look at the countryside and read the traces of past humanity. It
was enough to open Homer and to see a tableau, sometimes with
nostalgia, an imaginary world which, for the Archaic Greeks and

their successors, seemed as distant as that of Charlemagne in *The Song of Roland* seems to us. In the first century AD Pausanias, visiting Tiryns and Mycenae, did not fail to muse:

Still, there are parts of the ring-wall left, including the gate with lions standing on it. They say this is the work of Kyklopes, who built the wall of Tiryns for Proitos. In the ruins of Mycenae is a water-source called Perseia, and the underground chambers of Atreus and his sons where they kept the treasure-houses of their wealth. There is the grave of Atreus and the graves of those who came home from Troy, to be cut down by Aigisthos at his supper-party.[4]

Pausanias was not a historian but, as we shall see, the prince of antiquaries. However, he was intrigued by the exceptional architecture of these two sites and so he tried to interpret them by establishing a chronology which was compatible with the archaic mythical history. This persistence distinguished him from the Mesopotamian and Egyptian scribes by its effort to *interpret*, the desire to put at a distance and to explain. He did not seek to establish continuity at all costs, but on the contrary to make clear the reasons for a perceptible rupture, comparable to that between what we now call the remains of the Mycenaean period with Archaic and Classical Greece. Architecture was not the only trace of the Greek past which prompted his enquiries:

The Lion Gate at Mycenae. In the fifth century BC all that was left of Mycenae were a few monuments, including the famous Lion Gate. These ruins were the subject of several descriptions by Thucydides, Pausanias and others.

As for the weapons in the heroic age being all made of bronze, I could argue that from Homer, from the lines about Peisander's axe and Meriones' arrow; the opinion I have given can be proved anyway from the spear of Achilles, which is dedicated in the sanctuary of Athene at Phaselis, and Memnon's sword in the temple of Asklepios at Nikomedia: the blade and the butt of the spear and the whole of the sword are made of bronze.[5]

To enquire: Pausanias was on the lookout for any information which would make his guide intelligible, and his *historia* rested on tradition – word of mouth – but also on sight. The arms of Homer's heroes could still be seen in the temple treasuries; in verifying methods of execution and materials it was possible to verify the tradition. It makes little difference that Pausanias gives us no information on

Miniatures illustrating Homer's *Iliad* in a manuscript of 1477.
Homeric epic was the source of all Greek thinking on the
antique tradition. These miniatures, by a northern Italian master,
illustrate the Greek text and the Latin translation. Here, Chryses
confronts Agamemnon and Apollo avenges his priest by
sending the plague to the Greeks. Greeks and Trojans wear
antique armour.

A view of the
principal monuments
of Sparta.

how the temples could have collected such weapons, the important thing is that he established a connection between tradition and material objects.

Of course in terms of Greek history Pausanias is a late author, writing at a point in time when a passion for antiquities had become fashionable, but we can easily find in a historian as conceptual as Thucydides at the end of the fifth century BC what must be considered an archaeological analysis of the past. The ruins of Mycenae suggested to him thoughts quite different to those of Pausanias. How could a fifth-century visitor accept that this place had been, at the time of the Trojan War, the capital of the Greek world?

Mycenae certainly was a small place, and many of the towns of that period do not seem to us today to be particularly imposing; yet that is not good evidence for rejecting what the poets and what general tradition have to say about the size of the expedition. Suppose, for example, that the city of Sparta were to become deserted and that only the temples and foundations of buildings remained, I think that future generations would, as time passed, find it very difficult to believe that the place had really been as powerful as it was represented to be. Yet the Spartans occupy two-fifths of the Peloponnese and stand at the head not only of the whole Peloponnese itself but also of numerous allies beyond its frontiers. Since, however, the city is not regularly planned and contains no temples or monuments of great magnificence, but is simply a collection of villages, in the ancient Hellenic way, its appearance would not come up to expectation. If, on the other hand, the same thing were to happen to Athens, one would conjecture from what met the eye that the city had been twice as powerful as in fact it is.

We have no right, therefore, to judge cities by their appearances rather than by their actual power, and there is no reason why we should not believe that the Trojan expedition was the greatest that had ever taken place. It is equally true that it was not on the scale of what is done in modern warfare. It is questionable whether we can have complete confidence in Homer's figures, which, since he was a poet, were probably exaggerated. Even if we accept them, however, it appears that Agamemnon's force was smaller than forces are nowadays.[6]

This lesson in historical and archaeological methodology continues to be the basis of historical practice. As Thucydides was not content simply to enquire, he compared sources, one with another, and established levels of similarity which made possible a critique.

Even if modern archaeology is dismayed by a less than precise chronology, innovation is the important thing here. Of course Thucydides' contemporaries could visit Mycenae, Sparta and Athens and see the impact on the countryside and the townscapes of the different sites. But seeing was not enough, and just as the poet freely embellishes his tale, one city can take better care of its monumental surroundings than another. The observation which follows from the *opsis* is a given which must be subject to reason: the power of a town is not directly linked to its visible monuments. To the eyes of a fifth-century Greek, Mycenae seemed only a small abandoned village, but the historian's eye could already see what would become of proud Sparta in a few centuries: a little heap of ruins. As Thucydides' analysis is a constant dialectic between past, present and future, it is a true exercise in historical method, revealing in its first form the elements of critical history initially suggested by Herodotus.

A view of Athens.

But the paradox is even more provocative. In Greece itself, in the last ten years, a certain number of archaeologists have tried to complete, indeed to replace, the classic practice of archaeology (excavation and description of monuments) with sophisticated surveys capable of revealing what the present landscape hides: monuments, of course, but also agrarian buildings and communication routes ... in short, an archaeology which is not content with the *opsis* but with the *dynamis* inscribed in the soil of the ancient countryside. From the moment when historical narrative freed itself from the rigid frame of the annals and royal propaganda, the way was open for the critique of sources, and this is what Thucydides revealed in magisterial fashion. If he undertook the writing of the history of the Peloponnesian War, it was because he witnessed it from the start. Contemporary history, and thus a history of events – but this particular history, precisely because it aimed at the truth, had to create the instruments of its own validation. There is a qualitative difference between modern and ancient history:

For though I have found it impossible, because of its remoteness in time, to acquire a really precise knowledge of the distant past or even of the history preceding our own period, yet, after looking back into it as far as I can, all the evidence leads me to conclude that these periods were not great periods either in warfare or in anything else.[7]

The laws of Gortyn, inscriptions engraved in Doric dialect on stone slabs at Gortyn, Crete, in 450 BC. These laws are one of the most outstanding examples of epigraphy from antiquity. In the first century BC these slabs were reused to adorn the wall of a theatre.

Where direct enquiry is not possible, it is necessary to invent the means to verify the oldest traditions and to compare the chronological elements. This observation of facts linked to critique allowed Thucydides to write the most synthesising and best informed of the Greek histories. And the commentators were not wrong when they called this part of the books of Thucydides 'archaeology', not in our sense of the word but in the proper Greek sense: the study of ancient things. The novelty applies as much to the quality of analysis – Thucydides gives us in several pages a critical history of Greece before the Peloponnesian War – as to the quality of method directed at a global explanation based on indicators which could be examined and verified. That this form of archaeology could intersect with what we now call archaeology is easily shown, and the famous passage about the purification at Delos provides an excellent example.[8] In this sense, knowledge of the past – *archaiologia* in the Greek meaning of the term – is very close to that specialised branch of history which for the last two centuries we have called archaeology. It is true that for the Greeks the research and interpretation of ancient remains did not constitute an autonomous discipline (as we shall see, they had many other things to do to classify the complex web of information available on past mankind), but in trying with the rigour of a logician to put order into tradition, Thucydides came very close to what we regard as the modern science of archaeology: seeing visible traces in the ground, relating these to tradition, attempting a material, stylistic and functional analysis.[9] This was a surprising and fleeting advance in thought, the modernity of which was not evident until the nineteenth century. Thucydides, clearly, was neither the first nor the last to be interested in the material remains of the past. The Greek taste for mythology, a mythology incarnate in certain places and landscapes, led them to observe and account for the remains which their curiosity and persistence brought to light. Just as the oriental monarchs affirmed the splendour of their lineage in rediscovering the palaces and tombs of their forebears, the Greeks of the cities sought to find and honour the graves of fabled heroes of the past.

THE ARCHAEOLOGY OF THE SACRED:
THE CULT OF RELICS
Plutarch and the transfer of the bones of Theseus

After the Persian Wars, Plutarch tells us, the Pythia commanded the Athenians to retrieve the bones of Theseus from the island of Syros where, according to tradition, they had been buried:

But it was very difficult to recover these relics, or so much as to find out the place where they lay, on account of the inhospitable and savage temper of the barbarous people that inhabited the island. Nevertheless, afterwards, when Cimon took the island [...], and had a great ambition to find out the place where Theseus was buried, he, by chance, spied an eagle upon a rising ground pecking with her beak and tearing up the earth with her talons, when on the sudden it came into his mind, as it were by some divine inspiration, to dig there, and search for the bones of Theseus. There were found in that place a coffin of a man of more than ordinary size, and a brazen spear-head, and a sword lying by it, all which he took aboard his galley and brought with him to Athens. Upon which the Athenians, greatly delighted, went out to meet and receive the relics with splendid processions and sacrifices, as if it were Theseus himself returning alive to the city.[10]

For this hero cult to be effective, it had to be based on some minimal reality. The search for the bones of heroes was thus a cultural and political exercise which drew on complementary knowledge: the capacity for observation and piety, but also action. Cimon had to interpret the oracle and observe the landscape and animal behaviour, and this knowledge inspired by the gods allowed him to bring to light the hero's grave. The identification did not allow for discussion: the preceding signs and the size of the body proved the authenticity of the discovery. The procedures of the search and the cult of relics

The princely tomb of Eretria. Dating from around 720 BC and later covered by a heroön (monument of a hero cult) in about 680 BC, it provides archaeological evidence of the ideological salvage of Bronze Age objects during the Geometric period. Among the grave-goods was found a bronze sceptre from the Mycenean period. Visible in the photograph is the stone triangle of the heroön.

constitute a sort of archaeology of the holy. Moreover, the remains of the hero were a part of him, revived by the piety of the excavator: thus the earth knew how to respond to interrogation, provided one questioned it with fervour and attention. Herodotus tells us a story which is equally edifying but rather more belligerent. The Lacedaemonians and the Tegeans were at war and the former asked Pythia, 'How do we defeat the Tegeans?' She told them to bury the remains of Orestes, son of Agamemnon, on their land. Once again, what were they to do? Everyone knew who Orestes was, but where was his tomb? Pythia then added:

> Level and smooth is the plain where Arcadian Tegea standeth;
> There two winds are ever, by strong necessity, blowing,
> Counter-stroke answers stroke, and evil lies upon evil.
> There all-teeming Earth doth harbour the son of Atrides;
> Bring thou him to thy city, and then be Tegea's master.

After this reply, the Lacedaemonians were no nearer discovering the burial-place than before, though they continued to search for it diligently; until at last a man named Lichas, one of the Spartans called Agathoërgi, found it. The Agathoërgi are citizens who have just served their time among the knights. The five eldest of the knights go out every year, and are bound during the year after their discharge, to go wherever the State sends them, and actively employ themselves in its service.

Lichas was one of this body when, partly by good luck, partly by his own wisdom, he discovered the burial-place. Intercourse between the two States existing just at this time, he went to Tegea, and, happening to enter into the workshop of a smith, he saw him forging some iron. As he stood marvelling at what he beheld, he was observed by the smith who, leaving off his work, went up to him and said,

'Certainly, then, you Spartan stranger, you would have been wonderfully surprised if you had seen what I have, since you make a marvel even of the working in iron. I wanted to make myself a well in this room, and began to dig it, when what think you? I came upon a coffin seven cubits long. I had never believed that men were taller in the olden times than they are now, so I opened the coffin. The body inside was of the same length: I measured it, and filled up the hole again.'

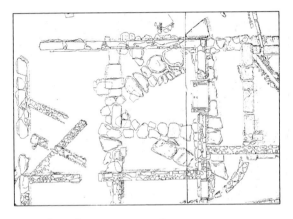

Plan of the Eretria tomb.

Such was the man's account of what he had seen. The other, on turning the matter over in his mind, conjectured that this was the body of Orestes, of which the oracle had spoken. He guessed so, because he observed that the smithy had two bellows, which he understood to be the two winds, and the hammer and anvil would do for the stroke and the counter-stroke, and the iron that was being wrought for the evil lying upon evil. This he imagined might be so because iron had been discovered to the hurt of man. Full of these conjectures, he sped back to Sparta and laid the whole matter before his countrymen. Soon after, by a concerted plan, they brought a charge against him, and began a pros-ecution. Lichas betook himself to Tegea, and on his arrival acquainted the smith with his misfortune, and proposed to rent his room of him. The smith refused for some time; but at last Lichas persuaded him, and took up his abode in it. Then he opened the grave, and collecting the bones, returned with them to Sparta. From henceforth, whenever the Spartans and the Tegeans made trial of each other's skill in arms, the Spartans always had greatly the advantage.[11]

Here even more than in the story of the transfer of Theseus' bones, the marvellous, the symbolic and the fantastic played a decisive part in the account. The discovery of the tomb was not the result of observation but the consequence of the interpretation of an oracle. We have no details of the arms or clothing of the hero; only his gigantic size distinguished his from any other burial. In fact, to locate the grave it was not necessary to interpret countryside or soil but to decipher a message. Identification was not linked to a material sign but to a place of symbols which had to be decoded. Lichas is an archaeologist of words rather than of the soil. Plutarch, like Pausanias, was more attentive than Herodotus to the discoveries revealed by the soil, because the spirit of the times in the second century AD favoured the collection and interpretation of antiquities. One of the witnesses is asked about the discovery by Agesilaus, king of Sparta, of the grave of Alcmene, the mother of Hercules:

Inscribed tablet from Bronze Age Crete. It shows an example of the script known as Linear B, deciphered in 1954 by the English archaeologist Michael Ventris. These signs were incomprehensible to the Greeks of the Classical period.

'You come most opportunely and as if by design,' said Theocritus. 'I had been desiring to hear what objects were found and what was the general appearance of Alcmena's tomb when it was opened up in your country – that is, if you were present when the remains were removed to Sparta on orders received from Agesilaüs.'

'I was not present,' Pheidolaüs replied; 'and although I expressed to my countrymen my strong indignation and exasperation at the outrage, they left me helpless. Be that as it may, in the tomb itself no remains were found, but only a stone, together with a bronze bracelet of no great size and two pottery urns containing earth which had by then, through the passage of time, become a petrified and solid mass. Before the tomb, however, lay a bronze tablet with a long inscription of such amazing antiquity that nothing could be made of it, although it came out clear when the bronze was washed; but the characters had a peculiar and foreign conformation, greatly resembling that of Egyptian writing. Agesilaüs accordingly, it was said, dispatched copies to the king, with the request to submit them to the priests for possible interpretation. But about these matters Simmias might perhaps have something to tell us, as at that

time he saw a good deal of the priests in Egypt in the pursuit of his philo-
sophical inquiries. At Haliartus the great failure of crops and encroachment of
the lake are held to have been no mere accident, but a judgement on us for
having allowed the excavation of the tomb.'[12]

Plutarch gives us a description, inadequate in our eyes but much
more detailed than we might have hoped, of Alcmene's grave. And it
does not take too much imagination for today's archaeologists to
recognise a Mycenean burial. As to the strange inscription, which
Plutarch tells us a little later the Egyptian priest Konouphis had great
difficulty in reading ('for three days he collated all sorts of characters
in the old books'), it poses problems because we know of no Mycenean inscription in bronze. In any case, it could be wagered that the
Egyptian priest's translation, which suggested
to the Greeks the creation of a competition in
honour of the Muses, had only a tenuous
connection with the text.

This passage from Plutarch is not the only
one to mention Greek Bronze Age writings.
During the reign of Nero an earthquake
destroyed the Cretan site of Knossos and
lime-bark tablets were found by shepherds.
The specialists at Nero's court took them for
Phoenician and translated them into Greek.
We possess a Latin edition by L. Septimius. As
the English archaeologist Robert Wace has
suggested, we cannot blame the scholars in
Nero's palace for not having translated a language they did not know. Whatever the con-
tent and imaginary nature of their translation, it gives us valuable
information on the psychology of the past in the Graeco-Roman
tradition. Not only were Mycenean and Minoan structures part of
the landscape which could not escape the notice of travellers, but
also, in the course of more or less casual excavations, fragments
which we now know to be the first writings in the Greek world
were sometimes found. Whether they attributed them to the
Phoenicians or the Egyptians, the Greeks knew that these incomprehensible inscriptions were quite different from the archaic letters
which they *could* decipher, and which they rightly traced back to
Phoenician invention — Herodotus had no trouble in reading the
'Cadmean' inscriptions (that is, following the Greek tradition, of

*Minerva and her
Inventions,* from a
fifteenth-century
manuscript. Minerva,
goddess of reason and
intelligence, is
represented as patron
of the invention of the
arts. At her feet figures
can be seen engaged
in weaving, carding
wool, metalwork and
playing the flute.

ΛΘΟΙΛΥΤΗΕΙΝΤΙΙΟΤΟLΟΤΙSΓUΕΚΙΝΝΝΝΑSSΙΕ
ΟΛΛΕΚΟΙΕΡΑΝΤΕΑLΙΕΙΤΑΥΙΝΙSΙOLLΙBUSΛΥRAS
ΛΟΟΙΕΙUΝΤΚΕΟDUΝΤΟΜΙΑLUSΙΑΙDΕΝΤΙΛΤΙΝΟUΝΙ
ΑΙΑΑLΑΟUΟΙΑΙLΤΙΝΤΟSΙΤΙSΙΝΟUDΙBUSΑΝΙΕRUΑΙ
ΙLLΙSΙΝΤΕΚSΙΕSLΜΛΟΝΝΛUΙΟΒΛΟΟΗΙΑΤΟLLUΝΤ

The Cyclops manufacturing Jupiter's lightning bolt. The Vatican Virgil (end of the fourth/ beginning of the fifth century) is one of the rare antique manuscripts of the later Empire to give us images from classical epic. Here the poet watches the Cyclops, masters of metallurgy, at work at their forge.

Mid-sixth century Greek vase. The Attic painters of the Archaic period were fond of the theme of the presentation of the arms of Achilles. On this vase the elements of the warrior's arms and armour are carefully illustrated.

Phoenician origin) carved on three tripods in the sanctuary of Apollo at Thebes in Boeotia.[13] The innumerable references to ancient objects deposited in sanctuaries are there to remind us that the temple treasure chambers were also, in a certain way, galleries of antiquities. These objects – tripods, arms, statues, clothing – were not displayed for their antiquity but because they recalled a particular event, incident or individual. Following Pausanias the entire history of Greece passes before the eyes of the visitor without a concern for the chronology that accompanies it, but with the firm desire to tie each object to an event, a person, or a particular object. This social role of the temples finds its origins in the tradition of presenting gifts, so often found in Homer. The objects which the heroes used – the arms of Achilles made by Hephaestus; the helmet of Odysseus which came to him from his uncle, the magician Autolycus; the bow of Philoctetes which was a gift from Apollo – all had a long history and the list of their owners was inseparable from their intrinsic qualities. In Greece social rank was linked with fame, a fame which attached to each weapon and each precious object. The exchange of objects was part of a complex gift-exchange system between heroes, kings and nobles. Thus there emerged a genealogy of objects just as important as that of men. From this grew the importance of the work of scholar-travellers and antiquaries who were the repository of knowledge of this kind.

THE GRAECO-ROMAN WORLD
AND ARCHAEOLOGY

THE TASTE FOR ART AND THE
TASTE FOR THE ANTIQUE
Pausanias, Pliny, Tacitus and the misadventures
of a treasure-hunting emperor

Unlike the treasures of the heroes, the temple treasuries had a collective function: they displayed objects of which the quality, rarity and, often, antiquity were a source of wonder to innumerable pilgrims. Soon the objects were distinguished not only by refined technique or precious materials, but by being the work of known artists. Competition between art and antiquity? Pausanias, before leaving the Parthenon, advises his readers, 'He who places works of art before antiquities, here is what can be seen',[14] and goes on to describe the masterpieces which the visitor should not miss. Once again Pausanias, a Greek author of the Roman period, addresses a public brought up on antique works and used to the splendour of urban settings and the arts of painting and sculpture. From the eighth century BC the Greek cities engaged in fierce rivalry over the building of sanctuaries and various monuments, the splendour of which was designed to proclaim their excellence. In experimenting with a political system which allowed each city to create its own institutions, the cities at the same time invented a life-style for the community in which monumental structures, statuary and paintings played a role as decisive as that of music and poetry. From this came the infinite sequence of works which were interdependent and evoked memories for artists, visitors and pilgrims. Artistic creation relied on these memories to justify, compare and foster each innovation which sprang from the sensibility of each artist. Plato later condemned that liberty which, in his eyes, so strongly distinguished the Greeks from the Egyptians. The latter, he said, maintained the same canons over thousands of years, since it was forbidden for sculptors, painters and other artists to distance themselves from traditional models; the Greeks by contrast never ceased to innovate, perfect and modify their forms of expression. This rapidly evolving art

Bronze tripod from Olympia, eighth century BC. In the Geometric period tripods formed an important part of the treasures of the great sanctuaries.

demanded an accompanying knowledge, a formation of taste following recognised and shared criteria, in short the invention of a history of art. When, around the second century BC, Greek art opted for a slower evolution, the role of art history became dominant and we shall soon see that politicians, Roman governors and even the emperors had a shared devotion to the most renowned artists and sought, by theft if needs be, to acquire their works for themselves. The enormous success of Pliny's history of art and Pausanias' guidebook cannot otherwise be explained. In developing a new discipline of the individual the Greeks had not only invented history but had created the necessary conditions for the appearance of an art market and thus a shared artistic knowledge. Not that the eastern courts had been lacking in artistic or historical sensibility, but there art could not be separated from the royal court, and the palaces of the dignitaries had to conform to this central model.

Aeneas at the construction of Carthage, a fifth-century miniature. For the illustrator of the Vatican Virgil the building of Carthage belonged to the cycle of the invention of the arts. The image of the foundation of a town is rare in antique art. Here, the heroes Aeneas and Achates watch the construction of the city.

If the taste for fine objects and collecting awoke the aesthetic sense, it also encouraged looting. After a victory, each city made it a point of honour to display the objects pillaged from the defeated city. The Roman governors moved to elevate artistic acquisition to the rank of a new branch of art, and Cicero has left us a colourful picture of the excesses of Varro. The hunt for treasure was often mixed with the most frenzied cupidity. Tacitus tells us with delight of an archaeological adventure by Nero:

Fortune soon afterwards made a dupe of Nero through his own credulity and the promises of Cæsellius Bassus, a Carthaginian by birth and a man of a crazed imagination, who wrested a vision seen in the slumber of night into a confident expectation. He sailed to Rome, and having purchased admission to the emperor, he explained how he had discovered on his land a cave of immense depth, which contained a vast quantity of gold, not in the form of coin, but in the shapeless and ponderous masses of ancient days. In fact, he said, ingots of great weight lay there, with bars standing near them in another part of the cave, a treasure hidden for so many ages to increase the wealth of the present. Phoenician Dido, as he sought to show by inference, after fleeing from Tyre and founding Carthage, had concealed these riches [...]. Nero upon this, without sufficiently examining the credibility of the author of the story, or of the matter

C·FVLVIVS·CALVIS·HARVSPEXS·D·D

Roman relief from Ostia, dating to the first century BC. On the right, fishermen draw up a Greek bronze in their net. This relief is one of the few instances in antique art where an archaeological object is clearly portrayed as such: the statue 'caught' by the fishermen can be easily recognised as a Greek bronze, probably a Herakles (Hercules) from the beginning of the fifth century BC. Hercules himself occupies the centre of the relief, and the personification of the god contrasts with his statue. He offers a tablet taken from a casket to a young boy. On the left, a third scene represents the consultation of the tablet; the person in the toga holds a half-open diptych, above him is a Victory.

itself, or sending persons through whom he might ascertain whether the intelligence was true, himself actually encouraged the report and despatched men to bring the spoil, as if it were already acquired. They had triremes assigned them and crews specially selected to promote speed. Nothing else at the time was the subject of the credulous gossip of the people, and of the very different conversation of thinking persons. It happened, too, that the quinquennial games were being celebrated for the second time, and the orators took from this same incident their chief materials for eulogies on the emperor. 'Not only,' they said, 'were there the usual harvests, and the gold of the mine with its alloy, but the earth now teemed with a new abundance, and wealth was thrust on them by the bounty of the gods.' […] Bassus indeed dug up his land and extensive plains in the neighbourhood, while he persisted that this or that was the place of the promised cave, and was followed not only by our soldiers but by the rustic population who were engaged to execute the work, till at last he threw off his infatuation, and expressing wonder that his dreams had never before been false, and that now for the first time he had been deluded, he escaped disgrace and danger by a voluntary death.[15]

A classic image of the treasure-hunting which obsessed an entire people carried away by the lure of gain, but also a portrait of the tyrant who saw the past as a resource capable of ensuring wealth in the present. The vain Eldorado of a mad emperor, who would not be stopped out of respect for antiquity or tradition. If the emperor was a treasure-hunter, if the well-being of the empire rested on the discovery of the riches of the past, it was as well that all rules were abolished: we shall see that the theme of the avaricious and deluded antiquary is a recurrent image in the history of archaeology.

ARCHAIOLOGIA AND ANTIQUITATES
Hippias, Varro and Polybius

The observation of ruins and the collection of prestigious and exotic objects was necessary for the Graeco-Roman scholars to understand, interpret and in a certain way exploit the world in which they lived. This curiosity, combined with the development of what Herodotus had been the first to call 'history', would lead to the founding of new disciplines: *archaiologia* in Greek, *antiquitates* in Latin.

Archaiologia: the knowledge of the past. In a famous passage in Plato's *Hippias Major*, Socrates debates with the sophist of Elis, Hippias, who is famous throughout the Greek world. The reputation and the honours awarded the scholar were not without striking and staggering rewards. His travels and embassies enabled the sophist to hold courses and conferences, attracting an immense public who remunerated him for his efforts. All the cities sought to hire his services, except Sparta, where the law forbade foreigners to teach the young. However, according to Hippias, the Lacedaemonians were as aware of the sophist's art as the other Greeks. In the course of questioning by Socrates it rapidly became clear that they were only interested in a particular branch of knowledge: neither astronomy, geometry, arithmetic, nor even the sciences of language or queenly rhetoric. The success of Hippias among the Spartans was limited to one science and one alone, that which dealt with 'the genealogies of heroes and of men ... and the settlements (how cities were founded in ancient times), and in a word all ancient history [*archaiologia*]'.[16]

Pub. terentius dacinus iarro

Bust of Varro (116–27 BC), one of the figures most revered by the Renaissance antiquaries.

The austere Spartan teachers categorically refused the sophist's lessons, but made an important exception for the science of the past. Still, this knowledge of the past was restricted to a very simple form of history: lists of names, of foundations, of sequences of events and the symbols necessary to legitimise the present – all this rather than thought. The most conservative of Greek cities, whose efforts, thanks to the sophistication of its institutions, were geared towards the abolition of time and the maintaining of the fiction of a never-changing, eternal city, this city had more need than any other of the past. A past which was to begin with a line of descent, a demarcation, a reference system, but which could not escape much greater questions. Assuredly what attracted the crowds was initially the element of *mythos*, the fine stories carried in the tales of ancient times. As expressed by Socrates, Hippias held for the Spartans the role of a grandmother 'telling stories to children'. But behind the stories of singular men there soon arose complex questions: the history of the cities called for more complete accounts, excursus and descriptions, in brief, 'everything to do with knowledge of the past'. *Archaiologia*, appearing for the first time under these circumstances, was thus a new word, one of those technical words dear to the refined language of the sophists. This *archaiologia* was not defined as a special discipline aimed at a specific type of knowledge. It was a convenient innovation to speak about everything that dealt with origins, with antiquity as a period, and with antiquities as objects of knowledge. In this sense, the term revealed an interest in the past less determined by explanation (history in Herodotus' sense, as an enquiry) than by description. Unfortunately tradition has not preserved for us the contemporary works on which this *archaiologia* was based: the treatises on 'peoples', on 'the names of peoples', 'the origins of peoples and cities' and the 'barbaric customs' attributed to Hellanikos (496–411 BC), or the books by Hippias on neighbouring subjects.

Arnaldo Momigliano has demonstrated that the emergence of two distinct types of history can be identified at this time (around the middle of the fifth century BC). The one, developing on its own account the Herodotean tradition of analysis, was interested in the recent past, that which we might call contemporary history, and sought with the unequalled mastery of Thucydides to construct an explanation of human behaviour, to lay the foundations of a science of politics. On the other side, Hippias, Hellanikos and many others were interested in a more distant past and in establishing the premises of a history of cities, morals and customs, directed more at their anatomy, at minute description, in short, at erudition. The Greek historians anticipated a classic distinction in the practice of history which Momigliano has summarised as follows:

1. In their writings, the historians stuck to chronology while the antiquaries followed a systematic plan;

2. The historians presented those facts which served to illustrate or explain a given situation; the antiquarians gathered all the material relevant to a given subject, whether or not they had a problem to solve. The subject in hand only helped distinguish the historians from the antiquaries in so far as, traditionally, it was considered that certain subjects (for example political institutions, religion, private life) lent themselves more to a logical plan than to chronological treatment.[17]

The antiquary is distinguished from the historian in that he collects objects or facts, whilst the latter relies on questions which ultimately lead him to the objects and facts. This subtle distinction has not ceased to weigh upon the organisation and development of the historical sciences and on man's feeling for the past. The opposition between historians and antiquaries – tacitly posed since its Greek beginnings – is not a difference of material but of method. Each deals with human affairs without following the same path. Momigliano considered the appearance of the term *archaiologia* with Plato as the indication of an awareness of these differences, as an attempt to define *archaiologia* against *historia*. But he qualified this statement himself in recalling that this term, which had become common in the Hellenistic period, had already lost its specificity: the Roman archaeology of Dionysius of Halicarnassus and the Jewish archaelogy of Flavius Josephus were histories in the first sense of the Romans and the Jews. The explosion of historical genres at this time is striking. The blossoming of works and the diversification of titles heralded the arrival of the age of specialists in the past, who can equally be called *kritikos, philologos, polyhistōr, grammatikos* and, in Latin, *doctus, eruditus, litteratus.*

Lectures on Varro with textual notes, composed in 1484 by Pomponio Leto, one of the most famous Roman antiquaries of the fifteenth century.

With the development of their institutions the cities created systems for archives, publication and communication. Soon, men began to collect, study and compare these. The principles stated by Herodotus and Thucydides had found in the fertile ground of the political practice of the cities the conditions necessary for their success. Historians since the Renaissance have searched in the classical tradition for prolegomena and keys to their theoretical debates. Where does ethnography start and history finish? What is the boundary between chronography and political history, or between local and universal history? These questions were familiar to the ancient historians, and they brought to them a variety of responses. Momigliano's analysis revealed the conquests of Hellenistic erudition by emphasising the variety of approaches and the advances in technique. Following on from these, the facts were not contradictory: if the Graeco-Roman scholars had invented most of the fundamental knowledge of the science of the past — publication, collection, description, chronological and textual critique — they were at the same time exploring the avenues opened up since the sixth century *Geographia* by Hecateus of Miletus. Capable of observing landscape and earth, they also set out the limits of interpretation and descriptive systems which made possible the establishment of a cumulative and ordered knowledge.

Unfortunately we do not have Hippias' *Archaiologia*, and we have seen that those of Dionysius of Halicarnassus and Flavius Josephus are in fact Histories. But at least we have at our disposal parts of a treatise on *Antiquitates* by a man whom Cicero tells us was an *investigator antiquitatis*. As a collaborator with Pompey and correspondent with Cicero, Varro was a man of stature in society and the scholarly world at the end of the Republic. For Cicero, Varro was the 'rediscoverer of Latin culture':

Indeed, when we were sojourning and wandering like foreigners in our own city, your books, I may say, escorted us home, and enabled us at length to perceive who we were and where we lived. You have revealed to us the age of our fatherland, its chronology, the laws of its religion and priesthoods, the plan of our home and foreign administration, the position of our territories and districts, the titles and descriptions of all things divine and human, with the duties and principles attaching to them.[18]

Varro's inquisitiveness was immense and his knowledge limitless. However, only a few meagre fragments allow us to discover this massive compilation. In Varro's work the architecture was as important as its construction, and we can partly reconstitute the project thanks to an impressive description by Saint Augustine:

Varro wrote forty-one books under the title Antiquities. *He divided his matter under two headings, human and divine, devoting twenty-five books to*

Manuscript of Herodotus with a Latin translation by Lorenzo Valla (1407–57). One of the most famous philologists of his time, Valla helped make known the work of ancient authors, notably Herodotus, who enjoyed great prestige during the Renaissance.

the former and sixteen to the latter. He followed the plan of devoting six books to each of four subdivisions under the heading 'Things Human': Persons, Places, Times, and Actions – dealing in the first six with persons, in the second six with places, and the third six with times, in the fourth and last six, with actions. These four sixes make twenty-four. At the beginning he placed one book by itself, as a general introduction to the whole. In general, he followed a similar plan in regard to divine things, as far as the subject matter allowed.

Sacred actions are performed by persons in certain places at definite times. And these are the four topics he treats, giving three books to each. The first three deal with the persons who perform the rites, the next three with places, the third with times, the fourth with the rites. Here, too, he is careful to make the distinctions: Who, Where, When and What. The main topic he was expected to deal with was: To whom. Hence, the last three deal with the gods; the five threes making fifteen in all. To make up the total of sixteen which I mentioned, he placed one book by itself at the beginning to serve as a general introduction.[19]

Varro's four-part division proposed a systematic and logical framework for the description of 'matters human and divine'. It established an order within the universe which otherwise would have been purely enumerative; above all it established a successive relationship between the characteristics of men and the characteristics of deities. Saint Augustine was not mistaken in emphasising that Varro addressed godly matters after those of mankind because he considered that the latter proceeded from the former. Moreover, it was not the essence of divinity which Varro studied but the way in which the gods were honoured, celebrated and regarded by mankind: 'Varro gives a reason for treating of human things first and of divine things later, namely, because cities came into existence first and only later instituted religious rites.'[20]

Varro envisaged a religious sociology which, for the bishop of Hippo, was sacrilegious because it could lead to the supposition that the existence of deities was a human creation. Ignoring the true faith, Varro, when dealing with the gods, spoke of the relationship of men to the gods and his theology was as fragile as his knowledge of antiquities was secure: 'In what he writes about human matters, he follows the historians who deal with facts [*historiam rerum gestarum*]. In what he writes about what he calls 'divine' matters, what does he do but give us feelings about fancies [*opiniones rerum vanarum*]?'[21]

Saint Augustine set out to destroy Varro's conclusions; however, his relentless critique is the best homage to the quality of the work. The antiquary won that which the theologian lost. No other Latin author before him had accumulated so much historical evidence and presented it so perfectly. Confronted with a historian's history, Varro produced an ordered corpus of knowledge, the importance of which rested not only on its proven learning, but also and above all on the logical – one could almost say phenomenological – nature of its approach. If social types, places, time and things (material and non-material) created by human societies were susceptible to ordered, progressive and complete knowledge, then the relationship of human and divine affairs could claim a rigour similar to that of the natural sciences. Varro thus provided the long line of antiquaries with the elements of a positive knowledge of past societies. The description of men, their actions, their institutions and their products was both the means and the end of antiquarian studies. The question of methodology came not before the collection of data or its cataloguing, but after. It followed from rigorous observation and the quality of classification. Here, assuredly, was a way of looking at the past which was different from the investigations and stories, however authoritative, of the historical tradition from Thucydides to Polybius. The latter expressed vividly these contrasting ways of reading the past:

The genealogical side appeals to those who are fond of a story, and the account of colonies, the foundation of cities, and their ties of kindred, such as we find, for instance, in Ephorus, attracts the curious and lovers of recondite lore, while the student of politics is interested in the doings of nations, cities, and monarchs.[22]

The type of history with which Polybius contrasted his political conception was exactly that which Hippias used to delude the Spartans: specific facts over general history, antiquarian history over history in the strict sense. This is the (almost) natural state of the debate which runs through the ancient history of the West and whose terminology continues to haunt the complex relationship between archaeology and history.

Scenes from one of the most luxuriously illustrated manuscripts (1473) of *The City of God*, the major work of St Augustine (354–430). Composed at the end of his life, this book is supposed to be a response to the pagans who reproached the Christians for forcibly imposing the abandonment of polytheism.

On this page in the upper frame St Augustine responds to the objections presented to him. Behind him pagans are worshipping idols: the pagan statues are placed on columns like busts in a Renaissance villa. Below, a Christian announces to the crowd the destruction of their town because of their sins.

Opposite above, the emperor Octavius surrounded by Varro, Cicero and St Augustine. The choice of authors is evidence of the interest in the work of Varro and his tradition from the late Empire to the Renaissance.

Opposite below, an example of stupidity: the pagans ask Bacchus for water and the nymphs for wine. On the left, the god of wine (*liber pater*), on the right, goddesses of water; devils hover above. The Romans address the divinities:

Das nobis aquas: give us water
Detis nobis barbas: give us beards (the philosophers', i.e. wisdom?)
Detis nobis vinum: give us wine
Detis nobis fortitudinem: give us courage.

The nymphs lead the men astray: a man flounders in a well under the weight of an upturned donkey: 'These were devils who by night mocked people and led them from the path.'

L ue femble que raye aſſez
diſpute es cinq liures pre
cedens contre ceulxo qui ai
dent que pour le prouffit
de ceſte vie mortelle et des
choſes terriennes len doie
honnourer z aourer par
telle ozdonnance z ſtatute
Eeſt adire de vraie religi
on qui en ꝓpre eſt appellee
latria. la quelle eſt deue a
vng vray dieu. pluſ ꝝ di

eux et ſaulx leſquelz la verite creſtienne conuaint
eſtir ydoles non prouffitables ou ors eſpzits et
maluais dyables ou certes creatures et no vne
arateur. Et qui eſt cellui qui ne ſache que
ces cinq liures ou autres de quelconques trans
nombzes ne peuent pour certain ſouffire a treſ
tgrande folie ou obſtinacion quant len cuide que
ycelle ſtloire de baincte ne donne lieu a aucunes
fozces de verite en la maluaiſtie. Toutesuoies de
cellup en qui ſittrant vice a ſcie nourrie. Ear no
mie par la maluaiſtie du medecin mais du
malade ſa maladie eſt faicte non auzible et m

GRAECO-ROMAN PREHISTORY
Diodorus Siculus

The discovery of fire, wood engraving by Cesare Cesariano, 1521, from his translation with commentary of Vitruvius' treatise *On Architecture*, written in 27 BC. Illustrations for this book provided the occasion for an iconography of the discovery of the arts which threw off medieval traditions. The reading of Graeco-Roman 'primitivists' was the source of Renaissance interest in the origins of humanity.

The *antiquitates*, established in a descriptive discipline by Varro's efforts, could not restrict themselves to the study of a history immediately preceding that of the cities. The question of human origins in the Graeco-Roman tradition was not just philosophical but also a subject for history, and Varro did not fail to echo this:

It is a necessity that from the remotest antiquity of human life they have come down, as Dicaearchus teaches, step by step to our age, and that the most distant stage was that state of nature in which man lived on those products which the virgin earth brought forth of her own accord; they descended from this stage into the second, the pastoral, in which they gathered for their use acorns, arbutus berries, mulberries, and other fruits by plucking them from wild and uncultivated trees and bushes, and likewise caught, shut up, and tamed such wild animals as they could for the like advantage. There is good reason to suppose that, of these, sheep were first taken, both because they are useful and because they are tractable; for these are naturally most placid and most adapted to the life of man. For to his food they brought milk and cheese, and to his body wool and skins for clothing. Then by a third stage man came from the pastoral life to that of the tiller of the soil; in this they retained much of the former two stages, and after reaching it they went far before reaching our stage.[23]

This passage from Varro's *Agronomy* faithfully demonstrates the three-age theory – the dark age, the age of myth, the age of *polis* – as initiated by the Greeks. We must also look to the Greek authors for a clarification of the vision of human origins to which Varro adhered.

In Greek tradition the origin of humanity was, above all, a philosophical question. Thucydides' distrust of everything that was not contemporary history was shared by most of those who held to a political and analytical concept of the historian's trade. The history of the Dark Ages and even that of the Heroic Age was thus a field of reflection reserved for philosophers, ethnographers and those who, along with Momigliano, we may call the antiquaries. The Greek tradition – particularly Ionian – was distinguished by the idea, which was affirmed, argued and developed in various ways, of constant human progress and a direct relationship between technical and social evolution. Certainly, ever since Hesiod, the idea of progressive

human decline from an original Golden Age was relatively current, but it emerged from mythological discourse and it did not restrain the development of concurrent theories on human origins. This history of human progress could take many forms, from the theory of discovery to the idea of stages best represented by Dicaearchus. The speculative quality of most of these models has lost none of its seductive capacity. It is even obvious that the modern three-stage theory – prehistory, protohistory, history – has its origins in the Greek three-age model. The cataclysm theory in the third book of Plato's *Laws* had also influenced numerous considerations of the relations between human history and geological time. The 'modernity' of prehistory as imagined by Greek thinkers and their Roman successors is such that it seems to us to develop into contemporary theories of evolution.

The paradox lies elsewhere; whilst the philosophers and theoreticians did not hesitate to deal with the question of human and societal origins with a surprising inventiveness, political history – but also ethnography and antiquarianism – profited little from this conceptual framework. Even if the Greeks were aware of the decisive relationship between men and their environment and were able to suggest, as Lucretius later did, the technological succession of stone, bronze and iron, whose enunciation was the keystone of nineteenth-century prehistory, not a single antiquary, at least in the texts left to us, undertook a detailed account of the dwellings, clothes and tools of prehistoric man. The opposition between theory and practice ran through Greek science. To be convinced we need only look at the scenario of primitive humanity set out by Diodorus Siculus in Book I of his *Bibliotheca historica*:

The foregoing, then, is what we are told about the first beginning of the universe. As for the first-born men, it is said they endured a precarious and subhuman existence. They roamed about individually in search of food, plucking the most digestible plants and natural fruits from the trees. The attacks of wild beasts taught them the advantage of mutual assistance; and, once thrown together by fear, they gradually came to recognize each other's features. Then, from inarticulate and confused sounds, they little by little refined their power of speech: they agreed with each other on verbal symbols for everything they encountered and made the meaning of all words clear among themselves. But, with such conventions arising all over the world, every group did not speak the same language, since each one chose its vocabulary at random. In this way all the different varieties of human speech came about, and these first existing societies were the origin of every nation.

With none of the useful things of life as yet discovered, these first men lived but miserably. They were innocent of clothes, unacquainted with houses or fire, and lacking the very notion of cultivated food. In fact, ignorant even of how to store their wild foodstuffs, they made no stockpile of provisions against future needs, wherefore many perished in the winters from cold and lack of food. But in the course of time, taught by experience, they sought the shelter of caves for the winter and put aside for later use those foods capable of being preserved. And, after gaining knowledge of fire and other conveniences, by degrees they discovered the arts and other things of advantage to

human existence. For generally speaking, in all things necessity itself served as man's tutor, and she grudged not her lessons on all subjects to a creature naturally adept and having the benefit of hands, speech, and shrewdness of mind in all endeavors.

But, to observe reasonable proportions in our work, we shall let what has already been said of man's beginnings and earliest way of life suffice us.[24]

Undoubtedly, no such coherent description of human prehistory was again put forward until the arrival of Boucher de Perthes in the nineteenth century. But this reconstruction – based as much on ethnographic observation as on the random discoveries of the sort recounted by Herodotus and Thucydides – did not become a pragmatic knowledge which could have led antiquaries to find the answers to their questions in the soil. The Greeks had not created an active archaeology, and this was not through lack of curiosity or inventiveness. And just as

Piero di Cosimo, *The Hunt*, c.1495–1505. This composition was part of a cycle of paintings which Cosimo devoted to the origins of humanity. Hunting is one of the major stages in the human experience. Here, there is 'nothing but horror and death [...]: a fight in the jungle with all against all' (E. Panofsky).

history remained the art of story-telling, in which critique, and above all the establishment of the sources, was of secondary importance, so, in the case of prehistory, the quality and ingenuity of the reconstruction was the prime objective. The antiquaries did not, any more than the historians, feel obliged to state and justify their sources.

Men building cabins and huts, wood engraving by Jean Goujon, 1547, from a French translation of Vitruvius' treatise *On Architecture*. The text presents animals as a model for primitive man.

M.I. Finley has brilliantly shown that Thucydides, despite the genius of his writing, was not in the mode of von Ranke; nor were Varro and Lucretius like Boucher de Perthes; the curiosity of the Ancients about the past remained philosophical and did not give rise to the profession of historian as we understand it today.

The philosophers and antiquaries of the Graeco-Roman world knew where to place the antiquity of man and how to establish a relative chronology which, even if not calibrated, suggested a considerable difference in age between the men of the Dark Ages and those of mythical times. They sensed that natural phenomena, or even the evolution of plants and animals, could contribute to lay the foundations for a natural history of mankind. In elaborating a theory of stages – hunting, pastoralism, agriculture – they introduced for the first time a rationality in the development of life-styles and techniques. They did not hesitate, as Lucretius suggested, to affirm that human progress was technical progress which, from stone to bronze and up to iron, was linked to man's ability to extract raw minerals of nature. However, we must not for all that think that this vision of

Scene of primitive life, wood engraving by Cesare Cesariano, 1521. Primitive man is shown using stone tools – an interesting image for a time when certain scholars were beginning to question the real nature of 'thunderbolts'.

the past was commonly accepted. At the same time, primitivist ideas about human decline since the Golden Age, cyclical theories and myths as a means of explanation all battled against the rationalist methods which our vision of the history of human science is led to prefer. If what we now call archaeology did not emerge fully-armed from Greek tradition, it is because, as M.I. Finley reminds us, Greeks and Romans did not have the same idea of history as ourselves:

The ancient Greeks already possessed the skills and the manpower with which to discover the shaft-graves of Mycenae and the palace of Cnossus, and they had the intelligence to link the buried stones – had they dug them up – with the myths of Agamemnon and Minos, respectively. What they lacked was the interest: that is where the enormous gap lies between their civilization and ours, between their view of the past and ours.[25]

In its dazzling intuitions and unpublished observations, the vision of the past handed down to us from Graeco-Roman antiquity constitutes for historians, and especially archaeologists, a call for humility, for the questioning and criticism of evidence.

CHINESE AND JAPANESE ANTIQUARIES
IN THE SEARCH FOR THE PAST

Bronze of the Shang dynasty (1650–1066 BC) and porcelain of the Qianlong period (1736–95). In China, bronze vessels were associated from the beginning with royal power. Rediscovered under the Song dynasty in the eleventh century AD, when important chance finds were a powerful stimulus to archaeological exploration, these bronzes became a source of inspiration for potters. Imitations of ancient vases, enhanced by the 'yellow imperial' colour or a dragon design, the porcelains of the Qing dynasty reflect the archaising taste of the Emperor Qianlong, a passionate collector of ancient pottery and bronzes.

Bronze vessels feature on the Coromandel lacquers exported to Europe in the seventeenth and eighteenth centuries, as on this medal-cabinet in the Bibliothèque Nationale, Paris. Here three bronze vessels of the Han dynasty (206 BC–AD 220) are clearly identifiable.

We have seen with Sima Qian the distinguished role which the Chinese of antiquity assigned to knowledge of the past and observation of the earth. Thanks to the formidable continuity of their ideograms, scholars were able, over the centuries, to decipher inscriptions and maintain an infallible contact with the past. The existence of a centralised empire and the increasingly important role of the scholars certainly constitute an advantage which explains the success of a particular form of Chinese historiography. Texts such as those of Xie Huilian in the fifth century AD vouch for the curiosity of imperial bureaucrats and the ritual devotion given to the discovery of ancient burials, just as we find, from the fifth century onwards, attempts at epigraphical critique. In a work entitled *yanshi jiaxun* an author used an inscription to rectify an erroneous title.[26] Later Zhao Mingcheng, in his preface to a book on antiquities, characterised the establishment of proof by means of inscriptions in the following terms:

After reading the classics in my youth, I found the deeds of princes and ministers recorded in detail in the histories, and although right and wrong is praised and criticized, this is based on the subjective opinions of the writers and may fall short of reality. [...] But take such things as chronology, geography, official titles, and genealogy, for example. When archaeological materials are used to examine these things, thirty to forty per cent of the data are in conflict. That is because historical writings are produced by latter-day writers and cannot fail to contain errors. But the inscriptions on stone and bronze are made at the time the events take place and can be trusted without reservation, and thus discrepancies may be discovered.[27]

So, almost ten centuries before western defenders of the pre-eminence of epigraphy over tradition, Chinese scholars affirmed with astonishing precocity the special nature and historical quality of epigraphic sources. The Greeks attributed to one of their earliest historians, Acusilaus (sixth century BC), the idea of writing genealogies from bronze tablets: '*Akusilaos [...] a very early historian. He wrote genealogies based on inscriptions on bronze which according to tradition his father had found while digging in some corner of his property.*'[28]

This fragment, even if apocryphal in part, nonetheless emphasises that the presence of inscribed texts is a guarantee which establishes the legitimacy of historical discourse. Chinese historians went still

further in affirming the pre-eminence of epigraphic over literary sources. The inscription had superior authenticity because it was a direct testimony of events produced by contemporaries themselves. In China, inscriptions were associated with sacrificial tripods, even more valued because they witnessed a past which only diviners and the literate were capable of interpreting. Prestige objects and instruments of worship, tripods were *sémiophores par exellence* and as such necessary to the accession of the new emperor, the harvesting of crops and resistance to invaders. Sima Qian devoted much of his *Records of the Grand Historian of China* to the discovery of ancient tripods; the learned strove to decipher the inscriptions on these as proof of their knowledge and their devotion to the emperor. Here, from 133 BC, is the story of Li Shaojun, sage and magician, who passed himself off as immortal:

When Li Shao-chün appeared before the emperor, the latter questioned him about an ancient bronze vessel which the emperor had in his possession. 'This vessel,' replied Li Shao-chün, 'was presented at the Cypress Chamber in the tenth year of the reign of Duke Huan of Ch'i [676 BC].' When the inscription on the vessel was deciphered, it was found that it had in fact belonged to Duke Huan of Ch'i. Everyone in the palace was filled with astonishment and decided that Li Shao-chün must be a spirit who had lived hundreds of years.[29]

Everything in this story is archaeological: the ancient vase which belonged to the emperor, the dating confirmed by the inscription, the marvelling of the court at a magician whose age was confirmed by the epigraphy. For the contemporaries of Li Shaojun, archaeology came to the aid of magic and not magic to the aid of archaeology. Sima Qian related this story with a certain irony. Like Pausanias he possessed a real interest in antiquities but he reveals himself to be closer to Herodotus in his feeling for factual history and his taste for solid detail. His work confirms what we already know to be the image of the past held by the Chinese scholars of antiquity and the Middle Ages. Various documents confirm the role of ancient objects and inscriptions in social life. There are varying accounts of the finding and accurate decipherment of inscribed bronzes in the second and first centuries BC,[30] and a *Treatise on Omens* compiled at the end of the fifth century AD contains a description of fifteen different discoveries concerning forty-one vases, briefly described with their origins carefully indicated. In the same period the first treatises on numismatics appeared, which were also linked to the interests of collectors. One of these collections has survived and consists of two big ceramic jars and a silver vase containing crockery, jewellery, rare medicines and a group of coins including one of Khusrau II (AD 591–628), last king of the Sasanian dynasty of Iran. This treasure belonged to a governor-general of the Shen-Xi region, Li Shouli, who died in 741, and contained, besides the Byzantine coins, a variety of Chinese coins of which the oldest dated back to at least the fifth century BC, and Japanese coins of the eighth century AD.[31]

With the establishment of the Song dynasty in the ninth century the taste for antiquities seems to have become still more pronounced. It was the time of catalogues of antiquities. A little later we see the appearance of the first woodcut-illustrated books on antiquities: the *Kaogu tu* in 1092 and the *Bogu tu* in 1122. Each of these works presents drawings of vases and facsimiles of inscriptions. They are organised along typological lines and the objects are dated; 224 catalogue entries made up the *Kaogu tu* and 839 the *Bogu tu*. The production of copies for cult purposes, and even fakes to satisfy the collectors, are proof of the contemporary craze for this type of object. We possess an extraordinary autobiographical testimony to the spirit of the collectors of the time. It is the postscript written in 1132 by the wife of the aforementioned antiquary, Zhao Mingcheng as an addition to her husband's book, *Metal and Stone Archives*. If we contemplate the moving portrait of this enterprise traced by Owen,[32] we find, in this lady's astute writing, the most literate and feeling critique of the collection:

When the book collection was complete, we set up a library in 'Return Home' hall, with huge bookcases where the books were catalogued in sequence. There we put the books. Whenever I wanted to read, I would ask for the key, make a note in the ledger, then take out the books. If one of them was a bit damaged or soiled, it would be our responsibility to repair the spot and copy it out in a neat hand. There was no longer the same ease and casualness as before. This was an attempt to gain convenience which led instead to nervousness and anxiety. I couldn't bear it. And I began to plan how to do away with more than one meat in our meals, how to do away with all the finery in my dress; for my hair there were no ornaments of bright pearls or

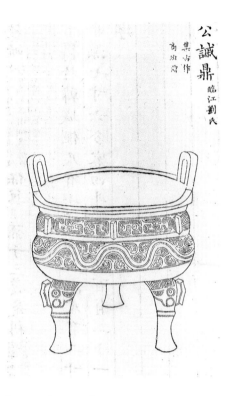

In the eleventh century Chinese scholars compiled the first catalogues of ancient vases of the second and first millennia BC. Here is a vase of Ding type, taken from a 1752 edition of *Kaogu tu*. The caption gives the name of the collector. On the back is a reproduction of the rubbing of the inscription which details the casting process of the ritual vase. A label indicates the find-spot, dimensions and weight of the object.

A collector of ancient vases appraises his collection, painting by Tu Chin, end of the sixteenth century. In a terrace garden a rich amateur shows his purchases to a friend, who examines the archaic bronzes laid out on the table.

kingfisher feathers; the household had no implements for gilding or embroidery. [...] Books lay ranged on tables and desks, scattered on top of one another on pillows and bedding. This was what took our fancy and what occupied our minds, what drew our eyes and what our spirits inclined to; and our joy was greater than the pleasure others had in dancing girls, dogs, and horses.[33]

The common passion for the collection which united the spouses was transformed into oppression; the exceptional widow of the noted collector makes us gradually aware that she and her husband (particularly herself) became objects in their own collection. She had to abandon books, objects and paintings to the mercy of invaders of the empire in the long flight towards the capital; with the last book, the last inscription remaining to her, she realised that she was herself the last trace of the collection.

Not until the eighteenth century in the West, and then not from a woman's pen, will we find as subtle an assessment of the alienation which seized the collector. Be that as it may, scholars of the Song period discovered with passion the attraction of the past when this was ordered into a collection. They made collecting into both an art and a vice, and this art clamoured for knowledge: first one should collect objects and, to do this, go into the field and observe. From this period also date the first archaeological accounts of travels, which led scholars to describe and recover the remains of ancient cities. Thus we have a plan of Xi'an, the Tang capital, made in 1080 and based on much earlier sources. It shows with great precision the mapping of different parts of the town. To maintain their interest the Song scholars did not restrict themselves to drawing: they classified and interpreted their finds. At the beginning of the eleventh century Liu Chang explained that the study of ancient bronzes could satisfy three different points of view: religious historians could determine the use of vases, genealogists could establish the sequence of historical figures, and etymologists could decipher the inscriptions.[34]

Where did this passion for antiquities come from? From tradition and from a strong continuity, as we have seen in China as elsewhere, but also from the existence of a social class able to collect and study. This accompanies a sense of time and of the erosion of history which is perfectly expressed by another contemporary: 'But mountains are levelled and valleys filled and the elements wreak their destruction. When we come down to the time of the Cheng Ho and Hsüan Ho periods (1111–1125), eight-tenths of those ancient objects had already been lost.'[35] This attention to the past, so characteristic of China, appeared also in Japan. In a Japanese chronicle of 713, the *Hitachi Fudoki*, there is a description of a shell-mound accidentally discovered in the archipelago: one of the oldest references to prehistoric remains to exist in a medieval text. Dating from the same period is the *Chronicle of Ancient Things*, which is an attempt to establish a mythological history of Japan.[36] A little earlier (689–97) the practice of *shikinen sengū* is attested, consisting of razing and rebuilding in identical fashion every twenty years the Imperial sanctuary at Ise. This ritual was designed to preserve the purity of the sanctuary across the centuries, whilst its appearance never aged. The original wooden architecture thus remained immutable thanks to the archaic skill of the carpenters and joiners. Compared to the Chinese, the Japanese had thus developed a technique of craft memory which, to the eyes of a Hellenist, recalls the concurrence of word and marble (see p. 22); here the skill transmitted cyclically is supposed to prevent the material deterioration of the sanctuary. The repeated action of the artisans led in the long run to the most solid of constructions.

THE MIDDLE AGES CONFRONTED BY THE RUINS OF ANTIQUITY

THE COLLAPSE OF THE GRAECO–ROMAN MODEL AND THE CRISIS OF HISTORY
The era of the hagiographers

Since the first Ionian philosophers, the people of classical antiquity
had striven to understand the past. This effort led to the creation of a
knowledge strongly tied to a historical genre. What differentiated the
Greeks and Romans from the Egyptians or the Assyrians was not, as
we have seen, an interest in the past, but the form which this interest
took, the way of writing history. In the intellectual field thus cleared,
several types of history saw the light of day, and this diversity explains
how a descriptive history which strove to classify societies, institutions and objects could flourish alongside political history. This project, which Varro incarnates towards its end, was the result of a
movement derived from curiosity and reflection which considered
the relationships of men, of institutions and monuments from a theoretical and classificatory viewpoint. It cannot be separated from the
work of the philosophers who, in trying to define the special nature
of mankind, laid the foundations for a history of evolution in which
man was the biological and social focus. Certainly, the idea of primitive man was opposed by the myths of the Golden Age, but people in
antiquity had little difficulty in visualising lost cities of the past, the
herdsmen of ancient times and their primitive weapons, the caverns
and huts of men of the earliest periods.[37] With the progressive collapse of the Roman Empire, it was not only institutions and the
social order that disappeared, but also an intellectual frame of reference. Even if, for several centuries more, western culture drew on the
Graeco-Roman tradition, it was never possible for intellectuals of the
medieval period to have the freedom, time and facilities which the
people of antiquity enjoyed.

The difficulties of the time – the wars, the effects of multiple invasions – cannot explain everything. The loss of influence of the model
of ancient education and the affirmation of Christian culture, which
was suspicious of the idolatry manifest in the texts, monuments and
ancient objects, counted for something. In the great upheaval which
ravaged the West, bishops and monks became the curators and

conmemorartione scōrx,

riæm nobir ,pfit. æd

Pacem nor dñe. tuorx

pælutir augmenta sint

inquib; tumixxbilir p

die inuentio Scī

§ qui inpr

inuentio

surcitast

pręcio. et ne

§ cui cuncta oboe

uerbo tuo ferift

Ineffæbilem clemti

crucir fili tui pio

Greek manuscript dating to AD 510, illustrating the discourse of St Gregory of Naziannus (329–89) entitled *Against Julian*. The Emperor Julian, called Julian the Apostate (332–63), had rejected Christianity and restored paganism. In the top section he is shown leaving a round tower and dragged against his will by a pagan priest towards an open cave beneath a tomb, in which can be seen an active crowd of demons. Led by the same priest (in the lower section), Julian, followed by two officials, is present at the immolation of a bull sacrificed by the priest.

defenders of literacy and literature, exercising this function with a devotion that would be hard to reproach. The collapse, not only of the Empire, but of the city as a place of local culture, progressively swept away a certain type of man and, with him, a philosophical way of 'making history'. So came the time of the hagiographers, and the clergy had to rid the countryside of the still numerous remains of paganism, because the type of history which the new ruling dynasties demanded had to justify their rapid rise to prominence and affirm their descent from a prestigious past. The clergy set out not only to expurgate ancient literature of works which could threaten Holy Scripture but, above all, they showed little interest any more in digressions on human origins. They had too much to do to establish that the Franks, like the Romans, were descended from the Trojans, and to reconcile the Revelation with Graeco-Roman history, which was all that was available.

It should not be forgotten that the arrival of the 'barbarians' in the Empire was at first characterised by a massive hunt for treasure. Rome itself did not escape pillage by Alaric and his successors. Procopius gives a detailed description of the Vandals sailing towards Africa, laden with Imperial treasures. Palaces, temples, private houses, villas abandoned by their owners and servants were easy prey, and the 'barbarians' were not the only ones to take advantage. This immense upheaval of people and possessions engendered a progressive redistribution of property and belongings. In fact the monuments of Rome did not begin to fall into ruin with the arrival of the 'barbarians'. In 376 Valens, Gratian and Valentinian issued an order that forbade house-builders to use marble and stone from monuments.[38] In 458 Majorius issued a decree ordering the prefect Aurelius to put an end to further destruction. Theodoric himself was careful to preserve the monumental setting of the city and charged his agent:

With the upkeep of ancient things in their original glory, and to see to it that the new did not spoil the old, for in the same way that one's clothes should match in colour for one to be suitably dressed, in order for a palace to be splendid every part of it must be as beautiful as the rest.[39]

Such a pronounced interest in monuments naturally led him to adorn his palace in Ravenna with the finest columns and most beautiful marbles from Rome. The acquisition of statues and colossi still went on, but what of excavating graves and sarcophagi? Theodoric was to give juridicial expression to the right of escheat which affected the most protected places, the graves and funerary monuments:

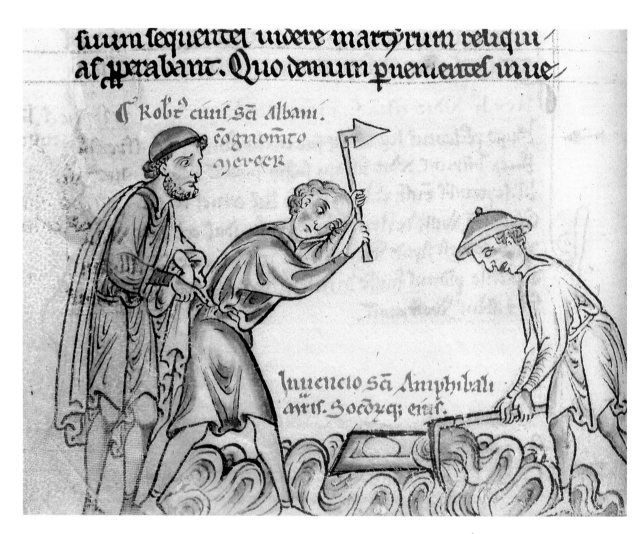

Discovery of the relics of St Amphibalus (286–303), depicted
in a thirteenth-century manuscript, the *Chronica majora*.
Under the eye of Robert, Earl of St Albans, the workmen
dig in the earth.

form the remains of the Empire into a framework for the new way of life, there had to be an art of exploiting the ruins. This is why the sixth and seventh centuries, before what we have come to call the Carolingian renaissance, seem so dark to us; this is why the interest in the past seems more utilitarian than cultural. Already, however, some clerics had returned to the path of tradition, and Gregory of Tours in his *History of the Franks* gives evidence of this desire to maintain links with classical culture. It was Childeric, for example, who was preoccupied by the state of learning and gave the order to: 'rewrite the books of the Ancients, which had been worn away with a pumice stone.'[42]

In matters of architecture, much more than pumice was required to make the monuments in the landscape disappear. Ever since Christanity had become the state religion under Constantine in the fourth century, the pagan temples had fallen into disuse. In 382 temple assets became taxable, and in 391 Theodosius forbade the use of temples for all cult celebrations. The Christian empire sought less to destroy the symbols of the ancient cult than to remove them from pagan practice. However, the path of the missionaries was long and strewn with pitfalls, because the people often resisted this authoritarian proselytism. The lives of the saints abounded with more or less comical episodes in which the heroes were confronted with the defenders of the ancient religion. Here again the bishop's concern was more to transform than to destroy, as witness Gregory the Great in the sixth century: 'Do not destroy the pagan temples, only the idols which are found in them. As for the monument, sprinkle it with holy water, erect altars and place relics there.'[43] It was not a time for taking stock, for analysis or emotion, but for continuity, for the dogged substitution of one religion for another in buildings where the afflictions of the time did not allow for reconstruction. But equally, beyond the ruins or the intact monuments which were easily visible everywhere, the hope of finding treasure was common to kings, villains and abbots. Here is the edifying story of the abbot Lupicinus:

Because he lacked means, having spent so much for the benefit of the community, God revealed to the abbot Lupicinus a place where ancient treasures

The search for the relics of St Etienne, from the Echternach Gospels, eleventh century. Christians in quest of relics are shown opening a tomb.

were hidden. He went to this place alone, and brought back as much silver and gold as he could to the monastery.[44]

Here was an abbot luckier than Nero, but it is true that he sought treasure in the cause of God. The worthy monks or saints of the time were not simply preoccupied with the pagan temples or the treasure of the past buried in the soil; they had to come to terms with even more remote sites, such as the discovery by Saint Ruprecht of the town of Iuvavum in Norica (Salzburg):

He came to realise that, in a place near the river Ivarum, which was called by its ancient name of Iuvavum, there were in ancient times numerous and wonderful buildings, almost in ruins and covered by the forest. Having understood this, the man of God wished to verify it with his own eyes, and the thing was proved to be authentic. He asked Duke Theodosius to authorise him to say a mass to purify and sanctify the place and he undertook to rebuild it, first raising a beautiful church to God.[45]

Ivory panel carved with a homage to music, fourth century AD. In the eleventh century it was used as a cover for the Autun Tonary, a collection of scores. Such ivories played a significant role in the transmission of classical art to the Middle Ages.

The above anecdote reveals the symbolic conquest undertaken by the Church in the sixth and seventh centuries. It was a matter of ensuring the control of space, of replacing with Christian trademarks the opulent signs of a pagan past. To affirm their expropriation of the territory the bishops or the saints had to know how to observe, locate and briefly identify the 'ruins of ancient times'. They displayed no interest in the past as such, no curiosity in the monuments or objects, only a desire to purify the world of the pagan miasma which was still so deeply rooted. The contemporaries of Abbot Lupicinus or Saint Ruprecht were no less attentive to the past than the friends of Cicero or the bureaucrats of the court of Nero, but nothing drove them to ask about the men who built the monuments they observed, only to battle against their beliefs.

RECONSTRUCTION AND RECOVERY
OF THE PAST
Charlemagne's clerks

The clerks of the high medieval period were perfectly capable of drawing historical conclusions from the study of the landscape. Historians from Caesar to Orosius in the fifth century AD had kept alive the memory of the site of Alesia. No one doubted that this was the place where Vercingetorix surrendered to Caesar, but it is fascinating to discover that during the ninth century AD the Bishop of Auxerre and his brother, the famous Abbé Loup de Ferrières, were already preoccupied with the identification of the site of the capital of a little-known Gallic tribe, the Mandubians. Loup, who was staying at Fulda, discovered in the library of the rich Carolingian abbey the text of Caesar's *Commentaries*, which he immediately sent to the Bishop of Auxerre. This discovery enabled Heric, a monk of Saint-Germain d'Auxerre, to suggest several years later that the site of Mont Auxois could be identified with Caesar's Alesia:

> *You too, Alesia, whose destiny was set by Caesar's armies / It would be wrong for me to refuse to celebrate you in my verses / Protectress of the frontiers of the territories / Caesar attacked you in fearsome combat / And held the Roman lines with difficulty in unequal combat / Learning what Gaul could achieve / An army defending its independence / Of that ancient fort there are but a few remains.*[46]

The christianisation of Gaul was not limited to the founding of churches and monasteries or the conversion of the masses. The clergy sought to learn the history of these lands, the better to insinuate themselves into accepted tradition. During the Carolingian period they did not disdain from taking an interest in a remote past of which a good ecclesiastical administration occasionally allowed them a glimpse. Why were Loup and Heric so interested in Mont Auxois, if not because that hill was the scene of the miracles of Saint Reine? In 866 the Bishop of Auxerre organised the transfer of the martyr's relics from the chapel on Mont Auxois to the monastery of

Bronze statuette of Charlemagne (724–814) on horseback, dating from 860. The influence of antique art is evident in the treatment of the cloak folds and in the statuette's close resemblance to the equestrian statue of Marcus Aurelius in Rome, which had survived the centuries as a visible monument.

Flavigny. The narrator of this event takes the opportunity to remind us of the history of the site:

So that the cause of the destruction of Alesia may not remain hidden, the attentive reader will learn that the mighty emperor of the Romans, Julius, who secured the monarchy and who, with his great armies, brought almost the whole world beneath Roman authority, as he himself wrote in his book The Gallic Wars, *after having subdued all Gaul, established his camp. The Gauls formed a conspiracy; by means of great military operations and many battles he crushed the rebellion which had spread to all the cities, which had joined their armies against him [...]. He struck them down, and made sure that the town was destroyed and that nothing resembling it was ever rebuilt [...]. The site, which was completely razed, is in a very favourable position, as anyone can see. But whether its restoration was subsequently begun, or finished, by some unknown person, we have no document to tell us.*[47]

The narrator engages with the interplay of history and its causes. The description of the landscape leads him to explore the passage of time, the succession and the chain of events. His viewpoint is that of an observer attentive to local topography – he was, after all, present during this archaeological process, the exhumation of the body of the saint. The site is perceived in its history, which continued after the victory of Caesar. He clearly noticed that some of the Gallo-Roman monuments were constructed after the siege. Here is a sense of place and a precision of observation which was to elude some of his distant successors until the nineteenth century.

The remains of the pagan past with its funerary customs did pose numerous problems to the clerics. In 866 Michael I, King of Bulgaria, consulted Pope Nicholas to determine whether one could dedicate prayers to those who died in the old faith. The Pope replied

QVANTA STRA
GE VIRVM SVBLI
MIS ALEXIA CESSIT
CÆSAREIS AQVI
LIS. PICTA TABEL
LA NOTAT

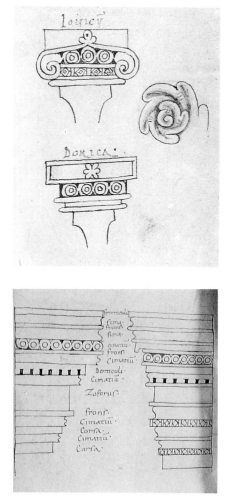

Drawings from an eleventh-century commentary on Vitruvius' treatise *On Architecture*.

with a formal edict: 'For those of your ancestors who died outside the Faith, it is impossible to pray by reason of the sin of unbelief.' Priests were obsessed with the eradication of ancient funerary customs, and prohibited the burial of Christians near to pagan tombs. Such customs did not cease overnight, as is shown in the numerous warnings issued by the clergy in central Europe and Scandinavia. The presence of the ancient and protohistoric past was evident in the shape of tumuli and megaliths. Polish archaeologists have observed the extent to which tumuli are present in the medieval chronicles and inventories of their country: *Trans montem ad tumulos paganorum* (across the hill towards the tumuli of the pagans), *in tumulo gigantis* (near the mound of the giant), *ad tumbas paganorum* (towards the tombs of the pagans). All of these expressions clearly indicate the part played in the topography of the medieval landscape by archaeological remains.[48]

If, little by little, churchmen and princes showed other interests than hunting for treasure, it is because something had changed. In laying claim to the western empire, Charlemagne set himself up much more than his predecessors as heir to the might of Rome – a claim not without cultural consequences. For, in refounding the empire, the new emperor surrounded himself with celebrated clerics (such as Paul Diacre or Alcuin), he established or expanded the monasteries and re-established relations between the surviving representatives of European scholarship. This first 'renaissance' (there would be others) saw the rediscovery of the classical tradition. In the more important monasteries (Bobbio, Saint-Gall, Saint-Riquier), the ancient authors occupied a new place by the side of the Church Fathers. This was the time of the great mentors, of whom Loup de Ferrières, in the succeeding generation, would be one of the most celebrated. The craze for antiquity drove Charlemagne to ask Pope Adrian for permission to excavate in Rome and to extract 'marbles and columns' to adorn Aix-la-Chapelle and Saint-Riquier. A fashion developed for using ancient sarcophagi for the burial of the great of the land.

Charlemagne himself was buried in a sarcophagus depicting the burial of Persephone, Louis the Pious in another showing the drowning of Pharaoh's soldiers in the Red Sea.[49] Beyond the recovery of treasures, beyond territorial expansion, a new taste for antiquity was born: statues, half-columns and sarcophagi became precious objects, to be used in the decoration of churches; vessels, jewels and cameos took their place among the treasures of castles and abbeys. During the tenth century the emperor Otto and his successors took up the torch of Romanism which had been progressively abandoned by Charlemagne's heirs. This was the era of the controlled return to pagan roots, which, like the Midianite woman of Scripture with her cropped hair and nails, would not be out of danger until it had been thoroughly cleansed and wrapped about in the rigour of theological commentary. At the monastery of Saint-Gall the ancient works were kept in a separate library reserved for *materialis lectio*. Furthermore, in

Hunting scene (*below left*) on the tympanum of the Abbey of Saint-Ursain at Bourges, twelfth century. Antique iconographic themes reappeared in Romanesque art. This hunting scene has been identified by J. Hubert and R. Crozet as that depicted on the Roman tomb of St Ludre preserved in the crypt of Déols Abbey.

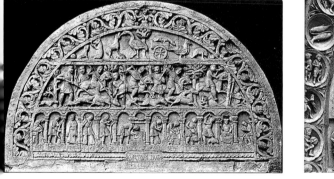

the middle of the eleventh century the rules of Cluny suggested that, to request a pagan book, one should scratch one's ear with one's finger: 'as a dog does with his paw, for a heathen can only be compared with such an animal'.[50]

For the clergy, the intellectual attraction exercised by the lure of classical tradition was as strong as the lust for treasure which occupied the common herd. However, the popularity of ancient literature was accompanied by an increasing taste for travel to the sources of Graeco-Roman culture. Monks journeyed from one end of the Latin world to the other. The great abbots of the eleventh and twelfth centuries, those of Saint-Benoît-sur-Loire, Cluny and Saint-Denis, had made the pilgrimage to Rome and had come back with a direct knowledge of the monuments of antiquity. At the same time the first accounts appeared of travels in Italy, such as the letter written by

Pagan cattle sacrifice (*above*), interior portal of the Saint-Madeleine basilica at Vézelay, twelfth century. Antique influence is further demonstrated by the close parallels with depictions of cattle sacrifice in Gallo-Roman bas-reliefs.

Conrad of Querfurt, chancellor of the Emperor Henry VI, who in 1194 visited and described many sites: the baths at Baia, the antiquities of Naples, the 'labyrinth of the Minotaur' at Taormina. Visiting Rome at the same period, Hildebert de Lavardin was overwhelmed by the number, quality and diversity of the buildings, and was virtually dumbfounded at the vision of the ancient town swallowing up the new: 'So many monuments are still standing, and so many are falling into ruin, that nowhere in the town is let alone but the buildings are destroyed or restored.'[51] Even in Rome there was an awakening interest in the protection of buildings. In 1162 the Senate decreed that Trajan's column should be protected: 'We wish it to remain intact, without decay, as long as the world shall last [...]. Anyone attemping to damage it in any way shall be condemned to death and his goods seized for the treasury.'[52] The city statutes, although much later (1363), contain an article devoted 'to ancient structures which must not be destroyed'. During the eleventh and twelfth centuries antiquity enjoyed a new-found prestige among the clergy linked with the affirmation of the intellectual role of Rome, the development of scholarship, and the admiration for Roman techniques, especially architectural. When, towards the year 1000, Europe wrapped itself, in the words of Raoul Glaber, in 'a white mantle of churches', the great Roman revival led princes and churchmen almost everywhere to examine the soil.

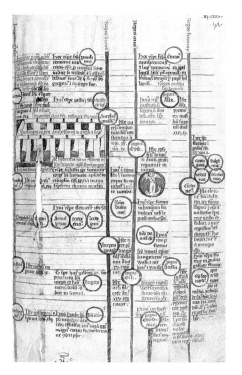

Imaginary view of Stonehenge in a fourteenth-century manuscript.

Greek and Roman remains were not the only antiquities to capture the attention of the learned and the curious. There were other monuments in the landscape. In 1009 a cartulary of Quimper states that Rudalt and Orscand, son and grandson of the bishop of Vannes, gave lands to the monastery of Saint-Cado. On these lands were several piles of stones (*acervum petrarum*), which can today be identified as megaliths.[53] The writer distinguishes between a *petra jacaens* (a fallen menhir) and a *petra stantiva* (a standing menhir). These references to monuments whose place in the landscape deserved some kind of topographical description have no further commentary. However, they are probably the first literary references to Breton megaliths. While such notes are not standard in medieval documents, neither are they rare. A cartulary of Redon at the end of the eleventh century records the presence of *lapides quaedam ingantes* (large stones) in the village of Treheguier.[54] The clerics and lawyers also interested themselves in Gallo-Roman remains. The chronicle of Lambert d'Ardres (end of the eleventh century) tells of a place to the north of the town, 'where all kinds of pagan remains may still be found, red tiles, the sherds of red vessels, fragments of little glass vessels, a place where a metalled track or a road made of solid stones has been discovered'.[55] None of the realities of the landscape escaped the trained eye of the land-surveyors, the meticulous attention of the lawyers. At the same time it occurred to none of them to comment on it.

Guibert de Nogent took a quite different view. Abbot of Notre-Dame de Nogent-sous-Couey in 1104, he died in 1124. His autobiography contains the following account:

The place in question is Novigentum. It is 'new' in its monastic guise, but its secular occupation goes back a very long time. Even though there is no written evidence for this, the unusual, and in my opinion non-Christian disposition, of the graves found there is proof enough. Around the church and within it, antiquity itself has brought together so many sarcophagi that this mass of corpses heaped in such a place must show how great was the renown of such a sought-after spot. The placing of the tombs is not at all as we know it; they are arranged in a circle about one of their number; besides, within these tombs were found vessels which resemble nothing in use during Christian times. The explanation must be this: that these are tombs which are either pagan, or belong to a Christian era so long ago that pagan usages were still observed.[56]

Guibert is probably describing a Merovingian cemetery. It is striking how similar his remarks and his detailed description are to Strabo's in his account of the discovery of the ancient tombs of Corinth by Caesar's soldiers: the same astonishment when faced with the sudden materialisation of an ancient past out of the earth, the same difficulties with dating and interpreting the remains.

In both ancient and medieval times the earth was not understood as a potential source of history. If antiquity revealed itself, or rather, if a consciousness of the antiquity of remains was awakened, it is

Helena presides over the exhumation of the Holy Cross, *The Golden Legend*, fourteenth-century manuscript. Helena, mother of the Emperor Constantine, had reportedly discovered Christ's cross at the time of her voyage to the Holy Land. According to the commentary by St Ambrose (330–97), 'she discovered the board [which bears the name of Christ], she worshipped the king and not – as in the case of pagan error and impious vanity – the piece of wood itself. She adored Him who had been suspended on the wood and whose name is inscribed on the board'. An epigraphic ability was needed here to distinguish Christ's cross from those of the thieves.

Discovery of the Holy Spear, from *Crossing the Seas*,
fifteenth-century manuscript. The discovery of the Holy Spear
which pierced Christ's side became associated with the tradition
of the discovery of the Holy Cross. It was at Antioch,
en route to the Crusades, that the Christian princes
found the Holy Spear.

always in a fortuitous fashion, like a rupture of the impervious barrier which separates the present from the past. Scholars were not incapable of observing or even commenting upon the remains which were revealed from excavating the soil, but the process owed nothing to any methodical study of the past. Like the Greeks and Romans, the men of the Middle Ages could turn their hand to digging in the traditional pursuit of treasure or relics. In order for those objects to function as historical signals, they must be observed in a historical way – something which happened even more seldom during the Middle Ages than in the ancient world.

THE EXHUMATION OF THE PAST
The discovery of Arthur's tomb at Glastonbury

The exhumation of relics, *Legend of St Hubert*, fifteenth-century manuscript. One by one, as they are exhumed, the relics are carefully placed on the altar. The discovery is attributed to Charlemagne.

The twelfth century was to an extent the first point since Charlemagne's efforts at which a methodical consideration of the past began to develop in the West. But the period was no longer the domain of imperial history. On the contrary, after the Romans and Franks had accepted the myth of Trojan origins, England joined in with Geoffrey of Monmouth's *Historia Regum Britanniae* (History of the Kings of Britain). The book was produced in the manner of a *vetustissimus liber* – an ancient chronicle of English history – which allowed the English their place within the *longue durée*, in a direct line from the Trojans. Even if the rather extreme and fanciful nature of Monmouth's book attracted immediate criticism, scholars of English history were to be inspired by it for many years to come. This was a time when Norman princes were setting out to research their Saxon, Celtic and Trojan predecessors. The most famous event of the day was, notably, the discovery of what was believed to be the tomb of Arthur and Guinevere at Glastonbury. According to Giraldus Cambrensis,[57] in 1191 the monks of Glastonbury Abbey were rebuilding this famous sanctuary, which had been destroyed by fire in 1184, when they found the tomb of a man of extraordinary stature and a woman; close by was a cross bearing these words: 'Here lies buried the famous king Arthur, with Guinevere his second wife, in the isle of Avalon.' The excavation appeared factual, tangible, and as Kendrick suggested, it brought a sense of reality: 'King Arthur was now as real as Alfred the Great or William the Conqueror.'[58] At almost the same time (1191) Richard I of England gave Tancred of Sicily[59] the famous sword Excalibur, and the legend was brought to life; precious symbols of the past became objects which one could touch, admire, or give as gifts.

Glastonbury was not the only medieval abbey to arouse archaeological interest. According to the chronicle of Matthew Paris, the abbots of the powerful abbey of St Albans, founded upon the Roman city of Verulamium, began to excavate the town's foundations early in the eleventh century. Abbot Aeldred began to dig methodically (according to Matthew Paris it was necessary to protect the monastery from thieves and to control the erratic course of the river). As the abbot dug out and filled in, he carefully saved tiles and stones to use in the fabric of the church. He aimed to use the site systematically, like a quarry, with a view to constructing a new sanctuary. During excavation he found the remains of boats and of shells, which proved that the sea had reached that point in times gone by. Notably he uncovered an enormous cavern which he attributed to a serpent. He declared that he would preserve his discovery for posterity. Here, close observation and due consideration of natural forces are mixed with the classical theme of the supernatural. The good abbot had probably unearthed the passage or sepulchral chamber of a burial mound; to him this looked like the lair of a monstrous serpent, but he left things as they were, as if to leave judgement to posterity. His successor, Elmer, continued to dig in one of the town buildings. He found a kind of book store, which a monk identified as the sacred texts of the ancient Britons. Among them was a book in Latin which related the life of St Alban. The monks burned the pagan books, but copied the life of the saint. Once transcribed, the book crumbled into dust.

The transcription of the life of St Alban must be treated with caution, like the decipherment of the tomb of Alcmene, or the tablets of Knossos, but the discovery deserves attention. Were there papyri

Ammonite carved in the form of a snake. To medieval scholars the ammonite represented a fossil snake: to prove this it was enough to carve a snake's head on the fossil shell.

(*rotuli* in the text)? In any case it is probable that the life of St Alban is nothing but a pious fraud which sought to give a religious dimension to the discovery. Matthew Paris's text ends with a description of the excavation of the urban zone: columns, tiles, dressed stone. All this made the abbot curious. He went on to find pots, amphorae, glass vessels, ashes – in short, he records, the remains of a pagan cemetery. The range of material discovered and the mixture of detail and fantasy which characterises Matthew Paris's account render this one of the finest examples of the medieval practice of archaeology.

The memory of this famous site was to persist in British archaeology: Francis Bacon was created Lord Verulam by James I, and Mortimer Wheeler chose the site as the most important training excavation of its time in Great Britain.

King Arthur's sword, Excalibur, being drawn down into the waters; the king is shown in the foreground; fourteenth-century manuscript.

If the eleventh and twelfth centuries saw a multiplication of the evidence of ancient finds, there is nothing astonishing about that. New building work abounded and a more attentive clergy looked on, supervising the activities of masons and developers. An archdeacon of Meaux, Foulcoie de Beauvais, has left a poetic commentary upon a discovery made on the site of a 'pagan temple' at Meaux:

There was a wall in the town which showed where the ruins were. Time has passed, but the name persists; the old peasants say it is the temple of Mars – to this day, peasant, you call these stones the temple of Mars. You would say so without knowing why. A discovery has given us proof of this name. A peasant ploughing over the ruins found a statue, it looked like a living person. He found a carved head which looked like nothing alive or made by men. A dreadful head, yet the style suits it well, it grimaces terrifyingly and terror becomes it. Its laugh, its savage mouth, its strange ferocity, the deformed form of a fitting style. Even before I had visited the site, then, the carving was brought to me, so that I could determine what it represented, for whom and by whom it was made. Having heard the perverse name by which the place is known locally, I examined the head – it's impossible not to see how clearly the place itself instructs us, giving us both the name and the savage head. This place is the temple of Mars, this head is that of the heathen Mars wrongly thought to be a god. In ancient times when the cult was alive – thus went my reasoning – fear brought gods into being. This is demonstrated by that place. The god has no validity and needs the hand of man and the medium of stone in order to exist. Neither mouth, nor eye, nor hand, nor foot, nor ear may stir. Art bestows resemblance, not presence. He was not created God, because God created all. He was created Mars; he is therefore not God, and if he is not God, he must not be honoured.[60]

Pagan divinities depicted in a Remegius manuscript, *c.*1100. Saturn, standing at the right, resembles one of the statues of saints given by Henri II for the altar of Basle Cathedral. Jupiter is seated on his throne in the manner of a medieval king, and his prophetic crow resembles St John's eagle. Apollo in his chariot holds the Three Graces like a bouquet.

This curious artefact, appearing as it did out of the earth, held a strange fascination for the worthy archdeacon because it was the embodiment of the abominable practice of idolatry. At the same time as he was developing the classic Christian arguments against the folly of false gods, Foulcoie was bewitched by a perverse influence emanating from the statue. The role of images in worship was one of the major points of theological debate at the time. How could pagan images be abominated and Christian ones accepted? How could one reconcile the rejection of images with the need for them which drove innumerable churchmen to decorate their churches sumptuously, and even to reclaim pagan figures with the intent of turning them into objects of Christian worship? Foulcoie's diatribe calls to mind St Jerome: 'The gods adored by nations are now alone in their niches with the owls and the night birds. The gilded Capitol languishes in dust and all the temples of Rome are covered with spiders' webs.'[61]

This Christian derision is not unlike that of Lucian, who mocked the bats and rats which chose to live among the statues of the greatest gods of Olympia. The pagan image is thus the most subtle and dangerous of the temptations of antiquity. In his condemnation, even destruction, the cleric is not merely being faithful to theological canons, it is a convenient way of consigning one part of the antique heritage to hell, whilst putting the remainder to a better, or different, use. Treasures – the capitals of columns, building materials – these were not only tolerated in churches after the year 1000, they were actively sought with a passion amounting to frenzy. That said, Foulcoie was much more than a proselytising priest. In his poem he

Scene from the life of St Sylvester, fresco painted by Maso di Banco, c.1336, on the walls of the Bardi Chapel in Santa-Croce, Florence. St Sylvester resuscitates two magi; the scene is supposed to be taking place at the time of Constantine, but the Forum is already in ruins...The saint performs his miracles amidst the remains of the ancient city, under the eyes of the Emperor Constantine surrounded by his retinue. This fresco contrasts the red-brick buildings of Christian Rome to the white marble of the ancient city.

illustrates the profound contradiction embedded in the relationship between medieval culture and antiquity. Without ancient culture there would be no Christian culture; at the same time Christian culture must be formed upon choice, an awkward separation from the Graeco-Roman heritage. Perhaps the contemplation of statues is as dangerous as reading evil books: Foulcoie was forced to struggle against his own taste for antiquity.

To the population at large and especially to the peasants, the observant cleric was seen as a scholar capable of interpreting and occasionally dating an object plucked from the soil; he was a man of no small ability. He could draw upon oral tradition and relate this to finds — in short, deal with sources both direct and indirect. Foulcoie's very individual style lends a special dimension to his testimony, but he was not alone. At the same time Anselm of Havelberg described with precision the Roman enclosure at Reims, and the *Chronicles of Tournai* told of ancient cemeteries in the town comparable with those of Laon and Reims. These texts, like those of Guibert de Nogent or Matthew Paris, reveal a sensitivity to antiquities and a naive but dogged taste for archaeology. As for Suger, the illustrious abbot of Saint-Denis, he dreamed of excavating in Rome to enrich his abbey.

The taste for antiquity turned the heads of churchmen in no small measure, and for the good of their consciences they invented a special prayer to christianise the pagan vessels found in excavations: *Benedicto super vasa reperta in locis antiquis [...]*, deign so to cleanse these vases fabricated by the art of the Gentiles, that they may be used by the believers in peace and tranquillity.[62] From the moment of their entry into the daily canon, the ancient pots occupied a defined and accepted place within human consciousness. Walls, fortifications, treasures, works of art and humble funerary offerings: the material remains of ancient times revealed themselves everywhere to the eyes of those curious enough to observe them. Lawyers or surveyors, abbots or princes, even the simple peasant with his plough – no one could avoid the sense of anxiety attendant upon confrontation with the invisible but real distance which the past assumed. The patient activity of the most well informed men led them to regard monuments, objects, even fugitive traces, as so many intelligible signs, at least partially explicable. As Jean Adhémar pointed out:

Reliquary statue, preserved in the church of Sainte-Foy at Conques. The statue is made of a wooden core covered with gold leaf. The head dates to the fourth century and represents a Roman emperor. Its place in this eleventh-century Romanesque church underlines the attention given to the remains of the past.

> *For five hundred years, from the eighth to the twelfth century, there were monks, clerks and kings who did not hesitate to say and to show that they were struck by the grandeur and beauty of monuments, statues and all the works of the artists of classical antiquity.*[63]

The prayer for ancient vessels demonstrates that the interest in ancient remains was not limited to art but extended to everything which the earth might reveal. The men of the Middle Ages, who during Merovingian times destroyed ancient ruins, now learned to domesticate, utilise and naturalise them, finding the means to incorporate them within the framework of their lives. Salvatore Settis showed how, in Modena, in Pisa and even Arles, the construction of religious monuments in the eleventh and twelfth centuries inserted themselves into an artistic vision essentially dependent upon the Roman model. It was no longer enough to clear an area and pick up the pieces, the aim was to make use of any architectural or other artistic remains. The emperor Frederick II is a perfect example of the kind of medieval prince who strove by any means available to establish continuity between the ancient and the medieval worlds. He represented himself as the successor, not of the emperors, but of the founder of the Empire himself: Augustus. He created a gold coinage, the *augustales,* on which he is depicted bearing all the attributes of a Caesar; in Capua he built a triumphal arch in the Roman style; he was a passionate collector of any ancient object he could find. In his town of Augusta in Sicily he even commissioned an agent charged with the excavation of 'the places where the maximum number of finds are to be expected'.[64]

Ristoro d'Arezzo, a twelfth-century author, gives a fine example of how the men of the Middle Ages were excited by Roman pots:

I could obtain of these vessels, a small bowl decorated in relief with such natural and subtle things that the experts, when they saw it, cried aloud, lost their composure and behaved like idiots – as for those who knew nothing of them, they wanted to break it and throw it away.[65]

The sculptured motif on a capital in the former abbey of Moissac (eleventh-twelfth century) is directly inspired by a Roman motif that appears on the upper part of the Cortona Sarcophagus. In the fifteenth century this same sarcophagus depicting the battle between the Centaurs and the Lapiths inspired Donatello and Brunelleschi.

(In fact, Arezzo was one of the most famous of the workshops which produced the glossy red ware called *terra sigillata*.) The admiration which Ristoro's contemporaries had for Aretine vessels is a fair match for that of Caesar's soldiers for the Corinthian pots. Roberto Weiss detects here a shift in taste, an emotional reaction to art which contrasts with the more solemn approach of previous centuries. We shall see how the thirteenth-century sensitivity to ancient art already suggests the stirrings of the Renaissance sensibility.

THE FORERUNNERS OF THE RENAISSANCE
CONFRONT THE NEGLECT OF
THINGS ANCIENT

Northern Europe and the wholesale destruction of Roman monuments. The Italian precursors: Petrarch and Boccaccio

It is tempting to link the testimony of Ristoro d'Arezzo to a major event in the history of Italian art: the completion of Nicola Pisano's baptistry in the cathedral of Pisa in 1260. The work itself contains numerous details which illustrate a particular taste. The Virgin is depicted in the same way as Phaedra on ancient sarcophagi, and the soldiers are dressed as legionaries rather than men of the thirteenth century. Christ and his companions are shown in the Early Christian fashion, without haloes. It is, in short, a work which uses ancient art as a creative model. The tremor which ran through art and literature in Italy at this time contrasts with the situation observed in France by someone as knowledgeable and well informed as Jean Adhémar:

The enthusiasm for ancient things is cooling. The chroniclers are ceasing to celebrate the Roman monuments and ancient sculptures in their towns. The collectors have given up the hunt for antique works of art, the artists are neglecting the marble bas-reliefs and the consular diptychs [...]. At the beginning of the thirteenth century the classicists have disappeared, classical studies have all but vanished from the monastic and abbey schools, and the interest of the clerks has been subdued in the face of the exigencies of a more ardent faith.[66]

While Italy was caught up in a progressive movement to return to antiquity, the other European nations seemed to be relaxing their interest in the Graeco-Roman past. There were reasons for this paradox; the eleventh and twelfth centuries saw the final integration of the barbarian invaders into classical history. The English and the Franks were asserting their Trojan origins, and certain documents added to these accounts an element of Jewish history. In Glastonbury in 1184, after the fire which destroyed their abbey, the monks not only produced the bodies of Arthur and Guinevere, but also proclaimed that St Joseph of Arimathea came to Glastonbury in AD 63 and was buried there. So Glastonbury glowed with the fire of a double legend in which medieval epic was crossed with the history of the Church. Such historical short circuits had their consequences; chronological confusion led the people and part of the clergy to a

very different reading of the landscape from the model which persisted from Carolingian times. The fathers of the Church were no
longer called upon to explain the surrounding world and the ruins
strewn upon it. Besides, these no longer possessed the freshness or
the triumphal air which they had in Merovingian times. With the
passage of time, the Romans were confused with Charlemagne and
the Graeco-Roman deities with the Islamic demons of medieval
epic. Minstrels and troubadours unconsciously contributed to this
modification of the image of the past. Theatres, amphitheatres and
temples became towers of Roland, palaces of Pepin le Bref, gates of
Ganelon. In the middle of the thirteenth century all ruins were by
definition Saracen: the crusades had replaced the Germanic invasions in popular imagination, and Apollo became a familiar spirit of
Mohammed. This was the time when the destruction of Roman
monuments through urban growth attained dimensions which were
never again to be repeated. From then on, the chronicles record
large-scale demolition of the amphitheatre at Trier, the walls of
Poitiers, the amphitheatres of Nîmes and Le Mans. Here was a difficult and sometimes fatal trial for antiquities. The urban and rural
landscapes were profoundly altered, and so, in consequence, was the
concept of regional history.

Northern and Central Europe turned their backs for a time upon
the ancient past, whilst the men of the South – of Avignon, Rome
and some Italian towns – took up the torch. In 1283 the Paduan
judge Lovato Lovati interpreted the discovery in the city of a skeleton of gigantic dimensions as the remains of the legendary founder,
Antenor.[67] The event would have been of little importance had it
not been followed by a resurgence of interest in ancient Rome. In
fact it was not so much the history of Rome proper which mat-
tered, as the regional history of each of the towns which, in Italy,
could claim a certain notoriety. This is better seen, perhaps, in the
context of a second fortuitous discovery forty years later in the same
city of Padua, one which attracted the attention of the learned. A
funerary inscription revealed the name of Titus Livius, and at once
the scholars were thrilled at the idea of having touched with their
own hands the tombstone of the celebrated historian. It little mat-
tered that this was the tomb of a simple freedman who had nothing
to do with his great namesake. The idea had been implanted in
scholarly circles that the collection and decipherment of inscriptions
was a valid historical pursuit.

Opposite: Crucifixion and Nativity scenes, details from the pulpit in the Baptistery at Pisa, by Nicola Pisano, 1259. Inspired by classical Roman art, Nicola Pisano created a new type of composition with his reliefs, using knowledge as an instrument of sculptural art: the Phaedra of Béatrice de Lorraine's sarcophagus is transformed into Nicola Pisano's Madonna.

In Padua, and soon Verona, learned men threw themselves into the writing of works on Roman history. Of course these were only compilations, but sometimes they contain unexpected curiosities. A manuscript of the learned Veronese Giovanni Mansonario has in the margin, alongside illustrations of Roman coins, the first known plan of a Roman circus in the history of archaeology.[68] This specifically Italian interest in ancient history, which was at the same time local history, found its master and its guide in Petrarch, the most celebrated of the editors of the works of Livy and Cicero. It was his predilection for the ruins of Rome which marked the rediscovery of that city. In Petrarch's view the capital of the ancient world was a site which had to be visited, and with the ancient authors to hand. This was the decisive step which separated the medieval from the

Above: Antique sarcophagus depicting the story of Phaedra and Hippolytus. This sarcophagus was incorporated into the external ornament of Pisa Cathedral when Béatrice de Lorraine was buried there in 1076.

Renaissance attitude. To read the urban landscape meant also to read the ancient authors; it was not enough to wander blindly among various *mirabilia* of the pilgrims. Rome must be put in perspective; not just the medieval city traversed by Petrarch, but the imperial city which was set apart from the medieval one by time's destructive agency. It was necessary to admit to the break which separated the present from the past, and to treat antiquity as an historical object. Sites should be studied by visiting and describing them, by making full use of the available inscriptions and coinage. The age of Petrarch was also the age of a new approach to numismatics – no longer the collection of medals, but a thorough interpretation of coinage.

Politics in the Thucydidean sense was also to play a part in the rediscovery of antiquity. Cola di Rienzo, in his desire to recreate an independent Rome, went even further than Petrarch. In 1346, the Roman dictator rediscovered Vespasian's *Lex de Imperio* at St John Lateran. He deciphered it straightaway, and so established the superiority of the people over the emperors. In consequence the resounding appeal for the political independence of Rome was posted on the church wall, and on 20 May 1347 Cola organised an event – a true political meeting – at which he read the text aloud before adding his commentary, the tenor of which can be imagined.

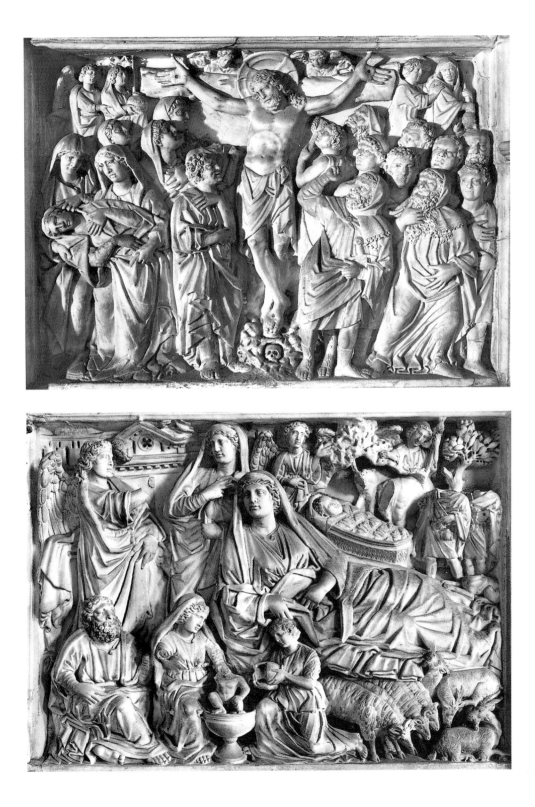

The story of Laocoon, from a fourteenth-century manuscript. What could be more moving than the story of the Trojan priest Laocoon, who, as he sacrificed an ox to Poseidon, saw two serpents emerge from the sea to attack his children? The illuminator has separated the image into three scenes which seem almost discrete: the serpents; the sacrifice; the children.

Such happenings proved to the people of Rome that stones could indeed speak, if interrogated. Soon afterwards, in the Angevin court of Naples, another great voice as powerful as Petrarch's would be raised in favour of a return to classical antiquity: that of Boccaccio. His interest in epigraphy, and especially his knowledge of Greek, rendered him even more than Petrarch a forerunner of the Renaissance.[69] Boccaccio's contribution[70] was his critical appraisal of the monuments and his rejection of folk-tales as a means of identifying them – victims as they were of neglect and destruction, as much as of the undirected enthusiasm of medieval scholars. Petrarch and Boccaccio favoured a critical approach to documents which signalled the beginning of a new era. A Florentine doctor, Giovanni Dondi, was one of the boldest of the Italian innovators. Combining an interest in documents with precise description based upon survey, he was probably the first of the scholar-travellers of the Renaissance. He was a disciple of, and an expert on, the Roman architect Vitruvius, and attempted to write an architectural description of the monuments he visited, comparing them to the Vitruvian model.[71]

The foundation of the town of Augsburg, plate from the *Chronicle of Augsburg* by the German Humanist Sigismund Meisterlin, 1522 edition. This image, like the two on the following page, illustrates episodes from Meisterlin's compilation: in this scene primitive people inhabit caves and huts.

The Italian scholars of the fourteenth and fifteenth centuries followed the path of Humanism in preparing for a return to classical antiquity – one not satisfied with a purely literary experience, or even with the rediscovery of certain art forms. They laid down the foundations of a historiography based upon a theory of knowledge: critical assessment of sources, that is to say the establishment of ancient texts, but also the systematic comparison of monument and text. They thus rediscovered the Varronian necessity for an order of

Von der Erbawung der stat Augspurg
Wie die menschen zü dem ersten gewonet hond vnnd

wie die Schwaben dise stat gepawen hond/vnd von der stat gelegenhait das
erst Capitel des andern büchs/vnd hie vacht das ander büch an. ic.

 Es nach der sindtfluß/vñ des thurñß zü Babiloni baw
ung/vñ der sprach verendrüg die geschlecht/vnd dye sych
taylten/da besaß ain yetlichs ain gegent/aber die võ dẽ
sun Noe der genant wz Japhet geporē warent/die na
men ein dz drittail der welt/dz genant ist Europa/gãtz
vñ über al von den selben gedeylten/ist auß geschayden
ein volck/dz da genãt ward Senoñ/dz ist die scharpfen
die mã zü diser zeyt nennen ist Schweuoß/aber in teütsch

antiquarian knowledge. Epigraphy, numismatics and historical topography were progressively added to the study of texts. Cyriac of Ancona is the epitome of this type of antiquary. He was born in 1391 and died in 1454, the product *par excellence* of an Italian merchant bourgeoisie thirsty for knowledge. From 1423 until his death Cyriac did not cease to visit most of the archaeological sites of the Mediterranean region, feverishly copying inscriptions and drawing monuments. As much at ease with the emperors of Byzantium as with the Sultan Mehmet II, whose secretary he was, this man broadly proclaimed his Humanist archaeology by dint of his sense of

The worship of the goddess Cisa, plates from the *Chronicle of Augsburg* by Sigismund Meisterlin. Extracted from two different editions, these images show how, over several decades, the vision of primitive humanity changed. The 1457 image shows the goddess in a loggia; that of 1522 emphasises the urban context and the wooden city walls.

reality and his mission to describe landscapes and buildings with the maximum precision. Quite apart from the extraordinary story of his life, he asserted himself with a radically new concept which he brought to the analysis of architectural remains. He was one of the first since Varro to question the veracity of sources. Monuments, coins and inscriptions were the *sigilla historiarum,* the 'seals of history' which verify in the same way that an epistolary document is verified. If the monuments possess a *fides* (truth) and a *noticia* (knowledge) greater than that of the texts, then here tradition is challenged – the accepted practice is subjected to the merciless agency of criticism.

Germany, too, was touched by the new wave of historical and antiquarian criticism emanating from Italy. Living at the same time as Cyriac of Ancona, the German scholar Sigismund Meisterlin devoted his studies to the historical origins of German towns. His work was caught up in the great movement of affirmation among the free cities of the Holy Roman Empire which sought to resist pressure from the powerful feudatories of the Empire. Meisterlin's *Chronicle of Augsburg* was one of the first works of local history to make room for the study of Latin inscriptions and antiquities. His manuscript, illustrated by a famous illuminator of the day, Hektor Mülich, attracts our attention with one of the very first portrayals of cave dwellers. Proof indeed that the desire for knowledge of the past could free itself from the very restricted limits of Graeco-Roman history. A friend of Aeneas Silvius (Enea Silvio de'Piccolomini and the future Pope Pius II), Meisterlin went to Italy in search of direct contact with antiquity. He was the first in a long line of scholars to apply the methods of Italian Humanism to the history of his own country.

Boccaccio (1313–75) presenting his work to John of Naples; below, Petrarch (Boccaccio's *alter ego*) is shown writing at his desk; fifteenth-century manuscript. True theoreticians of the knowledge of the past, these two figures of the fourteenth century announce themselves as the forerunners of the Renaissance.

However, this period in the history of antiquities was ultimately shipwrecked. Whether an accident of scholarship, or just historical bad luck, the greater part of Cyriac's work was lost, just like Varro's before him. We do have a great many documents and his corpus of Latin inscriptions to give us an idea of his work. However, facts are stubborn: three works central to our understanding of the past are now dispersed, scattered or quite destroyed – works by Varro, Cyriac of Ancona and, as we shall see, Peiresc. There was no curse upon antiquarian studies; it was time itself which caused the eating away and ultimate destruction of these texts.

From the far-off philosophers of Ionia to the scholars of the Renaissance, from Herodotus to Cyriac of Ancona, a subtle thread runs, linking the antiquarians among them. For Herodotus, as for all the Greeks, the Trojan Wars formed the point of departure for all history. Faced with the ruins of Ilium, Mehmet II, conqueror of Constantinople, could not resist giving his own history lesson. The Greek historian Kritoboulos of Imbros records:

Once arrived at Ilium, the sultan viewed the ruins of the ancient city of

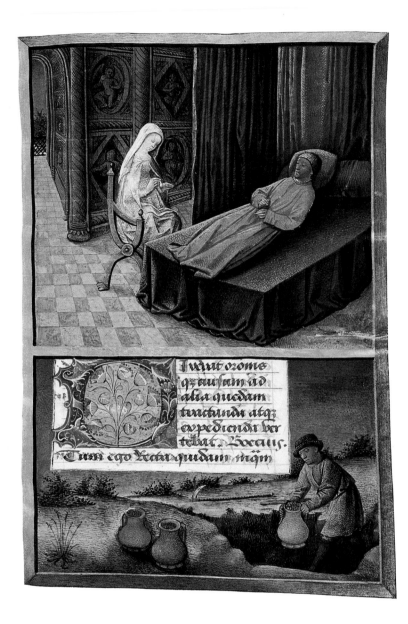

The discovery of the treasures, images from the *Consolation of Philosophy* by Boethius (480–524), fifteenth-century French manuscripts. The burial and discovery of a treasure in the earth became the theme for moral fables. Opposite, in a manuscript of 1477, Philosophy shows Boethius the spectacle of ill-gotten riches embodied by a magistrate with treasures spread out at his feet; to the bottom right a man digs a hole in the ground. Above is a miniature from a contemporary manuscript by the same illuminator. Philosophy and Boethius occupy the main part of the image; below them a peasant has laid down the hoe he has used for digging and takes in both hands a vase full of gold coins. Two other vases are seen at the edge of the pit. This is an allegory of chance: *If the peasant had not turned over the earth in his field, if the owner had not placed his treasure there, the gold would not have been discovered.*

Troy, its extent, its position, and the other advantages of the land, its favourable siting with regard to the sea and to the land mass. Then he visited the tombs of the heroes (I mean Achilles, Ajax and the others); he glorified them, praising their renown, their exploits, and their fortune in having the poet Homer to celebrate them. Then, it is said, he pronounced these words while nodding his head, 'It was reserved to me by God to avenge this city and its people, I have tamed their enemies, ravaged their cities, and made prey of their riches. In truth it was the Greeks, the Macedonians, the Thessalians and the Peloponnesians who ravaged this city in ancient times, and their descendants after so many years have paid to me the debt incurred by their impious excesses at that time, and often afterwards, against us, the people of Asia.'[72]

Any personal contribution by the sultan to this history lesson cannot be guaranteed. However, a man with whom Cyriac of Ancona was on familiar terms, even, it is said, discussing Greek and Latin authors with him, must have had some curiosity about the nascent Humanism. Moreover, his great enemy, Aeneas Silvius, was invited by the Holy Roman Emperor to harangue the German princes who had gathered at Frankfurt to deliberate the fall of Byzantium. In front of a dumbfounded audience, he appealed to the martial superiority of the Germanic peoples:

Mercury, in a drawing by Cyriac of Ancona, mid-fifteenth century. A traveller thirsty for archaeological knowledge, Cyriac of Ancona (1391–1454) copied and drew all the antiquities he could see. The Roman god Mercury was the protector of merchants and travellers.

You are great, you are warlike, you are powerful, you are fortunate, you are the Germans chosen by God, who has allowed you to extend your frontiers and who has given to you, above all mortal men, the honour of facing the might of Rome. Brave heirs of powerful ancestors, remember — keep before you the high deeds of the Ancients, see how many times your fathers crossed the Alps to Italy with mighty armies.[73]

Strong in his knowledge of Latin tradition on the Germanic peoples, Piccolomini was able to revive, for the first time, a Germany of the past forgotten by medieval scholars. It took an Italian to remind them that they were Germans and not Teutons, as they called themselves.[74] In describing to them their glorious military past he revived the memory of the legions of Varus mourned by Augustus, and he laid the foundations upon which the ancient history of Germany was built – thanks to the Italian rediscovery of Tacitus. In 1458 he

The ruins of Troy, sketch from a manuscript by Cristoforo Buondelmonti, fifteenth century. A Florentine cleric, Buondelmonti was one of the most adventurous antiquaries of the fifteenth century: for sixteen years he travelled throughout the Greek islands, illustrating his manuscripts with maps and sketches of the most notable sites.

developed this theme more widely, in response to criticism of the Germans against Rome. A new discourse appeared, rich in references to Tacitus and honoured with the same title: Piccolomini's *Germania* was published in Leipzig in 1496, and was to take its place alongside that of Tacitus in the minds of the German Humanists, endowed as they were with a burning curiosity. From one end of the Mediterranean to the other, history became an instrument of politics. The sultan, according to Kritoboulos, wished to be the heir of the Trojans, as the emperor wished to be the successor of the ancient Germans. But for Piccolomini the Turks were not Trojans, those who had just burned Constantinople were not merely enemies of the faith, but enemies of *belles-lettres*:

What misfortune; how many cities once powerful in reputation and deed are now destroyed. The sites of Thebes, Athens, Mycenae, Larissa, Lacedaemonia, the city of Corinth, and other famous cities – if you seek their walls, you will find only ruins [...]. And now that the Turks are victors and possess all that was Greek, I fear that all the Greek literature will be destroyed. And I do not think, as many do, that the Turks are of Asiatic origin, sons of Teucer [Teucer was the son of the river Scamander; he was the first king of the Troad, from whom the Romans were descended], *and that they do not hate letters. They are from the race of Scythians, separated from the Barbarian centre, who according to Aristotle inhabit the Pyrrhic*

Bernardino di Betto, called 'Il Pinturicchio', *Piccolomini Setting Out for the Council of Basle at Portovenere*. The Piccolomini Library of Siena Cathedral was built in 1492 by Francesco Todeschini Piccolomini, Archbishop of Siena, to honour the memory of his maternal uncle Aeneas Silvius (Pope Pius II). The frescos relating to Pius II were not finished until 1507, after the death of the archbishop in 1503.

Above: Aeneas Silvius is shown setting out for the Council of Basle in 1432 as secretary to the Bishop of Fermo, Cardinal Domenico Capranica. The procession nears the Tuscan port of Portovenere. Aeneas Silvius, at the centre on a white horse, turns round; the Cardinal is in profile on a bay horse preceded by a halberdier and squires.

Opposite: *Pius II Preaches the Crusade at Ancona*. At Ancona in 1464 Pius II announced the Crusade against the Turks: on 18 June the Pope, already ill, went to Ancona to wait for the fleet of the Doge Cristoforo Moro. He was to die in the same town on 15 August. The Pope is carried on a chair surrounded by numerous political figures of the time. Among them are Thomas Palaeologus, despot of Morea, bearded and dressed in a blue outfit with a large hat, and the Doge kneeling; to the right is Hassan Zaccaria, former Prince of Samos, wearing a turban and a green outfit, also kneeling. Behind the latter, facing the viewer, stands Calapino Bajazet, called 'the little Turk', pretender to the Ottoman throne. In the background is the city of Ancona with Trajan's Arch.

The Fall of Troy,
Italian manuscript of
the early fourteenth
century, once in the
possession of Petrarch.

mountains near the northern ocean: foul and infamous people, fornicators given to all kinds of evil practices.[75]

Piccolomini had more success with scholars than with princes. His calls to the crusades were to remain useless, and he died in Ancona without embarking upon his long-vowed crusade. However, the seed which he sowed in German scholarship would bear much fruit. Maximilian I, the last medieval knight and the first Humanist emperor, must have been an admirer of his: at the time of the Diet of Worms in 1496 he excavated the tomb of Siegfried at Worms. Less fortunate than the monks of Glastonbury, he found only water.

1 Reiner 1985, p. 3, lines 26–46.
2 Heeren-Diekhoff 1981, p. 222.
3 Herodotus, *The Histories*, I,1, trans.
   G. Rawlinson, London, 1992.
4 Pausanias, II.xvi, trans. P. Levi,
   Harmondsworth, 1984.
5 Pausanias, III.iii, trans. P. Levi,
   Harmondsworth, 1984.
6 Thucydides, I,10, trans. R. Warner,
   Harmondsworth, 1972.
7 Thucydides, I,1, trans. R. Warner,
   Harmondsworth, 1972.
8 See p. 26
9 Snodgrass 1987.
10 Plutarch, *Life of Theseus*, 36, Chicago, 1990.
11 Herodotus, *The Histories*, I, trans.
   G. Rawlinson, London, 1992.
12 Plutarch, *Moralia*, 577–78, Camb., Mass.,
   1959.
13 Herodotus, *The Histories*, V, trans.
   G. Rawlinson, London, 1992.
14 Pausanias I.xxiv, trans. P. Levi,
   Harmondsworth, 1984.
15 Tacitus, *Annales*, XVI, 1–3, Chicago, 1990.
16 Plato, *Hippias Major*, 285e, trans.
   P. Woodruff, Oxford, 1982.
17 Momigliano 1983, p. 247.
18 Cicero, *The Academics of Cicero*, I.iii, trans.
   J. Reid, London, 1880.
19 St Augustine, *City of God*, VI, 3, trans.
   D.B. Zema and G.G. Walsh, Washington,
   1977.
20 Ibid., VI, 4.
21 Ibid.
22 Polybius, *The Histories*, IX.i, trans.
   W. Paton, London, 1922.
23 Varro, *De Re Rustica*, II.i, 3–5, trans.
   W.D. Hooper and H.B. Ash, London,
   1934.
24 Diodorus Siculus, *Historical Library*, I.viii,
   trans. E. Murphy, North Carolina and
   London, 1985.
25 Finley 1975, p. 22.
26 Rudolph 1962–63, p. 170.
27 Zhao Mingcheng, in the preface to his
   Jin shi lu, after Rudolph 1962–3,
   pp. 169–70.
28 Jacoby 1957, p. 47; see also the
   commentary in Mazzarino 1989, pp. 61
   and 547.
29 *Records of the Grand Historian of China* by

Sima Qian, translated by Burton Watson,
   2 vols, New York, 1971, vol. 2, p. 39.
30 Shaugnessy 1991.
31 Thierry 1993.
32 Owen 1986, pp. 80–98.
33 Ibid., pp. 86–7.
34 Rudolph 1962–3, p. 175.
35 Ibid., p. 170.
36 Bourdier 1993, p. 85.
37 Kendrick 1950, p. 1.
38 Rodocanachi 1914, p. 17.
39 Ibid., p. 18.
40 *The Letters of Cassiodorus*, IV, 34, trans.
   T. Hodgkin, London, 1886.
41 Photius, *Letters* no.81.
42 Gregory of Tours, *History of the
   Franks*, V, 14.
43 *Patrologie Latine*, LXXVII, 120.
44 Zappert 1850, p. 759.
45 Ibid. p. 788.
46 Le Gall 1973, p. 140.
47 Ibid.
48 Abramowicz 1983, pp. 17–18.
49 Adhémar 1937, p. 79.
50 Ibid., p. 18.
51 Ibid., p. 94.
52 Mortet 1911, I.
53 Ibid., I, pp. 53–4.
54 Ibid., I, pp. 280–81.
55 Ibid., I, p. 181.
56 Guibert de Nogent 1981, pp. 211–13.
57 Armitage-Robinson 1926, pp. 8–9;
   Kendrick 1950, p. 15.
58 Kendrick 1950, pp. 14–15.
59 Stubbs 1865, p. 159.
60 Adhémar 1937, pp. 311–12.
61 Ibid., p. 81.
62 Wright 1844, p. 440.
63 Adhémar 1937, p. 99.
64 Weiss 1988, p. 12.
65 Weiss 1988, p. 13, footnote 4.
66 Adhémar 1937, p. 112.
67 Weiss 1988, p. 18.
68 Ibid., p. 23, pl. 5.
69 Ibid., pp. 43–7.
70 Settis 1984, III, p. 455.
71 Weiss 1988, pp. 51–3.
72 Reinsch 1983, p. 170.
73 Piccolomini 1551, letter CXXXI, p. 685.
74 Ridé 1977, p. 168.
75 Piccolomini 1551, p. 681.

rsi
tume .
torsi .
tanto
rsi .
nto
cta
nanto .
ta
gno
chiacta .
no
i
regno .

u noi
mei .

ntile
i suoi .
ntile
ire
o stile .
puo dire

CHAPTER

THE EUROPE
OF THE
ANTIQUARIES

Par course subite:

Théatres, colosses

En ruines grosses

Le temps precipite.

Que sont devenus

Les murs tant connus

De Troye superbe?

Ilion est comme

Maint palais de Rome

Caché dessous l'herbe.

•

JOACHIM DU BELLAY

(Time swiftly casts down the theatres and colossi and turns them into broken ruins. What has become of the walls of proud Troy, once so familiar? Ilium, like many a Roman palace, is hidden beneath the grass.)

Illustration to the poem *Dittamondo* composed between 1318 and 1360 by Fazio degli Uberti, fifteenth-century manuscript. Uberti imagines a conversation between the poet and the personified city clothed in mourning which acts as his guide. His view of Rome is still very close to the *Mirabilia*: the Colosseum at the centre is treated as a temple. The drawing is still medieval in style, but the interest in the monuments is already that of the Renaissance.

In considering the origins of Europe (and thus the origins of civilisation) the scholars of the late medieval period had only fragments of ancient history at their disposal; the rest was lost. In the monasteries and royal courts, scholars were desperately trying to reconcile scraps of Greek and Roman history with the biblical account. In the West, history never really made sense of this impossible marriage, this constant tension, and the emergence of the Indo-European myth during the nineteenth century could be seen as the last stage in that long march in which Herder and Renan were pioneers.[1] By invoking a primitive language the supposition that 'spiritually, we are all Semites' may be exorcised.

ROME, THE CAPITAL OF HISTORY

THE BIRTH OF THE ANTIQUARIES
The Roman obsession with ancient remains

We have seen how Italian scholars from the fourteenth century onwards were the first to undertake a systematic critique of the mythical origins of the western kingdoms. The princes of Europe were, of course, in part the heirs of the Roman Empire, but this was above all a spiritual and political heritage. The savants of the European courts were no longer compelled to bring the Trojans into the history of the ruling houses. These embarrassing ancestors had had to be expelled from national histories. The process was begun in Italy from 1450, and ended in Germany in 1520 with the affirmation of the indigenous origin of the Franks.[2] This had been a difficult task for scholars, involving as it did the destruction of things once beloved – particularly in France, where great pains had been taken to indulge the hitherto neglected Gauls by demonstrating their Trojan origins:

The Gauls were greatly renowned for chivalry above all the nations of the world [...] they were descended from Trojans like the Romans [...] proud and contemptuous of all subjection.[3]

If the tremor which shook history – and the sciences – in Europe began in Italy, it was because Italy stood at the confluence of two major formative movements of the Renaissance. The Italians were the best placed to provide themselves with Latin and Greek manuscripts, and it was easy for them to establish the presence of the ancient past in their towns and countryside. In 1432 Leon Battista Alberti embarked upon a plan of Rome, based upon detailed survey; Flavio Biondo wrote a systematic description of Rome which embodied new ideas in topographical history, *Roma instaurata,* in 1446, soon followed by *Italia illustrata* in 1453 and *Roma triumphans* in 1459. Biondo's ambition went far beyond detailed topography. His *Italia illustrata* was constructed along the same lines as Varro's *Antiquitates,* the influence of which was lasting. The system applied to all antiquities – sacred, public, military, private, triumphal,[4] *Qui homines agant, ubi agant, quando agant, quid agant:* 'who are the agents, where, when and how?' (Varro).

He defined antiquarian practice by the application of three categories: the topography of monuments, geographical survey, and the analytical description of the works of civilisation.[5] Such enterprises were possible because the description of the monuments of Rome was regarded not merely as an application of history, but as a contribution towards the birth of a new political philosophy and to the renaissance of the arts and sciences. Rome would become *Speculum, exemplar, imago omnis virtutis:* mirror, example and image of all virtue.

The recording and research of the antiquities of Rome in the fifteenth century were not totally speculative and impartial. The enterprise was necessary for the development of the city and could bring financial returns. The ancient monuments were a cheap source of building materials for the palaces of princes and cardinals, and the building contracts specified the reuse of any materials found *in situ*. In this way, like the Assyrian cities, Rome's present is literally constructed upon its past. The surveys and excavations had an economic and utilitarian function which devolved upon a particular type of agent, the *cavatori*, who exploited the city's soil in all ways possible – so much so that the popes attempted to limit destruction and to reserve at least part of the profits for the papal coffers. In 1515 Leo X commissioned Raphael to build the church of St Peter, with the express instruction to take charge of any antiquities which would adorn or form part of the building. He was also ordered to avoid any destruction which had not been authorised by the Pope.[6] A bull of Pius II forbade builders 'to demolish entirely or in part, or to turn into lime, any monument or its remains'. The Vatican administrator in charge of antiquities did not bear for nothing the title bestowed by Papal bull in 1573: Commissioner of Treasures and other Antiquities, and of Mines.[7] This was a clear and practical demonstration of the confidence which the Renaissance Romans had in their role as the administrators of the past. That past was certainly expressed in the matchless splendour of the city, but it also represented a challenge which was both material and symbolic: the disposition, control and exploitation of antiquities amounted to an important stake in the social and economic arena. Elsewhere in

Celestial Jerusalem, miniature by Nicolo Polani, 1459. Made as an illustration for St Augustine's *The City of God*, this miniature presents the two model cities, both recognisably based on Rome: the ancient Rome of pagan monuments; and fifteenth-century Rome, the capital of the Christian world.

However, in 1519 Raphael had set out his conception of the surveying of monuments in a memorandum to the Pope.[9] Not only should the survey be faithful, exact and orientated, but it should give an intelligible representation of the monument: plan, external elevation and internal elevation. In this sense the expertise of the antiquary was inseparable from the practice of the architect.

Extract from the method of archaeological survey developed by the first Renaissance topographer, Leon Battista Alberti, in 1433. This page is taken from his cartographic project on the monuments of Rome.

Plan of Rome made in 1533 by Pirro Ligorio. In this plan Ligorio integrates modern topography with an archaeological survey. His plan of the Palatine is shown as an anatomical study of the remains.

SURVEYING THE MONUMENTS
Pirro Ligorio, artist, architect and scholar

The execution of Raphael's programme fell to Pirro Ligorio. He was born in Naples in 1513 and died in Ferrara in 1583. More than any other he personified the Roman antiquary of the second half of the century. 'Antiquary' to Cardinal Ippolito d'Este, he was at once a painter, an architect and it goes without saying, a scholar. Ligorio was both a man of action and a savant, even though the famous Archbishop of Tarragona, Antonio Agostino, Spanish mentor of the antiquaries of Rome, reproached him for not knowing Latin. Charged by his patron with the planning of the Villa Tivoli on the site of the former villa of Hadrian, he was probably the first antiquary to undertake such a large-scale excavation.[10] He is described in a letter to the Duke of Ferrara from his ambassador to the Vatican, and the qualities expected of a court antiquary of the time are detailed:

An antiquary, the foremost in Rome, a man of fifty-five years [...] the very best [...] not only in the art of medals, but in that of drawing, of fortifications, and many others; he was inspector of the workmanship of the fortifications of Rome, he has served the whole world and the Cardinal of Ferrara in particular: his name is Pirro Ligorio.[11]

The Renaissance antiquary owed as much to Archimedes as to Herodotus. He was indispensable to every architectural project, for at the time there was no architecture without archaeology in Italy. Excavation and the development of survey techniques swiftly affected the way in which monuments were regarded, and this mirrored the revolution in the study and editing of ancient texts. The antiquaries needed to maintain their link with scholarly circles in order to be able to interpret coins or to restore and decipher

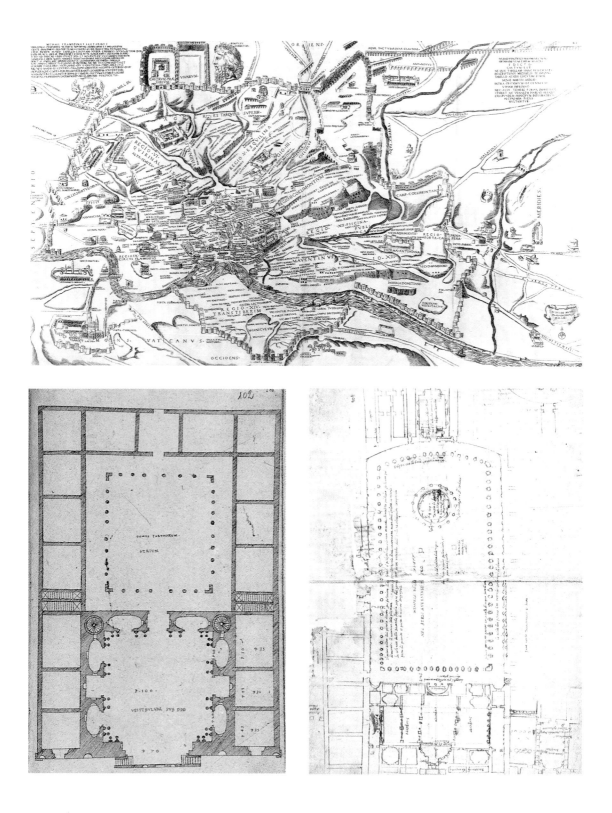

Time conquers all, it embraces all human endeavours
  And all human handicrafts
Yet antiquity, universally revered
  Always comes to an untimely end.
As you can see, and carved marbles
  Show the virtue of human trials.
Triumphal arches and beautiful walled cities
  The chiselled faces of antique medals
Bear witness today to the greatness of spirits
  Whose names have not yet been penned for posterity.

The love of antiquities, according to Johannes Sambucus, *Emblemata*, 1564. Emblem books were popular in the fifteenth century; dedicated to the Vatican Prefect, this image is one of the first to illustrate excavation as a means of historical research.

Illustration from the manual *Roman Antiquities* by Bartholomeus Rosinus. This work is notable for its landscape views of the most remarkable ruins in Rome; shown here are the Baths of Diocletian.

inscriptions, and they thus became familiar with methods of textual criticism – the *emendatio*, or correction, and the *recensio*, the checking and comparison of manuscripts. The learned of the Roman court coexisted with the artists and entrepreneurs charged with the building of the new Rome. Differences can certainly be observed between the fastidiousness of the philologists working towards the most faithful restoration possible of manuscripts and inscriptions, and the enthusiasm of the artists for the restoration of the works which they discovered. But the mood of the time favoured the creation of an intellectual milieu in which such differences were ironed out. Antonio Agostino, a harsh critic of Ligorio and of many others, was nonetheless swift to admit that he considered him one of the foremost specialists of his time. Whilst Ligorio's works on epigraphy are famous for their mistakes and inaccuracies, his plans of Rome are impressive and convincing, both in their execution and their factual content. Primarily an active spirit, Ligorio published little, but his wonderful notebooks show that he was no mere cataloguer.[12] He interested himself in the ordering of his material and applied his mind to questions of archaeological method. Should antiquities be grouped systematically by type, or should the approach be topographical? How might one unite archaeological with textual criticism?

All of these issues were tackled vigorously by the antiquaries of Rome, stimulated by scholars and sceptics like Agostino, who was one of the first to bring back into question the supremacy of text over object: 'I have more faith in medals, tablets and stones than in anything set down by writers.'[13] Revolutionary words, coming from someone who was also a philologist, but one who was not afraid to provoke his colleagues; he emphasised the necessity for a science of historical evidence which distinguished itself from a blind faith in text. The Archbishop of Tarragona wished for a more open-minded approach to the past, one based upon detailed description and drawing:

From their works [those of Ligorio and some of his colleagues] you would

PARS INTERIOR THERMARVM DIOCLETIANI.

PARS EXTERIOR THERMARVM.

imagine that they had read all the Latin and Greek books ever written, but what they have done is to use the knowledge of others. The value of their works lies not in their writings but in their drawings.[14]

Roman methods spread to numerous other Italian courts. The Italian antiquaries had transformed an interest in the past into an interest in the present, and more. They demonstrated the existence of a material antiquity which was just as important as the idealised antiquity of the texts, but their true merit lay in their development of techniques – epigraphy, numismatics, the study of topography – which made a science of the subject, or at least gave to those who were dissatisfied with the emotional and aesthetic approach the means to build their knowledge upon a discipline.

Titian, *Portrait of Jacopo Strada*, 1567. The painter and collector Jacopo Strada of Mantua was the leading purveyor of antiquities to the German Imperial Court: a pupil of Titian, he owes part of his reputation to this striking portrait of him by his master.

Martin van Heemskerck, *The Good Samaritan*, 1568.
In this composition, the painter associates the parable of the
Good Samaritan with the discovery, in the Pope's presence,
of a statue of Capitoline Jupiter. Does he suggest by this
that the Pope and his court lavished on the statue of Jupiter
the same care as was shown by the Good Samaritan to the
unfortunate victim of thieves? Does this canvas signify in
the manner of Ulrich von Hutten, a German Humanist
who was unsparingly critical of the clergy, that the Pope and
his cardinals were more occupied by the search for
pagan idols than by respect for biblical knowledge?
Is it a matter here 'of archaeologists or Pharisees'?
(E. Gombrich)

Egyptian mummy, drawn by Rubens in 1626 and sent to Fabri de Peiresc. This drawing attests to contemporary collectors' fascination for this type of antiquity. The little annotations in Italian are by Peiresc.

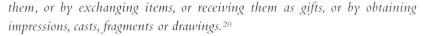

them, or by exchanging items, or receiving them as gifts, or by obtaining impressions, casts, fragments or drawings.[20]

This dazzling portrait of an antiquary at work was born at least as much of the wish to create a vision of erudition as to give a faithful description of Peiresc and his feverish activity. Gassendi summons up for us a picture of the antiquary's *métier* in the context of Rome at the beginning of the seventeenth century. Like Raphael or Ligorio, Peiresc was driven by an insatiable appetite for knowledge. Like his predecessors too, he was sure that he was practically the first to see the objects, monuments, inscriptions or manuscripts which he discovered. The difference lies more in the circumstances of discovery than of observation. Peiresc's way was not to dig up wonderful new things, to seek components, ornaments or ideas for the building of a palace. His palace was of the mind, of erudition. Here the antiquary's role is not to bring objects to light, but to bring his own sharper perception to bear in order to reveal what his predecessors could not see, or compare, or restore. Before Peiresc the antiquary's job was to frame the present so as to restore the past in a form acceptable to his contemporaries. Afterwards, the past was the proper domain of the expert, who could recognise true and false, who could enter restricted territory, identify places and collections, occupy a region in which he was likely to be challenged by others who watched for his faults or pursued the same rare object. Here, in a sense, the antiquary had lost the direct, emotional relationship with the past enjoyed by Petrarch's contemporaries, but he had gained in expertise and analytical skills – in short, in knowledge. For this kind of work to progress there must be access to cabinets of curiosities, public or private museums, and craftsmen able to undertake the restoration work, the drawings and the casts necessary for research. Essentially, Peiresc is telling us that since the specialist justifies himself through his knowledge, it is no longer necessary to be a Roman or an Italian in order to be an antiquary; it's enough to travel to Italy. The knowledge of antiquities thus became a shared resource:

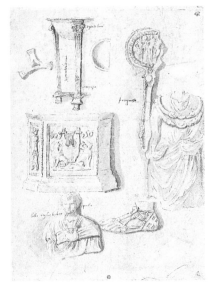

Etudes d'antiquités, by Nicolas Poussin, *c*.1645. Poussin exemplified the taste for antiquities that seized seventeenth-century artists.

Many people loudly scorn our studies, saying that they bring no glory to those who pursue them and no usefulness to others. The only ones who deserve such reproach are those who seek scholarship of a meretricious sort, or

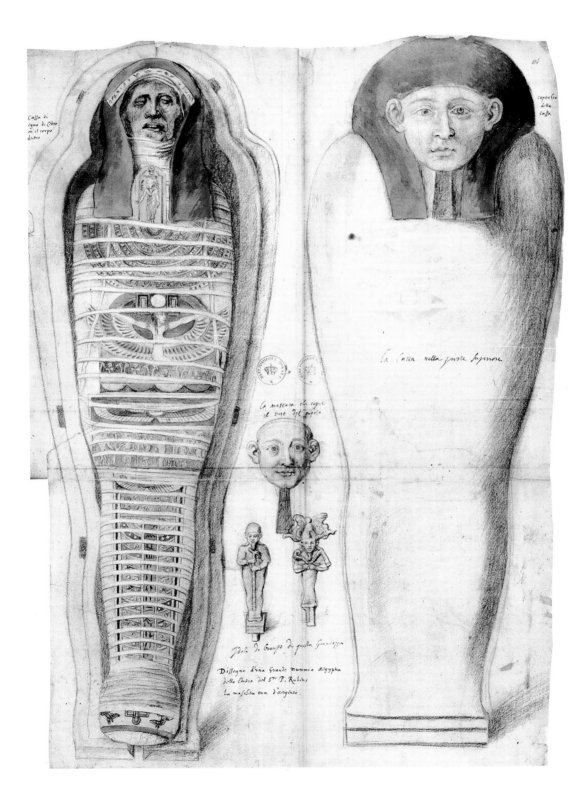

even worse, content themselves with collecting antiquities to adorn their cupboards and decorate their houses, only desiring them in order to be seen to possess them. On the other hand there are those who are entirely praiseworthy and do not waste their time in any sense – they research the antiquities, study them and publish them in order to throw light on the works of the classical historians, to illustrate the unfolding of history, the better to impress upon the minds of men its personalities and their deeds, and great events.[21]

Peiresc's defence of the antiquary is presented in terms of objects and appears to disregard the monuments. He is evidently thinking of portable antiquities – inscriptions, statues, vessels – objects which could be grouped together and ordered according to recognisable type, without going into the elaborate procedures demanded by monumental archaeology. Not that Peiresc neglected monuments; but for him, the heart of archaeology was collection. He was a collector of a particular sort, in contrast to the accepted model – an antiquary who put the knowledge of objects before their enjoyment. There is a truism implied here on the function of antiquaries, which nevertheless hints at an underlying value system. Antiquities were first a matter of taste, then a status symbol, and lastly a means of gaining knowledge …

Peiresc, or archaeology incomplete: one cannot follow the career of this remarkable antiquary from Aix without the sense of work cut short, of an inquisitive energy which burned out because of its very intensity. And the works themselves – the dispersed collections, the lost manuscripts – could have sprung from the imagination of one such as Borges, the true story of the antiquary who knew everything, understood everything, but never had time to write it all down. Fortunately, as we shall see, Peiresc did leave a real if impalpable mark, measurable by the influence which it never ceased to exert over his contemporaries and successors.

ENGLISH SCHOLAR-TRAVELLERS AND GERMAN DIGGERS

GEOGRAPHY AND ANTIQUITY IN THE BRITISH ISLES

William Camden and the exploration of British antiquities

Peiresc had shown the learned world that if there was a chosen country for all antiquaries, antiquity itself was omnipresent wherever enquiring minds wished to discover it. The lesson was extended beyond the Roman palaces but kept in close communion with the most fervent classical scholarship. From the Norwegian fjords to the banks of the Thames, the plains of Moravia to the canals of Holland, men began to scrutinise the soil and the countryside, not charged with the task of building palaces as luxurious as those of Caesar, and not digging for treasure but, like Peiresc's good antiquary, seeking to understand. Among them was a man whom Peiresc knew well from a youthful work which had shown him to be the Flavio Biondo of the kingdom of England: 'In 1586, a thirty-five-year-old schoolmaster named William Camden published an historical and geographical description of the British Isles entitled *Britannia*.'[22]

This book, due to its innovative character and the quality of its observations, was soon to become the bible of British archaeology and to see repeated editions, added to and enriched, from the death of Camden to the present day. Camden was not the first English antiquary, but he emerged as a model and an example to an even greater degree than Peiresc, because his work was easily accessible. His personal aim of compacting within a single volume a historical description of England was not new. Such a project had been conceived and begun by John Leland, librarian to Henry VIII and a pupil of Guillaume Budé in Paris, who planned a *De Antiquitate Britannia*, the prologue of which appeared in 1546.[23] Unfortunately this 'Pausanias of Tudor England', who understood so well how to combine his talent for description with visiting and examining sites, was struck by a sudden madness

Portrait of William Camden, painted by Marcus Gheeraerts the Younger in 1609.

and had to abandon his researches in 1550. Be that as it may, he was the first in England to put forward a method which combined the study of sources with a 'peregrination', something which was to become the defining characteristic of British archaeology.

Leland had been the discoverer and talented observer of a historical landscape overthrown by the Reformation and Dissolution of the Monasteries between 1535 and 1539. Camden was to reveal himself as a successor who surpassed the master. Born in 1551, the son of a painter (which might explain his interest in the visual arts), Camden studied the classics at Oxford. In 1575 he was appointed Second Master at Westminster School, and from this modest position was to revolutionise the knowledge of English antiquities. Taking advantage of school holidays, each year he visited a different part of the country in search of antiquities. His method was topographical and, using Roman geography as his starting point, consisted of constructing a local history for each English city. But his interest was not limited to remote antiquity. The ancient geography had to form a basis for a history which considered the Saxon and medieval periods as part of the history of a kingdom claiming a place in the learned world. Precision as to time and precision as to space were Camden's two imperatives, and to this end he invented the rules of historical cartography: the linguistic study of place-names to determine their Gallic, Saxon and Roman origins, the reconstitution of territorial history from tradition, and the study of coinage. He was the first to establish the existence of native mints in Roman Britain and to decipher the coin inscriptions to identify the cities which issued them. Contrary to the Trojan legends and Roman tradition, he emphasised the Anglo-Saxon nature of the origins of the British people.

Camden's work emerged with such authority in the still little-cultivated field of European archaeology that it seems a spontaneously generated phenomenon. But Camden's originality knew how to take advantage of a Humanist tradition attested not only by Leland, but also by the direct spread of Italian and Continental Humanism to Great Britain. It was to an Italian, Polydore Vergil, that the history of England owed the rebuttal of the Trojan theories of Geoffrey of Monmouth in his *Historiae Angliae Libri* (1534). In the learned circles which he frequented, Camden encountered people like Jean Hotman, son of the author of the *Franco-Gallia*, and the Dutch geographer Abraham Ortelius. Moreover, he was certainly one of the hosts of Peiresc when the latter visited England. Camden embodied a British archaeology, which was open to Continental influence, but which knew how to draw on local traditions as well as details of the landscape to lay the foundations of a national historiography. His fame never matched that of Peiresc but, unlike him, he had the means to take part in a collective project which was that of an entire generation of men moved by the distant past of England. He was surrounded by men such as Sir Robert Cotton, John Spelman and many others who worked together in a College of Antiquaries which constituted one of the very first scholarly societies of archaeology in Europe. In 1592 Camden was named Clarenceux King-of-Arms (i.e. one of the three senior heralds in the realm), and this role contributed to the development of his studies and connections: successive editions of the *Britannia* were enriched with plates of coins and transcriptions of inscriptions. In 1622, at the height of his achievement, Camden himself founded a chair in his name for the teaching of history at Oxford. Camden had not made the study of antiquities into a science, any more than he had approached the history of the pre-Roman populations of Great Britain in a radically new way, but he gave British archaeology a framework of reference (regional history), a method of observation (the combination of literary information with description of the landscape) and a technique of exploration (the close study of topynomic and numismatic sources) which dominated archaeology from the seventeenth century to the start of the eighteenth. Above all — and this is undoubtedly one of the reasons for his success — he was not isolated scientifically; in 1607 Sir John Oglander moved to the Isle of Wight and his attention was attracted by the ancient monuments and tumuli:

At my fyrst cominge to inhabit in this Island Anno 1607, I went to Quarr, and inquyred of divors owld men where ye greate church stood. Theyre wase but one, Fathor Pennie, a verye owld man, coold give me anye satisfaction; he told me he had bene often in ye church when itt wase standinge, and told me what a goodly church itt wase; and furthor sayd that itt stoode to ye sowthward of all ye ruins, corne then growinge where it stoode. I hired soome to digge to see whethor I myght finde ye fowndation butt cowld not.[24]

This most interesting testimony demonstrates that there were great prospects for excavation as a control mechanism, as evidence capable of confirming or denying a story. But Oglander went further,

Plate from *Monumenta inedita rerum germanicarum* by E.J. de Westphalen, published in 1739. This volume also contains the works of Nicolaus Marschalk. The very disparate iconography of this plate owes more to medieval tradition than to the spirit of the Renaissance and the Enlightenment. It is interesting to compare the image of the dolmen associated with devils and other zoomorphs with Meisterlin's illustrations (see pp. 109–10).

for him excavation could also be a means of exploration which might explain features of the landscape:

You may see divors buries on ye topp of owre Island hills, whose name in ye Danische tounge signifieth theyr nature, as beinge places onlie weare men were buryed [...]. I haue digged for my experience in soome of ye moore awntientest, and haue found manie bones of men formerlye consumed by fyor, according to ye Romane custome [...]. Wheresover you see a burie in any eminent place, moste commonlye on ye topp of hilles, you may presume that there hath beene soome buryed; according to ye etimoligie of ye woord, – digge, and you shall find theyre bones.[25]

Here was someone who had understood the topographic and toponymic lessons of Camden and, with his practical background, was ready to undertake excavations, not in search of treasure, but to satisfy his curiosity.

EXCAVATORS IN GERMANY
Nicolaus Marschalk

Digging up the soil is not in itself an activity which requires ability or particular technique, and we have seen that in certain circumstances the men of antiquity themselves had considered that excavation could provide answers to questions of a cultural, technical or even historical nature. Alongside the hunt for treasure, doubtless practised since treasure first existed, as the Egyptian, Assyrian or Chinese texts show, there existed a hunt for information, to which certain medieval chronicles testify;[26] but there is little evidence for the spontaneous archaeology

Megalith in the form of a dolmen, detail of plate opposite.

practised by spirits as innovatory as Oglander. In so far as the documents allow us to judge, it was a Thuringian scholar, Nicolaus Marschalk (1460/70 – 1525), who seems to have been the first to apply his Humanist background to the solving of a historical question by means of excavation.[27] He examined the difference between megalithic alignments and tumuli, and well-versed in the Latin sources dealing with Germanic peoples, attempted to attribute the one to the 'Herules', the other to the 'Obetrites'. Not

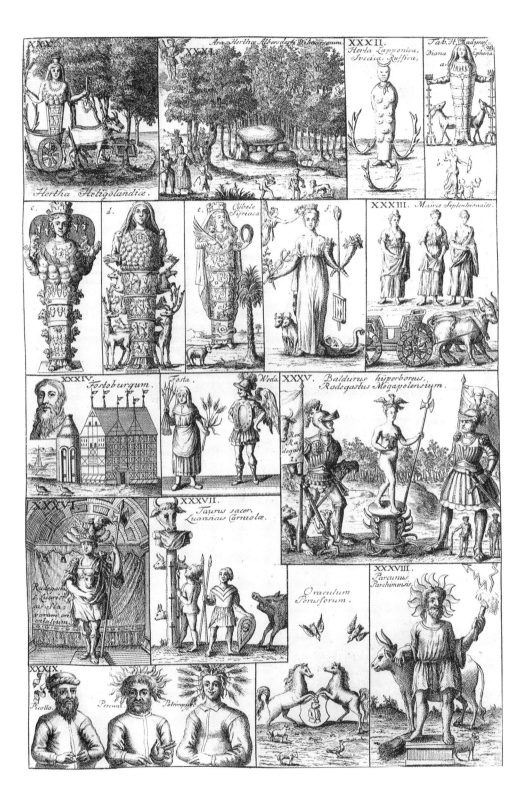

Vases rising from the earth, after Barthélemy de Glanville, *Le livre des propriétés des choses*, fifteenth-century manuscript (above) and incunabula published in 1485 (below). In the medieval period the discovery of ancient vases in the ground was the object of numerous interpretations. In the two scenes these vases are represented as born spontaneously from the earth.

content with studying the monuments themselves, he noted that cremation urns had been found nearby and regarded these as the burials of the servants of the chiefs interred in the funerary monuments:

Some of them were left to burn

Placed in urns directly on the ground.

Like the 'thunderbolts' (shaped flints), the megaliths and tumuli, the prehistoric urn cremation cemeteries were part of the 'archaeological landscape' of medieval and modern Europe. But the presence in the plains of central Europe of immense 'urnfields' was an extra element of curiosity. Discovery, mainly fortuitous, took on a particular prominence when persons of importance were witnesses. In 1529 Martin Luther visited the church at Torgau and was shown urns which had been recently discovered. A commission concluded that 'there must have been a cemetery there.'[28] Similarly, in 1544 a citizen of Breslau (Wrocław), Georg Uber, wrote to a friend after the discovery of pots at Lübben in the Spreewald:

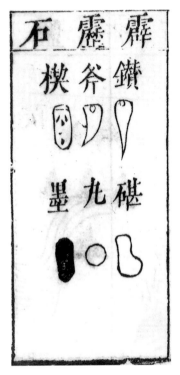

I believe we are in the presence of a funerary ritual of a people who, having no proper urns, used earthenware vessels as a substitute, which, as a sign of piety, they filled with the ashes and left-over implements from the pyre.[29]

Not everyone, however, accepted this view; the *Cosmographia* of Sebastian Münster, which appeared in the same year, took up the old myth of pots 'born spontaneously in the soil'.[30] But this time the story was badly received. In the light of a quite widely shared scepticism, Princess Anne of Saxony asked for an enquiry, and ten years later the Prince Elector of Saxony celebrated the acquisition of a certain number of urns in the following terms: 'It is likely that, in times gone by, in the pagan world, since it was customary to burn the dead, they were buried there [in the 'urn fields'].'[31] Like the 'thunderbolts' the urns (which we now recognise as vessels of the Lusatian culture) were regarded as curiosities appropriate for the royal cabinets of rare objects (*Wunderkammer*).

Representations of 'thunderbolts' from a Chinese encyclopaedia by Li-Shi-Tschin, 1596. The flints interested Chinese antiquaries and naturalists of the sixteenth century.

These precious objects were frequently embellished to adapt them to the tastes of the time; the museums in Frankfurt and Hamburg still have two pots, one of Lusatian culture adorned with a tin covering, the other of the Germano-Roman period (*terra nigra*) elaborated with silver decoration.

The funerary deposits of vases and other objects in the ground made for one of the most debated issues among central European antiquaries during the sixteenth century. The princely courts took an interest, the pots acquired monetary value, collectors sought after them and, of course, the learned were called on for advice. The explanations could be fantastic ('the product of dwarves who worked deep below ground'); natural – as in the Polish tradition of J. Dlugosz, who believed them to be formed by a sort of subterranean firing; or archaeological. But this last interpretation, although offered since the end of the fifteenth century, was not the prevailing one, at least before the start of the eighteenth century. The question, however, had been splendidly summarised by Georg Agricola in his famous book *De Natura Fossilium*:

Page from *Cosmographiae universalis*, written by the German geographer Sebastian Münster in 1544.

> *The ignorant masses in Saxony and Lower Lusatia believe that these flasks were generated spontaneously within the earth; the Thuringians believe that they were used by the monkeys which formerly inhabited the caves of Seeberg. On careful consideration, they are urns in which the ancient Germans, not yet converted to Christianity, preserved the ashes of the burnt corpses.*[32]

The protohistoric urns posed a problem for sixteenth-century scholars, not only when the knowledge of the latter was compared with popular belief, but also because the urns appeared in the earth in a form that did not obviously accord with their experience of funeral practices. An intimate of the Duke of Schleswig, Paulus Cypraeus, described thus a site discovered in 1588 during work for the construction of a road: 'One had scarcely put down one's foot or driven in one's shovel, when the urns and the remains of bones appeared to the point of covering the ground.'[33]

These strange accumulations of vases in the earth, which it seemed could not be reconciled with known practices, were interpreted with a certain logic by a Lutheran pastor named Johannes Mathesius, in 1562:

> *It is indeed remarkable that these vessels are so varied in shape that no one is like the other, and that in the earth they are as soft as coral in water, hardening only in the air [...]. It is said that there was once a grave on the spot, with the ashes of the dead, as in an ancient urn [...]. But since the vessels*

are only dug up in May, when they reveal their position by forming mounds as though the earth were pregnant (which guides those who seek them), I consider them to be natural growths, not manufactured, but created by God and Nature.[34]

The pastor's fanciful text tells us more than the critiques of the learned rationalists because it specifies the circumstances under which the urns were discovered. The pots were sought out by those who collected them and to an extent traded them. These open-air antiquaries had observed that in particular climatic conditions prospecting was easier than in others, and from this they derived practical lessons on the best method of discovery. The 'harvest' of

Protohistoric vase (*far left*) of Lausitz culture. In the sixteenth century it was decorated with engraved leaves and provided with a zinc lid marked with the name of the Imperial councillor Haug von Maxen (*c.*1560).

Vase of the Germano-Roman period (*left*) found at Basenheim, near Koblenz, in 1563. Decorated in silver, this vase is capped by a bell-shaped lid. On its crest a putto holds like shields two coins, one of Galba and the other of Otho (68–9 AD). A dedication inscribed on the vase specifies that 'this antique vase was found on the lands of the noble and eminent Anthoni Waldposten of Basenheim with a pot and earthen bottle in a vineyard where there were other vases of the same sort, [...] two copper fibulae used by the Ancients [...] and everything remaining in the earth for many hundred years. Found at the end of April 1563 by an inhabitant of Basenheim.'

vases took place in May, doubtless because at that time of year vegetation growth revealed observable anomalies (greater density of vegetation or different soil colour). It was not the earth that gave up the antiquities, but men who invented observation methods which allowed the discovery of remains. Even if this shocks our modern concept of archaeology, the pastor's theory was not absurd and poses a fundamental question for the epistemology of archaeology. The observer detects an anomaly in the earth – colour variation or change in relief or in the vegetation cover, the presence of tiles, sherds or flints – and he makes an archaeological deduction which he labels site, burial, settlement. But are these the primary indices (due to the direct action of the people who produced them), or the secondary (due to erosion, to soil movements)? Should one relate a climatic piece of data (more vases found in the spring) to a modification of surface contours – a modern hypothesis – or to an internal

Drawing of the excavation of a Roman *castellum* at Benningen, in Württemberg, made by Simon Studion in 1597. This plan indicates a desire to place the monument in its geographical setting.

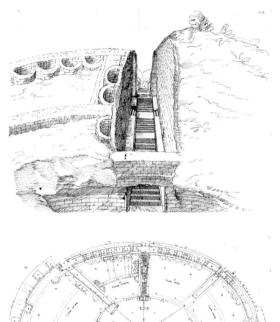

Drawings of the excavation of the theatre at Augst, made by Basilus Amerbach in 1582. These excavations at Augst, near Basle, were probably the first in Europe to be organised by a public institution (municipal council). The surveys were as precise as those of the Roman antiquaries.

change in soil composition? The error made by Mathesius is proven, but it is rich in implications.

The interest of the curious, the princes and the learned for funerary urns was a constant in sixteenth-century archaeology. The recurrent finds, notably on the sites of Maslow and Gryzyce in Silesia, were the most famous. In 1546 the Emperor Ferdinand I dispatched a commission of enquiry to Maslow, and in 1577 the Emperor Rudolph II undertook research at Gryzyce. Delighted by the discovery of urns, Rudolph had a wooden column erected on the site as a memorial of the excavation.[35] This interest was assuredly linked to the development and function of cabinets of antiquities, which illustrated as it were by endorsement the story of the taste for antiquities.

THE ARCHAEOLOGY OF ARCHAEOLOGY
The Wunderkammer

Before considering how the Scandinavian antiquaries managed to synthesise the archaeological knowledge of the Renaissance by integrating its diverse branches into an organic whole which paid as much attention to material sources as to written tradition, it is useful to pause for a moment over the picture of European archaeology at the end of the sixteenth century.

Let us imagine the history of archaeology as a stratigraphy. It reveals to the observer the recent layers, juxtaposed according to national influences, as well as an ancient foundation formed by a common tradition. The oldest layers are those of the medieval oral and written tradition: the 'giants' footsteps', the 'sorcerers' beds', corresponding to the scattered presence across the European landscape of megaliths and tumuli which appeared, as we have seen, in medieval iconography but of which the illustrators of the sixteenth century were especially fond. The oldest 'modern' image of Stonehenge is a watercolour by Lucas de Heere, a Dutchman who was

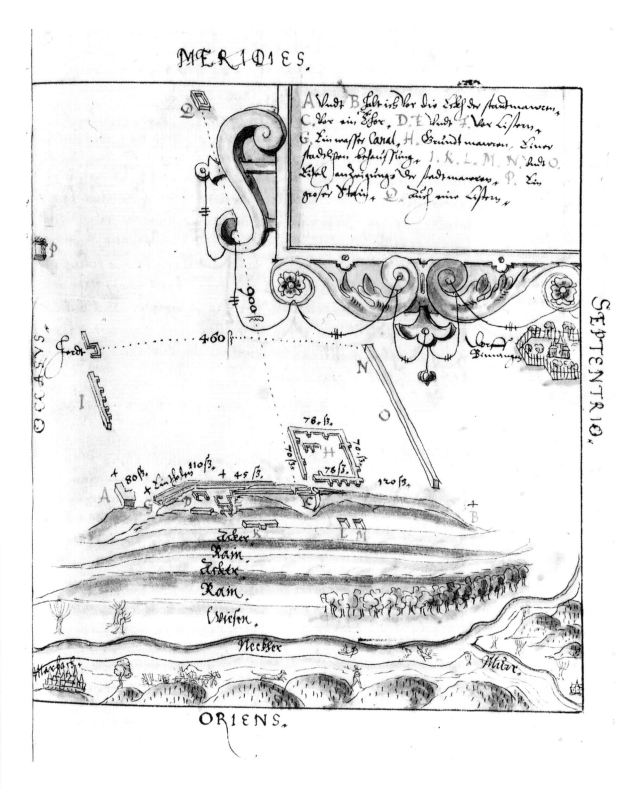

The site of Jelling, published by Peter Lindeberg in 1591. Done at the request of Heinrich Rantzau, governor of the province of Holstein, this illustration is accompanied by technical descriptions, which attest to a quasi-anatomical analysis of the monuments. The votive stone, situated between the two tumuli of the kings of Denmark, bears runic inscriptions translated at the bottom of the drawing.

the subject. *Many believe that they are cast down by lightning; yet those who study history judge that before the use of iron they were struck from very hard flint for the folly of war. Indeed, for the most ancient peoples, pieces of flint served as knives.*[38]

What is striking about the history of the interpretation of flints, pottery, megaliths and tumuli is the perfect parallelism of interpretations. Against the mythological tradition a small number of scholars produced convincing theories, but these were never fully accepted by the learned world. This duality between knowledge and tradition constitutes the foundation, the oldest layer in our vertical section through the archaeology of the sixteenth century. Closer to the surface come archaeological practices. These can be divided into distinct regional schools, which form contemporary deposits that are not, however, composed of the same sediments. The Italian layer is dominated at the outset by the rediscovered antiquity which emerged under the picks of the builders of modern Rome. The Italians benefited from three advantages. Firstly, the cities of Padua, Bologna, Rome and Naples constituted centres of intellectual, artistic and philological activity: artists and antiquaries gathered, engaged by kings, princes and cardinals to classify, restore and study their collections, and to collaborate in urban and architectural projects. And in Italy Humanist culture was at home: attention to the earth and the collection of remains were prompted as much by necessity as curiosity, and philogical, pictorial and architectural knowledge was immediately available. Finally, the straightforward history of Italian towns was inseparable from the history of the Graeco-Roman world.

It was not the same in France, England, central or northern Europe. In these four cultural zones – assessed a little arbitrarily – history was there to be conquered, founded and established on foundations newly liberated from the weighty presence of the Trojans and the tribes of Israel (this was not always the case, however, as we shall see in the work of the Swede, Olof Rudbeck). In these circumstances the antiquaries naturally tended to construct an anachronic history, which started with the present in order – with the help of rare ancient texts – to establish the lineaments of an ancient history which joined up with medieval history. From this process derived the key role of particular Latin texts – Caesar for France and England, Tacitus for the Germanic and even the Slavic world (to the degree to which the Slavic identity rested on the recognition of traits characteristic of the ancient populations of central Europe). But the texts were few, and the first antiquaries of the sixteenth century were above all epigraphers. To their marvelling eyes arose the vast memory of Roman epigraphy, or the runic stelae which graced the Scandinavian churches. However, the epigrapher's province was not limited to a display case, he had to go out into the field; peregrination replaced the promenades of the Roman antiquaries. Marschalk, Peiresc, Camden and in particular Ole Worm in Denmark and Johan Bure in Sweden were indefatigable travellers who found their own reasons to traverse the landscape and above all to observe it. In the country-side of temperate Europe, with the exception of

Votive pyramid of Heinrich Rantzau, governor of the province of Holstein. In memory of the kings of Denmark, Rantzau raised in 1578, on his own estate, a votive pyramid which bears the following Latin inscription: 'The year 5540 since the creation of the world, the year 3484 since the Flood, the year 1578 since the birth of Christ, the year 985 since the birth of Mahomet.'

Roman towns which had partly retained their fortifications and monuments, it was necessary to use one's eyes to identify megaliths and tumuli, to observe the ground to distinguish deserted villages or necropoli. Peregrination, chorology, geography – these were familiar words to the antiquaries of the sixteenth and seventeenth centuries, whose inquisitiveness matched that of the learned, the scientists, astronomers, mathematicians and botanists who abandoned their libraries to observe the earth and the sky. Stuart Piggott emphasises that 'surveying' was part of the culture of gentlemen who had received their training at the Inns of Court, the English law schools.[39] A new type of antiquary linked to the rural world appeared: gentry, townsmen and even farmers, preoccupied with their harvests and the administration of their land. These antiquaries did not exercise their learning in the service of a prince or royal administration, or if they were given this role – as when Camden was created a herald – it was because of success in their peregrinations. For these men excursion, travel on foot or horseback into the countryside, was both a second education and a pleasure. Thus in 1621, Robert Burton states in his *Anatomy of Melancholy*:

> *What more pleasing studies can there be than the Mathematicks, Theorick or Practick parts? As to survey land, make mapps, models, dials &c., with which I have ever much delighted myself.*[40]

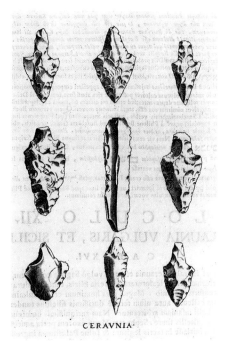

CERAVNIA

Representations of different 'ceraunites', from the first edition in 1717 of the *Metallotheca Vaticana*, written by Michele Mercati in 1570. The learned Italian explained that these alleged 'thunderbolts' were in fact flints worked by the hand of man.

There were, of course, notable differences from one country to another. The British, following Camden's national and regional tradition, excelled in archaeological cartography, in the description of the landscape and the listing of monuments. The central European antiquaries were more active in excavation and attempts at ethnic interpretation of the remains found in the earth (the influence of Tacitus). The French, with the notable exception of Peiresc, were more interested in cabinets of curiosities, in the cataloguing of 'thunderbolts', coins and inscriptions, than in traversing the countryside. In France, history remained dominated by the written model evident in all the literature concerning the Gauls. Perhaps, as has been seen, because too much was asked of the Gauls – whether they were German or Roman, Catholic or Protestant, royalist or republican – the antiquities offered less help than the texts. This archaeology of archaeology, as far as it can be taken, could yet reveal infinite variations in a world where relationships in the field of scientific enquiry were astonishingly close (let us remember that a direct or indirect correspondence linked Camden, Peiresc, Rubens, Worm, Gassendi and Galileo) but where the small numbers of the learned made for the halting development of specific disciplines, as one sees yet again with the premature disappearance of Peiresc. As ever, to complete the 'sectional view' of the subject, we must turn to Scandinavia, which had seen the birth of a new mode of archaeological practice, and because it was there, for the first time in European history, that the state was given not only to legislation on the conservation of the past but also to the creation of archaeological institutions.

The cabinet of Michele Mercati. In 1585 Mercati created one of the first mineralogical cabinets in Europe. This gallery followed an ordered architectural arrangement which distinguished between minerals on one side and metals on the other.

THE SCANDINAVIANS

THE BIRTH OF LANDSCAPE ARCHAEOLOGY
The synthesis of the archaeological knowledge
of the Renaissance

In the snow-bound North the past does not reveal itself in the friendly way that belongs to temperate lands. The scholars of the northern Renaissance lacked not only the rich resources of the Italian and German monasteries, but also the continuity that Roman ruins at Trier, Basle and, of course, in Provence and Italy, established with the distant past of ancient Rome.

But for those who took the trouble to look at the landscape, the earth revealed its secrets: megaliths, barrows and even runic inscriptions (the first Scandinavian writing) were everywhere. At the end of the twelfth century Saxo Grammaticus had already noted strange monuments here and there:

In the distant past there were giants, an ancient people whose existence is attested by the massive stones which formed the roofs of burial monuments and dolmens. Should anyone doubt that these are the work of giants, they should tell us who else could have placed such enormous blocks in such positions. [41]

Contemporary theologians agreed that the Goths, ancestors of the Scandinavians, were descended from Gog, the heir of Japhet, and this biblical authentication was not lost on the medieval population.

In 1434 at the Council of Basle, Nicolaus Ragvald, the Swedish Bishop of Växjö, successfully claimed precedence over his brethren as representative of the oldest race in Europe, disputed only by a Spanish bishop in the name of the Visigoths. [42] This form of historical legitimation continued into the Renaissance, as shown by learned clerics such as Olaus and Johannes Magnus, Swedes loyal to the pope and exiled to Rome by the Reformation. Olaus Magnus, Bishop of Uppsala, used his enforced leisure to write one of the first historical, geographical and ethnographical descriptions of the Nordic people. His book, published in Rome in 1555, is lavishly illustrated with engravings which reveal an extraordinary vision of the Scandinavian countryside: forests of megaliths, barrows, stones with runic inscriptions, pictures of dwarves and elves mining precious metals. This humanist scholar stayed close to medieval tradition: 'In ancient times, when giants lived in Northern lands, well before the Latin alphabet was invented […], the kingdoms of the North had their own writing.'[43]

Olaus Magnus was indeed a Humanist with wide experience of the classical tradition but he did not test the available evidence against the texts in the manner of the Italian and German scholars of the time. He concentrated on the distinctiveness of the Nordic landscape, on the monuments and inscriptions, which he sought to interpret not for their own sakes but in relation to classical tradition: giants and runes attested to the antiquity of the Nordic peoples at a time before writing was known to Greece or Rome. At this time Olaus Petri, the great reformer of the Swedish church,[44] was more critical in his approach to northern history, calling for a systematic treatment of documents, archives and inscriptions. He was cautious on the question of origins and refused to pronounce on the dubious primacy of the Danes and Swedes.

However, it was not until the end of the sixteenth century that people began the systematic collection of Nordic antiquities and started to link knowledge of sources with travel – so dear to the Roman and British antiquaries. Heinrich Rantzau, Governor of Holstein, commissioned richly detailed engravings of the Jelling barrows. In 1588 he also organised an excavation of the Langben Rises Hoj dolmen, to the north of Roskilde, in search of the giants.[45] More ambitious projects were undertaken by more rigorous minds. One such was Johan Bure, son of a pastor in Uppsala and educated within a strict classical tradition, who in addition to his Latin and Greek had taught himself Hebrew. In 1602 he became tutor to Crown Prince Gustavus Adolphus, future king of Sweden and one of the greatest warriors of the century. In the fervid intellectual and nationalistic climate of the Swedish court, Bure soon turned to the decipherment of runes. This was no novelty – after all runic characters were still being carved on funerary and religious monuments in some parts of Sweden – but Bure was one of the first to collect and systematically analyse the ancient inscriptions. He established a precise alphabet, suggested rules for transcription,

Frontispiece of *Danicorum Monumentorum Libri Sex* by Ole Worm, published in 1643. The association here of the Graeco-Roman tradition with the Scandinavian and biblical traditions reminds one that the story of antiquity was not limited to the Graeco-Roman tradition.

proposed a dating system and, above all, undertook a corpus of Swedish inscriptions. From 1599 Bure, with two assistants, organised regular topographic and archaeological surveys. By comparison with Camden in Great Britain his methods were not original, but they are distinguished by the care devoted to the illustrations and the attention given to the epigraphy, the recording of which was the main purpose of his travels. At a stroke he transformed the traditional antiquarian tour into a systematic study – the first professional archaeological survey. His personal links with the Swedish court provided resources of which his contemporaries could only dream: royal commissions, the help of artists and engravers and, especially, the unswerving support of the monarch.

The results were staggering. In a few years Bure and his team recorded a quarter of the known inscriptions in Sweden. The kingdom of Sweden was thus the first state to endow an archaeological service which fore-shadowed in many ways the role of our modern agencies. Bure's success would not have been complete with-out one vital factor – competition. At the beginning of the seventeenth century Swedes and Danes were locked in keen political and diplomatic rivalry. The two double monarchies (Denmark–Norway, Sweden–Finland) were determined to create an image of their past appropriate to their political and diplomatic roles in a war-torn Europe. History played a vital part in the great diplomatic game between the two kingdoms, and in Scan-dinavia archaeology was the handmaiden of history. The decipher-ment of the runes allowed the reading of the earliest records of the northern kingdoms, and the country-wide corpus revealed monu-ments which, while less familiar to scholars, were assuredly as spec-tacular as the ruins of Roman towns.

Forest of signs, wood engraving from *Historia* by Olaus Magnus, 1567. Both prehistoric remains and medieval burials were attributed to the ancient Scandinavians: they constituted a kind of repertory of architectural forms embedded in the landscape like enigmatic letters.

Two views of the Scandinavian countryside: wood engravings illustrating Olaus Magnus' *Historia*, 1567. Magnus wondered whether the standing stones of the Norwegian mountains were the work of pagans or giants. He attributed to the same giants the megaliths and stone alignments of Sweden. Ole Klindt-Jensen has, however, emphasised the visionary nature of the author, who was already preoccupied by the protection of antiquities: the runic inscription below the altar reads 'Respect the antiquities'.

TRAVELLING THROUGH TIME
Ole Worm

It was to be a Dane who made the next important contribution to the new science which linked the antiquarian tour to survey, collection and interpretation. Ole Worm was born in Aarhus in 1588 and was educated to the highest standards of the time. After college in Aarhus he went on to the Johanneum in Lüneburg, a noted centre of classical studies, frequently attending lectures at the *Stiftschule* in Emmerich, a Jesuit institution which accepted Protestants. After this solid grounding, Worm embarked on an extensive period of travel and study (mainly of medicine) in Europe which took him as far as Italy – to Padua (where the young Peiresc had preceded him by several years) then to Rome and Naples. His appetite for knowledge was matched by a taste for collecting everything. Like Peiresc he did not restrict himself to antiquities but was intent on a reference collection which brought together medical and philological material and reunited *naturalia* with *artificiosa*. In Naples he was an avid visitor to the cabinet of antiquities formed by Ferrante Imperato, one of the most noted collectors of the time. His contacts with the school of 'chemical science' created by Pierre La Ramée (Petrus Ramus) – the then expert on 'Gaulish antiquities' – secured introductions everywhere, in Paris and also in Montpellier, where he stayed during 1609–10. With all Europe his classroom he spent time in Kassel, then a noted intellectual venue under the patronage of Prince Moritz of Hesse, and in Heidelberg, Amsterdam and London. In 1613 this international scholar became Professor of Latin at the University of Copenhagen. Here he would exercise an unmatched influence on the human and natural sciences. At the time the university was undergoing reform, with the keen support of Worm. By turn Professor of Latin, Greek, Physic and Medicine, from 1622 he threw himself into the study of runes. His extensive correspondence, quite as brilliant as that of Peiresc, reveals his unflagging curiosity in the fields of natural history and antiquity. Among his regular correspondents we find members of Peiresc's circle: Pietro Gassendi, Gabriel Naudé and Lapeyrère.

Danicorum Monumentorum Libri Sex, six volumes on Danish monuments, was published in Copenhagen in 1643. It is a general treatise on Danish antiquities, which made a name for itself both for its

Reconstruction of the cabinet of Ole Worm, after the frontispiece of *Musei Wormiani Historia*. Worm's cabinet was his life's work: it symbolised a vision of the world which established a continuum between animal, vegetable and mineral.

Ole Worm's cabinet, frontispiece of *Musei Wormiani Historia*, 1655.

methodology and for the quality of its illustrations. The first volume, following the classical tradition, consists of a definition of the subject but is effectively a veritable practical manual of archaeology. Monuments, objects and text: the recollection of the past is universal and it is the antiquary's task to perform a comparative 'post-mortem' on these different historical sources. Any historian wishing to study Nordic antiquities must have the courage to prefer national history over that of the classical world:

Because our antiquities seem intractable most of us turn aside from our patriotic duty and, neglecting our local antiquities devote ourselves to the foreign, but to neglect the home ground in favour of that which is far away, to adhere to the distant at the expense of the familiar, is vice not virtue. So it naturally follows that the actions, rituals, customs, institutions, laws, victories, triumphs and all those Danish achievements would be swallowed in darkness and be consigned to oblivion for eternity.[46]

The work was cultural and patriotic. Antiquity was not restricted to the Graeco-Roman tradition but must take into account domestic, or as we would now say, national remains. The Danes were no less worthy of interest than other ancient nations. Worm did not attempt to achieve the impossible in a complete catalogue of all the forms of antiquity, but to record those antiquities which would appeal to scholars by virtue of their rarity, grandeur or great age. Here the naturalist was at work as much as the philologist, creating order in a vast and as yet unexplored material world. Objects must be classified by composition and above all, function. Antiquities were defined by their purpose: sanctuaries, altars, tombs, epitaphs, public places, circuses, boundaries and frontiers. This is a strange list, which can only be taken as the application of Roman categories to Danish antiquities. In order to devise a descriptive system of archaeology, Worm drew upon the classical tradition. His methods reveal an obvious contradiction between his desire to create a new discipline and to reconcile this with the tradition of Varro's *Antiquitates*.[47] Worm never once questioned the validity of establishing whether (or not) institutions such as the Roman forum or circus existed in ancient Scandinavia. His archaeology was based upon clear and identifiable evidence in the landscape for activities seen as common to all societies. The inventory had an underlying order: first ritual (monuments and funerary practices), followed by records (inscribed on wood or stone) and finally social monuments (fora, circuses, boundaries, frontiers, sanctuaries). This was not the naive view of a collector acquiring whatever the ground might turn up, but a considered attempt to make use of tradition to read the landscape and decipher the signs and inscriptions seen there. Worm went beyond the classification and interpretation of remains, seeking to understand their function and to link them to the landscape which he could observe. After recalling the work of his predecessors, especially that of Olaus Magnus, he noted that the remains of the 'pagan' period were fewer in Denmark than in Sweden:

In Denmark, so far as I know, there are few ruins anywhere, perhaps because our ancestors, once converted to Christian mysteries, sought every means to eradicate the shame of such idolatry and completely destroyed the old cult places [...] or that they replaced them with temples to the true God, seeking to root out all memory of the false. Thus it is not uncommon even now to find the broken and scattered remains of their altar-tables in the fields and woods.[48]

If archaeology began with the collecting of antiquities, it came of age with their interpretation. Worm's originality lay in setting out clear descriptive methods and in relating the monuments in their landscape to the historical record. Archaeological interpretation needs a historical explanation of the way in which knowledge survives from the past. Monuments do not remain in their original state, and their preservation depends upon histories of which archaeology must take due account. Worm's scheme was progressive: after defining the types of monument he studied successively sanctuaries, divinities, sacrifices, standing stones and the meeting places of the ancient Danes. In this way he created a new form of antiquarian discourse, revolutionary for its time. Description and a ragbag of detailed observations were not enough – knowledge had to be ordered into an intelligible system. This fundamental progress did not see – as the sixteenth-century antiquaries did – the monuments as disparate ciphers which had lost their meaning, but as missing pieces of the historical jigsaw. 'Time's shipwreck', a concept dear to Bacon and Vossius[49] might be salvaged; the jetsam on the shore of history could, if properly interpreted, reveal facts, practices and behaviour which could take us to the heart of past societies.

Taking a new look at the world which surrounded him, the antiquary discovered in the present the material remains of the past and in doing this freed himself, partially but decisively, from tradition. From that time on, history no longer consisted of interpreting ancient texts but of using monuments as a starting point for later –

and only later – drawing on tradition. In this sense Worm's method was Baconian:

With regard to authority, it is the greatest weakness to attribute infinite credit to particular authors, and to refuse his own prerogative to time, the author of all authors, and, therefore, of all authority. For truth is rightly named the daughter of time, not of authority.[50]

The Lejre site, drawn for Ole Worm in 1643.

The Jelling site, drawn for Ole Worm in 1643. Taken from Worm's *Danicorum Monumentorum Libri Sex*, this survey differs a little from that of Rantzau a few decades earlier (see p. 152).

The exploration of the soil is a voyage in time. For this there is no need of Latin or Greek sources, but an enquiring mind, a sharp eye, a grasp of landscape and a taste for drawing. Worm's work had greatly impressed his contemporaries by the quality of its descriptions and the beauty and precision of its plans and drawings. The royal site at Lejre in Sjaelland was the subject of an extraordinary topographic and archaeological study. Worm's approach was not to start with a single monument as a means of constructing the history of a place; he inserted every particularity of the site to create a complete view, rendering precisely the traits of the landscape. Antiquaries in the Roman tradition started with the monument and finally put it in context. The Scandinavian method, already apparent in Jelling's recording for Governor Rantzau, was wholly different. Worm's analysis of the royal site of Lejre featured every detail of the topography – lowlands, hills, woods. Contemporary land-use was related to each monument:

A. *The monument of Harald Hyldetandi bounded to north and south by large stones, in the centre a huge square block resting on smaller stones.*

B. *Area of stones, the summit almost entirely occupied by a slab of rock in the shape of a chair; the people call it 'Droningstolen', the Queen's throne, where according to tradition the Queen presided, wearing the imperial diadem.*

C. *The former site of the royal palace, still known as 'Konigsgarden'.*

O. *The place of coronation, enclosed by a ring of stones. Nearby is hill D, where the newly crowned king stopped to be seen by the people and receive their fealty.*

E. *'Ertedal' in the woods, a pleasant valley thought to be named after the goddess Hertha.*

F. *Lejre's river.*

G. *'Steenhoj' hill.*

H. *Monument and tomb of king Olaf.*

I. *'Maglebrae', the main bridge.*

K. *Supposed site of the king's stables, formely called 'Hestebierg'.*

L. *Place named the royal foals, 'Folehoj'.*

M. *'Kirkehoj' where a temple stood, according to some traditions.*

N. *'Früsshoj'.*

P. *River which crosses 'Kornerupio', called 'Kornerup Ae'.*

A modern reader would have difficulty in acknowledging the constant confusion between the analysis of the archaeological remains and a mythical vision of royal life. Worm's interpretation of the landscape was still within the medieval tradition when he identified the queen's throne and the royal coronation site, but it is consistent with an analysis of the spectacle of royal power which was still favoured by modern day absolutist monarchs.

The work is inevitably of its time, but beyond this historical conditioning there is much to admire: the global vision of landscape, the way in which practical survey drew upon tradition (place-names, sagas) and the recording techniques. Worm in action rigorously followed the method set out in his famous letter of 1638 to the Bishop of Stavanger in Norway, and which may be seen as a model for contemporary archaeological travel.

The triumphal arch of Maximilian I according to a scheme by the architect Kölderer
and Albrecht Dürer, 1515–17. The author of *Der Weisskunig* (the scholar-king or white-king),
Maximilian I had this triumphal arch engraved in order to record on paper the glory which
he did not have the means to commemorate in stone. His antiquary J. Stabius had written
a commentary in rhyming verse which demonstrated each of the emperor's activities,
including architecture, the learning of languages, heraldry and collecting. Maximilian
had dreamt of an archaeological and historical description of a Germany to which
the greatest scholars of the time, Stabius, Konrad Celtis,
Wilibald Pirckheimer, had to contribute.

COLLECTION AND CLASSIFICATION
An instrument of learning and experimentation

Theory and practice in the field qualify Bure and Worm as the founders of a landscape archaeology which is the forerunner of our modern surveys. The innovation lay not solely in the examination, cataloguing and plotting of each site, but in the topographical approach, in the attention paid to the drawings and in the care taken with publication. From start to finish, Worm was in charge of a chain of complementary operations which could not be carried out by any one person, but which demanded a degree of collaboration and co-operation facilitated by the extent of his knowledge, his offices and his international contacts. Worm sought to win the Danish and foreign diplomats he met to his cause, he mobilised the bishops, the ministers and the king's representatives in far-flung provinces. If necessary he did not hesitate to use his authority. Worm was not only a thinker, he was also a collector in the best Humanist tradition, eager to know and to classify all the curious objects which chance and enthusiasm brought before him.

The passion for collecting, perfectly demonstrated by Pomian, is as ancient as human curiosity. During the sixteenth century scholars and the nobility began to assemble collections which were not merely treasures, but had a didactic function in terms of an ordered explanation of the world. A difficult problem indeed – to classify such a diverse range of *sémiophores*, whose place in a collection was won primarily because they were curious, precious or rare. Barbara Balsiger has clearly demonstrated how the classification process answered a philosophical imperative: concentrate the maximum number of objects, as diverse as possible, into the minimum amount of space. The collection is a microcosm of the world, interpreted as a macrocosm. These efforts led directly to a redefinition of collecting: this was an age of scepticism. The *sémiophore* can invoke the invisible; it is beyond time and space, a fragile link with a lost and frequently poorly understood world. The attraction of collecting, in Pomian's sense, lay in the metaphysical

Detail of the triumphal arch of Maximilian I. Maximilian's collection was not made for display but to be hidden in a side room, hardly accessible.

The cabinet of Ferrante Imperato, a plate from his *Natural History*, 1599.

consequences of that reductionist process. There are many ways of 'harvesting' objects.

The princely and royal courts were particularly proud of the reputation attached to their treasures. They were enriched by a variety of political and economic transactions. But beside the traditional areas of competition for those things already deemed to be collectable, there were other things which entered the arena by dint of a catholic approach to acquisition – things which were diverted from their customary use, or plucked from the oblivion into which they had fallen. The sixteenth-century vogue for American objects was of that nature, like the collection of types of fossils, mineralogical samples and, of course, archaeological and ethnographic objects. This transfer of interests and awakening of new tastes made room for another sort of collection: 'We are not dealing with the appearance of new objects, but with a new class of *sémiophores* composed of objects undergoing study which takes its place alongside existing classes.'[51]

The cabinet of Francesco Calzolari, a plate from *Museum Calceolarium*, 1622.

Beside the relics or other precious materials which had hitherto formed the heart of every great collection there appeared objects whose interest lay in what they revealed about the past or present, be it in their appeal to the senses (such as statues and paintings), or in their intrinsic qualities as objects of learning (such as scientific instruments). Certainly the precious or sacred nature of items was a necessary feature of a collection, but at the same time the collection itself became a mechanism for the generation of knowledge. In 1565 Samuel von Quicchelberg, a doctor from Antwerp and friend of the Duke of Bavaria, had already expounded his theory on the subject. In the work which he published that year he introduced the first imaginary museum in history to the world of learning. His aim was to construct a scaled-down model, a structured sample, of the material world. Quicchelberg's book was the guide to a virtual collection used as an aid to learning and experimentation. He divided the objects into five sections which, materially and intellectually, structured his imaginary museum.[52]

The first was devoted to a history of the museum, to the images, maps and models which establish collections in time and space. The second dealt with *artificiosa*: statues, stones, architectural fragments, metal objects, coins, pictures, engravings. The third, *naturalia*: the animal, vegetable and mineral world. The fourth, *instrumenta*: objects or machinery from musical instruments to clothes, including measuring and surgeons' instruments, hunting equipment and agri-

RITRATTO DEL MVSEO DI
FERRANTE, IMPERATO

IO·BAPT·BARTONVS   HIERONYMVS·A·SCARPVLIS

emphasis was more upon continuity between the different orders rather than contrast. At the bottom right of the engraving are all the carefully labelled specimens: parts of animals, shells, minerals and plant material grouped by type; above, the smaller stuffed animals alternate with sculptures and an assortment of instruments; finally, there are the larger animals, huge tortoises, polar bears, weapons, machinery, clothing and even a life-size human being.

These introductory images cannot, of course, be taken as a faithful illustration of the catalogues, but because they set out to give an idea of the whole collection they do reveal a choice and an intention. One's first impression of the *Museum Wormianum* is of a microcosm in the tradition of Quicchelberg, in which man occupies a decisive place. To Worm, *artificiosa* and *naturalia* were inseparable, their close and complementary nature derived from the link which united man and nature in the past. The originality which distinguished Worm from his immediate predecessors as well as from the encyclopaedic works of such as Konrad Gesner and Ulisse Aldrovandi stems from his views on the relationship between nature and man. The first four sections of the *Museum Wormianum* correspond to Quicchelberg's scheme: mineral, vegetable and animal in deliberate sequence (neither Imperato nor Calzolari employed such a progression). The same methodical approach is evidenced in his Chapter IV, which is probably the first general treatise on archaeological and ethnographic material. Worm divided his artefacts into twelve classes: clay objects, amber objects, stone objects, gold and silver objects, bronze and iron objects, coins, glass and similar materials, objects made from plant materials, wooden objects, *fructibus,* objects made from animal products and unclassifiable objects.

Worm had a methodical mind, but he was no revolutionary, and his conservatism sometimes played odd tricks on him. He still believed in thunder-stones, something which Michele Mercati had rejected many years before. Worm did not possess Mercati's talent for interpretation, or the fondness for excavation shown by German prehistorians such as Nicolaus Marschalk. He did have other qualities, though, which some of his predecessors lacked. Worm combined observation with organisation, and saw a project through from the gathering of information to its publication. The breadth of his learning combined with the range of his professional acquaintance have justly earned him the title of father of the archaeology of the Age of Reason. After his death the *Museum Wormianum* collection was

The cabinet of Athanasius Kircher, engraving 1678. With the famous Jesuit father Athanasius Kircher, the taste for Egyptian antiquities became fully established in collecting: the obelisks were partly integrated into the furnishing.

incorporated into the museum of King Frederick III in Copenhagen. Worm thus bequeathed to posterity a method (the analysis of the archaeological landscape), a collection which fulfilled the most progressive criteria of the time, and above all the idea that archaeology could, when necessary, make up for the absence of texts and inscriptions. The careful study of material remains, the detailed plotting of finds and the survey of monuments, contributed to the birth of a new discipline in which history and natural history combined. Thanks to the work of Bure and Worm the Scandinavian monarchs, and the scholarly concensus, discovered that the earth responded to interrogation. The lesson was understood: in 1622 Christian IV of Denmark passed the first edict concerning the protection of antiquities, and on 20 May 1630 Gustavus Adolphus published a statute covering Swedish antiquities. These actions marked the passing of archaeology into the public domain – for the first time beyond Rome there was a heritage to defend.

The cabinet of Sainte-Geneviève, engraving, 1692. This cabinet was one of the most famous French cabinets of the seventeenth century.

From the Roman antiquaries of the Renaissance to the Scandinavian scholars, from Biondo to Worm, the same spirit of enquiry motivated men in their study of the material remains of the past. Observation, excavation and survey came to be established as a method of gaining historical knowledge. This materialist revolution in history came about at the same time that the scientific world was being rocked by experimentation and the discovery of new worlds:

We must also take into consideration that many objects in Nature fit to throw light upon Philosophy have been exposed to our view and discovered by means of long voyages and travels, in which our times have abounded. It would indeed be dishonourable to mankind, if the regions of the material globe, the Earth, the Sea, and Stars should be so prodigiously developed and illustrated in our age, and yet the boundaries of the Intellectual globe should be confined to the narrow discoveries of the ancients.[53]

Patiently, the Humanists constructed their learning in the territory once occupied by the myths of ancient history, where tales of demons and elves had held sway. That learning was not just an exploration (to use Bacon's term), but strove to become an explanation. The Scandinavian antiquaries, perhaps because they were in more of a hurry than the others to take advantage of new historical resources, were the first to attempt a synthesis in collecting and interpretation. These new resources, which they fell upon with a beginner's enthusiasm, enabled them to write a history quite different from that of the Greeks and Romans, one which had to be coaxed out of the earth and the landscape. During the second half of the seventeenth century a new generation would set to work. Worm's achievement was at once the last ripple of the Renaissance and the prelude to a new literary genre: the manual of antiquities.

1   Olender 1989.
2   Beaune 1985, p. 19.
3   Duchesne, 'Les Commentaires de César en français', BNFR, 38.
4   Momigliano 1983, p. 250.
5   Mandowsky 1963, p. 14.
6   Lanciani 1902, 1, p. 166.
7   Wataghin 1984, p. 197.
8   Manuscript of Naples XIII B 7, pl. cited in Mandowsdy 1963, pp. 49–50.
9   Golzio 1936, pp. 82–92.
10 Ibid., p. 8.
11 Ibid., p. 5.
12 Ibid., pp. 35–51.
13 Agostino 1587, p. 377.
14 Ibid., p. 117.
15 Beaune 1985, p. 33.
16 Dubois 1972, p. 92.
17 Ramus 1587; Hotman 1583.
18 Taillepied 1585.
19 Gassendi 1641.
20 Ibid.
21 Ibid., p. 235.
22 Levy 1964, p. 70.
23 New Year Gift to King Henry VIII, London, 1546.
24 Long 1888, pp. 198–9.
25 Ibid., pp. 117–18.
26 See chapter one.
27 Gummel 1938, pp. 10–11; Stemmermann 1934, pp. 18–22.
28 Gummel 1938, p. 11.
29 Ibid.
30 Ibid.
31 Ibid.
32 Ibid., p. 12.
33 Ibid., p. 16.
34 Sklenar 1983, p. 36.
35 Stemmermann 1934, p. 77; Gummel 1938, p. 21.
36 Piggott 1990, p. 75.
37 See chapter one, p. 68.
38 Metallotheca, XII, chapter 16.
39 Piggott 1976, p. 111.
40 Ibid.
41 Saxo Grammaticus 1911, p. 23.
42 Klindt-Jensen 1975, p. 11; Svennung 1967, p. 34.
43 Magnus 1567, p. 41.
44 Petri 1917.
45 Klindt-Jensen 1975, p. 15; Schück 1932, p. 68.
46 Worm 1643, introduction, p. 2.
47 See p. 63.
48 Worm 1643, p. 7.
49 Bacon, '[…] antiquities are history defaced, or some remnants of history which have casually escaped the shipwreck of time', Advancement of Learning, II, 2, section 1. Vossius, De philologia liber, 'Antiquities are the remains of ancient times, similar to the debris of a shipwreck' (cited in Momigliano 1983, p. 255).
50 Bacon 1840.
51 Pomian 1987, p. 48.
52 See Taylor 1948, p. 126 and Schlosser 1908, p. 79.
53 Bacon 1627.

THE HISTORY OF
THE TEMPLES
OF THE ANTIENT
CELTS.

O qui me gelidis in vallib Hæmi
Sistatq ingenti ramorum protegat umbra!
Fœlix qui potuit Rerum cognoscere causas!

Atq metus Omnes & inexorabile Fatum
Subjecit pedibus, strepitumq Acherontis
avari. Virg.

CHAPTER 3

FROM ANTIQUARY TO ARCHAEOLOGIST

Tu ris de leur rodomontade

Ce sont Habicot, leurs escrits,

Car tu leur rends telle dentade

Qu'ils s'en vont sans ris avec cris [...]

Or il faut que tu t'assures

Que ceux qui ont mords sont remords

D'une si profonde morsure

Que s'ils sont plus mords ils sont morts.

NICOLAS HABICOT, *ANTIGIGANTOLOGIE OU CONTREDISCOURS DE LA GRANDEUR DES GÉANTS,* PARIS, 1618.

(You laugh at their swaggering;

They are outlandish, their writings,

For you give them such a savaging

That they make off not laughing

but shrieking [...]

Now you must make sure

That the biters are bitten

With such deep remorse

That were they bitten deeper

they'd be dead.)

In the middle of the seventeenth century a new figure appeared in the world of European scholarship: the antiquary. Whilst the Renaissance – especially in Italy – had produced scholars such as Pirro Ligorio and Bartolomeo Marliano who had dedicated their lives to the study of antiquity, these did not represent a particular class of scholarship. The Renaissance savant had too many strings to his bow to allow himself to be restricted to one branch of knowledge – his thirst for learning was too great. In this sense Nicolas Fabri de Peiresc and Ole Worm were still Renaissance men. Even if antiquity was their preferred domain, they were motivated by an equal enthusiasm for medicine, astronomy and geography. By contrast, during the second half of the seventeenth century these were men who set out explicitly to construct a science of antiquities as a discipline in itself. After the age of the explorers came the age of the

The Druids as portrayed in a drawing by William Stukeley, 1723. Stukeley epitomised the ambivalence of the eighteenth-century antiquary: doctor, Anglican vicar, illustrator, fieldworker. His brilliant imagination revealed to him the magic world of the Druids, builders of megaliths. However, his passion for discovery also made him one of the best contemporary observers of landscape and the soil.

179

Frontispiece of Nicolas Bergier's *Histoire des grands chemins de l'Empire romain*, 1622.

builders: where the men of the sixteenth century had tried to construct a historical method,[1] scholars throughout Europe now set out to establish a theory governing antiquities. It was no longer a case of simply describing the monuments, but of explaining their use and function.

The pioneering Ole Worm had already written that one had only to examine the earth and to excavate in order to bring back to life those peoples who had no written history.[2] Reviving the past called for a willingness to learn which, for a northern European, meant liberating oneself from the bonds of classical history, and from the fascination for Graeco-Roman antiquity. To construct a history of the Danes, we have seen how Worm had to interpret the landscape and examine the earth in order to discover a past that had been lost to human memory. Beyond the cities of the ancient world, no historian had gathered together the annals of the past. Without writing there was no memory, other than that embodied in buried remains — the language of another kind of history, intelligible to those who were aware of this material evidence of the past. If everything contained within the soil formed part of human history, then it was the task of the antiquary to classify and interpret this vast body of potential evidence, *generis infinita*.[3] Nicolas Bergier, in his *Histoire des grands chemins de l'Empire romain,* which appeared in Paris in 1622, explained even better than Worm the need for a descriptive typology of roads:

> It is thus of material and formal matters that we must speak [...] and show that there were no works in the world in which so many materials were used, and so much patience, vigour and industry applied to their setting out. It is all the more difficult to deal with this subject because it is little clarified by history: there are few authors who have described precisely and clearly the diversity of the materials of which these roads were made.[4]

The history of roads was first of all a history of techniques, then a complementary social history of lines of communication. Bergier and Worm, working in very different ways, both attempted to explain, interpret and order their material. This raises a fundamental question: what was the nature of the learning of the antiquaries? And further, how much value can be ascribed to the documents they produced?

The progress made in historical research had led the Humanists to question the methods applied, and to reflect upon the notion of historical proof. Somewhat later the antiquaries asked themselves the same questions, but their response was different. The interpretation of a text does not obey the same rules as the evaluation of a monument. An archaeological 'autopsy' relies more upon the senses (sight, touch) than a philological analysis. The antiquaries themselves propounded to the Pyrrhonists[5] the integrity of object over text:

There is no greater security for us than that to be found in coins or ancient marbles. Certainly neither theory nor fact can contradict this. Whereas our remaining sources have the dubious reliability of texts which are continually retranscribed, only these [the coins and marbles] have the initial authority of the original versions.[6]

For Ezechiel Spanheim, a brilliant diplomat and excellent numismatist, objects prevailed over texts because their evidence was more reliable and better established (this did not apply to all objects, but to those whose authenticity was beyond question). What could be more trustworthy than an inscription, compared to tradition? Coins and inscriptions were to the classical world what runes were to the Scandinavian: a new source of historical knowledge, more immediate than tradition. Moreover, they revealed to the antiquaries landscapes hitherto concealed. Certainly, one could collect coins for one's cabinet by using a reliable network of informers and dealers, but inscriptions were more demanding. To find them it was necessary to travel, to search the soil and to examine the monuments. In this way archaeology won its independence – by delivering a text of another nature than that of the literary tradition. To summarise, the men of the seventeenth century (like some of our contemporaries) were able to reveal the historical meaning of objects only by treating them as texts, by deciphering them. Behind the meticulous work of the antiquaries one can clearly discern the philological metaphor which tends to frame material object systems as language systems.

THE EARTH IS A HISTORY BOOK

ARRANGING OBJECTS AS TEXT, MAKING HISTORY READABLE

Spon, Spanheim and the invention of numismatics
Bianchini and comparative iconography

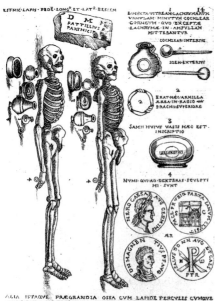

Plate from the catalogue of antiquities by Paul Petau, 1612. The objects shown here come from two Gallo-Roman tombs found during work on the old *Hôtel d'Anjou*. Clearly, all these remains are not contemporary, but they attest to the desire to present excavated finds *in situ*.

Frontispiece of *Antiquariae supellectilis portiuncula*, collection of Paul Petau, 1612. This album of plates was the first illustrated catalogue of antiquities to be published in France. Here, as the border of the frontispiece, Petau drew an Egyptian sarcophagus seen back and front. Below appears the foot of a bronze cist (wrongly identified as 'Isis aerea' or 'Bronze Isis'. Above, in a medallion between two Erotes, Petau inscribed the following Latin squib, playing on his own name: 'I want (*peto*) nothing which is not antique.'

Nobody has expressed better than Jacob Spon the idea that the study of antiquities is a textual matter:

> But without imitating the passion of those who mistrust any other science than that of their books, let us be content to have demonstrated our subject, and to show that there are wonderful things to learn from inscriptions as well as from books. Or if they must have books, let us say that our antiques are nothing if not books, whose pages of stone and marble were written with iron and chisel.[7]

Spon shares with Spanheim the same curiosity and interest in a living antiquity, complete in itself and unobscured by any intermediary, revealed through coinage and especially through inscriptions. But for Spanheim, coinage alone reaches us with an integrity which lifts its importance above any other material trace of the past:

> Other works, gloriously carved or constructed for their glory, even those which are famous, were completely obliterated in a short period, either for their materials or through the ravages of time. There are outstanding references in which Cicero states that monuments were erected to citizens who died for the good of the Republic: 'Therefore a great mausoleum will be laboriously and magnificently constructed, its inscribed letters a permanent testimony to your sacred virtue, that in exchange for your mortal state you attained immortality.' (Phil., I, XIV). Yet has not this too been demolished, consigned to oblivion, has not posterity slighted it or erased it? Temples, theatres, arches, trophies (I shall sum up this principle point in a few

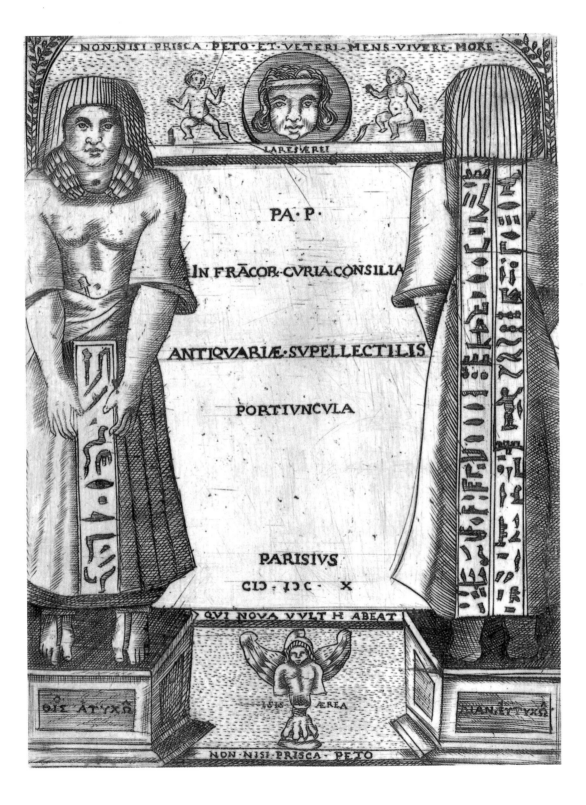

Representation of the remains of the amphitheatre at Lyons, from *Recherche des antiquités et curiosités de la ville de Lyon*, written by Jacques Spon in 1673. Jacques Spon captioned his drawing: '*A* is the circle of the theatre where people were accommodated. *B* Niches where one could stand or sit, or the ends of galleries or staircases. *C* One of the vaults [...] used as a cage for the beasts that were made to fight. *D* The orchestra, where the next in line waited. *E* The arena [...], once a flat area but now only a hillside vineyard.'

survive today? Those monuments which were built not for the current time, but, like the theatre of Scaurus, which Pliny describes, were built for posterity, have fared as badly; they have achieved their hope of eternity, these whose ruins or remains have remained just visible for many centuries. The terrible fate of ancient texts subject to so much damage, and their destruction, so often bewailed and yet which cannot be mourned enough, which man, even though illiterate, does not know of this and groan?[8]

All human works are doomed to disappear in one way or another, and every object carries within itself the seeds of its own destruction, but coins *are in fact more solid, indestructible, thanks to the nature of their substance and the immediacy of their art; and they prevail through the multitude of places in which they are found, and moreover, in their number and variety.*[9]

The quality of coins as evidence does not depend entirely upon their physical and artistic properties, but is also linked to the conditions of preservation and discovery. A serious archaeological analysis enables them to be identified and dated. This kind of observation indicates exactly how far the antiquaries had progressed. The philological model led the new antiquaries to construct a critical method just as precise and meticulous as that employed by the Humanists in their work on manuscripts. The authenticity of a document depends on evidence, and that evidence, according to Spon, is easier to establish for inscriptions than for manuscripts and books. The latter may always be falsified:

Moreover it is less easy to counterfeit an antique inscription than to falsify a book or to attribute it to an author other than the true one: one needs a greatly refined wit to recognise that a piece is not by a certain author. But to pronounce an inscription to be not ancient I think is not so difficult, provided that one has studied the subject a little. The stone chosen by the Ancients, its given shape, and the exact form of the letters, together with their depth, are not things easily imitated by ignorant workmen. Finally, the style, the orthography, and even the full stops if you will, which are usually triangular rather than round, can uncover the deceits possible in this medium, more easily than in an ancient book.[10]

Spanheim and Spon were the inventors of numismatics and epigraphy as positive sciences, because they were not content just to collect their source materials and present them to enthusiasts, but thought of a way of turning them into the instruments of analysis.

A generation later Francesco Bianchini was to attempt the same thing with images. Let us admit, he says, that profane history (being a good Vatican official he was careful with regard to divine history) is knowledge − it depends upon sources accessible to human reason, and which proceed from purely natural causes. In this way the historian turns to tradition, to written sources. But these are not enough, because alongside oral and literary tradition, antiquity has given us images, and the analysis of images does not depend on the same methods as the analysis of discourse:

The addition of the figures and symbols pertaining to each part is not a frivolous ornament to my work; rather, it was my resolve and intention by means of these to make the collection of histories presented here more immediate for the mind and more easy for the memory. The force of an idea comes from the robust image with which in its conception it was, so to speak, stamped on the mind. And the impression is usually strengthened by that robustness as the body is by the imagination, and intellect is by evidence. But the figures, which aid the senses, do not always add strongly

Portrait of Charles Patin engraved for the frontispiece of his *Thesaurus Numismatum*, 1672. Charles Patin, a Parisian jurist and doctor, epitomised the seventeenth-century antiquary. Seated before his medal cabinet, he holds a coin. On the medal cabinet are placed shells and a Roman bust. Two engravings of Louis XIV and the emperor Leopold I are hung on the wall.

to intelligence. They must bring some evidence of truth with them, if they are to press home their meaning [...]. I can avail myself of a painting by Raphael or Titian as an aid to the imagination in representing the triumph of Titus. But when I see the relief on the Arch of that same Titus, which shows him in his chariot, if I read the inscription added by the Senate, if I gaze at ancient coins where he is shown in a victor's robes, these images make a much more profound impression on the mind; they do not serve simply to attract the eyes with well-executed yet vague designs, but they are able to touch our minds with those ancient symbols, which serve as true witnesses to that which is represented.[11]

Frontispiece of Bianchini's book, showing different periods in the history of religions, 1697. See caption opposite for a full description.

With this project Bianchini opened up a new and original route into the past – that of comparative iconography. Archaeology during the Renaissance, and sometimes afterwards, paid scant attention to the status of the images used to give substance to history. In the manuals of antiquities equal place was given to illustrations of ancient works and to purely imaginary creations. Bianchini, who was not only president of the Vatican's antiquities commission but also the Pope's astronomer, tried to put order into the complex world of images, and pleaded for the use of original works which should be treated with the same care as other types of documents, coins, inscriptions and monuments:

So I, keeping careful sight of these principles, whilst trying to make the idea of history vibrant and strong, have elected to express that idea with figures; but figures which support the point being made, rather than being vague in that which they represent. This can be achieved by recovering images of the works of the ancient Romans [...]. This we hope to have achieved by limiting the images to certain classes, and by assigning one of them, according to its own character, to each part.[12]

Bianchini's method was emblematic as well as iconographic. Every historical period since the Flood could be illustrated by a monument or combination of monuments to signify the 'age of silver' or the 'age of copper', to use certain of his traditional divisions. Bianchini was the first to anticipate the important role played by the illustration of the monuments in the knowledge of antiquity, but his conclusions and his rigid way of looking at the problems of historical

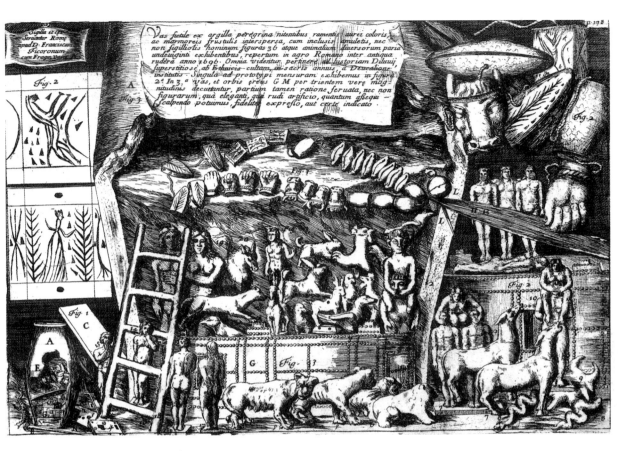

Above: the Flood. Plate taken from *La istoria universale provota con monumenti, e figurata con simboli*, by Francesco Bianchini, 1697.

Francesco Bianchini here shows us the contents of a vase which had been discovered in the Roman countryside. This archaeological discovery apparently attested to the ancient cult of Deucalion, worshipped after the Flood: 'If we consider the complex in its general meaning, it seems that it could not concern anything other than a superstitious representation of the Flood, as celebrated in Greek tradition, with the famous sacrifice intended both for the dead who were lost in this extermination of mankind and to safeguard those who were destined to repopulate the earth.' (Bianchini, 1697, p. 181.)

Description of frontispiece opposite: at the foot of an Egyptian obelisk St John holds a pen and a parchment on which are seen an alpha and an omega. At his feet an eagle, from whose beak flows the fountain of life. The synagogue (symbolised by the veiled woman), crowned with the chi-rho symbol by Rome, baptises four continents: the Indian, identifiable by his feathers: the Black; the Asian; and the European, who offers the Pantheon under which is seen the terrestrial globe, a Christian crown and a rayed crown. Rome wears the armour of an ancient soldier. Leaning on a shield with the initials SPQR (the senate and the people of Rome) she holds in her left hand an upturned torch. Her left foot rests on a hieroglyphic codex, her right foot against a wicker basket representing paganism, from which spill Artemis of Ephesus, the snake of Aesculapius, the wheatsheaf of Demeter and various ancient coins. In the left background appears Roman landscape, to the right the basilica of S. Giovanni in Laterano.

Vignette from a chapter of *La istoria universale provota con monumenti, e figurata con simboli,* by Francesco Bianchini, 1697. Bianchini captioned his drawing: '1 & 2 bas-relief taken from Pietro Santi Bartoli; 3 medal of Philip; 4 medal of Lucilla; 5 Jupiter as god of rain, as on the Antonine column; 6 a Japanese idol.'

knowledge led him to confuse image with symbol and symbol with cause. In spite of this his work remains seminal, demonstrating that along with numismatics and epigraphy, iconography was a necessary branch of archaeological knowledge.

THE SURVEYORS OF THE PAST
John Aubrey and comparative archaeology
Thomas Browne and the resurrection of history

The concerns of the epigraphers, numismatists and iconographers were very different from those of scholar-travellers such as Camden and Worm. Their business, unlike that of the latter, was not the revelation of a world previously untrodden – they had to justify themselves in the face of the scepticism of the philologists and historians who obliged them to accept literary rules: presentation of the sources, internal criticism of the documents, delivery of proof. For the study of antiquities to progress, it would be necessary to marry strict philological method to analysis of landscape, travel to the knowledge of literary sources but also of local traditions, toponymy and regional linguistics to a mastery of tradition. This synthesis was

Numismatists at work, plate from *La Science des médailles*, by Jobert, 1739. The spaciousness and luxury of this cabinet attests to the craze for medal collecting.

to be achieved by an Englishman, who ushered the antiquaries into a new world. John Aubrey was born in Wiltshire in 1626 and died towards the end of the century, in 1697. He lived the life of an impoverished gentleman, a wanderer in search of a haven, but this admirer of Francis Bacon and Descartes was an active member of the Royal Society of London, a friend of Thomas Hobbes and William Harvey (who discovered the circulation of blood), the colleague of Newton and Locke – in short, a man at the centre of British intellectual life. His interests were those of a man of the Renaissance; he was a scholar-traveller, folklorist and antiquary, but also a physician and naturalist, a man of letters and an excellent draughtsman. A man of influence with an enquiring mind, his major antiquarian work, *Monumenta Britannica,* met a similar fate to Peiresc's, not because it never proceeded beyond rough draft, but because he never found a publisher. However, the manuscript was circulated, read and admired as one of the most important archaeological works of the seventeenth century. In its most complete version, which dates to the last years of Aubrey's life, the book falls into three parts. The first is devoted to 'the religion and customs of the Druids', the second to architecture, and the third to what we would today call archaeological structures: barrows, urn burials, tombs, earthworks, and so on. The whole is completed by the *Miscellanea,* a kind of appendix necessary to the understanding of the book, which is divided into four chronological typologies:
- *chronologia architectonica* (classification of the orders of architecture);
- *chronologia graphica* (classification of writing systems);
- *chronologia aspidoligica* (classification of shields depicted on tombstones);
- *chronologia vestiara* (classification of clothing).

More than any of his predecessors, including Worm, Aubrey sought to construct a system of antiquities which relied as much on descriptions as on a series of clearly stated rules. His goal was manifestly theoretical; this is attested by a quotation from Guez de Balzac's *Conversation with the Marquise de Rambouillet:*

Even all that is written down is not certain to survive, and books perish, just as tradition is forgotten. Time, which can conquer iron and marble, does not lack strength against more fragile things. The northern peoples, who seem to have arrived to make time pass faster and to hasten the end of the world, declared war in particular on written matters. It is no thanks to them that even the alphabet itself was not abolished.[13]

The antiquary's craft as perceived by Aubrey could answer just that sort of question. The imperfect chronicles had to be replaced by careful observation of the landscape, the earth and objects. As Michael Hunter emphasised, Aubrey's originality stems from his sensitivity to the past. A man who had lived through the Civil War and its trail of devastation could hardly be less aware than William Camden had been of the destruction of all kinds which was affecting the countryside: *'Mors etiam saxis, nominibusque venit,* death comes even to stones and names'.[14] What attracts the antiquary is not only the individual character of an object, but the qualities in a monument which bring the past into the present, as Aubrey quotes from Meric Casaubon:

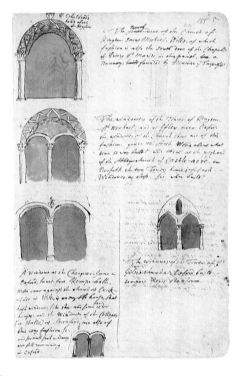

The typology of medieval windows, drawing from *Monumenta Britannica* by John Aubrey, written in 1670. The classification of the orders of architecture, developed by Aubrey in his work, is one of the finest examples of medieval archaeological typology.

That Antiquaries are so taken with the sight of old things, not as doting upon the bare forme or matter (though both oftentimes be very notable in old things) but because these visible superviving evidences of Antiquity represent unto their minds former times, with as strong an impression, as if they were actually present, and in sight, as it were.[15]

Never had an antiquary written so emphatically that knowledge of the past demanded that application of observation and imagination which alone led to archaeological reconstruction. Aubrey did not neglect the power of emotion, but pressed it into service as a means of analysis, an instrument of knowledge. Aubrey's method consisted of combining the observation of past and present, ethnology with written tradition, analysis of the landscape and the anatomy of monuments. He differs from Worm in the wider range of his interests and methods, but also in his disregard of description for its own sake, and his wish to establish rules of interpretation to govern observation:

These Antiquities are so exceeding old, that no Bookes doe reach them: so that there is no way to retrive them but by comparative antiquitie, which I have writt upon the spott from the Monuments themselves.[16]

Comparative antiquity: this singular expression is flown like a banner – Aubrey was acutely conscious of his originality. He was certainly not the first to consider the comparison of monuments with each other as a means of identifying them, but he did invent the typological-chronological method which consisted of systematically classifying the archaeological categories, as witnessed by his *Miscellanea*. Palaeographers had for a long time been working on the chronological classification of scripts, and Jean Mabillon was at that time working on the creation of a theoretical and practical framework for the study of official documents. Aubrey's crucial contribution was to suggest that architectural features, blazons and clothing could be subjected to the same kind of classification. Aubrey's proposed method was to order objects and monuments chronologically, to identify the variables which permitted that ordering, and to compare the types thus identified with each other – a method which had all the appearance of a new science. His ambition was not to enrich an enthusiast's collection, or to construct a microcosm of the universe after the fashion of the *Museum Wormianum*, but to restore

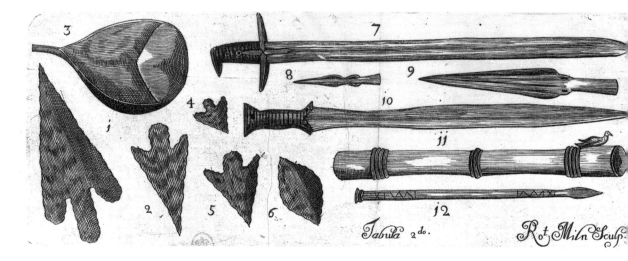

Classification of weapons, drawing from *Miscellanea quaedam eruditae antiquitatis* by Robert Sibald, 1707. The flints, long considered as 'thunderbolts' are correctly interpreted here. Worked as arrowheads, they take their place alongside other weapons.

antiquity in a palpable form by marrying the rigour of the naturalist with the passion of the historian. Aubrey was certainly aware of the 'paradigme de l'indice', which allowed the antiquary to restore the whole from the part:

As Pythagoras did guesse at the vastnesse of Hercules stature by the length of his foote [...], so among these ruines, are Remaynes enough left for a man to give a guesse what noble Buildings &c: were made by the piety, charity, & magnanimity of our forefathers [...].[17]

His ambitions were not limited to a palaeontological restoration of the past. He suggested to the antiquary that his ultimate goal was to discover the way of life, behaviour and even the psychology of vanished populations. This he did with the humour of a man who had travelled the English countryside, who had noted his fellow countrymen's estrangement from the past, and in some cases, their deleterious enthusiasm, as Michael Hunter describes:

He then compared the ruins with fragments of a shipwreck [an image very close to Francis Bacon] *'that after the revolution of so many yeares and goverments, have escaped the teeth of time, and (which is more dangerous) the hands of mistaken Zeale. So, that the retriving of these forgotten things from Oblivion in some sort resembles the Art of a Conjurer, who makes those walke & appeare that have layen in their graves many hundreds of yeares: and to represent as it were to the eie the places, Customes and Fashions, that were of old Time.'[18]*

Archaeological map of Wessex, drawing from *Monumenta Britannica* by John Aubrey, written in 1670. This map is a fine example of Aubrey's archaeological method.

The antiquary was no sorcerer guided only by the force of his imagination; his task was to bring to light objects and monuments, but also rules for their interpretation. 'Comparative antiquity' was a speculative method which attempted to decipher the language of monuments. For someone with Aubrey's mathematical skills, it was tempting to draw an analogy from algebra:

In that deluge of history, the account of these British monuments utterly perished: the discovery whereof I do here endeavour (for want of a written record) to work-out and restore after a kind of algebraical method, by comparing them ... to make the stones give evidence for themselves.[19]

Chambered tomb
known as Waylands
Smithy on the
Berkshire Downs,
drawing from
Monumenta Britannica
by John Aubrey,
written in 1670.

Frontispiece from the
work by Joachim
Oudaans, published in
Amsterdam in 1644.
In this image the taste
for medals is
associated with the
interest in excavation.
To the left, in a palace,
collectors examine the
survey or restoration
of a monument; to the
right, beyond the
terrace, men dig up
the earth.

Not content with establishing an exact typology of monuments, Aubrey set out to support his reasoning by reference to a range of facts expressed algebraically. In other words, he invented what we would today call 'theoretical archaeology'. In view of these brilliant insights, it hardly matters that Aubrey, in his work, did not really follow his own rigorous model. One could hardly expect him to date megalithic structures correctly (even though his refutation of the theory of Inigo Jones, the famous architect who regarded Stonehenge as a Roman temple, is not without interest). He suggested a typology of fortifications, contrasting the square Roman camps with circular ones, demonstrating once again his talent for observation. Even though he hesitated to attribute the latter to the ancient Britons or the Danes, he had laid the foundations of a new way of thinking. The pioneers of aerial photography were to follow the same process. The misfortunes of his private life, like the setbacks he suffered in his attempts at publication, resulted in Aubrey's being deprived of the place he deserved in the history of archaeology; recent work by British archaeologists, however, has allowed us to rediscover a personality just as important and original as Peiresc. Aubrey was certainly archaeology's first true formalist. Even if his message was scarcely heard, he helped to give archaeology in Britain, in other respects so pragmatic, a theoretical dimension. Aubrey shared with Spanheim and Spon a faith in the antiquarian method, in the

need to reach the most ancient history through original documents which were very different from the manuscripts of the Humanist tradition. The difference lies in his realisation that he must take into account humbler objects than coins, and that for the most ancient history of England, inscriptions would be of no help to him. Unlike Bure and Worm, he was not driven by the attraction of deciphering an unknown script, but rather by an enormous appetite for landscapes and their monuments, as well as by his sense of the fragility of the testimony of the earth. The science of his day was a more experimental matter than in the time of his learned Scandinavian predecessors, and so he was less passionate than they about descriptions, and more eager for explanations. We should not be surprised.

In Britain during the second half of the seventeenth century the discourse on antiquities formed a literary genre of which the masterpiece was penned by one of the best prose writers of the time, Thomas Browne. A physician, he was born in London in 1605 and died in 1682. Like Worm, he learned his medicine in Padua and Montpellier; he settled in Norwich in 1637. The discovery of funerary urns in a field near Norfolk led him to publish, in 1658, a pamphlet entitled *Hydriotaphia, Urn Buriall, or, A Discourse of the Sepulchrall Urnes lately found in Norfolk*. It was not his purpose to produce an excavation report in the modern sense. It was more a philosophical meditation upon the fragility of human life, a widely discursive essay on death. The past which made such such a vivid impression on the author's imagination appeared to resemble no well-defined period, even though he attributed burials to the Roman period which we now know to be Saxon. With its varied and sometimes extravagant style, and the subtle interplay between scholarship and emotion, Browne's book demonstrates the archaeological sensitivity of the contemporaries of Locke and Hobbes:

In a field of old Walsingham not many months past were digged up between forty and fifty urns, deposited in a dry and sandy soil, not a yard deep, nor far from one another. Not all strictly of one figure, but most answering these described: some containing two pounds of bone, distinguishable in skulls, ribs, jaws, thigh-bones, and teeth, with fresh impressions of their combustion. Besides the extraneous substances like pieces of small boxes or combs handsomely wrought, handles of small brass instruments, brazen nippers, and in one some kind of opal.

Near the same plot of ground for about six yards' compass were digged up coals and incinerated substances, which begat conjecture that this was the

ustrina *or place of burning their bodies, or some sac-*
rificing places unto the manes, *which was properly*
below the surface of the ground as the arae *and*
altars unto the gods and heroes above it.

That these were the urns of Romans from the
common custom and place where they were found is
no obscure conjecture [...].[20]

Browne's attitude to the discovery was that of
the conscientious doctor, more interested in the
site and the nature of funerary deposits than in
possible finds. His analytical method was, however, that of the antiquary. He went beyond
comparison of the remains with others found in
the region, and fitted his description into a
topographical and chronological study of finds
in that part of England. Having defined the history of the place and its various phases of occupation, he went on to deal with the funerary
customs, having evidently read Italian anti-

Funerary urns,
drawing by Thomas
Browne from his
Hydriotaphia,
published in 1658.
These funerary urns,
now regarded as
Saxon, had been
attributed by Thomas
Browne to the
Roman period.

quaries like Bosio as well as the Scandinavians (Worm). In fact his
commentary is a general discourse on the techniques of cremation,
in which he invokes both classical tradition and the works of past and
contemporary antiquaries. It is first and foremost a meditation upon
funerary customs:

He that lay in a golden urn eminently above the earth was not like to
find the quiet of these bones. Many of these [royal] urns were broke by a
vulgar discoverer in hope of enclosed treasure; the ashes of Marcellus were
lost above ground upon the like account. Where profit hath prompted, no
age hath wanted such miners, for which the most barbarous expilators found
the most civil rhetoric: 'Gold once out of the earth is no more due unto it,'
'What was unreasonably committed to the ground is reasonably resumed
from it,' 'Let monuments and rich fabrics, not riches, adorn men's ashes,'
'The commerce of the living is not to be transferred unto the dead,' 'It is no
injustice to take that which none complains to lose,' and, 'No man is
wronged where no man is possessor.'[21]

This extraordinary refutation of Roman funerary laws, this apolo-
gia for Theodoric's edicts on the disinterment of treasures,[22] is also a
formidable defence of the antiquaries' right to dig up whatever they
pleased. Browne the stoic made common cause with the antiquary to
ridicule human vanities and to deride the sumptuousness of tombs.

The text is remarkable for its dual nature. On the one hand, the archaeological discovery is an occasion to reflect upon death and the ephemeral nature of the body; on the other, the act of reflection is based upon a minute description of the urns and their position in the soil, and on the survey of the zones of deposition. Protohistoric, Roman and medieval cemeteries were a never-ending source of fascination to the men of the Renaissance; Thomas Browne's work transformed that curiosity into knowledge because it sought more to explain than to describe.

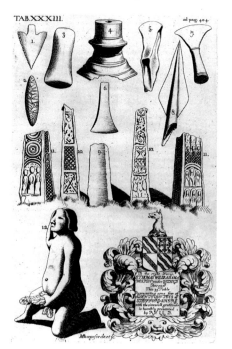

Plate from the *Natural History of Stafford-shire* by Robert Plot, representing a variety of objects including a flint, bronze axes, a statuette, an early Christian cross and ancient stone monuments.

The innovative work of men such as Aubrey and Browne illustrates the changes which characterise the second half of the seventeenth century. Strong in the knowledge gathered by their predecessors, the new antiquaries were encouraged to excavate, to construct chronologies, and to attempt reconstructions based on the detailed observation of the earth and its monuments. Men such as Robert Plot and Edward Lhuyd are typical of the new generation, who regarded the study of antiquities as part of natural history.

Plot was the first keeper of Oxford University's Ashmolean Museum, and Lhuyd was his immediate successor. Antiquities were included in his books the *Natural History of Oxford-shire* (1677) and the *Natural History of Stafford-shire* (1686), but as he explained himself, these were not to be confused with 'the pedigrees or descents either of families or lands [...] nor of the antiquities or foundations of Religious houses [...]'.[23] Plot's aim was to study not traditions but material remains: 'ancient Mony, Ways, Barrows, Pavements, Urns, ancient Monument of stone, Fortifications, &c.'.[24]

THE ANATOMISTS OF THE LANDSCAPE
'Anatomical dissection' and the discovery of Childeric's treasure

---

Since the discoveries made by Camden and the first Scandinavian antiquaries, archaeology had progressed as much in the methods of field survey as in the appraisal of sources and the application of botanical and geological knowledge. But the principal progress came from excavations, and in this area the Scandinavians were at the fore. The most advanced were the Swedes, who were the first to establish a national antiquities service. In 1662 the chancellor of Sweden, Magnus Gabriel de La Gardie, founded a Chair of Archaeology in Uppsala for the antiquary Olof Verelius. In 1666, again in connection with the University of Uppsala, he established a College of Antiquities. This organisation, under the guidance of the secretary of the University of Uppsala, Joseph Hadorph, had by 1675 an impressive list of associates: a specialist in Icelandic sagas, two assistants, two illustrators, an administrator, a secretary, a printer, two engravers, a proof-reader, a messenger and a factotum — everything necessary to collect, identify, write up and publish the results of investigations directly financed by the royal treasury. Not content with being an unrivalled organiser and scholar-traveller, Hadorph was quick to undertake excavations and publish the results of his findings at the site of Birka. At just about the same time Verelius presented the description of the excavations of a tumulus near Broby:

That is why I am not really convinced that in Brunaold's time all men were cremated as St Olaf's saga and Snorri have indicated. On the contrary, the kings and heroes made use of slaves whom they intended to bury as part of a funerary ritual. And I cannot refrain from adding to that the funerary mounds raised after the primary cremation. It seems likely that they were built in Brunaold's time, when all the bones and ashes gathered together were covered with earth and stones so that they should not be scattered, or suffer other harm. In order to test this hypothesis, I set out last summer to open, by means of the appropriate works, an enormous tumulus near the Broby lands in the Ullerakers territory. As it would have taken a very long time to demolish the whole mound, and furthermore having no wish to disturb the shades of the departed, I opened a way into the middle of the tumulus, extending it forward from the base of one of the earthen sides. In the process I very soon found stone structures; they stretched from north to south, and it seems that oaken timbers had been placed above them, the cinders of which had not all been consumed. And there, amongst the cinders, was the burnt body of the deceased, turned I believe towards the south. Once the pyre and the body had been cremated a tomb was built, protected by more stone placements and by soil, such that none might harm them. To the north, I think at the head of the deceased, were placed some very eroded urns of which only fragments could be recovered. Inside I found nothing but earth. There were no more bones or ashes, just the remains of funeral meals and sacrifices to the gods and to the dead, destined for the shades. In this tumulus I found five structures on top of each other, and what I most wondered at was that at the base, top and middle, among the ashes and the bones burned together, I found other bones and skulls in the same place which had been untouched by any fire but which were, however, friable: certain proof that in the same one family some individuals were cremated and others buried. [25]

This progress did not rely solely on recourse to excavation to support reasoning, but was linked to the attention given to detail, to the composition of layers, the analysis of the context of traces in the soil – in short the underlying idea that the earth was composed of remains of different kinds which allowed the reconstitution of its history. Without realising it Verelius employed, if one may say so, the idea of stratigraphy.

This was an idea embraced by the most renowned and brilliant of his Scandinavian contempories, Olof Rudbeck. Much has been written about Rudbeck's work as historian, comparativist and anthropologist, but his work as an antiquary has been relatively neglected.

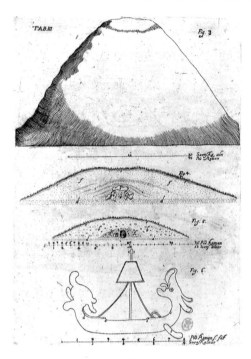

Stratigraphical section of a tumulus, from Olof Rudbeck's *Atlantica*, 1697. This view of the tumulus is probably one of the first published stratigraphical sections.

Born in 1630 at Vasteras in Sweden, Rudbeck was elected Professor at the University of Uppsala in 1653. He soon left off his botanical and medical studies to launch into a visionary prehistory which sought to establish the superiority of Nordic man, embodied by an original land of Atlantis which coincided with Scandinavia. In his conception of archaeological methods, Rudbeck was not different from his predecessors Worm or Hadorph. Like them, he considered travel to be the prime discipline, that which unlocked an understanding of the landscape, and like them he associated toponymy with the study of sagas, medieval sources and the survey of runic inscriptions. But he was without doubt one of the first to regard excavation as an act of anatomical dissection, an operation which consisted not just of removing objects from the soil, but of understanding the relationships of the remains to the layers which preserved them. This conception of fieldwork led him to make cuttings into the Uppsala tumuli which he had undertaken to excavate.[26] The funerary chamber was carefully drawn and the layers clearly distinguished one from another. Rudbeck regarded the landscape with an anatomist's passion and combined bird's-eye views, classic since Worm, with the production of contoured plans which gave the relief great precision of detail, such as in the plan of the old town of Uppsala.[27] Observation of the soil even led him to propose the establishment of an absolute stratigraphy calculated by the thickness of the layers.[28] Being a good Lutheran he began his chronology with the Flood; however, it cannot be denied that within the limited means at his disposal, Rudbeck laid the foundations of stratigraphic method. He demonstrated an innovative intuition in resorting to observations of the successions of strata to establish an absolute chronology.

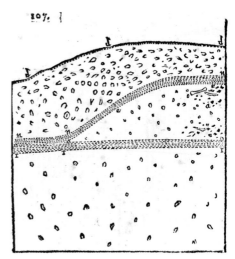

Stratigraphical analysis, from Olof Rudbeck's *Atlantica*, 1697.

However, the idea of looking at the soil first as the container of objects from the past, but also and above all as a succession of fossilised deposits, was not entirely invented by the Scandinavian antiquaries. Men as different as the Roman antiquary Flaminio Vacca at the end of the sixteenth century, or Nicolas Bergier at the start of the seventeenth, had already expressed almost comparable views. Flaminio Vacca confidently ascribed the Tiber deposits to the Flood:

I recall that in the foundations of St Peter's in the Vatican, towards St Mary's church, in the chalk layer were found some pieces of wood four hands long and one wide, which had been humanly worked using an axe or another iron tool. And that must have been before the great ark, since the layer of chalk is the work of the great Flood, and the wood was covered by the latter without any trace of digging; these pieces of wood were like stone: heavy, black and hard, and I have heard that they were placed in the Pope's wardrobe.[29]

Vacca's outlook, however, was that of an interested onlooker observing an uncommon natural phenomenon. He was a long way from the vision of a man such as Rudbeck; it is perhaps possible to detect the germ of his theory in a man like the astute Bergier, who brought an engineer's precision to the study of the remains of the past:

Yet again I reach for Pliny and Vitruvius and again refresh my memory of the different materials used by the architects, paying attention to the ordering of their layers, each named by historical sequence [...]. That done,

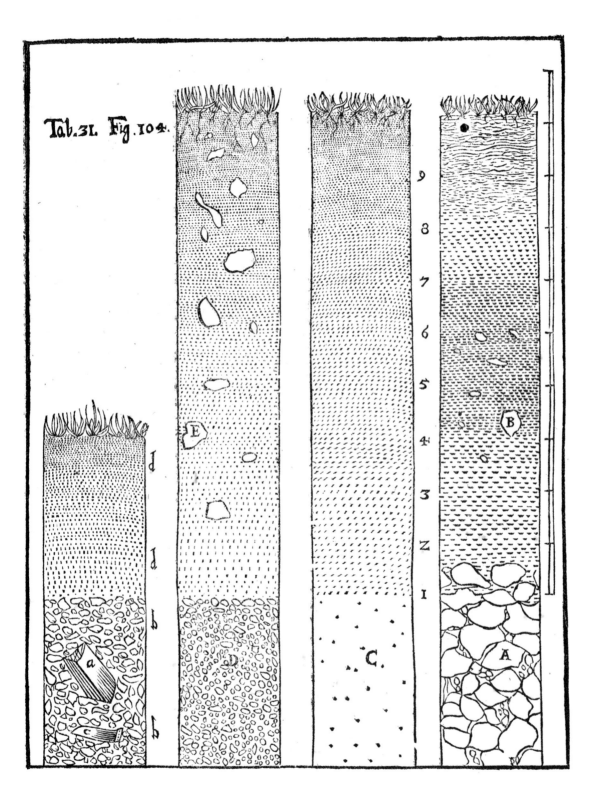

Tab. 31. Fig. 104.

I was resolved to have the great routes dug in my presence [...] to see how far they resembled domestic paving, in the diversity of materials and the way in which they were laid. In this my time was not wasted, because having had the ground dug to bedrock and turned over from top to bottom, I found distinct materials clearly separated and layered. The first of these three routes had the same number of layers, organised in sequence just as that familiar to us. In the second I found a slight change in ordering, and in the third, the number of layers was multiplied. But really there are so many similarities between the paving of the old houses and the materials used in our great routes, that the order of those of the houses can fill the gaps in our knowledge and can re-establish the proper names for each of the layers of which I was previously ignorant. I wait for the happy chance that I might find books to give me a more exact and specific direction.[30]

Nicolas Bergier brought to the soil the same careful attention as Rudbeck, but from a different perspective. For him exploration of the landscape was just a means of filling out the written sources, and his trial diggings allowed him to establish parallels with the vocabulary of house and road-building. Excavation helped to complete and sometimes to verify information derived from written sources; its principal mission was not to discover objects or monuments. It consisted of considering the different layers which make up the earth as an ensemble, the components of which merited analysis and comparison without ever constituting a whole. To work in this direction the antiquaries had to employ the tradition and methods of Scandinavian archaeology, or to set about the study of remains with the practical curiosity of a man such as Bergier. At the time this was not, of course, the prevailing model. To see this clearly one has only to refer to the most famous archaeological discovery of the time, the treasure of Childeric.

On 27 May 1653 a tomb was discovered at Tournai full of magnificent objects: gold coins, golden bees, a sword with enamelled goldwork, a ring with an inscription which revealed its owner's name, *Childirici Regis*. This discovery aroused enormous interest in Europe because this Childeric was none other than the son of Meroveus, the father of Clovis who died at Tournai in 481. Jean-

Study of the principle of sedimentation, from Olof Rudbeck's *Atlantica*, 1697. Rudbeck here attempts a chronological measurement of the sedimentary deposits.

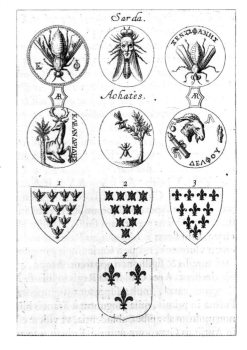

The metamorphosis of the bee into the fleur-de-lis, drawing from *Anastasis Childerici* by Jean-Jacob Chifflet, 1655. The golden bees discovered in Childeric's tomb are represented here as the originals of the fleur-de-lis motif. Chifflet was happy to retain an artistic approach to archaeological finds.

Jacob Chifflet, son of the personal physician of Archduke Leopold, Governor of Belgium, hastened to publish a study of the finds in 1655 with the famous publishing house Plantin. It was a fine work of rhetoric devoted to the discovery of treasures from the Bible up to Childeric's tomb, but the description of the tomb was poor. Among the very fine plates illustrating the major pieces there was no plan, no view specifying the archaeological context of the discovery. Without unduly castigating the learned Dr Chifflet, one sees clearly that he lacked his Scandinavian contemporaries' taste for and curiosity about landscape. In France and Italy (despite the pioneering work of Antonio Bosio on the subterranean remains of Rome), archaeology was still primarily a hunt for objects or monuments rather than an attempt to uncover the history of the earth.

THE ERA OF SYSTEMATIC DESCRIPTION

BRINGING HISTORY TO LIFE
Germany in search of its origins

Once again the northern antiquaries gave proof of a greater attention to antiquities than their French and Italian contemporaries. This was, in the first place, for archaeological reasons. The lively interest in protohistoric tombs shown by the antiquaries of the Renaissance continued through the seventeenth century and the beginning of the eighteenth. The cabinets of antiquities of princes and bourgeois alike

Frontispiece of *Sepulchretum gentile* by J.H. Nünningh, published in 1714. It depicts the meeting of classical and local history.

continued to be filled with protohistoric vessels – often the excuse for extraordinary museological set-pieces, such as the illustrations of the cabinet of Johann Christoph Olearius, or the 'pyramid-museums' of Leonhard David Hermann. Alongside these spectacular displays mounted by collectors of curiosities, the fantastic illustrations of such men as Picardt, with their Brummagem giants and Germani, seem to belong to another epoch entirely.

The time of systematic description had arrived, and a great cohort of German scholars took the initiative. The works of Johan Daniel

Major (*Bevölkertes Cimbrien,*1692), and J.H. Nünningh *(Sepulchretum gentile,*1714) are sufficient to show that times had changed. On the flyleaf of Nünningh's book, the opulent figure of History holds her pen high, whilst Hermes turns the pages of the book she is preparing to fill under the scrutiny of Time, portrayed as an aged man with wings, scythe in hand and hourglass at his feet. Next to History a Cupid perches on an open cabinet of medals. This imagery in the classical tradition contrasts with the figure of another Cupid in the foreground, under History's throne: in his hands he holds an urn, and on the ground are the instruments of the new history: bronze and stone axes, lamps, arrowheads, pots, coins. The image explicitly suggests that a new range of antiquities will contribute to the writing of a history that owes nothing to classical history. To emphasise the difference the author includes engravings of a series of objects presented in typological order: vessels, axes, coins, spearheads. What is more, one of the plates is devoted to excavation: in the foreground two men are extracting a vessel from a tumulus; behind them is a cluster of burial mounds, and in the background, megalithic structures.

Archaeologists at work, engraving from *Sepulchretum gentile* by J.H. Nünningh. The archaeologists appear rather as treasure-seekers than as excavators, but the graves and megalithic alignments are very carefully represented.

It is not surprising that these profound changes in the nature of archaeology took place in Germany, and especially in northern Germany. From the Renaissance onwards every scholar was aware that local history depended upon antiquities to fill the gaps in the classical texts. Thus the transition from the Renaissance to the Age of Enlightenment in Germany (and in the rest of central and northern Europe) corresponds with a displacement of historical interest from the universal to the local. Leibniz himself had called upon his compatriots to use their observations of the earth in order to reconstruct the ancient history of Germania.[31] That prescription was followed to the letter by his friend and disciple J.G. Eccard, who wrote an essay entitled *De origine Germanorum,* published in Göttingen in 1750 by L.W. Scheidius.

In a Germany in quest of its origins, it was the clergy who took the leading role in writing a new history which paid equal attention to both text and landscape. They took over from the Humanists, but

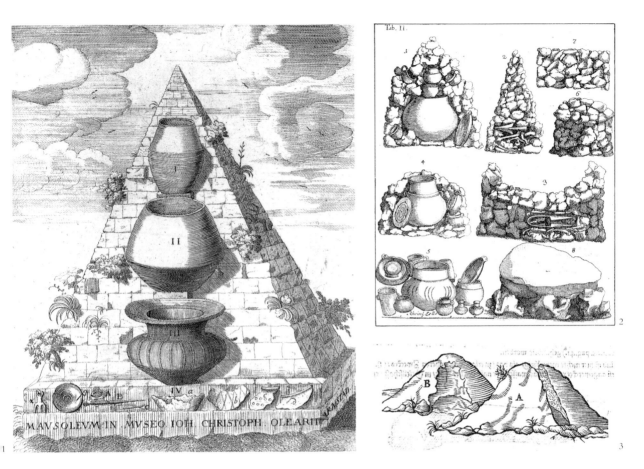

1. Frontispiece of *Mausoleum in Museo* by Johann Christoph Olearius, 1701.
Here the classic image of the pyramid is linked to a new class of antiquities, symbolised
by the three piled urns and the sherds placed at the base of the pyramid.

2. Leonhard David Hermann, in his *Maslographia* (Brieg, 1711), was one of the first to show
connected finds: each object was associated to its context, depending on its state of preservation
in the soil. This form of illustration revealed an anatomical interest in deposits.

3. Exploration of tumuli, drawing from *Bevölkertes Cimbrien* by Johan Daniel Major, 1692.
Major wondered about the best way to explore a tumulus: (A) shows a transverse
section, and (B) a segmentary cut.

Frontispiece of the *Gottorfische Kunstkammer*, 1666. The eagle reveals a bucolic landscape inhabited by figures in typical costume, a kind of ethnographic introduction to the collection.

Megalith, drawing by Andreas Albert Rhode, from his *Cimbrisch-Holsteinische Antiquitäten Remarques*, 1720.

Plate from the *Gottorfische Kunstkammer*. In the choice and presentation of objects, the influence of archaeological discoveries in Germany is as notable as the influence of ethnography: (1) Roman lachrymatory vase; (2) Roman lamp; (3) Lusatian urn; (4) Indian mummy; (5) Egyptian mummy.

with the avowed intention of verifying the cogency of their theories through personal observation and experiment. Christian Detlev Rhode and Andreas Albert Rhode exemplified this new generation of antiquaries who were not afraid to dismount from their horses and excavate with their own hands. They were both Protestant ministers from the region of Hamburg, father and son (C.D. Rhode, 1653–1717; A.A. Rhode 1682–1724). They combined a sound classical education with a feeling for landscape which recalls the antiquaries of the British tradition. But they owed to German scholarship a familiarity with excavation hardly known elsewhere in Europe. In 1699 and 1700, Christian Rhode had already published a report on his explorations in *Nouvelles littéraires de la mer Baltique,* where he speculated on the function of weapons placed in tombs. Andreas Rhode, who from 1717 continued his father's collecting and excavation activities, had a more ambitious aim. He wished to bring about a sharing of direct experience of the past, and to use the results of excavation as a means of learning about local history. To this end he edited a weekly magazine, *Cimbrisch-Holsteinische Antiquitäten Remarques,* one of the most engaging publications in the history of archaeology. These were modest eight-page leaflets, each one carrying on the flyleaf an illustration preceded by Latin verses and a free translation in German. Each of the engravings represented a monument or an object found during excavation. The style is individualistic, mixing humour with concise description and notes on methodology in a popular German, but also full of French and Latin words. This was scientific journalism of an informed kind, which allowed the reader to keep up with the discoveries of an eighteenth-century archaeologist on a weekly basis. The subject matter, as announced in the first week's title, was funerary archaeology: 'It is the law of nature that all the dead must be buried.' Rhode's view of his discoveries contains all the freshness of first wonder, plus the combined naivety and acuity of a true fieldworker. Excavation was no inferior manual task, but a technique of exploration which was subject to rules. Johan Daniel Major had already suggested various techniques for the exploration of tumuli: excavation by trench or by segment, designed

Tab. XXXVI

Frontispiece of the *Historia de Arianismo olim Smiglan infestante* by M. Adelta, published in 1741. The vases and weapons in the foreground symbolise the marking of the past on the earth.

to avoid the blind destruction of funerary structures. Rhode was equally assiduous in his reading of the earth:

Finally, when we had dug down to a depth of eight/nine feet, there appeared a green earth which seemed to suggest that something would quickly be found; I therefore stopped the labourers and undertook the rest of the work myself with the aid of a knife and a little trowel brought for that purpose.[32]

Like Rudbeck and Major, Rhode was an observer used to spending long hours in the field, a man with an eye for detail, and his meticulous style renders him one of the pioneers of excavation technique. His curiosity was not limited to observation, but extended to interpretation, to the extent where his interest in the uses of flint in the daily lives of the ancient Germans led him to knap his own artefacts in an effort to reconstruct ancient techniques.[33] The apparently chaotic products of the minister's pen progressively resolved themselves into a treatise on the protohistoric burials of Holstein. All the important questions of prehistoric archaeology were deliberated intelligently, and often humorously – cremation and inhumation rituals, the interpretation of grave goods, the relationship of these finds to their ancient makers. Admittedly his remarks are somewhat vague from a chronological point of view, and though he allowed that the bronze objects were older than those of iron, the decisive stone–bronze–iron paradigm was not familiar to him. Rhode did not possess Aubrey's brilliant insights into typology, and unlike Rudbeck he paid no heed to the topographical recording of his excavations, but with his multiple interests he was more typical of the field archaeologist in the Age of Enlightenment than either of these two. He had thus fulfilled

Frontispiece of an issue of *Cimbrisch-Holsteinische Antiquitäten Remarques*, by Andreas Albert Rhode, 1720. On his drawing of the tumulus, Rhode inscribes a verse from Ovid, 'It is an old wood, not frequented for many years; this is the sacred place of a cult.

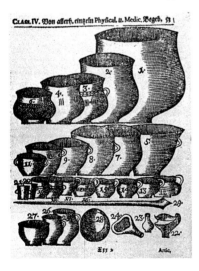

Typology of funerary urns, drawing from the book by Engelhard Guhr, published in 1722. The typological approach is obvious in the ordering of the vases.

the programme set out for him by J.A. Fabricius, who wrote of the preface to his book:

For some time all kinds of good patriots have had it in mind that the deeds, tales, behaviour and customs of our ancestors, the ancient Germans, should not be suppressed or abandoned to negligence. One has only to think of all the trappings and customs which the Ancients of Germany devoted to their dead and to their burials, and one is astounded by the pains taken by those interested in observing them in as much detail as possible. How many have taken it upon themselves to supplement the testimony of the authors of the past, by their own labour and at their own expense to research the tombs and to present the evidence down to the minutest detail.[34]

Both patriotism and Pietism are present in this work – in the taste for detail, the enthusiasm for reconstruction, and the will to present facts which were as irrefutable as the accepted texts; for the men of the Enlightenment knowledge of the past was indissociable from their religious convictions. The pastors of northern Germany had a thirst for knowledge which was inseparable from their application of reason to religion – in this they resembled their British counterparts, who went in search of the Druids in order to establish a new kind of Anglicanism.

THE DRUIDS: AT THE WELLSPRING OF HISTORY
Stukeley and the role of the Celts in the origins of Europe

It all began in an atmosphere of serene positivism. William Stukeley was born in 1687 to a middle-class family in Lincolnshire, at the time one of the most isolated parts of England (according to his biographer, Stuart Piggott), and at a very young age began his medical studies in Cambridge. There, and later at St Thomas's Hospital in London, he mixed with the foremost English scholars of his day: Isaac Newton, the astronomer Edmund Halley, and Richard Mead, director of the hospital and one of the most brilliant physicians of his time. In this scientific milieu the taste for antiquities was allied with enthusiasm for botany, astronomy and mathematics, and Stukeley, a gifted draughtsman, showed himself to be a peerless observer. In 1717 he set up as a doctor in Lincolnshire and undertook a series of archaeological expeditions which were to determine his scientific career. In a series of archaeological guides to Britain, Stukeley seized

Record of a megalith, drawing from an unpublished manuscript by George Owen, *History of Pembrokeshire*, 1603. Contemporary with the first records of megaliths, this drawing attests to an anatomical interest in the study of megalithic architecture. Owen was not just a scholar-traveller but also anticipated geological stratigraphy.

Camden's torch, *iter domesticum, iter curiosum, iter cimbricum*. Compared with the German excavators, British tradition was more than ever a peripatetic one. Even though Stukeley was not the first to discover Stonehenge, his description and survey drawings were seminal, and his account of the nearby prehistoric site of Avebury was to enter the annals of British archaeology. Stukeley combined a knowledge of the landscape with acute observation: at Stonehenge he was the first to discover 'the Avenue', which led to the River Avon; at Avebury he produced the first complete plan and accurate topographical interpretation of the site. To the description of landscape he added excavation skills, and his approach was that of a modern archaeologist who observes the stratigraphy in the soil. Here is what he wrote about the excavation of a Bronze Age tumulus near Stonehenge:

> *The manner of composition of the barrow was good earth, quite thro',
> except a coat of chalk of about two foot thickness, covering it quite over, under
> the turf. Hence it appears, that the method of making these barrows was to
> dig up the turf for a great space round, till the barrow was brought to its
> intended bulk. Then with the chalk, dug out of the environing ditch, they
> powder'd it all over.*[35]

What characterised the new antiquarian spirit of the late seventeenth and early eighteenth centuries was an interest in the landscape, and a vision of the earth not just as a potential treasure-chest but as a repository of interpretable traces. Stukeley's habit of recording his

Landscape notes at Stonehenge, drawn by Stukeley on 7 August 1723. Stukeley was above all a landscape archaeologist. Through his drawings he emphasised that survey was an indispensible means of understanding the past.

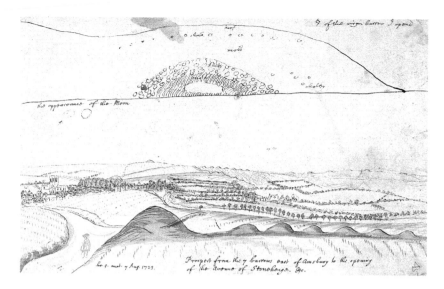

Notes on the lie of the land at Avebury, drawn by Stukeley in May 1724.

discoveries in detailed drawings set him well to the fore along the path that led to the foundation of landscape archaeology. His contribution extended beyond the development of topographical analysis, or the addition of excavation to the antiquary's scientific resources: it led to a chronological analysis of the past which put paid to theories that megalithic structures were Roman or Saxon, declaring them to be Celtic monuments. In the absence of a long chronology that could accommodate the existence of a 'history before history', all British monuments before the Roman period were deemed to be Celtic. The consequences for science would not have been so dramatic had Stukeley not regarded the Druids (who were thought to be Phoenician colonists) as the civilisers of Britain – preliterate Christians of a sort who, well before the advent of Christianity, had tried to introduce the seeds of civilisation to Europe. This was the heart of the matter. If the Renaissance scholars had succeeded in expunging the myth of Trojan origins from the history of Europe, the theologians of the seventeenth century had not freed themselves from biblical chronology. As a result they were obliged to combine the beginning of history in Europe with sacred history. Many scholars and theologians attempted this, for example Simon Bochart in his *Geographia Sacra* (1646). In such a context one should not be surprised at Stukeley's vision of the Druids. When in 1728 he took the cloth as vicar of All Saints, Stamford, he was not only solving a problem of domestic finance; he brought to the Church of England a gift which the Archbishop of Canterbury, William Wake, held to be of the

the ground in Abury declines very much o. ew. moderately N. & S.
13. May 1724. this day I saw several of the few stones left on overton
hill carryed downwards towards W. Kennet & two thirds of the temple
plowd up this winter & the sods thrown into the cavitys so that next year it
will be impossible ever more to take any measure of it.

this afternoon I pacd over Kennet avenue, the intermediate distance
betw. overton hill & Silbury thence to the termination Bekampto
avenue thence along bekampton avenue to Abury again
I find each avenue is 8000 f. long, from Silbury to either
of the extremitys 6000. the whole making 30000 foot or
6 miles. I drank at Swallow head to the pious memory
of king cunoda it runs pretty strong now out of the solid chalk
& the water is altogether as clear as Horace's fons blandusia
& admirably soft. I found some paeony clia hereabouts upon
the north sides of banks a palm long & flowers extravagantly
large the folio rutaceo I mean about this bulk
much brook lime watercresses at Swallowhead
thalictrum call the meadow plants thereabouts
the temple at the end of Bekampton avenue was
at the extremest corn field just under a square
enclosure at the S. side of bristol road betw.
it & Batteroad in a straight line with Silbury &
overton hill. the ditch round Abury is not so broad as the
vallum by a great deal but very deep & steep cut out of
the solid chalk very curiously tho' they have not been so
carefull in heaping up the vallum but left it irregular
this is the pfile of it.

tho' the stones of the avenue are but 100 on a side & generally
70 f. interval yet 1000 f. is gaind by the curvity of the
avenues for sometime the two stones are near 100 f. asunder
& haps they regarded the harmonic Number of 8 or the proportion
of Silbury. the entrances to both druids house that under overton
way hill & that S. of Stonehenge is outer with a sort of causway

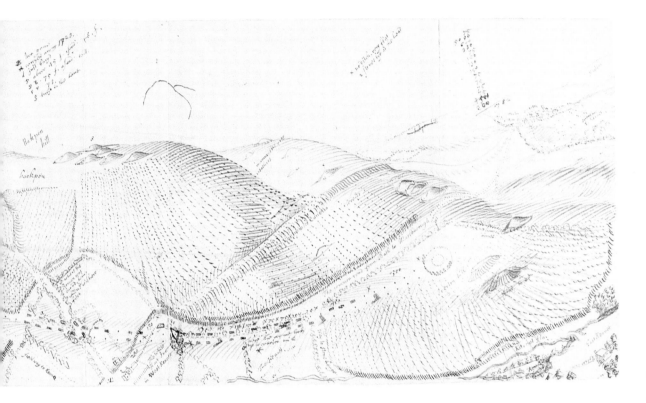

Overhead view of Avebury, drawn by Stukeley in 1723. Stukeley was to produce an overall plan of Avebury, complete with detailed topographic survey. Stukeley's drawings compel as much by their precision as by their quality.

2

Ars longa. Vita brevis. Judicium fallax. Memoria labilis.

30 Junij 1720. Isaac Newton.

Dona praesentis cape laetus horae

Jan. 10 1720/1 Edm: Halley

Pondere Numero et Mensura.

Chr: Wren. Mar: 10: 1721.

— Sequiturq Patrem non Passibus Aequis

Chr: Wren. C Fil.

Ὁ Θεὸς ἀεὶ γεωμετρεῖ.

Sept. 20 1731. Gul: Whiston Matheseos Exprofessor Lucasianus apud Cantabrigiensis

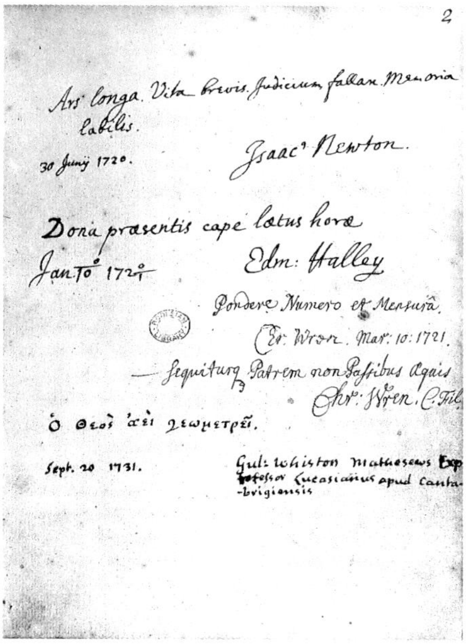

Stukeley's *Liber amicorum*. Stukeley belonged to a circle which included the leading spirits of the age. Among the signatures and dedications of his friends shown here are those of Newton and Halley.

first importance – the re-establishment of the ancient history of the nation as part of sacred history. Roger Gale, Stukeley's friend and companion on his excursions, wrote to him:

Your reconciling Plato and Moses and the Druid and Christian religion may gain you applause, and perhaps a Patron, but it is good to be sure of the latter upon firmer motives than that scheme may inspire people with at present.[36]

His old friend's scepticism concerning his chosen path is equalled only by the criticisms voiced by others close to him of the new and startling enterprise undertaken by the self-styled arch-Druid. From then on Stukeley's imagination, interest, knowledge and gift for draughtsmanship were bent on reconstructing the imaginary world of the Druids which he had created. The works of Rudbeck and Stukeley are in fact extraordinarily similar in some ways. Two doctors, two critical minds, both fieldworkers used to practical outdoor observation – and both their approaches undermined by a highly poetical, fantastical vision of the past. In both cases (differences of time and nationality apart) the reason is the same: in their exploration of the origins of man, the scholars of the Enlightenment were obliged to take account of sacred history. This was their downfall, for they were forced to weave into the complex fabric of their observations and theories a thread which had no other justification than scripture. A strange destiny indeed for these robust men, who began their quest by digging the earth and ended by indulging in the crazy dreams of the kind gently satirised by William Cowper:

Nor those of learn'd philologists, who chase
A panting syllable through time and space,
Start it at home, and hunt it in the dark,
To Gaul, to Greece, and into Noah's Ark.[37]

1   See Huppert 1973, pp. 93–109.
2   Worm 1643, Introduction.
3   Ibid., p. 2.
4   Bergier 1622.
5   The Pyrrhonists – from the name of the Greek philosopher Pyrrho – objected to any historical discourse, saying that history was unknowable because it depended upon a series of falsehoods and errors of interpretation.
6   Spanheim 1664, p. 44.
7   Spon 1673, Introduction.
8   Spanheim 1664, p. 11.
9   Ibid., p. 14.
10 Spon 1673, p. 7.
11 Bianchini 1697; the quotation is taken from the 1747 edition, pp. 20–21.
12 Ibid., p. 21.
13 *Monumenta Britannica*, MS Oxford, Bodleian Library, MS. Top. Gen. c24, p. 43.
14 Hunter 1975, p. 166.
15 Ibid., p. 171.
16 Ibid., p. 181.
17 Ibid., p. 178.
18 Ibid., p. 179.

19 Aubrey 1980–82, p. 32.
20 Browne 1658, 1966 edn, p. 10.
21 Ibid., p. 24.
22 Browne refers explicitly to Cassiodorus, *Variae* I, 4; see p. 84.
23 Plot 1686, p. 392.
24 Plot 1677, p. 315; see Piggott 1990, pp. 90–93.
25 Verelius 1664, pp. 81–2.
26 Rudbeck 1937, volume III, fig. 3.
27 Ibid., volume III, fig. 27.
28 Ibid., volume I, pp. 85–91.
29 Vacca 1704.
30 Bergier 1622, pp. 141–2.
31 Letter from Leibniz to Georg Friedrich Mithof, 17 May 1691, cited in Gummel 1938, p. 101; Leibniz 1717, p. 335.
32 Rhode 1719, p. 40.
33 Ibid., p. 320.
34 Ibid., preface, p. 2.
35 Piggott 1985, p. 93; Stukeley 1740, p. 44.
36 Piggot 1985, p. 98, letter from Gale to Stukeley, 14 June 1729.
37 Cowper, *'Retirement'* 691–4, from *The Complete Poetical Works of William Cowper*, ed. Robert Southey, London, 1849.

THE ANTIQUITY OF MAN AND
THE ANTIQUITY OF THE EARTH

THE BIBLE QUESTIONED
Isaac Lapeyrère and Judah Halevi

Part of the answer to the above questions is exemplified in the life and work of a scholar who, if not the most learned of his generation, was certainly the most obstinate of the defenders of the long chronology, the 'black abyss of time' to recall Buffon's poetic definition. In February 1656 a wanted man went into hiding in the noble city of Brussels, but he was quickly taken by a company of thirty men who shut him in the tower of Treuremberg at the request of the ecclesiastical authorities. The arrested man, Isaac Lapeyrère, was no highwayman but the Prince of Condé's doctor, a former French ambassadorial attaché at the Danish court, the confidant of Queen Christina of Sweden and author of a book which was decried by the Protestant and Catholic world alike, *Preadamitae, sive exercitatio super versibus duodecimo, decimotertio et decimoquarto, capitiis quinti epistolae D. Pauli ad Romanos* (*The Pre-Adamites, or an Essay on Verses Twelve, Thirteen and Fourteen … of the Letters of Paul to the Romans*). To the scholarly world this book was no surprise. Its author's notoriety and the inflammatory nature of the subject had made it a much sought-after and anticipated work, which was published in five simultaneous editions, three of them by Elzevier in Amsterdam. Lapeyrère was born in Bordeaux in 1597:

> *The son of a King's councillor, triennial and provincial controller with special authority for the wars in Aquitaine, a Protestant from a respected family; such are the main features of Isaac Lapeyrère … a great reader and enthusiast for the unusual, inventor of a phonetic system of orthography, historian, engineer, perceptive ethnographer, he brings to his research a zeal so ardent and original that he seems only to be satisfied by paradox or heresy.* [1]

This man, so vividly brought to life by the discerning pen of René Pintard, was no beginner in the field of scholarship and criticism. In 1643 he had published a pamphlet, *Du rappel des juifs*, which called for a convergence of Judaism, Protestantism and Catholicism, and in 1647 he published in Paris a minor masterpiece of geographical and ethnographical information on Greenland, *Relation du Groenland* (*An Account of Greenland*). From his position on the fringes of

Protestantism and Catholicism (and even of Judaism, since some authors would like to see him as a kind of Marrano [Spanish or Portuguese Jew]), Lapeyrère appeared to be literally obsessed with the narrowness of the historical and geographical frontiers imposed by the Jewish Scriptures. He aimed to put into practice the programme prescribed by Bacon – to approach matters of intellectual and spiritual achievement with the same drive as that which carried the explorers and scientists to great discoveries. In all his works, from *Du rappel des juifs* to *Les Préadamites* (translated into English as *Men before Adam*) and including his *Relation de l'Islande* (another ethnographical and geographical essay published in 1663), a single thread links theological discourse, geographical exploration and critique of sources. However, his critical efforts collided with a text which no one in the seventeenth century could investigate with impunity: the Bible. Contrary to the accusations of his

RELATION
DV
GROENLAND.
Par le sieur de la Pereyre.

CVRVATA RESVRGO.

A PARIS,
Chez AVGVSTIN COVRBE', dans la
petite Salle du Palais, à la Palme.

M. DC. XLVII.
Avec Privilege du Roy.

Title page of Isaac Lapeyrère's work, *Relation du Groenland*, 1647. This was a considerable scholarly achievement in the fields of geography and ethnography, and a milestone in Lapeyrère's career.

numerous – and fascinated – critics, Lapeyrère was not out to undermine the foundations of Holy Scripture. His more modest – but equally dangerous – aim was to distinguish in the biblical text between what was owed to things human, and what to things divine. His reference to St Paul functioned as a kind of guarantee of the Christian orthodoxy of the project. In this he was continuing a much earlier tradition, which allowed humanity a far longer history than that authorised by the Bible:

> It is a natural suspicion that the beginning of the world is not to be received according to that common beginning which is pitched in Adam, inherent in all men, who have but an ordinary knowledge in things: for that beginning seems enquirable, at a far greater distance, and from ages past very long before; both by the most ancient accounts of the Chaldeans, as also by the most ancient records of the Egyptians, Ethiopians and Scythians, and by parts of the frame of the world newly discovered, as also from those unknown countries, to which the Hollanders have sailed of late, the men of which, as is probable, did not descend from Adam.[2]

Nothing too extraordinary in this, but the form is probably more important than the content. While considerable intellects had for a very long time been doubting the age of the world allowed by Scripture, none before Lapeyrère had devoted a systematic treatise to this delicate subject.

The idea that the history of mankind went back perhaps dozens of millennia was common to the Greeks, and before them to the Egyptians and to the Assyrians and Babylonians. But the Bible, from the moment it became accessible to the Greeks and Romans through its early translation known as the Septuagint, offered a much shorter chronology and an account of the creation of the world which was to become a central tenet of Christian orthodoxy. In the fifth century AD, St Augustine had definitively expelled from the Christian West 'the abominable lyings of the Egyptians', who claim for their wisdom an age of 100,000 years',[3] and dedicated another chapter of *The City of God* to the demonstration 'of the falseness of that history that says the world has continued many thousand years'.[4] Notwithstanding the good faith and the science of pagan authors, if they contradicted Scripture then they could not be telling the truth. The West was to live for thirteen centuries beneath the magisterial interdict of the Bishop of Hippo.

However, this historiographic dogma was subjected to criticism wherever ecclesiastical or rabbinical backs were turned. Judah Halevi's extraordinary book, the *Kazari*, was written in Spain at the beginning of the twelfth century (the Kazars were rulers of lands bordering the Black Sea, who hesitated for a long time before deciding to which branch of monotheism they would convert – Jewish, Christian or Islamic). In it the king asks the rabbi, 'Does it not weaken thy belief if thou are told that the Indians have antiquities and buildings which they consider to be millions of years old?' The rabbi replies proudly:

It would, indeed, weaken my belief had they a fixed form of religion, or a book concerning which a multitude of people held the same opinion, and in which no historical discrepancy could be found. Such a book, however, does not exist. Apart from this, they are a dissolute, unreliable people, and arouse the indignation of the followers of religions through their talk, whilst they anger them with their idols, talismans, and witchcraft.[5]

The rabbi's reply is couched in exactly the same terms as the Judaeo-Christian polemic of the Later Empire against pagans, but it is careful to avoid the fundamental debate. The Indians are dismissed by the same method as that used by St Augustine: because they do not accept the message of the Bible, their history has no reliable basis. The denial of the long history of man was thus at the heart of of monotheistic doctrine; it was typical of the sort of question which defined the classic debate between heathens and monotheists. And despite the denials of orthodox believers, of whatever persuasion, the question cropped up every time a small mixed group discussed the comparative history of the origins of man. Halevi himself was more prudent than the unknown rabbi; he suggested that his readers, if they were not completely convinced by the orthodox argument, should allow that at least one world – ours, that of Scripture – owes its existence to a progenitor called Adam.[6] In the Judaeo-Arab world, which in the Middle Ages was much more open to Assyro-Babylonian, Egyptian and Indian influence, the apparent simplicity of the biblical chronology was less easy to defend than within Christian culture. *Nabatean Agriculture,* a curious document written in Arabic at the beginning of the tenth century, already attributed to the Sabaeans (the inhabitants of ancient Arabia) the belief that the history of man went back several hundred thousand years, and some cabbalists were quick to postulate the existence of other worlds, much more ancient than ours. In the twelfth century Maimonides echoed these traditions:

The Sabaeans allowed the eternal nature of the world, because according to them the sky was God. They held that Adam was a person born of a man and a woman, like other human beings, but they glorified him saying that he was a prophet and apostle of the moon, that he encouraged the cult of the moon, and that he wrote books on agriculture.[7]

Down the centuries, despite the denials of the rabbis and the Church, the obscure tradition of a much longer history than Genesis permits was preserved, even though it may only be glimpsed through the refutations of the adherents of orthodoxy. It seems to run parallel to the theme of the 'three impostors' (Moses, Jesus and Mahomet), which feeds an entire body of clandestine literature and ideas denounced by the Church and the ruling authorities – a kind of permanent conspiracy against the religions based on holy writ. Right through the fourteenth and fifteenth centuries heresy trials bear witness to the existence of a critique of Scripture, one of the pivotal themes of which was the denial of the Adamite origins of humanity.

The discovery of America put this kind of critique back on the agenda in two ways. First because it posed questions about the origin of the American peoples, and second because there were many witnesses to the fact that these people used a much longer chronology than the biblical one. Even if Christopher Columbus had never considered that the Native Americans might be different from the Indians normally encountered on the Asian route, his immediate successors soon had to address the problem of the ethnic and racial character of the indigenous peoples. It had probably already cost the missionaries and *conquistadores* some effort to admit that these people were indeed human, and therefore souls which must be conquered. However, once the humanity of the native peoples had been accepted, there was immense speculation as to their origin: migrations of the lost tribes of Israel, Phoenicians, Arabs and even Norwegians were invoked in order to explain the first colonisation of the Americas. One notable voice, however, was raised in defence of the indigenous nature of these peoples, that of Theophrastus Bombastus von Hohenheim, otherwise known as Paracelsus, founder of chemical medicine, and Ole Worm's spiritual father:

Portrait of Paracelsus, by Quentin Metsys. Theophrastus Bombastus von Hohenheim, otherwise known as Paracelsus (1494–1541), was one of the first to propose the polygenesis of the human race, thus calling Holy Scripture into question.

Thus we are all descendants of Adam. And I can scarcely hold back from brief mention of the men who have been discovered in hidden islands and who are still unknown. It is not likely that we must consider them as descendants of Adam; what would any such be doing in the hidden islands? It seems to me wiser to think of these men as descended from another Adam, because it will be difficult to postulate that they are near to us in flesh and blood.[8]

This sort of theory is not, as Popkin points out, pure and simple confirmation of the polygenesis of the human species, but it does open the way – a way embraced by Giordano Bruno, and one which led him to the stake. In his *Spaccio della bestia trionfante* (1584), he treated the question of chronology as an element of biblical criticism. If the Americans were accepted as men, then one must also accept their chronology, in particular their suggestion that the world was more than 20,000 years old. It is quite likely that this allusion of Bruno's refers to the discovery in 1551 of the Aztec stone calendar which was buried seven years later by the Spanish ecclesiastical authorities in case of scandal.[9] Bruno's critique came very close to meeting the views of Paracelsus:

Because men are of many colours – the black people of Ethiopia, the red tribe that is native to America, the water-based people of Neptune who live hidden in caverns, the pygmies who have spent centuries bent under their yoke, inhabitants of the veins of the earth, the keepers of the mines, and the monstrous giants of the South – these are not similar as progeny and are not the descendants of one original parent.[10]

FAMOSO·DOCTOR   PARESELSVS.

SECRETS OF THE FREE-THINKING SALONS
The contemplation of man's place in history

The curiosity of the Renaissance and the more fanciful traditions of the medieval naturalists were united in the person of Giordano Bruno, whose views reflected the intense spirit of enquiry which moved his contemporaries. The progress of neither geography nor chronology allowed for a blind and literal reading of the Bible. To study mankind one must have the courage to place mankind within its historical context; such was the legacy of the Renaissance to the free-thinkers. It was the message bequeathed by Bruno and his English friends, the renowned explorer Sir Walter Raleigh, Thomas Harriot and the poet Christopher Marlowe (the irreligious of the court of Elizabeth). Bruno was burnt at the stake for his avowed heresy, but through such critical intellects as the renegade Giulio Cesare Vanini and the famous philosopher Tommaso Campanella, he was to influence Lapeyrère. Pintard has described beautifully this free-thinking milieu of the seventeenth century, which gave Lapeyrère the references, support and stimulation necessary for the publication of his work. Here is his portrait of Vanini, who disturbed the whole of Europe with his curiosity and his temerity:

For that godless man, whose blasphemies shrieked down the years and seem to have shaken the hearts of the faithful and filled the defenders of the faith with terror right up until the devout apogee of the reign of Louis XIV, attacking the faint-hearted as they prudently retreated – that impious man had travelled widely, studied in Naples and Padua, visited Germany and the Low Countries, shone at the French court and at the palace of the Archbishop of Canterbury, sailed on the Atlantic and the Mediterranean; he had been a priest, a Carmelite monk and probably chaplain to the Swiss Guard, and he had preached in the Parisian parishes after a conversion to Anglicanism and a recantation; he also appeared as a philosopher – bizarrely, one approved by the doctors of the Sorbonne, even while his body, still twitching from the gallows and stained with blood where his tongue had been torn out, was awaiting the flames by order of the Parliament of Toulouse.[11]

Evidently the threat hanging over the heads of the free-thinkers was not just formal, and in light of this it is perhaps easier to understand Lapeyrère's behaviour after his arrest. On 11 March 1657, in the presence of cardinals Barberini and Albizzi, Lapeyrère solemnly abjured his theories. It is not without interest for the history of archaeology that the abjuration took place in front of the cardinal with the strongest of antiquarian credentials, Francesco Barberini, whose secretary was none other than the famous Cassiano Del Pozzo, a friend of Galileo – the man with the 'paper museum', a correspondent of Peiresc, and the most learned and systematic archaeologist in Italy at that time, who, according to a letter to Bourdelot, was in 1640 already contemplating the conversion of Lapeyrère.[12]

Unlike Galileo, Lapeyrère had to wait a long time before the scholarly world accepted the evidence for men before Adam. The reason perhaps stems from the fact that the antiquaries of the day, in so far as they had read his work (and such men as Aubrey, Stukeley and Rhode might quite possibly have been interested in a work related to their field of enquiry), saw in the pre-Adamite idea only a philosophical suggestion. However, in *An Account of Greenland*, Lapeyrère showed that while he was not a professional antiquary, he was perfectly capable of putting forward a geographical and historical case. While he was in Copenhagen he had, after all, debated with the master of Scandinavian antiquities, Ole Worm, and visited his museum. It was Worm himself who had given him information on the first inhabitants of Greenland and Iceland, and it was thanks to him that Lapeyrère was able to contest the theory of Grotius, who saw the Americans as the descendants of the Vikings, who had come from Greenland to the coast of America, where they settled. The first inhabitants of these regions were not of Scandinavian origin:

I will therefore tell you what Mr Wormius, the most curious person that ever I met with in the affairs of the north, has communicated to me by word of mouth, and in writing. They were savages, the original natives of Greenland [...]. Mr Wormius is of opinion, that those Skreglingres were not far distant from the gulf of Davis, and perhaps were Americans [...].[13]

From his conversations with the learned Dane Lapeyrère gleaned not only facts but a comparative method which enabled him definitively to refute Grotius' theories and to prepare the way for a polygenetic interpretation of the peopling of the Americas:

This leads me to a discovery of the mistake of the author, who has published his dissertations concerning the origin of the Americans, which he deduces from the Greenlanders; the first inhabitants of which he would make us believe were Norwegians, and consequently that the first inhabitants of America, were originally of Norway. He pretends to justify his opinion by a certain imaginary affinity betwixt some American words that terminate in Lan and the termination of Land, so frequent in the German, Lombard and

Norwegian languages, and the resemblance of the manner of living; that is, as he tells you, betwixt the Americans and Norwegians, who are, if you will believe him, the Allemanni of Tacitus.[14]

Lapeyrère took ironic vengeance upon the haughty remarks made about him by Grotius, and in so doing conducted a methodical lesson in ethnography. Worm at least had taken the pre-Adamites seriously, and he wrote to Lapeyrère:

I was already suspecting that on your return from Spain, and for love of those peoples, you had taken yourself off to the Icelanders, Greenlanders, or even straight to the Americans. [...] While I was with our Prince we talked a great deal about your Pre-Adamites, and I had to explain your reasoning: he was charmed by the novelty of this discourse, and as I recounted various things about you and our talks together, he very much regretted that he had not enjoyed your company while you were with us.[15]

Lapeyrère's theories, which in France, Italy and Britain were only discussed in the secrecy of the liberal salons, were not held to be scandalous in Copenhagen, and were the object of deep discussion between the old antiquary and his disciple Crown Prince Frederick, who became King of Denmark in 1648. Unfortunately, Worm's archaeological work was then almost finished; he was working tenaciously towards the development and publication of his collection of curiosities which was to become the *Museum Wormianum*. Lapeyrère offered his theories on the great antiquity of man to the Scandinavian and British scholar-travellers, to the excavators of Germany and to the collectors of Italy and France, but they were hardly inclined to welcome them; in displacing the question of the origins of man from the field of description to that of interpretation, Lapeyrère had transformed a question of chronology into a philosophical problem. It is true that Girolamo Fracastori, Leonardo da Vinci and Bernard Palissy before him had suggested that the earth was much older than it seemed, and that fossils were not created by some spontaneous phenomenon by which mineral took on the shape of animal, but were living bodies, petrified and buried in the depths of the earth. Again, George Owen and afterwards Nicolas Steno suggested a stratigraphical theory of the formation of the earth which necessitated a long time-scale, but none of them took on the cardinal dogma of Adamism. Even if some, like Robert Hooke in his *Micrographia* (1665) and his *Lectures and Discourses on Earthquakes* (1668), had discreet doubts about the necessity of a universal Flood,[16] it was only to separate more effectively the history of mankind from the history of the earth. For the naturalists, the history of the earth ran parallel to the history of mankind, but the different lines of evolution never crossed. Natural history would have everything to gain from borrowing its methods from the human history of the antiquaries. Shells and fossils were 'the Medals, Urnes, or Monuments of Nature', they were:

The greatest and most lasting Monuments of Antiquity, which, in all probability, will far antidate all the most ancient Monuments of the World, even the very Pyramids, Obelisks, Mummys, Hieroglyphicks, and Coins, and will afford more information in Natural History, than those other put altogether will in Civil.[17]

These lively words of Robert Hooke are a good illustration of the paradox of the time: the naturalists enjoined their colleagues to construct a natural history upon the model of antiquarian history. It never occurred to them to ask whether antiquarian history might benefit from natural history. Shrewd intellects such as Steno or the Italian painter Agostino Scilla – the Bernard Palissy of the seventeenth century, who in 1670 published *Vain Speculation Disarmed by the Senses. A Reply Concerning the Petrified Marine Bodies Found in Various Terrestrial Places* – adhered to professions of faith which accommodated the biblical chronology, and one can understand them. The idea of the immensity of natural as well as human history was in the air. But precisely because he had proclaimed such an idea, Lapeyrère created a vast aura of suspicion about himself. Everywhere Dutch Calvinists, German Lutherans, and Anglicans and Catholics of all nationalities and disciplines were determined to refute the blasphemer. In eleven years no fewer than seventeen volumes appeared with the express intention of confounding the agitator.

Lapeyrère posed a fundamental historical question, and had to wait two centuries before his theories found any resonance among the antiquaries, with the discovery of the immense prehistoric time-scale. But when all was said and done, in spite of Leonardo and Palissy and Mercati, most of his contemporaries still believed in the spontaneous generation of fossils and the existence of thunderbolts. However, the ideas he had waved in the face of the scholarly world were to be taken up in another form in liberal circles. A case in point is a strange book

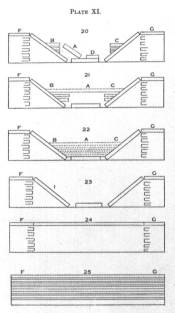

PLATE XI.

STENO'S FIGURES 20-25, IN EXACT SIZE.

Plate showing geological stratigraphy of Tuscany made in 1669 by Nicolas Steno (1638–86). Steno was Danish, but spent a long time in France and Italy. In dissecting a shark found in Livorno in 1666, he demonstrated the true nature of fossil shark teeth. Stephen Gould has pointed out that this graphic representation attributed to J.G. Winter, translator of Steno's work into English, was adapted in order to present time schematically as a linear succession of events (Gould 1990, pp. 90–97).

entitled *Muhammad the Turkish Spy: The Eight Volumes of Letters Writ by a Turkish Spy*, supposedly translated from the Arabic by a Genoese, Giovanni Paolo Marana.[18]

These apocryphal letters belong to a classic genre of later seventeenth-century literature in which the noble savage and the wise men of Egypt (Marana also commissioned an 'Egyptian' work) featured alongside Turks and Persians, who were to take the lead in such fictions before the Chinese made the Jesuits very unhappy. It allowed the narrator to stand back and flout convention – to give free rein to criticism in a less dangerous and more seductive form than the pamphlet. According to Paul Hazard, these are books in which 'it is said that the coming of Christ, because this is an embarrassment to reason, is not true; that the Bible, because it is not clear, is false; and that the only good lies in admitting only what is evident'.[19]

Our Turkish spy lost no time in interesting himself in the theories on the origin of man which were so cautiously tackled by the antiquaries of the day. Besides, the preface tells us that our author was passionate about antiquities:

Though he cannot be called an Antiquary, yet he appears a great Lover of Antiquities, and no less an Admirer of new Discoveries, provided they be both of them Matters of Importance, and worth a wise Man's Regard. For it does not belong to either of these Characters, that a Man is a curious Collector of Medals, Images, Pictures, and a Thousand other insignificant Trifles, which can neither serve to illustrate History, *regulate* Chronology, *nor adjust any momentous Difficulty in the* Records of Time, *but are only reverenced for their Rustiness, illegible Characters, and exotick Figure [...]. He loves* Antiquities, *but 'tis only such as draw the Veil from off the* Infancy of Time, *and uncover the* Cradle of the World. *This makes him insist with so much Zeal and Passion, on the Records of the* Chinese *and* Indians.[20]

We have been warned: the Turkish spy is an antiquary after Lapeyrère's own heart, a man unmoved by the fetishistic attitude to the past (an attitude also decried by Peiresc)[21] but animated by the desire for knowledge, who assumed the right of criticism and comparison. The historical and palaeontological doctrine of this spy in high places represents a perfect development of the pre-Adamite theses, one which had rid itself completely of any reference to the Bible:

Of all the people on the Earth, the Jews *seem to have been most guilty of imposing on the World an Opinion of their Antiquity, and aggrandizing their Line above all the Race of* Adam. *And from them the Error is transmitted to*

Frontispiece of Agostino Scilla's book, *La vana speculazione disingannata del senso*, published in 1670. Agostino Scilla (1629–1700) was a Sicilian painter known as 'Lo scolorito', and a lively advocate of the palaeontological analysis of fossils. He was interested in the natural sciences and also had a passion for numismatics.

the Christians; who giving a kind of implicit and blind Faith to the Hebrew *Historians, have confined the Age of the World within the Compass of six thousand Years; whereas, if other Chronologies be true, it may, for ought we know, be above Six hundred thousand Years old.*[22]

The 'spy' was not content with sober criticism of the antiquaries and chronologists of his time, and attacked the dogma which united them all (even the most enquiring minds among them) in deference to faith in the biblical tradition. In this he brought to its logical conclusion the critique of Lapeyrère, the man who discovered the idea of prehistory before the word had even been invented. Indeed, this Calvinist who ended his life with the Oratorian Fathers, a man of the Enlightenment before his time, passed on his conviction before his confession:

Here lies Lapeyrère, the good Israelite,
Huguenot, Catholic, then pre-Adamite.
Four religions mourn him with one voice,
And his indifference was so uncommon,
that after eighty years to make his choice,
The good man died, and chose not one among them.[23]

The men of the Enlightenment were thus well provided with the necessary tools for archaeological observation: numismatics, epigraphy, travel, topography, and in certain cases as we have seen, a sense of landscape and an interest in the relationship between what appeared on the surface of the soil and the layers of which it was composed. In addition there were the regional and national traditions. The Scandinavian taste for ruins and exploration; the passion of the central European antiquaries for taphonomy; the fondness of the British for the description of local antiquities; and the more traditional desire of the French and Italians to collect Greek and Roman antiquities – all these outlined an archaeology which had little in common with that of the Renaissance. It was necessary to put some order into the ever-expanding body of antiquities. It is true that the 'manual of antiquities' was not a discovery of the Enlightenment, and good minds such as Rosinus had already made the attempt at the end of the sixteenth century,[24] but the ambitions of men such as Bernard de Montfaucon and the Comte de Caylus were much greater, and more systematic, than those of Gronovius and Graevius, for example, who had tried to bring together the available Greek and Roman documentation at the end of the seventeenth century.[25]

THE ESTABLISHMENT
OF ARCHAEOLOGY

COMPILING IMAGES OF OBJECTS
AND MONUMENTS OF THE PAST
Bernard de Montfaucon

Bernard de Montfaucon (1655–1741) represents the great Benedictine tradition of Saint-Maur. Like Jean Mabillon he was also a palaeographer and a philologist, but during his travels in Italy (1698–1701) he decided to devote some of his considerable energy as an editor of patristic texts to the study of antiquities:

During the breaks which so often occurred in the editing of St John Chrysostom, even in the first volume, I published L'Antiquité expliquée et représentée en figures, *a work which I had been preparing for a long time; in Italy I had collected drawings of ancient monuments of all kinds which are to be found in greater number there than in the other countries of Europe. In France I continued to seek out and to have drawings made of everything which was to be found in the cabinets of curiosities, and monuments of every kind in town and countryside, and everything to be found in the other countries of Europe, which I collected either from printed books or through the agency of my friends.*[26]

Montfaucon's project, as the title clearly suggests, was to illustrate the monuments of antiquity in such a way as to make explanation possible. The image was fundamental but it complemented the text and had no value of its own proceeding from another branch of knowledge – in contrast with Bianchini's approach. The aim was above all philological, to establish a strict and intelligible relationship between text and object: 'These monuments are divided into two classes: that of books and that of statues, bas-reliefs, inscriptions and medals, two classes, as I have said, which are interdependent.'[27]

For this enterprise to be successful, it was necessary to organise the work according to a carefully thought out explanatory method. Montfaucon vacillated for a time between miscellany and system:

For a while I hesitated to decide upon the manner I would adopt: to deliver a corpus of the whole of antiquity together seemed to me to be very difficult; to present only isolated or unqualified examples having little relationship one with the other – this would not overcome the difficulties which would always be met by those wishing to inform themselves of the whole of antiquity, in having recourse to an infinity of books which are very difficult to find.[28]

The aim of the publication was not just scientific. The compilation of such a comprehensive and informed record took on an educational function which allowed the volumes of *L'Antiquité expliquée* to be used as a manual (and, moreover, Montfaucon suggested that his readers devote two years to the systematic study of his work). Its structure followed a functional order. First came the gods (and here Varro's plan can be recognised), then cults, thirdly the customs of private life and of civic life, 'wars, transport, major roads, bridges, aqueducts, navigation'. The last section was devoted to funerals, tombs and mausolea. Montfaucon's scheme was impressively structured. Illustrations, customs, material culture in both individual and collective spheres, sociology and funerary practices: there are certain predilections. His definition of archaeology was built up progressively. The first set of illustrations (the gods) was followed by a chapter on cults, which in turn depended on the appropriate apparatus, from daily life to great collective enterprises, and thence back to social matters. Montfaucon was not immune to the obsession with funerary matters which seemed to form the heart of archaeology; his last book was devoted to the memorial: memorials to the dead, whether buried, displayed, cremated, or simply evoked by means of symbolic monuments – standing stones, columns, cenotaphs. Montfaucon's enterprise was driven not so much by a simple interest in monuments as by an ambition to reconstruct the past within a global perspective. Even though Graeco-Roman civilisation was at the heart of his corpus, Montfaucon was happy to digress into eastern and even Gaulish or Germanic territory. His central Mediterranean vision of the past prefigured the concept of the *Altertumswissenschaft* (science of antiquities) which lay at the heart of nineteenth–century archaeology:

Frontispiece of Bernard de Montfaucon's *L'Antiquité expliquée*, published in 1722. This image epitomises the ideal of the antiquary at the beginning of the eighteenth century.

It is desirable that this work is as well-executed as it is interesting to the public. Here the whole of antiquity is treated; all branches are included and a great many figures are given for each; these figures are exactly and precisely explained to the best of my ability. When figures are lacking for certain subjects, I do not omit to explain these subjects and so complete the series [...]. What I am attempting here is to cover the whole of antiquity in one corpus: by the term antiquity I mean only that which can be seen, and which can be represented by illustrations; it is nonetheless of vast extent.[29]

Ideas, theories, the way things worked – all these were things which the antiquary could derive from texts. Objects and monuments offer knowledge of a quite different sort, and their interpretation depends upon the expert's eye and the draughtsman's hand. It was Plato's old distinction between the world of ideas and that of the senses which led Montfaucon to his view that archaeology was the image, and history the text. In a society where prints were the only means of reproducing images mechanically, the visual arts played a fundamental role. Illustration was the technique *par excellence* of the antiquary – it enabled him to reproduce the object, the monument, the landscape, the various traces visible to the practised eye. *L'Antiquité expliquée* was an exercise in methodology in which each object (or each representation of an object, for very often Montfaucon published things he had not seen) was assigned a text which gave it meaning. The learned Benedictine was thus a theoretician, postulating a relationship and a reciprocity between text and image, an idea which has remained within archaeological discourse ever since.

Urns and stone artefacts found in Hesse by J.C. Iselin and published in Montfaucon's *L'Antiquité expliquée*. Here, among the Graeco-Roman antiquities, appear worked flints, for a long time regarded as 'thunderbolts'.

As a good Benedictine, Montfaucon was a man for the written word. The order he sought to install into antiquarian studies derived from his unequalled knowledge of literary tradition, but it reflects a definition of antiquities which goes back to Varro. Since Camden, Worm, Aubrey and Rhode, some antiquaries had explored another path, one which began with objects, not texts, and one in which antiquities were collected, studied and described according to the way in which they were used, rather than according to the meaning ascribed them by textual tradition. The birth of this new kind of antiquary should come as no surprise in a context where texts were increasingly rare, and the monuments of the past were farther away from the models of Graeco-Roman antiquity.

THE FOUNDATION OF A SCIENCE
OF OBJECTS AND MONUMENTS
Anne Claude Philippe de Turbières
de Grimoard de Pestels de Lévis,
Comte de Caylus

Elevations and plan of Mount Gergovie, executed for the Comte de Caylus by Dijon, an engineer in the province of Auvergne. The precision of the topographical studies carried out under Caylus's supervision by bridge and highway engineers demonstrates the operation of rigorous standards.

The Comte de Caylus, as we have seen, proposed to replace the philological model with an experimental one, in contrast to the classical *descriptio* and *interpretatio*, and to turn the antiquary into a kind of physicist of the past.[30] The count was from a very different generation to that of the learned Benedictine, nor had he spent his life buried in esoteric tomes before becoming possessed by the demon of antiquities. Born in 1692, this scion of the high nobility had begun his career in the military (like Montfaucon before him), but attracted by adventure he accompanied the French ambassador to Constantinople and visited the coast of Asia Minor before in 1718 beginning his life as a dilettante and patron of the arts. He next took up a place in the Académie de Peinture, then in the Académie des Inscriptions et Belles-lettres. Caylus was not, however, a collector in the narrow sense. What interested him about the art of his time, and that of the past, was the ways in which it developed, and the techniques of drawing and painting (he was himself an excellent engraver). His wealth allowed him to extend patronage to Parisian artists, and to acquire antiquities through a network of devoted correspondents as far afield as Alexandria and Syria. He was a new Peiresc, and if he was less learned and less the encyclopaedist than his illustrious predecessor, he was just as thirsty for knowledge. He was surrounded by such men as Pierre Mariette, Jean-Jacques Barthélemy and Charles Le Beau, all of whom counted among the art- and history-lovers of Paris. This man of the world came late to antiquities, but with what passion! He was soon in touch with all the Italian antiquaries of his time, particularly the most active of them, Father Paciaudi. He seemed to be a 'hunting dog on the trail of antiquities', but he was no collector:

I am not creating a cabinet – vanity not being my objective; I care not at all for showy things, but for the bits and pieces of agate, stone, bronze, pottery, glass, which may serve in whatever way to discover some practice or the hand of a maker.[31]

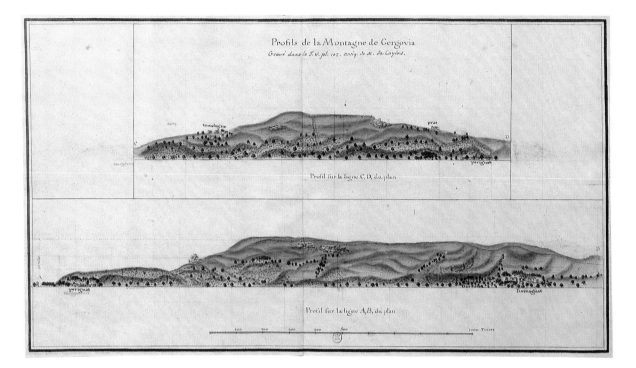

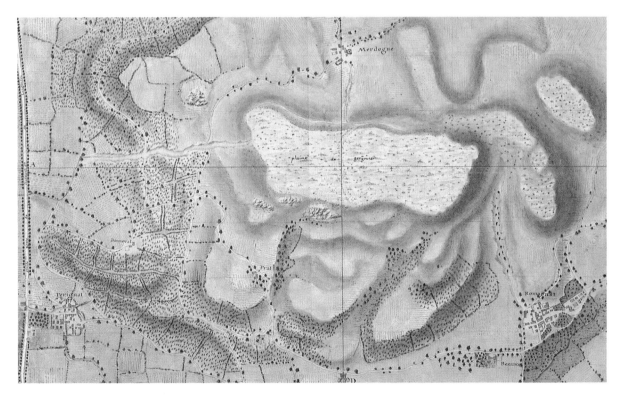

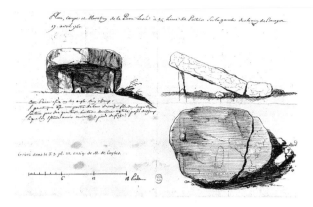

Drawing of the *pierre levée* in Poitiers, executed for the Comte de Caylus. This study by the engineer Duchesne is very different from that published in Braun and Hogenberg's atlas in 1600 (see p. 14). A comparison of the two drawings shows the progress made in two centuries.

He admitted to deriving more pleasure from fragments than from intact objects, from masterpieces, 'the beautifully-preserved pieces, those cold Apollos, those beautiful so-called Venuses'.[32] Once his crates of antiquities were unpacked his only thought was to make them available to the scholarly world, 'The antiquities arrive, I study them, I have them drawn by up-and-coming young people. This gives them the means to live and to study.'[33] In short, his collection had more to do with the laboratory than with the cabinet of an amateur. He sought to experiment rather than to illustrate. His contribution to archaeology is expressed by his numerous notes published by the Académie des Inscriptions, but his master work is still the *Recueil d'antiquités égyptiennes, étrusques, grecques, romaines et gauloises*. It was published in seven volumes in Paris between 1752 and 1768, and was distinguished from its predecessors by its determination to present only original documents:

I restricted myself to publishing in this compendium only those things which belong, or belonged, to me. I had them drawn with the greatest exactitude, and I dare say that the descriptions are no less faithful. Good fortune, and some small expenditure, are insufficient to swell personal pride and lead one away from the truth. My taste for the arts has not led to any desire for possession. [...] Antiquities are there for the extension of knowledge. They explain the various usages, they shed light upon their obscure or little-known makers, they bring the progress of the arts before our eyes and serve as models to those who study them. But it must be said that the antiquaries hardly ever saw them in this way; they regarded them only as a supplement to the proofs of history, or as isolated texts open to the longest commentaries.[34]

No antiquary before Caylus had expressed so clearly the primacy of knowledge over the desire to possess, or insisted so vigorously on that first-hand experience of the object which governs archaeological knowledge. No one before him (and very few after) had so explicitly criticised the philological interpretative model which the men of the Renaissance had applied to monuments. If the study of antiquities had anything to do with the experimental method, then the paradigm of textual interpretation was not enough, and the interpretation of the archaeologist, like the logic of the physicist, was capable of demonstration. To make that possible, some laws had to be established:

The drawing provides the principles, comparison provides the means of applying them, and this way of proceeding in some way imprints in the mind the predilections of a nation, so that if during excavation one finds something foreign to the country one might conclude, without fear of error, that it sprang from the hand of an artist who was himself foreign.[35]

The key role of the image in the definition of a culture and a period had already been emphasised by Bianchini, but Caylus went much further and made the graphic representation of every object one of the rules of the antiquary. Each object was capable of revealing constant traits which established its cultural and geographical origins. Caylus was proposing none other than a typological theory, which is the ancestor of all archaeological reasoning. The inferences he drew were not limited to the characterisation of origin. He set out to elucidate the diachronic dimension necessary for the construction of an evolutionary typology:

Once the cultural character of a nation has been established, one has only to follow its progress or its changes [...]. It is true that the second operation is more difficult than the first. The tastes of one people differ from those of another as clearly as the primary colours differ from each other, while the variations in national taste in different centuries can be viewed as the the very subtle shades of one colour.[36]

If every object could be assigned a place and time by virtue of an observable and quantifiable cultural determinism, then the antiquary had in his possession a powerful instrument of logic capable of ordering similar objects in series. In developing a double principle of evolution and cultural distinction, Caylus helped lay the foundations of a descriptive typology central to modern archaeology. Despite its lack of order and disjointed composition, the *Recueil* announced a new era in archaeology, one which was more attentive to objects, more sure of its descriptions and its definition of types, more interested in technology and the reconstruction of processes. Whether taking an interest in ancient painting, the manufacture of vases or the techniques of

Plate from Caylus's *Recueil d'antiquités* showing an archaic bronze figure of a hunter from Sardinia. It reveals Caylus's fascination for all kinds of antiquities.

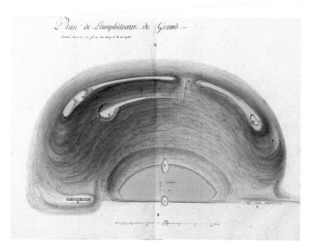

Plan of the
amphitheatre at
Grand, Lorraine, made
for the Comte de
Caylus.

coining, Caylus put the greatest importance on observation, on placing the object within the process of its manufacture. He emphasised to the antiquaries of his time that no study of antiquities would ever be satisfied with the repeated perusal of texts. On the contrary, a part of history was concealed within objects, and provided one approached them in the right way, they might be made to speak:

The more I read, the less I can confidently rely upon the authors with respect to the arts. One must see the works in order to speak about them, and have a very sure and well-established knowledge of them in order to write about them.[37]

Plan of the fountain
of Nimes, drawn by
Damun for the Comte
de Caylus. The
monument at the site
of the spring was
discovered in 1738.

THE BURIED CITIES OF VESUVIUS

While Montfaucon was bringing the publication of *L'Antiquité expliquée* to a conclusion in 1711, a colonel of the Austrian army, Prince d'Elbeuf, who owned a small property near Portici, discovered statues and inscriptions of exceptional quality at the bottom of a shaft dug by a peasant. He made a gift of three almost intact statues to Prince Eugene of Savoy, commander in chief of the Holy Roman Empire. After the Prince's death the statues were acquired by Augustus II, Elector of Saxony and King of Poland, whose daughter Amalia was to become queen as wife of Charles III, King of Spain and Naples. Archaeologists of the nineteenth century tried to show a link between the royal marriage and the renewal of explorations in 1738. For his part, the man in charge of the site, the Spanish engineer Rocco Joachin Alcubierre, claimed to have taken the initiative during the course of building works which he was carrying out on the royal property at Portici. Starting from Prince d'Elbeuf's shaft and galleries, which were fortunately placed in the centre of the theatre of Herculaneum, the excavators soon found the stuff of dreams: inscriptions, statues of bronze and marble, and above all, uniquely in the history of the Graeco-Roman world, paintings which had been rapidly buried, and thus protected, by the disaster

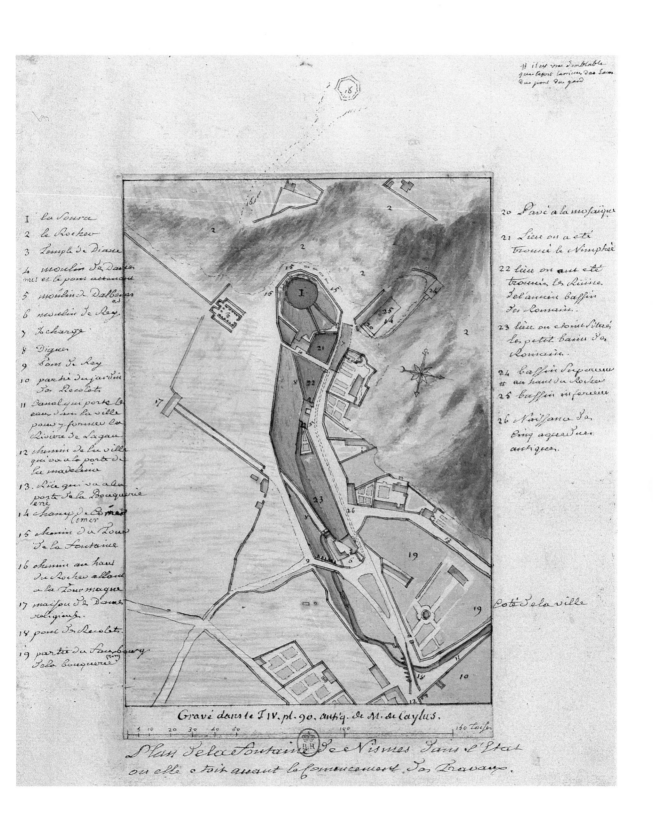

which overwhelmed the town. Ten years later, in 1748, the king opened equally spectacular excavations on the site of Pompeii under the direction of Alcubierre. It is hard for us to imagine today the excitement and interest these excavations unleashed, at a time when this was practically the only royal archaeological site in the whole of Europe. (When, some years later, the Duke of Parma summoned Paciaudi, the faithful correspondent and friend of Caylus, to direct excavations at Veleia, it was with the express aim of rivaling the Neapolitans.) Herculaneum and Pompeii, though, had something special that distinguished them from any other archaeological site, however prestigious. The two cities buried by the eruption of Vesuvius were caught in full swing, before their populace had a chance to save their most useful possessions. Neither had their successors used the site as a quarry for construction materials. With the help of Bernardo Tanucci, a cultured minister and disciple of the great scholar Muratori, Charles III undertook the excavation of the buried cities as a personal project, the success of which was to win for the kingdom the admiration of the whole world. Unfortunately the king and his minister had found in Alcubierre no Rudbeck or Aubrey. The Spanish engineer and his associates were in thrall to the treasure-hunting tradition of excavation, of the most rapid exhumation of the greatest number of antiquities possible. Instead of clearing the monuments by means of open trenches they continued the gallery technique begun by Prince d'Elbeuf and deprived themselves of any overall topographical understanding of the two sites. The more enlightened travellers attracted by the unique spectacle, like Horace Walpole, noticed this from the start of the operation:

There might certainly be collected great light from this reservoir of antiquities, if a man of learning had the inspection of it; if he directed the working, and would make a journal of the discoveries. But I believe there is no judicious choice made of directors.[38]

President de Brosses confirmed this opinion in his travel journal a few years later.[39] Alcubierre had organisational talents, but this officer in the Engineers believed more in the military technique of gallery-digging than in the surface excavation which was the rule when confronted with deposits less difficult to deal with than those of Herculaneum. Pompeii and Herculaneum posed a triple problem to the antiquaries of the eighteenth century: how to explore such a huge and teeming area, how to organise the museum and the protection of the site, and how to publish it. On all three counts the king

The discovery of Herculaneum and view of the main street in Pompeii, drawings from *Voyage pittoresque de Naples et de Sicile* by the Abbé Saint-Non, published in 1782. The discovery of the sites of Herculaneum and Pompeii during the first half of the eighteenth century gave rise to a great enthusiasm for excavation. However, the techniques depicted here were still rather rudimentary.

and his counsellors seem to have made bad choices – not because they were incompetent or stupid, but because Italian antiquaries of the period since the Renaissance had not managed to develop the field techniques necessary for the excavation, recording and presentation of evidence (with the isolated exception of Bianchini's work in Rome). In Scandinavia these questions had been mastered, as they went hand in hand with the concept of antiquarian work which put the excavators in the service of the state. In Herculaneum and Pompeii the excavations were primarily on behalf of the king, to collect objects suitable to adorn his palace at Portici. Thus there were measures to prevent the fraudulent sale and theft of objects which were as sought-after as the sites were famous. There was also a fierce ban on the drawing or description of the objects placed in the museum, the publication of which was reserved for the Academia Ercolanese founded by the king. The latter privately published sumptuous volumes, which were inaccessible to scholars at large. It is easy to understand how the enlightened visitors from throughout Europe who had seen the sites – from President de Brosses to Cochin, from Walpole to Winckelmann – protested against the management of the excavations. Scipione Maffei of Verona criticised the stupid gallery system and the ill-considered sorting of the objects whereby those less worthy of attention were simply thrown away; Winckelmann fumed against the treatment of the paintings, and the Comte de Caylus fretted. Conservation posed even greater problems than excavation. Because of the galleries, the paintings had to be cut into pieces to get them out, and so the murals were treated like ordinary pictures. As well as these technical problems, work was under way to treat the remains in the same way as modern objects: while the murals were cut up and framed to hang on the walls of the Portici palace, the vessels were viewed as pieces of Sèvres or Meissen. All this criticism and the great plethora of publications (mainly unauthorised) which the vast public interest brought did lead, however, to some belated improvements: from 1763 the excavation at Pompeii was open to the sky, and the Abbé Baiardi, who was responsible for publication – a good scholar but a poor antiquary – was replaced by more dynamic men. Due to the vicissitudes of history, it was to be a long time yet before expectations were met – the expectations of all the antiquaries of Europe, as well as those of the great travellers who, from Goethe to Chateaubriand, were so taken with the poetry of the buried towns of Vesuvius. Be that as it may, the discovery of Herculaneum and

Pompeii had transformed the taste for antiquity. Architects, scholars and travellers from all over Europe visited the site of the two towns and completed their picture of what they had already admired in Rome: daily life, the 'bits and pieces' of the past which were so dear to Caylus, all found their way into the image of antiquity.

SYSTEMATIC EXCAVATIONS
Observation, survey and explanation

If the scientific perspective of the antiquaries had changed so abruptly and radically with Caylus, it was because their relationship with the monuments of the past had been profoundly modified since the beginning of the seventeenth century. France, it is true, had not seen the kind of systematic development of regional studies that was supported by the state in northern Europe, or driven by scholarly curiosity in Britain. Something had changed, though, beginning in the last decades of the century. This was demonstrated by the work of Roger de Gaignières (1642–1715), among others.[40] De Gaignières was equerry to the Duke of Guise, then in 1671 to his aunt, Mlle de Guise, and had been governor of the principality of Joinville. His scholarly reputation was such that he played a part in the

Triumphal arch at Langres, a drawing taken from Roger de Gaignières's album *Antiquité des Gaules* (1700). He was one of the first to attempt a survey of the antiquities of France.

The amphitheatre at Arles, a drawing dated 1666 taken from Roger de Gaignières's album, *Antiquité des Gaules*. This view owes more to Renaissance taste than to the vision of eighteenth-century engineers.

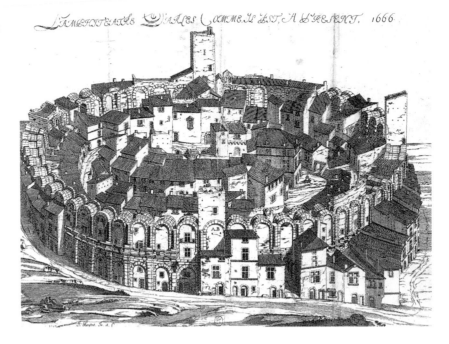

Illustrations of the antiquities of Aix, by Gaillard de Lonjumeau (1760). The precision and attention to detail show the progress made in the depiction of monuments and antiquities.

education of the heir to the throne, the Duke of Burgundy. Although Gaignières was a Parisian, he had spent most of his life travelling the kingdom, collecting curiosities and commissioning drawings of anything which he felt was worthy of interest. Aided by his valet, Rémy, and afterwards by a draughtsman, Louis Bourdan, he had copies made of everything he could in the way of manuscripts, funerary monuments and remains of every period. His great originality lay in the emphasis he placed on the medieval and modern periods. Renaissance collectors' cabinets were dominated by objects from antiquity. At the end of the seventeenth century attention was turned to more recent periods, as if the historical universe had expanded to touch the contemporary world. Gaignières' interest embraced portraits, the landscape, customs and festivals:

> *The enormous encyclopaedia of the world created and inhabited by man assembled by Gaignières forms a kind of counterpart or complement to the cabinets of curiosities in which the natural world is concentrated, and in which man is merely first among the animals. Gaignières is no more interested in ancient history than in natural curiosities, which are strictly banished from the collection.*[41]

Schnapper is right to highlight the novelty of the project and its execution, but his judgement of antiquity seems a little harsh. Gaignières, unlike Peiresc, did not put antiquity at the top of his list, but

1. un Autel dans l'anciene Maison du St. Fabri de Peiresc derriere le Palais de Sextius. 2. partie des debris d'un Pavé de plusieurs couleurs de mosaïque qui avoit 11. toises de longueur et 7 de largeur trouvé ainsi que la baze de 4. pieds de diametre dans les creusements faits dans le mois de 9bre 1749. a l'occasion de la batisse des greniers de la place de l'Hotel de Ville. ces debris sont dans la cour de la Maison de Mr. le Baron de Gaillard Lonjumeau Ventabren. 3. representation des ruines actuelles de la piramide triomphale et de l'enceinte quefit elever Cayus Marius a l'honneur de la Victoire quil remporta sur trois cents milles barbares placée au quartier apellé du triomphe le long de la Riviere de l'arc auprés de la petite Bogiere du St. cadet Barnoin sur le grand Chemin au devant de la Montaigne apellée alors de la Victoire vis a vis la Ville d'Aix. 4. parties destinées de marbre qui ont resté dans la maison du St. Fabre Borrilli 5. dans le Jardin du St. Peloutier et trouvé en 1720. dans les terres au dessus de la Ville. Chartreuse.

2. la Façade du Palais bati a Aix en 631. de la fondation de Rome par Sextius Calvinus qui se trouve cachée par les batisses du Palais des jurisdictions a l'exception de la Tour apellée du chaperon ou sont deposés les titres des anciens Souverains du Païs; 2. la Tour apellée de St. Mitre qui sert de Cachot aux Prisonniers. 3. la grande Tour isolée qui se trouve engagée dans les memes batisses. 4. de meme que la rotonde de 8 Colonnes de marbre vert caillouté de blanc.

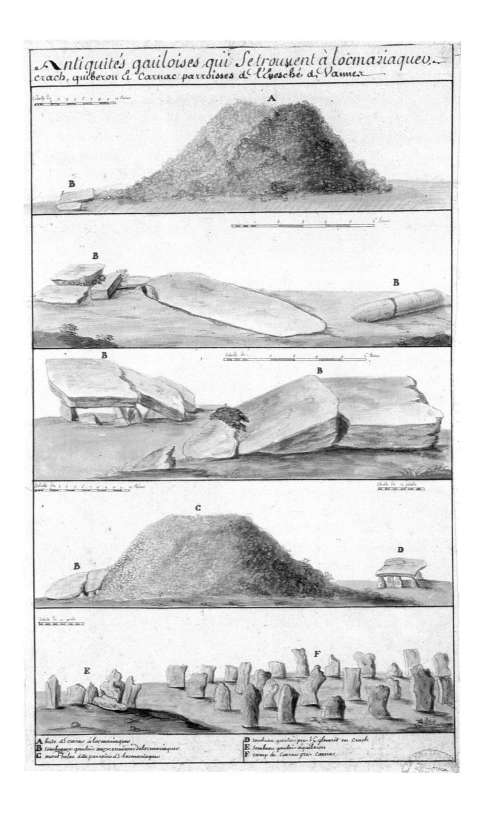

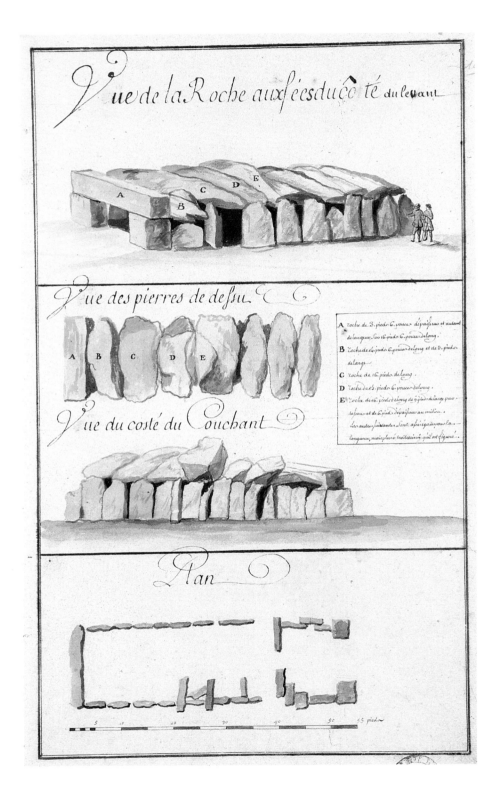

Gallo-Roman site at Châtelet, between Saint-Dizier and Joinville in Champagne. In 1772 an ironmaster from the neighbouring village of Bayard, Grignon, decided to excavate the site and swiftly managed to engage the goodwill of the Académie des Inscriptions et Belles-lettres, and the support of the king. Discoveries mounted up, and in 1774 Grignon was able to publish two numbers of the *Bulletin of Excavations Carried Out by Order of the King of a Roman Town, on the Little Mountain of Châtelet*. Grignon was one of those positive individuals who brought to archaeology the techniques of a true fieldworker: topographical survey and analysis, drawing and description of finds, observation of variations in the terrain and of conditions of discovery:

Topographical map of the town of Châtelet, by Pierre-Clément Grignon.

His Majesty ordered these excavations to continue [...]. Armed with this authority, we began by digging across the whole extent of the mountain a trench three feet wide, which varied in depth, and a second across the smaller dimension, which crossed the first at right angles. By this method we found that the whole surface of Le Châtelet had been occupied, and there had even been houses as far as the top of the mountain [...]. The total extent of the excavations to date is 8,573 toises carrées [c.17,000 sq. m], and we estimate the earth extracted from the various diggings at 4,654 toises cubes [c.9,000 cu. m]. All of this was dug thoroughly, down to the rock which forms the body of the mountain, and we have reproduced the plan and section in the plate which is attached to this short work. We also drew a very small-scale plan of the extent of the excavations taken from a large-scale topographical plan. These two plans are the work of my son, who, independently of this difficult work, has carried out all excavation work with as much zeal and energy as intelligence, the main directorial work being reserved to us, also the responsibility for the cleaning of the antiques, of reconciling the pieces, of classifying them in my museum, of drawing most of them and of writing their history.[46]

A worthy rival to Caylus, the ironmaster from Bayard followed his programme to the letter: to observe, survey and explain antiquities for their own sake, and to make them sources of knowledge by means of a clearly defined and controllable series of operations. Of course there was still a wide gap between Grignon's work and a modern stratigraphic excavation, but as Pinon has emphasised, he was one of the first in France to develop a complete programme of landscape archaeology.

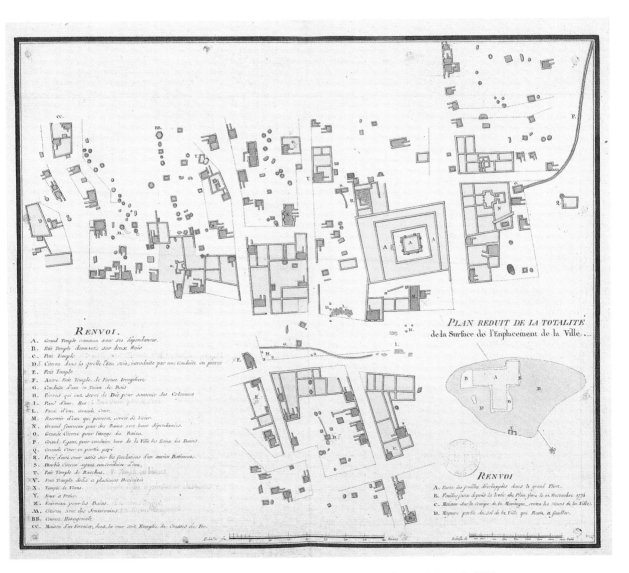

General plan of the excavations at Châtelet, drawn by Pierre-Clément Grignon in 1774.
The techniques of excavation and survey employed by the Grignons, father and son,
anticipated archaeological methods of the nineteenth century.

THE CRISIS IN
MEDITERRANEAN ARCHAEOLOGY
Johann Joachim Winckelmann

Opposite, above:
Las Incantadas,
Thessalonica, by James
Stuart. A Corinthian
colonnade surmounted
by a pillared storey,
second century AD.

Above: Archaeologists
at work, frontispiece
of Guiseppe Antonio
Guattani's *Monumenti
antichi inediti* (1784),
showing excavators in
a romantic setting.

Opposite, below:
Monument of
Philopappus, from
The Antiquities of Athens
by James Stuart and
Nicholas Revett
(1761). Their travels
and surveys revealed a
new image of Greece.

Throughout the eighteenth century able minds had tried to render intelligible the ever-increasing mass of discoveries, sometimes in the face of the jibes of their contemporaries, such as Diderot and Voltaire. It was left to the son of an obscure cobbler from Stendal in Prussia to revise completely the West's attitude towards Graeco-Roman works.

Mid-eighteenth-century Germany, which worshipped daily at the shrine of Greek art, was to find in Winckelmann an inspired singer of the praises of antique art, who expressed in a new kind of German prose the matchless quality of Greek art. There had been no shortage of scholarly works on the subject before, but Winckelmann proposed to put order into the chaos of learning, and dared to construct a stylistic chronology where his predecessors had been content with iconographic commentaries. However, his decisive influence was not due to his technical approach alone, but to his interpretation of the works of antiquity, which became the supreme bible of Neo-classicism. Seen thus, Greek art was not the agent of a particular, historically-determined response, but represented the ideal of a perfect and absolute beauty which was embodied in the works of Pheidias. Stylistic analysis was not, as Caylus thought, a technical device, but the key to the understanding of an aesthetic. Winckelmann transcended archaeology in the relevance of his analyses, but above all in the quality of his style and the ambition of his aesthetic. The social milieu of the *dilettanti,* writers, artists and antiquaries found in his work a frame of reference and a philosophy of art: a major event which had practical as well as intellectual consequences. From the middle of the eighteenth century the archaeological voyage to Italy, and soon after to Greece and Turkey, became both a social and a cultural necessity. Philology and aesthetics – the voyages brought the antiquarian tradition into the modern world. 'I came to Rome,' says Winckelmann, 'to open the eyes of

those who will come after me.'[47] Winckelmann immediately played a decisive role among the *connoisseurs* of Rome, who with their outposts in France, Germany, Scandinavia and Britain, formed a kind of summary of the arts in Europe. Around the cardinals' palaces, around the pope and the various ambassadors, there gathered a crowd of artists, aristocratic travellers and scholars. This was very fertile ground for the rediscovery of antiquity. It was not the revelatory kind of antiquity, which displayed 'a whole race of statues' to the dazzled eyes of the men of the Renaissance. It was related to a craze for the architecture, sculpture and pottery which was the fruit of the scholarly researches of the antiquaries of the preceding period. At the end of the eighteenth century it was no longer only Roman antiquities which became accessible: the Greek temples of Paestum and Sicily and sites in Greece and Asia Minor were available for inspection by the bolder spirits. The knowledge of antiquity expanded in space as well as in time. The Grand Tour was undertaken to view these ancient landscapes, but also to find among the evocative ruins and their architecture the yeast of inspiration, the elements of a new style of architecture which was to change the face of most European cities. The fashion for antiquities can be explained as much by the development of ideas as by a new social demand, and the explosion in travel literature was to sustain its momentum. The *Voyage du jeune Anacharsis en Grèce vers le milieu du IVe siècle avant l'ère vulgaire* by the Abbé Barthélemy, Stuart and Revett's *Antiquities of Athens* and the Comte de Choiseul-Gouffier's *Le Voyage pittoresque de la Grèce* all disclosed landscapes and monuments hitherto unknown to the general public. The great encyclopaedic descriptions of the preceding period were replaced by monograph studies. Scholarly travel was supported in France and England by the Crown, and the Society of Dilettanti of London gave financial support to expeditions. The architects who visited Greece – Stuart, and later Cockerell – were prolific builders through whom the new taste was imposed. The manner of publication changed; the overhead views of monuments were supplemented with sections and plans, and the accuracy of the surveys improved, all to public approval.

The taste for antiquities was not merely theoretical. The travellers of the eighteenth century, like the antiquaries before them, were collectors, but they displayed a new technical interest and a desire to imitate. The voyage changed in social status and dimensions. Ambassadors began to fund collecting expeditions. Richard Worsley, British

View of the site of Ilium (*left*) and ruins of a temple near the mound of Troy (*below*): drawings from *Voyage pittoresque de la Grèce* by the Comte de Choiseul-Gouffier, published in 1782. Choiseul-Gouffier's observations show more of an interest in the picturesque than in architecture.

ambassador to Venice; Choiseul-Gouffier, French ambassador to Constantinople; Lord Elgin, British ambassador to the same city; Sir William Hamilton in Naples – all had their 'antiquary', their illustrators, their cast-makers, and sometimes their permanent residents in Athens, like the Frenchman Fauvel for Choiseul and the Italian Lusieri for Elgin. In London the Society of Dilettanti, founded in 1733, was the heart and soul of these enterprises and the meeting-place of those English gentlemen who were the most determined and numerous of the travellers. This curiosity, coupled with the need to finance the expeditions, went hand in hand with pillage. Who would secure the Parthenon sculptures, the French or the British? Fauvel made a start, but Elgin beat him to it. In this game of fame and prestige everything was permissible, as a letter from Choiseul to Fauvel demonstrates: 'Take everything you can, lose no opportunity to loot everything which is lootable in Athens and its surroundings [...]. Spare neither the dead nor the living.'[48]

Winckelmann's astonishing and unsurpassable success, before his tragic and premature death in Trieste in 1768, can only be explained in terms of the establishment of the taste for, and knowledge of, Graeco-Roman antiquities at the heart of cultural attitudes in the European world. The ground had been prepared during the classical age, but the craze for monuments and objects was a cultural trait of

The French consul Fauvel in his house at the foot of the Acropolis. Lithograph by Louis Dupré, 1825.

the Enlightenment. Winckelmann offered an aesthetic to a Europe in which Greek art had been only a matter of taste. In justifying it he destroyed the antiquarian model which made history subservient to objects. His *The History of Ancient Art among the Greeks* is not a series of annotated works, but an ordered account which places those works in an historical context in an inimitable style. Generations of antiquaries had sought only to explain the objects, but Winckelmann set out to explain a culture by its objects. This was an impressive change of perspective which addressed the scholar as well as the artist. Better still, he did not reserve his disclosure of the attractions of the sublime for the ears of the German princes, Dutch scholars or Italian cardinals. He addressed *all* men of the Enlightenment, telling them that if Greek art had reached such a degree of perfection, it was because that art had developed within one of the freest societies that man had ever known. Beauty was the sister of liberty:

The independence of Greece is to be regarded as the most prominent of the

causes, originating in its constitution and government, of its superiority in art
[…]. The freedom which gave birth to great events, political changes, and jeal-
ousy among the Greeks, planted, as it were in the very production of these
effects, the germ of noble and elevated sentiments. As the sight of the bound-
less surface of the sea, and the dashing of its proud waves upon the rocky
shore, expands our views and carries the soul away from, and above, inferior
objects, so it was impossible to think ignobly in the presence of deeds so great
and men so distinguished.[49]

There was something of Rousseau in this man (we have this
observation on Diderot's authority). To his literary gifts Winckelmann
could add those of connoisseur, and his boundless
curiosity gave his contemporaries the impression
that with each of his books a new continent of the
past was to be discovered. The essayist was also a
scholar-traveller, on the trail of all the archaeological novelties of his time, from Rome to Herculaneum to Paestum. It was an era of excavation as
well as exploration, as is shown by the discovery of
Herculaneum and Pompeii and the 'state' excavations organised by the Duke of Parma at Veleia. In
the eyes of archaeologists, however, his work
became the victim of its own success; his history of
Greek art depended mainly upon Roman copies,
(original Greek statues were to emerge during the
nineteenth century with the development of excavation in Greece). This theoretician of imitation
had built his aesthetic and typological opinion
upon copies. His abbreviated life and his fear of

Sultan's edict written
in Turkish and Greek.
This document is the
official authorisation
for the export of the
Venus de Milo (1821).

reality had prevented him from braving the voyage to Greece, his
life-long desire. It was to be one of his successors at the head of the
Vatican museums, Ennio Quirino Visconti, who declared to the
scholarly world that the marbles taken from the Acropolis by Lord
Elgin were indeed authentic Attic sculptures of the fifth century BC.
Winckelmann, however, had achieved something of which no antiquary had ever dreamed. He had imposed a new vision of Greece
upon contemporary society, and an aesthetic which for decades
would be held as the key to understanding ancient art. The concept
of the sublime, and of liberty – these two poles of Winckelmann's
thinking – would not, however, carry the same longevity. For some –
Herder, Lessing, Humboldt and, of course, Goethe – the mystery of

The Apogee of Greece, Karl Friedrich Schinkel, 1825, copy attributed to Wilhelm Ahlborn, 1836. This painting could be seen as a visual expression of Winkelmann's and Goethe's theories on Greek art.

Greek art formed the heart of his legacy; for others, principally the revolutionaries, the message of the liberty of the ancients was born anew in the person of Winckelmann. David's paintings and the architectural projects of Thomas Jefferson – future President of the United States, his country's ambassador to Paris during the Revolution, and spare-time archaeologist – were part of the Winckelmann heritage.

THE HISTORY OF ART AND OF NATURE
Contradictions in the archaeology of the Age of Enlightenment

Through the enthusiasm and curiosity of the savants, the science of the antiquaries emerged as a completely distinct discipline. At the end of the eighteenth century the collections not only flourished but became (or were becoming) museums open to the public. Landscape studies made enormous progress, and the more observant spirits from this period onwards knew how to pick out those variations in the soil which foretold modern stratigraphic techniques. Thanks to the efforts of the numismatists and epigraphers, the antiquaries had at their disposal the means of dating and interpretation necessary to the understanding of any literate society. In addition, the insights of such men as Aubrey, Caylus and Winckelmann showed typology to be the cardinal method of seriating and dating objects. Paradoxically, however, one is treated to the spectacle of the best of antiquaries – like Maffei and Caylus – taking works of the Renaissance for ancient sculptures, and to Montfaucon's father referring to the Three Age system but not discussing it. Caylus, who had guessed the great antiquity of the Breton megaliths, did not have recourse to Buffon's theories to support his words, and La Sauvagère sought the authority of Voltaire to deny the existence of fossil shells.

The 'ceraunites' or 'thunderbolts' are a good indication of the difficulties encountered by the archaeologists of the Enlightenment when they tried to reconcile an experimental approach with antiquarian tradition. As early as the sixteenth century Michele Mercati had shown that the so-called 'thunderbolts' were in fact chipped stones used as tools by the ancient populations of Europe. However, his book was not published until 1719,[50] and the subject still seemed difficult enough in 1723 for Antoine de Jussieu to address it in a paper to the Académie des Sciences, and in 1734 the antiquary Nicolas Mahudel[51] did the same at the Académie des Inscriptions. While the two authors agreed with Mercati's opinion, their arguments were more developed; Jussieu insisted upon ethnographic comparisons and on the use of similar stones by the 'savages' of Canada and the Caribbean, concluding that:

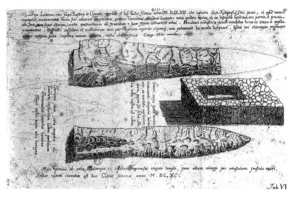

The populations of France and Germany and of other northern countries, but for the discovery of iron, are quite similar to all the savages of today, and had no less need than them, before the use of iron, to cut wood, strip bark, cleave branches and kill wild animals, to hunt for their food and to defend themselves against their enemies. They could hardly have done these things without such tools, which unlike iron, being not subject to rust, are found today in their entirety in the earth, almost with their first polish.[52]

Jussieu's conclusion clearly articulates the rule of actualism in archaeology: any ancient object made in the same material and following the same process as an object made by a modern-day population must have had a roughly equivalent function. The Jesuit Father Lafitau used the same rationale in *Mœurs des sauvages américains comparées aux mœurs des premiers temps* (1724), so giving his mark of approval to the comparative ethnology of ancient and modern peoples. In addition, the commentary of the Permanent Secretary of the Académie des Sciences, following Jussieu's paper reinforced his opinion:

Stone weapons from Kilian Stobaeus's book on the history of 'ceraunites' (1738). In Scandinavia, an interest in local antiquities led scholars to illustrate the 'thunderbolts' faithfully. Stobaeus regarded them as tools and weapons predating the use of iron.

If the other stones figured are monuments to the great physical revolutions, then these are the monuments to a great revolution which one might call moral, and the comparison of the New World with the Ancient serves to prove both revolutions equally.

In other words, the invention of flint tools was to the history of man what the appearance of certain fossils was to the history of the natural world; the two kinds of history shared the same kind of induction. A dangerous opinion, which established in a scientific context what Lapeyrère had suggested in a theological one.

Mahudel, in his paper to the Académie des Inscriptions, developed the technical arguments: the 'thunderbolts' were functionally similar to bronze and iron tools. One could therefore infer that these were objects which shared the same purpose, before the discovery of 'brass and iron'. Mahudel stuck to this explanation, effectively a typological one, without ever developing the actualist argument.

Why? Undoubtedly because it was thus easier for him to draw an acceptable conclusion: man used stone before metal, but there is nothing here which contradicts biblical tradition. While Jussieu developed an approach based on ethnographic parallels which supposed an equivalence of human and natural history, Mahudel followed the antiquarian method which gave precedence to sources and typological comparison, in which case there was no need to resort to evidence borrowed from natural history.

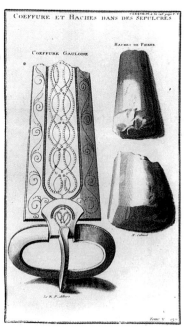

Plate from Monfaucon's *l'Antiquité expliquée*, showing protohistoric stone axes and a Merovingian buckle plate which was thought to be a 'gallic hair ornament'.

The discovery in 1685 in Normandy of the megalithic tomb of Cocherel may help shed light upon the difficulties encountered by the antiquaries of the eighteenth century when they tried to interpret monuments outside the classical tradition. This tomb, carefully described by the gentleman excavator, consisted of a burial chamber in which about twenty bodies were buried, accompanied by objects which were out of the ordinary: stone axes, worked bone, arrowheads, 'It seems that the barbarians there used neither iron nor copper, nor any other metal.'[53] In addition to this first grave there was a cremation burial, 'in ground eight *pouces* [inches] higher'. Montfaucon went for an ethnic interpretation of the different modes of burial, 'There can be no doubt that this was the tomb of two nations of the remotest antiquity.'[54] However, he was careful to avoid any chronological interpretation, and contented himself with attaching to his description a letter from an antiquary of Basle, Jacques Christophe Iselin, which added details on burials of the same type found in Germany and the Nordic countries. In his letter Iselin, who was a competent antiquary and a friend of Schoepflin, suggested simply that tombs of this type should be classified according to the tools and weapons found during excavation, following a stone–copper–iron succession. This was a fundamental paradigm inherited from Greek and Latin authors, but one which no antiquary had used explicitly to classify archaeological evidence.[55] Montfaucon added no commentary to Iselin's letter; to him it was merely a useful source of information on 'northern antiquities', which he employed in his supplement to draw attention to the megaliths of Brittany and the Vendée, and to establish their relationship with identical monuments in the British Isles, such as Stonehenge.[56] In an unpublished paper, *Sur les armes des anciens Gaulois et des nations voisines*, presented at the Académie des Inscriptions in 1734, Montfaucon once again returned to the idea of a Stone Age, but he did not modify his interpretation of Cocherel. Others, like his colleague, the Benedictine Jacques Martin, did state that the megalithic tomb of Cocherel was a double tomb, Gallic and Germanic, dating to the Migration period; one of the strong points in his argument was precisely that 'stone axes are therefore not at all the sign of great antiquity.'[57] It was for Caylus to give an overview on the question of megaliths, in the sixth volume of his *Recueil*, in the chapter devoted to Gallic antiquities. Caylus was better informed than his predecessors because he could refer to the works of local antiquaries, especially those of La Sauvagère and Président de Robien. He was, however, quick to distance himself from the views of his predecessors and informants who saw in the Carnac alignments Gallic structures, a Roman camp or the consequences of the 'great invasions' (or, according to the engineer Deslandes, a natural phenomenon):

Firstly the great number of these stones, which are in no way the work of a few years, proves our profound ignorance of the ancient ways of Gaul; for I am far from attributing these monuments to the ancient Gauls.

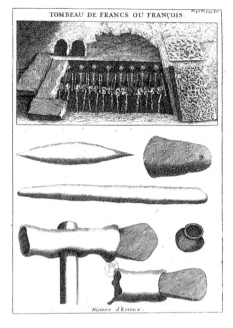

The Cocherel tomb, from *Religions celtes*, by Jacques Martin (1727).

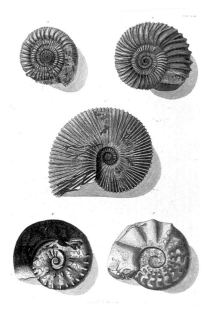

Fossil ammonites, a plate from a compendium of the wonders of nature by G.W. Knorr and J.E. Walch (1755).

I follow in this matter the opinion of M. de La Sauvagère; the monuments themselves attest that the Gauls can have no part in it, for it is a fact that being masters of the interior of the country they would have erected some of these stones in several parts of the continent, and they have only been found in some provinces situated on the coast, or at least not far away. Secondly, these stones suggest a well established cult, and we know the customs and religion of the Gauls well enough not to attribute to them this kind of superstition [...].

Thirdly, the arrangement of these rocks proves the desire of this nation (whatever it might have been) to pass into posterity. In fact, these monuments, very difficult to displace, and useless in every sense – for it would always be easier to take others like them from the earth than to throw down those which were set up, and which besides bore no ornament which might tempt the malice of men to destroy them – these monuments, I say, put me in mind to ask whether the most enlightened race could employ better or more certain means to leave testimony to their existence [...].

Fourthly, the number of stones placed on the coast of Brittany bears witness to the length of the sojourn made in this part of Gaul by peoples whose way of thinking was the same, at least in this respect; but it is simpler, and more in keeping with appearances, to agree that this kind of monument is the work of the same people. These reflections increase the singularity of the absolute silence which tradition itself has maintained on such repetitive usage; one can infer an antiquity even more remote than the time of the Romans, of which all trace is lost.[58]

Caylus could scarcely go further, except by inventing, half a century before the actuality, the idea of prehistory. Like Jussieu, he happened upon the idea of a long human history by a simple exercise of comparison and deduction – a history which was itself part of the history of nature. Buffon, in *Les Époques de la nature*,[59] had expressed beautifully that he did not have the solution to the question of continuity between human and natural history:

As in human history we consult books, and research among the coins and medals, and decipher ancient inscriptions to determine the timing of changes and the dates of events in intellectual history; in the same way in natural history we must dig into the archives of the earth, and pluck out the ancient materials from the entrails of the earth, pick up the debris, and assemble in one body of evidence all the indications of physical change which may allow us to go back to the different ages of nature. It is the only way of fixing some points in the immensity of that space, and of placing a certain number of milestones upon the eternal road of time.[60]

When, as Jussieu wrote, the material facts are also stages in human development, when man invents stone tools, then there is no longer any difference between human history and natural history. With the

prudence of someone who knew just what weight the interdicts of the theologians carried, Buffon suggested throughout his text that others might undertake in the field of human history what he had tried to do for the history of the earth and of animal species. No doubt his deep convictions were shared by Caylus, who wished to turn the antiquary into a physicist in the same way that Buffon suggested that the naturalist was an antiquary. Boulanger demonstrated the originality of his own thinking in taking up Lapeyrère's reasoning on the antiquity and diversity of men in the world:

This diversity of anecdotes [about the Flood] appears to hint that there were in various countries of the world men who survived these diverse accidents, which goes strongly against the Jewish tradition adopted by the Christians, who would have all the inhabitants of the present world descended from the survivors of the deluge, of which Moses spoke.[61]

All the same, if one is to believe a recent work by the German sociologist Wolf Lepenies,[62] one might think that Winckelmann, so much a child of the Enlightenment, would not have repudiated this

Discovery of the giant reptile in Maastricht in 1766, drawn by Faujas de Saint-Fond in 1799. In 1795, this French naturalist tried in vain to acquire the animal from Maastricht for six hundred bottles of wine. It was one of the greatest palaeontological discoveries of the eighteenth century.

In 1799 John Masten found some enormous fossil animal bones in peat bog. Charles Wilson Peale, a rich collector of natural curiosities, installed a wheel-driven drainage system on the site and discovered a mastodon. The site thus became a gathering-place for the curious of the entire east coast of the United States.

opinion – Winckelmann, who strove to establish a science of art founded upon a naturalist and evolutionist model, who, like Buffon, saw in style one of the mainstays of thought, and who was, according to Goethe, the first art historian to propose a hypothesis capable of being faked ... The drama of individualists like Buffon, Winckelmann and Caylus lay in their intuition of the revolution in human and natural history which was to take place during the nineteenth century, without access to the means of its execution: perhaps that is why we are still so receptive to their endeavours today.

1 Pintard 1983, pp. 358–9.
2 Lapeyrère 1656, *The Proeme*.
3 St Augustine, *The City of God*, XVIII, 40.
4 Ibid., XII, 10.
5 *Kazari*, I, pp. 60–1, cited by Popkin 1987, pp. 27–8.
6 Ibid., I, p. 67.
7 Maimonides 1970, III, XXIX, p. 222.
8 Hohenheim 1929, p. 186.
9 Popkin 1987, p. 35.
10 Bruno 1879, I, 2, p. 282.
11 Pintard 1983, p. 20.
12 Ibid., p. 359.
13 Lapeyrère 1732, p. 403.
14 Ibid., p. 426.
15 Worm 1751, 'Monsieur Peyrère, advisor to M. the ambassador of France at Christianopol', pp. 945–6.
16 Hooke 1705, pp. 408 and 412.
17 Ibid., p. 335.
18 Several editions of this text exist in diverse forms, of more or less equal length. This English edition is from 1748.
19 Hazard 1961, p. 24.
20 Marana 1748, Preface, p. xix.
21 See above, pp. 136–7.
22 Marana 1748, vol. VIII, Letter XII: 'to the venerable Mufti', p. 253.
23 Ménage 1694, II, p. 69.
24 See p. 128.
25 Gronovius 1694–1703, 13 volumes and *Thesaurus antiquitatum romanarum*, by J. G. Graevius, 1694–9, 12 volumes.
26 Bibliographical note by Montfaucon on his own works, in Broglie 1891, p. 321.
27 Montfaucon 1719, Supplement, Introduction, volume I.
28 Ibid., section III.
29 Ibid., volume I.
30 See pp. 36–7.
31 Nisard 1878, I, p. 4.
32 Ibid., p. 9.
33 Ibid., XXXVIII.
34 Caylus 1752, Foreword, I–II.
35 Ibid., VII–VIII.
36 Ibid., VIII.
37 Rocheblave 1889, p. 274.
38 Letter from Horace Walpole of 14 June 1740, from *Private Correspondence of Horace Walpole*, London, 1820, volume I, p. 67.
39 Zevi 1987, p. 15.
40 See the recent reassessment of this character by Antoine Schnapper, in Schnapper 1988, p. 291ff.
41 Schnapper 1988, p. 294.
42 Cited in Schnapper 1988, p. 295.
43 Pinon 1991, p. 42.
44 Ibid., p. 85.
45 La Sauvagère 1758.
46 Grignon 1774, pp. 96–8.
47 Letter to Berendis, in Holtzhauer 1969, p. 86, letter 17.
48 Letter from Choiseul–Gouffier to Fauvel, cited in Legrand 1897, p. 57.
49 Winckelmann 1880, volume I, pp. 289 and 293.
50 Mercati 1719 (see pp. 151–2).
51 Hamy 1906.
52 Jussieu, in Hamy 1906, p. 248. In 1728, in his *Fossiles of all Kinds Digested into a Method*, J. Woodward reached the same conclusion; part two, letter 39–40.
53 Montfaucon 1719, V, 2.
54 Ibid.
55 The precedence of bronze over iron is, however, a 'topic' of German archaeologists of the end of the seventeenth century: J.D. Major and Jacob Mellen, and indeed J.G. Eccard, clearly allude to it.
56 Montfaucon 1719, Supplement V, Book VII, chapter 3, p. 145ff.
57 Martin 1727, p. 317.
58 Caylus 1752, volume VI, pp. 386–7.
59 Buffon 1776.
60 Ibid., p. 3.
61 Boulanger 1756, VI, I, p. 296.
62 Lepenies 1986.

Megalithic Tomb, watercolour by Wilhelm Tischbein the younger, 1820. A talented painter, Johann Heinrich Wilhelm Tischbein (1751–1829) was a friend of Goethe. Like the latter he was interested in Graeco-Roman antiquities and drew the Greek vases in the collection of Sir William Hamilton. He devoted several paintings to man's ancient history, and was passionately interested in the survey and excavation of tumuli (see p. 291).

CHAPTER 5

THE
INVENTION OF
ARCHAEOLOGY

Here bring the last gifts! – loud and shrill
   Wail, death-dirge for the brave!
What pleased him most in life may still
   Give pleasure in the grave.
We lay the axe beneath his head
   He swung, when strength was strong –
The bear on which his banquets fed –
   The way from earth is long!
And here, new-sharpen'd, place the knife
   That sever'd from the clay,
From which the axe had spoil'd the life,
   The conquer'd scalp away!
The paints that deck the Dead, bestow –
   Yes, place them in his hand –
That red the Kingly Shade may glow
   Amidst the Spirit-Land!

FROM JOHANN CHRISTOPH FRIEDRICH VON SCHILLER, *THE INDIAN DEATH-DIRGE*, 1797.

Archaiologia, antiquitates, antiq-
uities: for over two thousand years these were the terms used to
describe the study of the material past in the West, and the men who
devoted themselves to this study were called 'antiquaries'. In the first
half of the nineteenth century a new term – archaeology – was
increasingly used, and this shift in vocabulary corresponded to a modification of the role and purpose of knowledge of the past. The scholars who explicitly asserted their archaeological credentials aimed to

View of the Valley of the Mississippi, John Egan, 1850. The tumuli of the Native American civilisations of the southern United States have formed one of the most debated subjects in American archaeology since Jefferson. The monumental grandeur of the Mississippi Valley is represented in a series of pictures created in 1850 by John Egan, a painter from Philadelphia, based on studies by Montorville W. Dickeson, explorer and excavator of the Mississippi burial mounds. Dickeson used these images painted on muslin to illustrate his lectures. The excavation is depicted realistically; particularly notable is the excellent rendition of the successive strata. Jefferson's influence is evident here.

create a new branch of knowledge which was not subservient to philology but embraced the entire material part of human history. In order to achieve this they undertook the construction of a specific tool for the classification of objects: typology. But typology alone could not provide a full framework for the reconstruction of the past. It was necessary to assign groups of objects and monuments to specific periods, and then to observe the soil, distinguish the layers and recognise the human activities of ancient times. To this end archaeologists salvaged the idea of stratigraphy, the foundations for which had been laid by geologists. Buffon had urged naturalists to behave like antiquaries; archaeologists themselves set out to approach the earth in the same way as the geologists. They thus discovered what Buffon had feared: that natural history and human history were one.

THE PRESUMPTION OF
MAN'S GREAT ANTIQUITY

ANTIQUARIES BETWEEN
THE FOG AND THE FLOOD

In the Humanist tradition – that of such men as Spon, Maffei or Montfaucon – the functional analysis of objects and monuments played only a secondary role. Educated by texts, and reared on classical culture, the Humanist antiquaries did not seek to interpret the function of remains *per se*. After all, it was sufficient to refer to tradition to know how baths, an amphitheatre or a triumphal arch were used, and Vitruvius was always there to offer helpful information.

As we have seen, it was different for the regional antiquaries, from Worm to Aubrey. Faced with the remains of the High Middle Ages or of prehistory, they had to confront the rigours of history *without* text. It was only with the greatest difficulty that Montfaucon himself could publish the megalithic burial at Cocherel, excavated in 1685 by a Norman gentleman of the same name.[1] And if, in a letter published as an appendix to his account, he made room for the observations of Jacques Christophe Iselin on the three-age sequence – stone, copper, iron – this was referred to only in passing, as if this revolutionary theory seemed to him a secondary matter. In short, the men of the Enlightenment were not ready to admit the consequences of what Caylus had so bravely suggested: the idea of a cultural history based on technological development. In itself the typological approach could not reveal its full virtues without being linked to the stratigraphic or technological study of objects. It was Legrand d'Aussy who, in a report to the Institut National in the year VII (1799), proposed not only the clearing of monuments, but their excavation:

The tombs must be opened because it is not just mineralogists who stand to gain from opening up and digging up the earth [...]. For archaeology and history too, there will often be found matter for observation and antiquities to gather.[2]

Legrand d'Aussy, as Annette Laming-Emperaire observed, was not just an explorer of the earth: he was undoubtedly one of the first in the eighteenth century to consider the problems of burials in an historical and geographical context. In an attempt to establish a

The Skeleton Cave, Caspar David Friedrich, 1803. This picture shows the artist's interest in archaeological landscapes. A friend of Goethe, Caspar David Friedrich (1774–1840) was the embodiment of German Romanticism.

chronology, he picked up the forgotten thread of Ole Worm's remarks on the means of distinguishing between funerary traditions. The Danish scholar had drawn on the difference between megaliths and tumuli in laying the foundations of a chronology of Scandinavian burials. Legrand d'Aussy continued his work in order to make a distinction between the Age of Fire, of which he believed Cocherel to be the prototype, and the Age of Mounds:

I have called the first period the primitive Age of Fire, and I will call the second the Age of Mounds. But since there are mounds which only contain burnt bodies [...] and others which only have complete bodies, such as those which I shall cite in a moment, I believe that we can further divide the mounds into two periods: mounds with burnt bodies, the second age of burial fashion; mounds with unburnt bodies, the third.[3]

The effort was not towards pure typology. To classify the tombs was also to attempt to construct a chronology. In this Legrand d'Aussy was clearly less at ease than his predecessors in Scandinavia or Germany, because he was less familiar with the terrain. But he was as aware as Caylus of the singularity of megaliths. Even if he did not, as the latter had, affirm that they could not be ascribed to the Gauls, he called them 'tombs of the first period of the nation', which dated back an 'immeasurable span of years'. Here was a modest observation which allowed us a giant step. The megaliths could no longer be considered as monuments which might be confused with those of the Gauls a few centuries before Caesar: Legrand d'Aussy recognised in

them an antiquity beyond the norms of traditional history. He had
had an intuition of the great span of history but nevertheless had not
got as far as deducing the existence of a prehistoric past because his
approach remained purely theoretical. He had certainly understood
the advantage the antiquary could gain from observation of the
earth, but he went no further than considerations which were as
ambitious as they were routine. Under the aegis of the Ministry of
Public Education he proposed a project aimed at keeping watch over
the landscape to prevent the destruction of burials, and organising
their excavation and study. He did not view the landscape with the
eyes of a treasure hunter; he envisaged having detailed plans made of
the monuments before beginning work on their excavation. He went
as far as to suggest keeping a detailed record of finds and measurements as in the manner of the samples entrusted to naturalists and
anatomists. He was as keen to display antiquities as he was anxious to
protect them, and he proposed nothing less than the setting up of an
archaeological section within Alexandre Lenoir's Museum of French
Monuments: an avant-garde project for a typological museum in
which each type of monument would be represented in strict order
by a full-scale model.

Well-versed in the writings of his leading antiquarian predecessors
(and especially those of Caylus), Legrand d'Aussy opened the way for
a modern practice of the antiquarian profession. For the first time
the fragility of archaeological monuments became the focus of attention, and for the first time means of protection and investigation
formed the object of a discussion on method which was no longer
limited to portable objects or the monuments in Graeco-Roman or
Eastern traditions. Antiquarian science took a global view of the
traces of human history. Legrand d'Aussy was also not afraid (and
here again he showed himself to be a disciple of Caylus) to emphasise
a national duty to protect and study monuments. Underlining the
special character of the Breton megaliths, he even proposed giving
them Breton names. As the last antiquary of the eighteenth century,
Legrand d'Aussy asserted that observation of the soil was a deeply
historical discipline; as the first archaeologist of the nineteenth, he
developed a programme for the disciplined professionalisation of
archaeological practice.

In the France of Napoleon and the Restoration the forward-
looking ideas of Legrand d'Aussy had to bide their time. Central
government seemed little interested in giving France an antiquities

service like those of Sweden, Denmark and even some German states, and the tradition of the aristocrat antiquary had stopped with Caylus. It was to reappear, to be sure, with such men as the Duc de Luynes; but he, like too many other French archaeologists of the period, was attracted by the Mediterranean world, and his contribution to the study of the antiquities of Gaul was limited. Legrand d'Aussy did not lack contemporaries and successors: August Louis Millin and his *Recueil des monuments pour servir à l'histoire générale et particulière de la France* (*Compilation of Monuments Useful for the General and Particular History of France*; 1790); Alexandre de

Plate from *Recueil des monuments antiques* (1817) by Grivaud de La Vincelle (1762–1819), a senate official. He was one of Caylus's successors, and an early exponent of the study of Gallo-Roman *terra sigillata* pottery.

Laborde and his *Monuments de la France classés chronologiquement* (*Monuments of France Listed Chronologically*; 1816–26); Grivaud de La Vincelle and his *Recueil des monuments antiques* (*Compilation of Ancient Monuments*; 1817) – contrasted with the works of those obsessed by the Celts, which dominated the output of French antiquaries at this time.[4] But their work was not that of men engaged in the everyday surveillance of the land, or in direct contact with the objects and monuments which emerged from the earth through building or other works.

France in the first half of the nineteenth century lacked observers of the earth; or rather, since the 'classic' antiquaries were mainly Parisians, cut off from the realities of the land, they did not play the role later to be undertaken by such newcomers as François Jouannet, Casimir Picard and Jacques Boucher de Perthes. The only antiquary of note to alter this attitude was to be a Norman, Arcisse de Caumont, the embodiment of a type of antiquary who had 'studied botany and geology before archaeology'.[5] Moreover, this turning point had not escaped Jules Michelet, who noticed that in Caen the history of antiquity and natural history proceeded together:

> *What struck me in Caen was that the same men, Caumont, Lair and Vaultier, were at the same time antiquaries and naturalists. My travelling-companion constantly mingled history with natural history. In fact, Caen reunited, on the one hand, Roman and Norman antiquities, on the other the antediluvian antiquities, fossils, etc.*[6]

Arcisse de Caumont was undoubtedly one of the most dedicated

Stratigraphic representation by James Douglas, from his *Nenia Britannica*, published in 1793. In the tradition established by Stukeley, Douglas combined his topographcial surveys with a stratigraphic vision of the landscape.

workers in French archaeology in the nineteenth century, as can be seen in his *Cours d'antiquités monumentales* (*Notes on Monumental Antiquities*), published in twelve volumes between 1830 and 1841. But his curiosity was directed more towards the Middle Ages and the urgent need to protect historic monuments than towards the more ancient periods. His vigorous advocation of the need to protect the past occupied much of his energy, which he directed towards the creation of learned societies and the establishment of a service for historic monuments. François Guizot's creation in 1834 of the Committee of Historic Works and the establishment of a public administration of monuments were largely due to his influence, even if this dedicated regionalist had often fallen out with the Parisian centralists, especially Prosper Mérimée. Arcisse de Caumont had an encyclopaedic knowledge of art history and was a man open to all the scientific currents of his time, a trait which linked traditional antiquaries with the archaeologists of the new generation. As Secretary of the Linnaean Society of Calvados, he stood for those antiquaries who wished to cross the bridge separating history from natural history, perhaps because, like Boucher de Perthes, he owed his training to the Abbé de La Rue — an emigrant priest who had brought back from England a confirmed taste for universal history.

During the first decades of the nineteenth century, in contrast to Germany and Great Britain, the soil of France remained little excavated. In Britain interest in the observation of the earth and in excavation had not ceased since Stukeley. The Revd Brian Faussett (1720–76) can be considered the record-holder among eighteenth-

century tomb-excavators. Driven by a kind of sacred ardour, he succeeded over a few years in 'opening' several hundred tumuli in Kent.[7]
He is a prime example of a particular circle of antiquaries who,
unable to indulge their passion through participation in the Grand
Tour, resorted to the exploration of regional antiquities. Undertaken
using methods that every contemporary archaeologist would con-
demn, Faussett's researches, which for a long time remained unpublished, gave his successors access to exceptional comparative material,
essentially of the Saxon period. James Douglas (1753–1819) was to
take up the torch. As an officer in the Royal Engineers, he began
with surveys of fortifications in Kent, which led him
to the discovery of Anglo-Saxon burials. Profiting
from his experience as a topographer and draughtsman, he made plans and sections of these graves. He
soon decided to publish a synthesis devoted to the
funeral practices of the Ancient Britons. Entitled
Nenia Britannica, it appeared in 1793. In his work, just
as in that of Faussett, the Romantic period of British
archaeology was declared, that of gentlemen enthused
by the opening of graves, who increasingly supplanted
the antiquaries of the Enlightenment.

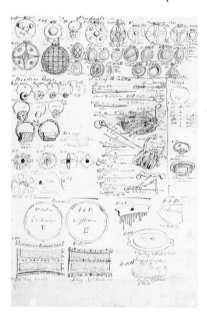

Series of objects
found in a medieval
tomb, drawn by
James Douglas, from
his *Nenia Britannica*
(1793). These finds
from Anglo-Saxon
graves are carefully
drawn. The
presentation
emphasises
Douglas's accuracy
and eye for detail.

Linked by their passionate enthusiasm, two men
embodied this new British archaeology: William Cunnington (1754–1810) and Sir Richard Colt Hoare
(1758–1838). Cunnington, a middle-class cloth merchant, and Colt Hoare, a rich and romantic baronet,
together encapsulated the spirit of England. In their
work they were accompanied by a good draughtsman, Philip
Crocker, and a team of workmen financed by Colt Hoare. With
them, grave-opening became a collective exercise, a professional
enterprise which sought to establish a particular quality of documentation based on plans and sections. Their curiosity went beyond
funerary archaeology: their intention was to found a regional archaeology. Work on the ground was preceded by preliminary survey, and
the excavation was supervised by Cunnington and his team. In 1808
Colt Hoare embarked upon the publication of a comprehensive
monograph, which was published between 1810 and 1822. With its
plans, exact surveys and regional dimension, *The History of Ancient
Wiltshire* was more than a simple catalogue of excavations, it was a
considered study of the archaeology of a region. Colt Hoare liked to

Richard Colt
Hoare and William
Cunnington
supervising the
excavation of a
barrow on Salisbury
Plain. Watercolour by
Philip Crocker, 1807.

think of himself as a true historian and, against Celtomaniacs of all kinds, declared 'we speak from facts, not theories'. He linked the passion for archaeology with a desire for understanding. For him excavations answered a precise question, 'to ascertain to which of the successive inhabitants of this island they [the prehistoric antiquities] are to be ascribed'. After ten years of work he could nevertheless return to the evidence and admit 'total ignorance as to the authors of these sepulchral memorials; we have evidence of the very high antiquity of our Wiltshire barrows, but none respecting the tribes to whom they appertained, that can rest on solid foundations'.[8] Proof was necessary in order to escape chronological uncertainty. In the absence of a comparative analysis of finds based on well-described assemblages, the prize could not be won and Colt Hoare, like Montfaucon, could draw little by way of positive conclusion from a cautious suggestion offered by one of his correspondents, the Revd Thomas Leman:

> I think we distinguish three great eras by the arms of offence found in our barrows. First those of bone and stone, certainly belonging to the primeval inhabitants in their savage state, and which may be safely attributed to the Celts. Second those of brass probably imported into this island from the more polished nations of Africa in exchange for our tin, and which may be given to the Belgae. Third those of iron, introduced but a little while before the invasion of the Romans.[9]

To make good use of these original thoughts it was necessary to develop a technique for the study of associated artefacts. Cunnington and Colt Hoare had little idea of how to go about this. It was also necessary to develop a procedure of recording the finds, the importance of which the Revd Leman, himself a collector, stressed in a letter to Cunnington:

You will excuse me I am sure when I take the liberty of pointing out to you the necessity of immediately pasting a small piece of paper on every piece of pottery, *or* coin *that you may hereafter find, describing with accuracy the very spot in which you find them. The people who succeed us, may probably know more about these things than we do, (or else I am confident that they will know but little) but we ought to ... afford* them *the Information we can, with clearness.*[10]

We can be sure that had Colt Hoare been able to take advantage of these complementary remarks, his work would have gained a demonstrable force which it lacks. But, as a gentleman, he had the courage of his convictions, and his conclusion resounds as a verdict on the era of the antiquaries: 'How grand! How wonderful! How incomprehensible!'[11]

Legrand d'Aussy had a synthesising mind which tried passionately to impose order on the antiquarian hotchpotch, while Colt Hoare and Cunnington had the powers of observation and enthusiasm for the land. But all three lacked the necessary means of relating material to the layers that made up the earth. For the study of the past to escape the vicious circle to which belief in a short chronology had confined it, it was necessary, as Rasmus Nyerup said, 'to pierce the thick mist' of time. Interest in stratigraphy was to lead, through its application to the question of human origins, to the discovery of a time-span so long that it would have to be termed 'prehistoric'. Certain seventeenth-century precursors, beginning with Lapeyrère, had created a belief in a long history for mankind. After all, hadn't Mercati, at the end of the sixteenth century, established that the 'thunderbolts' were tools, evidence of ancient human industry? But where did the boundary separating the old from the very old begin? Pioneers of research on fossils, such as Nicolas Steno or Agostino Scilla, had demonstrated some time before that the history of the earth revealed a very long process of geological formation. However, Mercati's ideas were echoed by William Dugdale in the middle of the seventeenth century.[12] Hadn't Robert Plot, in his *Natural History of Stafford-shire* (1686), affirmed that he had found flints which dated to a most ancient period? The brilliant theologian and geologist John Woodward – had he not, a few years later, held up to derision those who still believed in the natural origin of the 'thunderbolts'? As to the theoreticians on the history of customs, like Goguet and de Pauw,[13] they looked firmly to the men of the Enlightenment to trace an evolutionary picture of the earliest human history, where worked flints appeared prominently.

The most enquiring antiquaries could not fail to direct their attention to the discoveries which, following the example of Cocherel, attested to the existence of a worked stone industry that pointed to the great antiquity of mankind. In 1715 a London bookseller, John Bagford, described a flint point discovered in a London gravel pit, 'like a British weapon made of a flint point in a shaft of good length'.[14]

However, the discovery of an elephant (without doubt a mammoth) in an adjacent deposit led the antiquary to attribute the flint and the animal to the time of the Roman conquest. This clever solution allowed him to avoid the bolder hypothesis of certain of his contemporaries, who saw in the elephant skeleton proof of the biblical Flood. In 1797 John Frere, High Sheriff of Suffolk and later a member of Parliament, discovered a series of worked flints associated with animal remains in a Suffolk brick-earth quarry and did not hesitate to attribute them 'to a very remote period indeed; even beyond that of the present world'.[15] Not content with exact description of the position of his discovery, Frere added to his commentary a stratigraphic description of the find and a section of the deposit.

Despite his evidence and a publication in the journal of the Society of Antiquaries of London, Frere's spectacular discovery did not, at the time, give rise to any particular debate. After all, without directly questioning biblical chronology, great minds from the eighteenth century onwards had tried to identify the men contemporary with the Flood. In 1708 a Swiss doctor, Johann Jacob Scheuchzer, published a strange lampoon in defence of the fossil fish that had been victims of the Flood instead of men, but which were considered by men to be stones. And among these he produced a human skeleton as evidence of the Flood, which, a century later, Cuvier identified as a salamander.[16] More seriously, in 1774 a pastor of Erlangen, Johann Friedrich Esper, explored the Bayreuth caves in which he discovered a rich harvest of animal fossils mixed with worked flints and human remains.[17] He was convinced that he had found in the earth a material trace of the Flood.

Worked flint, found by John Frere in 1797. Plate from the journal *Archaeologia*, 1800.

Esper was aware of the originality of his discovery, but he had no available means of dating, nor any reference system which would allow him to analyse the animal remains. As Donald Grayson emphasises, the association of fossil animals with human remains posed no problem for him, since he could not determine the age of the fauna.

Although attestations of the great antiquity of mankind were accumulating, the learned world was not yet ready to admit to it. For the concept of continuity between human and natural history to be established, antiquaries not only had to increase their observations, they had to be able to relate these to the history of the earth and a history of species to which geologists and palaeontologists were applying themselves at the turn of the century. Georges Cuvier in France and William Buckland in Great Britain were to give geology the chronological means which it lacked. The work of each, in their supporting evidence, helped to prove that it was possible to consider human history as part of the history of the earth. Adopting Buffon's image, Cuvier saw geologists as the antiquaries of nature:

They have dug in the ruins of the globe to discover the monuments of its physical history, as the antiquaries dig in the ruins of cities to discover the monuments of the history of arts and the customs of the peoples who inhabited them.[18]

As a zealous antiquary, he applied himself to the collection and description of a vast quantity of animal fossils, so as to attribute them to well-defined strata and thus to lay the foundations of a general stratigraphy of extinct species. Cuvier's prodigious anatomical and stratigraphic work offered palaeontologists chronological markers which facilitated comparison between different sites and the geological profiles which distinguished them. Cuvier thus established an indissoluble link between the types of animal fossils and the strata which contained them: each type could be assigned to a defined geological formation. Systematically, and with tenacity, Cuvier offered naturalists the object of their dreams: a clock which allowed them to date the ages of the universe. At the same time the English geologist and theologian William Buckland increased his studies of the

Entrance to the cave at Gailenreuth and mandible of cave bear, drawings from a work by J.F. Esper published in 1774. Esper found fossil animal bones and human bones while exploring caves in Bayreuth. His drawings are of very high quality, but the accompanying anatomical descriptions are rather vague.

Opposite:
Traces of the Flood, a plate from *Physica sacra* by Johann Jacob Scheuchzer (1731). Scheuchzer's contribution to the analysis of fossil landscape features attracted the attention of the geologists. In 1708 Scheuchzer thought he had discovered a fossil man at Altdorf, but in 1812 Cuvier proved this to be a salamander.

Fig. 1

unexplored

Ground Plan of the Cave

Lead Vein

chronology and stratigraphy of caves
and his palaeontological, stratigraphic
and chronological observations. Cuvier
and Buckland thus opened the way
for a rigorous study of the association
between human remains and fossil
fauna; but paradoxically they were at
odds over the contemporaneity of
man and the extinct animals:

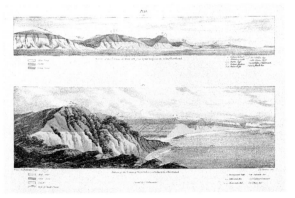

*Never, at least to our knowledge, have
human bones been found in the usual
strata of the earth, as those belonging to quadrupeds have been encountered. Human remains which have been found lay either in loose soil, or
in caves where they might have been carried by carnivorous animals, or
finally in ossiferous crevasses among fissured rock where they could have
been swept by landslides or other accidents. It is thus logical to think that
man did not appear on earth until after the other classes of mammal, just
as is expressed in the Book of Moses.*[19]

Stratigraphic sections
of the Dorset and
Devon coasts, from
Reliquae diluvianae
(1823).

It was to be less than twenty years before, on the basis of the same
principles as those of the two great geologists, the antiquity of man
was definitively accepted.

THE DIFFICULT EMERGENCE
OF THE IDEA OF CONTINUITY
Type, technology, stratigraphy

Cuvier's unwillingness to accept the great antiquity of man stemmed
from his 'catastrophism', his firmly-established conviction that fossil
species had disappeared suddenly as a result of a diluvial catastrophe.
Nevertheless, in Paris, Jean-Baptiste Lamarck had suggested that the
history of animal species could be far better accommodated by
another hypothesis, that of transformation. If we could find in the
earth the remains of animal species which were today extinct, it
might relate to the fact that these species were progressively transformed: the transformation of living beings seemed more certain and
verifiable than catastrophism. For those who argued for the continuity of man and nature, Lamarck's ideas offered a fertile source of
inspiration. Goethe's reaction to a debate which opposed Cuvier and
Etienne Geoffroy Saint-Hilaire at the Académie des Sciences of Paris

Opposite, above:
Section through the
Paviland cave, found in
1822. Drawing from
Buckland's *Reliquae
diluvianae* (1823). This
very precise drawing
shows that the human
skeleton (known as the
'Red Lady') was found
in sediments in which
fossil animal bones
were numerous.
However, Buckland
regarded it as an
intrusive deposit and
rejected it as proof of
the existence of a fossil
human being.

Opposite, below:
Rhinoceros skeleton
found in a cave in a
mine at Callow.
Drawing from
Buckland's *Reliquae
diluvianae* (1823).
The excavation
methods shown here
were quite meticulous
for the period.

in July 1830 bears witness to this. On 2 August of that year Soret, one of the tutors of the Prince of Weimar, was asked by Goethe, 'What do you think of the great event? The volcano has begun to erupt ...' Soret replied, 'It is a terrible story, but what can one expect of a government like this in a situation of this kind if not the exile of the royal family?' But Goethe was not interested in the abdication of Charles X:

We don't understand each other, dear friend, I'm not talking about those people; my subject is quite different. I'm talking of the quarrel which is so important for science which has just publicly opposed Cuvier and Geoffroy Saint-Hilaire at the Academy.[20]

No one could accuse Goethe of a lack of historical sensibility, but in the last days of July 1830 the catastrophism–transformation battle seemed to him much more decisive for history than the misfortunes of Charles X.[21] Goethe, an admirer of Winckelmann, embodied a rare curiosity which allied a taste for ancient art with unravelling the secrets of nature. His interest in geology and his anatomical discoveries made him attentive to all the debates on evolution. As a fieldworker who had participated in numerous excavations on the territory of the Grand Duchy of Weimar,[22] he was a strong supporter of the transformation theory because he believed, like Herder, 'that the animals are the older brothers of men'. This expert dabbler in all and sundry, this mind of insatiable curiosity, embodied the antiquary in the best sense of the term. With his friends Heyne and Meyer, and in the steps of Winckelmann, he had opened the way to a rediscovery of antique art, whilst his passion for natural history made him one of the forerunners of human palaeontology. Goethe's unflagging interest in human and animal anatomy, his taste for old junk – be it classical or prehistoric – perfectly symbolise the limits of the antiquaries' knowledge at the start of the nineteenth century. Like Colt Hoare and Cunnington he came up against the problem of chronology, and like them he had not the wherewithal to establish a periodisation of the remains which formed a sort of compact mass, impossible to put in order in the absence of a typological method. To break the deadlock it was necessary to combine geological

Portrait of Georges Cuvier, by Marie-Nicolas Ponce-Camus.

information with the comparative study of artefacts. The tradition of eighteenth-century antiquaries offered no preparation for this sort of exercise. Johann Gustav Büsching (1783–1829), the tireless explorer of Silesia's past, was an excellent example. Despite his desire to dissect every tumulus he found, despite the care with which he conducted excavations, his recourse to sieving of the spoil heaps,[23] it was impossible for him to begin to pierce the mists of chronology for the 'pagan period'. Romantic Germany, like England at the start of the nineteenth century, was full of enthusiastic antiquaries. Perhaps it was this very sense of a national past, so highly developed in the pastors of the eighteenth century, that became a national passion for a middle-class traumatised by the Napoleonic conquest. Was not Ernst Moritz Ardnt to write, 'We, the people of Germany, feel a

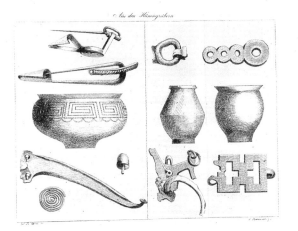

Protohistoric antiquities from a German collection. Drawing by Wilhelm Tischbein, 1808. In 1808, at the instigation of Duke Peter von Oldenburg, Tischbein visited a private collection in Eutin. His drawings were published by F.J.L. Meyer in 1816.

nostalgia analogous to that of the deer which snort in the Spring for setting out in search of our history'?[24] This enthusiasm, which was responsible for a huge increase in the number of excavations and archaeological museums, and which led to the development of new techniques of investigating the soil, ran into a fog, was blocked by belief in a Flood, just as had happened in Great Britain. This undoubtedly explains the lack of interest, and even the critical stance of the German archaeologists towards the Three Age theory, which seemed to them to obscure the central problem of ante-historic archaeology: the ethnic question.

Goethe, Vulpius, Büsching and of course Lindenschmidt, founder of the Römisch-Germanische Zentral Museum at Mainz, had contributed to create, like Colt Hoare and Legrand d'Aussy, the framework for a descriptive method — what may be termed an

Fossil bones and tools found in caves near Liège. Plate from Philippe-Charles Schmerling's book, 1833–4.

Tom. 2. Pl. XXXVI.

abilities of these three researchers enabled them within a few years to discover and publish material from several caves in which fossil fauna were associated with the remains of human activity. The Montpellier team constituted the first intellectual group to engage in the affirmation of the very great antiquity of mankind. The three friends published the results of their excavations and adhered absolutely to their identification of fossil animals and their analysis of flints,[30] not afraid, it seems, of boldly affirming their conclusions:

The geology which supplements our short annals will come to reawaken human pride in showing the antiquity of our race. For only geology can from henceforth give us some idea of the period of the first appearance of man on earth.[31]

As a consequence of this prophetic declaration of faith, and despite the reputation of Marcel de Serres, these results were not accepted by the majority of geologists and palaeontologists, especially after Cuvier's total opposition. Nevertheless, in stating that one must set out from 'present processes', from observation of contemporary geological phenomena, Tournal largely anticipated the uniformitarian geology of Lyell and the prehistory of Boucher de Perthes.[32] In discarding the idea of the Flood, so dear to the first prehistorians, he laid the foundations of belief in the continuity between ancient and modern times, between prehistoric and modern man.[33] A physician from Liège, Dr Schmerling, published in 1833 a volume entitled *Recherches sur les ossements fossiles découverts dans les cavernes de la province de Liège* (*Researches on the Fossil Bones Discovered in the Caverns of the Province of Liège*), which reached the same conclusions as his predecessors in Montpellier. Nevertheless, the learned world was still not convinced of the great antiquity of mankind ...

THE THREE AGE MODEL AND THE FOUNDATION OF COMPARATIVE ARCHAEOLOGY

For more than a century, above all since Aubrey and Caylus, intelligent minds had realised that it was possible to classify the remains of the past through using the intrinsic characteristics of these to order them in time. This method, common to anti-quaries and geologists, had not only drastically changed geology at the beginning of the nineteenth century, but had led equally to enormous progress in the field of historical, classi-cal and, soon, Near Eastern archaeology.

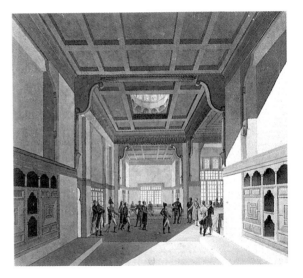

View of the great hall of the Institut d'Egypte, drawn by Protain in 1798. The Institut was inaugurated by Bonaparte.

From these beginnings nineteenth-century archaeological curiosity was not confined to geologists and palaeon-tologists but stretched to encompass the entire eastern Mediterranean. It certainly touched Greece, where the struggle for independence had mobilised European opinion and towards which an ever-increasing number of travellers were flocking, inflamed by the ideas of Winckelmann and the poems of Goethe, Hölderlin and Byron. Besides, this dreamt-of Greece was there to be admired in the galleries of the great museums of Europe. In purchas-ing the Parthenon friezes from Lord Elgin and putting them on public display, the British Museum led the way. There had been long battles before the *cognoscenti* were prepared to accept that these were Greek originals and not Roman copies, but once the matter was cleared up a true fervour for Greek art gripped the European bour-geoisie. This appetite for Greece was only just equalled by another passion, more exotic but quite as strong – that for Egypt. For millen-nia, ever since Herodotus, the mystery of Egypt had intrigued

Dominique Vivant
Denon measuring
the sphinx, from
*Voyage pittoresque dans
la Basse et Haute
Egypte*, by Vivant
Denon, 1802.

Opposite:
Frontispiece of Edme
Jomard's *Recueil des
observations et des
recherches qui ont été
faites en Egypte pendant
l'expédition de l'armée
française*, 1809–22.

Europe, but after the Arab invasion in the seventh century relations
were strained with an empire which, for the Greeks and Romans, was
one of the pillars of culture and religion, the model of a barbarian
wisdom without which the classical world could not have been
achieved. What was generally known of the ancient Egyptians were
the pyramids, the hieroglyphs – which since Cristoforo Buondelmonti's discovery in 1420 had attracted all the eager minds of the
learned world – and the mummies. With the expedition to Egypt and
the dozens of scientists who accompanied Bonaparte, Egypt became
as attractive as Greece. The various publications – notably the sumptuous *Expédition d'Egypte* published by an unrivalled organiser, Edme
Jomard – inspired an 'Egyptian style', which influenced architecture
as much as the plastic arts. Added to this the country, under the direction of a reforming monarch, Muhammad Ali, opened itself up to
western influences. The time of the lone explorer or bold merchant
who for centuries had been the only Europeans to travel in Egypt
was gone. Now came the engineers, diplomats and adventurers who
worked in the service of the kingdom and the two colonial powers,
England and France. Despite their defeat, the French retained a firm
presence in Egypt. The Consul General of France, Bernardin
Drovetti, who had been nominated by Napoleon, knew how to curry
favour with the authorities. He made the most of this by occupying
his numerous leisure hours with undertaking excavations and establishing a fabulous collection, destined for Europe. Henry Salt, the
English consul, worked to the same end, but with the prestige and
support of the victorious power. He rapidly enlisted the assistance of
Giovanni Belzoni, a colourful personality – adventurer, entrepreneur

and soon one of the most effective collectors of Egyptian antiquities, this giant had begun his career as a circus strong-man. There was no point in expecting from these excavators on a large scale the same precision or taste for knowledge as that of the landscape antiquaries of the eighteenth century. These men were the successors of Elgin and Choiseul-Gouffier, heirs of the expeditious methods of Fauvel and Lusieri. But they inundated the European museums with Egyptian objects. Drovetti was to sell no fewer than three collections: one to Turin, another to Paris, and the last to Berlin. Belzoni turned himself into a kind of Egyptological entrepreneur. In London in 1821 he opened the Egyptian Hall, an exhibition of Egyptian works which attracted great crowds. To the enthusiasm of governments and the audacity of adventurers was added a third element which succeeded in swaying opinion: a young and romantic scientist had just found the key to the decipherment of hieroglyphs. For four centuries hieroglyphs had seemed an unfathomable mystery of symbols. In demonstrating that they were a system of writing, and in establishing the pattern of development from this system to the demotic alphabet – in recognising in ancient Egyptian the language of the Christians of Egypt – Jean-François Champollion revealed to Europe a new world of knowledge. His discovery, which was contemporary with that of the decipherment of the cuneiform script, had much more impact because it resolved a problem which had exercised scholars for so many decades, and because it arrived just in time to allow the discoveries of the heirs to the Egyptian expedition to bear fruit. From the standpoint of the history of knowledge, the decipherment of the Egyptian language coincided with the apogee of modern methods of classical philology. Having laid the foundations of a comparative philology which revitalised the heritage of the Renaissance, the philologists successfully tackled the languages of the ancient East. Champollion's success was a stroke of genius, but it had been prepared for by the development of philological methods and their application to the Eastern languages: Abbé Barthélemy with Palymrian, and Sylvestre de Sacy with Old Persian had opened the way. In demonstrating that the hieroglyphs could no longer hold out against the knowledge of philologists, Champollion gave Orientalism the right to become a separate branch of knowledge. From this point on the entire Near East was open for archaeological exploration.

However, it was northern Europe which launched a model which was to revolutionise archaeology just as much as the decipherment of

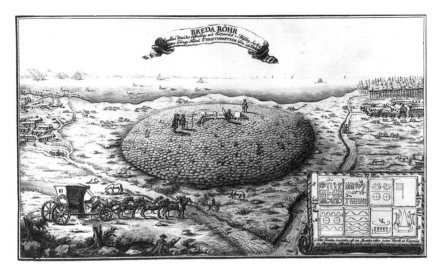

The Bronze Age tomb of Kivik, Sweden. On the lower right are depicted the carved designs from the funerary chamber. This is one of Scandinavia's most famous megalithic monuments.

hieroglyphs had transformed Orientalism. Christian Jürgensen Thomsen was the first archaeologist (in 1819) to design a museum around the stone–bronze–iron succession; above all he was the most determined advocate of the need for technological as well as typological comparison between archaeological and ethnographic objects.

Father Louis Hennepin, in his description of Louisiana in 1683, had already drawn on this type of observation, and there had even been a Danish Humanist, Johann Laverentzen, who suggested the usefulness of ethnography in the interpretation of archaeological objects.[34] But not until Thomsen were such suggestions put into practice: 'The experience demonstrates that comparable conditions and, in particular, an equivalent cultural level lead to equivalent instruments to produce the necessities [of life].'[35] In giving such precise expression to the law of cultural similarity, Thomsen added to the typological rules of Caylus a means of analysing objects which was not only descriptive but technical and laid the foundations of a prehistory which was no longer dependent upon texts:

It seems evident to me that at an early period all of northern Europe was inhabited by very similar primitive races. That they correspond to the North American savages seems to me certain in several respects. They were warlike, lived in forests, and possessed little or no metal.[36]

This first picture of a preliterate, prehistoric Europe coincided with the revelation of the great antiquity of humanity. Thomsen's originality did not just lie in his justification of the old Three Age model which, with occasional eclipses, had inspired philosophers, historians and antiquaries ever since antiquity. It was also evident in the practical consequences which he drew from this model – establishing a chronology which would be the basis of an exposition accessible to all. The importance of the method he proposed could be verified empirically in the galleries of the new Copenhagen museum. The revolution in chronology in European archaeology was born within a museum which, at the time, was the most complete tool for understanding the prehistoric past of Europe. Strengthened by their long tradition, the Scandinavian antiquaries had understood, ahead of their British, German and central European colleagues, that the exploration of the past required a new format which could not be confused with the cabinet of curiosities or the art museum: the museum of comparative archaeology. At the time no European museum could offer collections as full as those in Copenhagen. In 1836 Thomsen published his *Guide to Northern Antiquities*, but his system had already been elaborated and put into practice ten years earlier, when he was working on the ordering of his collections.

Development of Bronze Age ornament in Scandinavia, from Thomsen's *Guide to Nordic Antiquities*, 1836.

A museum man, Thomsen was set apart from his contemporaries because he sought to organise not single objects but the assemblages to which he had had access as a result of his role as secretary to the Commission of Antiquities of the kingdom of Denmark. With the help of young collaborators and the Danish army, he had undertaken excavations on the island of Bornholm. Some time later he organised an excavation of the site of Hvidegaard in Zealand. It was a well-preserved Bronze Age burial, and he ensured the most accurate results possible through entrusting the analysis of the organic remains to competent naturalists. The quality of excavation and the precision of the report published a few years later[37] attested to his qualities of observation. Thomsen's system was not a theoretical model spontaneously thrown together on its author's intuition, but the product of minute descriptions of assemblages, systematically compared one with the other. The essential obstacle to a bronze–iron succession lay in the fact that the Iron Age assemblages had both bronze and iron objects. Thomsen pointed out that Iron Age finds were characterised by the use of iron cutting-tools. In moving on from the analysis of the single object to the assemblage, Thomsen discovered the combinatorial method which allowed him, on the basis of increasingly large groups, to arrive at a general chronology:

The great stone-chambered tombs seem to have been constructed at a time when the first metals were gradually and slowly beginning to be used in Scandinavia. Mainly, we have only found in their interior, as already noted, unburnt bodies, often with coarse urns, rarely metal objects and in all these instances a little bronze or gold but never iron or silver, but most times only stone objects and simple amber ornaments.[38]

To construct such a chronology it was not enough to pay attention to the different types of objects; it was vital to establish the necessary associations, and to be assured of the quality of the observations which had validated them. Antiquaries who were sufficiently in control of assemblages to establish reliable associations were few and far between until Thomsen. His need to organise things in series and his attention to the landscape had led him to discover one of the cardinal principles of archaeological chronology. Thomsen's role in the development of Scandinavian prehistory was not only that of a formidable innovative thinker. He was also an organiser and keen advocate of landscape archaeology who did not hesitate, strengthened by his experience as a self-taught businessman, to organise, mobilise and convince. For the Danish society which sought confirmation of its coherence in the past, he knew how to offer a convincing picture of the origins of Denmark. The public crowded his museum, which he opened up to them with his unflagging good will. Thomsen knew how to inspire a vocation, and in particular he won the close collaboration of a young man who was to become his prestigious successor: Jen Jacob Worsaae. The latter was only fifteen when he began to frequent the museum and take part in the excavations. At twenty, Worsaae published his first excavation report which confirmed Thomsen's system; three years later he completed a synthesis which established itself as the most ambitious handbook of Scandinavian prehistory, *Danemarks Oldtid (Danish Antiquity)*. In a more polished style than that of his master, based on new excavations and a more exact

„Det første antiquariske Fund. Efter Nogles Beretning var det en Fyrrepind, men gamle paalidelige Koner i Jellinge have forsikret mig, at det var et Sværd".
(Minørmester Møller, Worsaae, Herbst, Steffensen).

A group of Danish archaeologists at work in Jelling, as seen by J. Kornerup, 1861: 'The first archaeological find was, after some discussion, thought to be a poker; but some old women of Jelling who were trustworthy assured me that it was a sword.'

chronology, he revealed to thousands of readers that it was possible to write a history *before* history, which could satisfy all the demands of establishing proof as well as being highly readable. But Worsaae did not stop at Scandinavian archaeology. He soon launched into a series of travels in England and Ireland which led to the publication of a book on Nordic civilisation in England, Scotland and Ireland and which was the first synthesis devoted to a comparative analysis of Nordic peoples in European prehistory. With Worsaae, and thanks to the Three Age theory, knowledge of the past could free itself from the weight of tradition. While drawing on written sources the archaeologist could employ a tool which enabled him to organise the finds in time. He was not afraid to search for missing information among the geologists and zoologists. Worsaae proved the worth of his system by resolving a Scandinavian problem through the application of his comparative method. Works on the coast of Jutland in 1848 had uncovered a massive heap of oyster shells mixed with flint and bone fragments. Assisted by the zoologist Japetus Steenstrup and the geologist Johann Georg Forchhammer, Worsaae addressed the problem and the three researchers soon demonstrated that these were cooking remains from the Stone Age:

In holding to the theory that oysters are found nowhere in the area around Mejlgaard except within the heap that I have described, which is very closely defined, and that the archaeological objects were dispersed in its interior at the same time as the charcoal and the animal bones, one cannot but think that at an early prehistoric period, when the shoreline was close to this deposit, there was a sort of canteen for the local populace. This would explain the cooking equipment, the charcoal, the animal bones and the flint blades (to open the oysters). [39]

In identifying the 'kitchen midden' (*Kjokkenmoddinger*), Worsaae did not simply answer an archaeological enquiry. He demonstrated that a multi-disciplinary approach to the finds and an effective excavation could allow the prehistorian to resolve an archaeological problem without recourse to written sources. It thus became possible to confront the problems of relative chronology for the Stone Age. How did the 'kitchen midden' relate to the civilisation of the Scandinavian megaliths?

In the accumulations of oysters, the flints are generally of a particular type, very rough; the same goes for the pottery, and one also finds bone objects of a particular class in great numbers. By contrast, the flints, stone tools, pottery, amber ornaments and other finds from the megalithic graves are much more developed and show a different method of manufacture.[40]

Step by step, with their characteristic quiet tenacity, the Scandinavian archaeologists (the Swedes soon joined the Danes in their work on prehistory) contributed towards the exploration, on ever more solid foundations, of the origins of mankind. Their progress, linked to close observation of the landscape, allowed the establishment of an evolutionary model which opened the way for a more general consideration of the history of the first human societies. Their success, which was more advanced than that of their English or French contemporaries, was undoubtedly founded on the fact that they announced their findings in the name of a discipline which was more readily accepted because it had been recognised since the seventeenth century as one of the components of national history. But they also held to the fact that the Three Age theory was born at the heart of antiquarian knowledge, certainly still diffuse but well defined. Elsewhere in Europe antiquaries had to take the critical step and appropriate the tools of the natural sciences to affirm a new discipline which united the two cultures, natural and Humanist. Of course in Scandinavia Thomsen had had his critics. But these were nothing in comparison with the storms raised by the explorers of man's antiquity in France and Great Britain. However, adversity had its benefits. The ferocious polemic which tore the scientific world apart, and the need to establish the finds by precise and incontrovertible observations, led prehistorians to pick up on all the arguments developed by their predecessors and to propose a stratigraphic, technological and typological analysis of remains:

It is not only the form and material of the object which serves to establish its great antiquity [...]. Further, it is its position; it is its depth from the surface; it is also that of the overlying layers and the debris which composed them; finally it is the certainty that here is its original soil, the earth trodden by the artisan who made it.[41]

What the founding fathers of prehistory gave to modern archaeology derived from a triangle of reciprocal relations: type, technology and stratigraphy. From these three concepts was to emerge the archaeological positivism which would give archaeology its scientific foundations.

THINKING OF ARCHAEOLOGY
AS A NATURAL SCIENCE

THE PHILOLOGICAL MODEL
Gerhard and the Instituto di Corrispondenza

With the idea of a natural history of mankind, through contact with geologists and zoologists and, soon, under the aegis of Darwin, pre-historians of the nineteenth century contrived to lay the foundations of a global prehistory, which is at the root of modern archaeology. However, the debate opened in the sixteenth century by Antonio Agostino continued. During the whole of the first half of the nine-teenth century classical archaeologists sought to free themselves from the influence of the world of collectors and artists, and strove to get archaeology, the twin sister of philology but decidedly independent, recognised as legitimate through an academic institution. In publishing his archaeological precepts in the *Archäologische Zeitung* in 1850, Eduard Gerhard, a militant advocate of a rational and historical archaeology, pleaded both for the independence of archaeology and for affirmation of its philological nature:

The study of the monuments of classical antiquity must begin with this literary knowledge on which rests that which one calls in a narrow sense philology. The archaeologist devotes himself to the monumental component by starting from philological evidence. All kinds of amateurs of antiquities unite to procure for him the primary material for his studies, just like the artists who advise and enlighten him. This dependence of the archaeologist on the amateurs of antiquities and the artists which has often led to the reprehensible development of what one might call antiquarian dilettantism [...] poses many problems.[42]

Since the Renaissance, with the development of collections, and as a result of Winckelmann's inspired work, Graeco-Roman antiquities had become not only objects of enquiry, status symbols – indeed a means of enrichment – but also the school of an aesthetic which considered Graeco-Roman civilisation to be unsurpassable. In seeking to free himself from 'antiquarian dilettantism', from philosophical symbolism and from the adulatory aesthetics of the men of the eighteenth century, Gerhard had to accept without questioning the precepts of German philology. It was a matter of replacing intuitive reverence for antiquity with something more reasoned but just as absolute:

To develop a philological archaeology it is not necessary to adapt its methods to the needs of amateurs of antiquities or artists - although it is recommended to involve them - but it must be founded on a close relation with philological teaching in its entirety [...]. If the philologists, following their aesthetic inclinations, remain distanced from the arts of the ancients, they forget that the antique monuments are of interest not just to themselves, but are indispensable sources for the understanding of antiquity.[43]

Antiquaries at work, by Giovan Battista Passeri, an enthusiast of things Etruscan, 1767.

Gerhard had to battle on two fronts: against the antiquaries of the old school, who were more concerned with the form of objects than with their evolution, and against those philologists, who in the style of Theodor Mommsen, took archaeologists for the illiterates of history. This was a social paradox which tended to narrow the scientific and technological horizons of classical archaeology, engaging it in an unequal contest with philology in order to give it an equivalent apparatus of scholarship. For the project of Gerhard and his contemporaries was to transform the science of the antiquaries into a science of antiquity – a semantic shift more important than it seemed, since it would lead to the creation of new types of institution.

Yet again it was in Rome that everything was to begin; the city was the merry-go-round of the learned. Whilst English travellers were more numerous in Greece, German professors felt at home in Rome. The way had been opened by a Dane, Georg Zoëga, who established himself as an archaeologist in 1784 and soon became the Danish Consul General. Then, in the procession of Prussian diplomatic representatives to Rome, came the glories of German intellect: Wilhelm von Humboldt (1802–08), the Roman historian Barthold Niebuhr (1816–23), joined once by the traveller and collector Jacob Bartholdy (in 1818), and finally, in 1827, the diplomat, theologian and archaeologist, Christian von Bunsen (until 1838). Bunsen's social graces, his great culture and relationships with men as diverse as Schelling, Creuzer, Lachmann and many others, made his house in Rome a meeting point for artists, archaeologists and scholars from every country: the sculptor Thorwaldsen, but also Chateaubriand,

Champollion and Leopardi.[44] A galaxy of archaeologists soon congregated around Bunsen; they included F.G. Welcker, professor at Bonn and one of the most renowned philologists of the time, and also young scholars of repute such as Theodor Panofka and Gerhard. The latter was to become the lifetime administrator of a quite extraordinary organisation which opened in 1828 thanks to the initiative of Bunsen: the Instituto di Corrispondenza Archeologica.

The Instituto was conceived as an international organisation charged with the regular publication of the most notable archaeological discoveries. It consisted of a central section in Rome which co-ordinated the work of the resident archaeologists of various nationalities, and the national sections, German, French and English. Bunsen's support in housing the Instituto in his embassy was com-

Drawing from the Etruscan tomb in Tarquinia known as the Tomb of the Triclinium, by Carlo Ruspi, 1832. It reveals the precision desired by archaeologists at the beginning of the nineteenth century.

pleted by a subsidy from the Crown Prince of Prussia (the future Frederick-William IV) and a personal contribution from a young French aristocrat devoted to archaeology, the Duc de Luynes. Here were assembled the flower of contemporary learning – from Germany, August Böck, Friedrich Creuzer, Carl Ottfried Müller; from France, Quatremère de Quincy and Charles Lenormand; from Italy, Carlo Fea and Bartolomeo Borghesi – as well as famous collectors, the Englishman James Millingen, the ducs de Luynes and Blacas, and leading diplomats like Metternich and Humboldt. With the Instituto, method (academic philology), aesthetics (embodied in the heritage of Winckelmann), and the tradition of the Grand Tour combined to give birth to a new enterprise. Collecting and the material acquisition of objects from that moment on counted for less than interest in the unknown; the desire for knowledge prevailed over sensibility. To achieve these goals there had to be adequate publications which individually answered specific questions. The Instituto was also a publishing house which produced various series: *Bulletino* for rapid information, *Annali* for scientific communications, *Monumenti* for monographs on monuments. The aim was to create a kind of living encyclopaedia of archaeology equipped henceforth with categories and specialities: museum catalogues, topographic description, epigraphy, ceramic studies, iconography.

The discovery of the Vulci tombs in 1828 opened up new realms for this conquering and confident archaeology. For Italy at the beginning of the nineteenth century was living an 'Etruscan dream'. Even if, since the sixteenth century, the Etruscans had played a critical role in the ideas that the Italians (and especially the Tuscans) had developed concerning their origins, and even if in the eighteenth

View of the home of the Instituto di Corrispondenza Archeologica in Rome, built in 1835.

century the Etruscan question had played the same role in Italian historiography as that of the Gauls in France, it was only around the 1820s that Etruscology became Etruscomania, with the systematic exploration of the Tuscan cemeteries. An awestruck Gerhard was present at the discovery of one of the greatest Archaic and Classical period cemeteries of the ancient world, on the land of Lucien Bonaparte, Prince of Canino. Vases and urns here became as covetable as statues. In selling his collection of painted vases to the British Museum, the British Ambassador to Naples, Sir William Hamilton, raised painted vases to the status of a symbol of the taste for the antique. This soon included such men as Lucien Bonaparte, who as a result made more money from the excavation of Etrurian cemeteries than they did from farming that same land. From here came the passion for 'Etruscan' vases (Etruscan because found in Etruria, Winckelmann having been one of the few to hold them as Greek), which was to develop into Etruscomania when the first painted tombs appeared.

Gerhard's archaeological theories provide an unparalleled review of the exact state of classical archaeology in the first half of the nineteenth century. For those who saw themselves as archaeologists as opposed to the more adventurous antiquaries, the age of random collecting and aesthetic pleasure for its own sake had gone.

Just as the school of German philology had liberated itself from theology, so the school of archaeology had to assume its autonomy. With one reservation, however, for this independence of archaeology existed only within the framework of the 'science of antiquity'. Archaeology shared the same goals as philology, but it was to achieve them through other means. For this to happen it had to become professional in the face of competition from artists and travellers, and also in view of the philologists' claim to precedence. After more than thirty years spent fighting for the intellectual independence of archaeology, Gerhard could speak out loud and clear. In Germany after the 1848 revolution, schools of archaeology flourished everywhere. At that time more than ten German universities had chairs of archaeology, whilst Great Britain and France had only one each. This success can be explained by the triumphal route established by the German schools of philology, but it was also based on the refined ideological model elaborated by Gerhard and his contemporaries. Faced with a more accessible Mediterranean, European culture could no longer content itself with the booty of knowledge and treasure-hunting which had so far prevailed. Archaeology could claim a place as a positive science founded on concrete results. The practical nature of the new way had not only theoretical consequences but could, and must, illuminate 'ancient life'. Antiquity became a source of innovation and no longer of imitation; it revealed technological solutions and practical knowledge which could be applied to the present. The achievements of architects and works by sculptors and painters could be enriched by archaeology, just as archaeology fed on the arts. Antiquity explained, the heritage of the eighteenth century, became a living antiquity that could be touched and analysed by its range of techniques and its regional diversity.

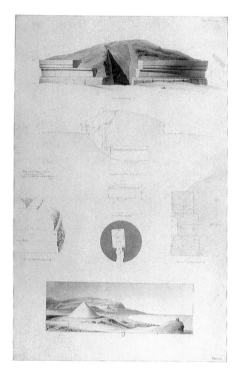

Elevation, section, plan and details of a tumulus and view of the necropolis of Tarquinia, drawn by Henri Labrouste in 1829. This drawing demonstrates the interest in the Etruscans shown by the architects attached to the Académie de France in Rome.

However, confronted by the philologists, Gerhard knew how to take advantage of the mystery of archaeology and the emotions that it engendered. He demanded recognition of the credit to be gained on the ground through association with diplomats and travellers. The archaeologists who succeeded the philologists at the universities had to assert themselves through their connections, through the interest they aroused in high society and the royal courts, in short, through being distinguished not just by simple academic merit.

However, Gerhard's full and ambitious programme fell down on one detail. His archaeological propositions made no solid reference to excavation other than implicitly: archaeology was conceived of as a collecting activity. If the workmen contributed, as at Pompeii or Canino, it was by sheer chance. True archaeological work began when objects were made available in collections or museums. For Gerhard's contemporaries excavation was no different to surveying or cataloguing but was just a means of extracting remains from the soil. However, it was only another ten years before French or German excavations in Greece posed the problem in a radically different way, and above all for the arrival of Heinrich Schliemann to remind the university establishment that it did not own the copyright to the image of antiquity.

In its step-by-step confrontation with philology Gerhard's archaeology progressively came to lose all historical pretension. If, to return to Wolf's distinction, the characteristic of history was *das Werdende*, then the characteristic of archaeology was *das Gewordene*.[45] An unequal struggle which left philologists in contact with living sources and archaeologists grappling with dead ones. If the ultimate goal of archaeology was to fabricate infinite groups and classes without allowing explanation of the past (i.e. to produce history), what good were the boring minutiae of typology? The path of positive archaeology, threatened by the intolerance of aesthetes and the acerbity of philologists, was very constrained. The philological paradigm certainly formed a good means of technical advance and social recognition in the service of archaeology, but in the final reckoning it proved itself an impediment. Basically Gerhard was much closer to Montfaucon than to Boucher de Perthes, as was expressed by Humboldt in a letter to Metternich defending the Instituto di Corrispondenza against the suspicions of the Vatican:

The Archaeological Society, by the nature of its cosmopolitan composition, by the purity of its purely artistic purposes, has already rendered massive services to the cause of the progress of the arts. It professes no political tendency other than that to reunite, as around a single hearth, the divergent lines of good taste, and no other belief other than that which lifts the soul to noble and great ideas.[46]

In short, Gerhard was a determined reformer, but in a particular way narrow-minded. He remained confined by the concept of classical antiquity formed at the University of Berlin under the sway of Humboldt and Böck. Wholly preoccupied with the publication of catalogue after catalogue, with following up discoveries, with 'keeping in with' artistic and collecting circles, he had no time to interest himself in what was happening beyond the frontiers of classical archaeology. However, it was from this remote antiquity, which had not yet the right to be named prehistory, that the decisive thrust would come.

THE TRIUMPH OF MAN'S GREAT ANTIQUITY
Boucher de Perthes

What was there in common between Gerhard, with his fascinated presence at the discovery of the Etruscan tombs at Vulci on the land of Lucien Bonaparte, Prince of Canino, and such men as Tournal or Schmerling, who scrutinised the depths of the soil with an amazement mixed with anguish, to discover a few animal bones or worked flints? A similar faith in the idea that objects, if one knew what questions to ask of them, could speak. The transformation of antiquarian knowledge into an archaeological discipline came about by a care devoted as much to objects and monuments as to the conditions of their burial. This new rigour called for the establishment of certain rules of observation, retrieval and publication. The Danish archaeologists had been the first to construct systematic rules in discovering the cardinal role of typology. By different routes classical archaeologists had arrived at the same conclusions, but for these methods to be applied to human fossils it was first necessary to admit to their existence. All the discoveries of the 'forerunners of prehistory' had run up against this centuries-old obstacle. In the first three decades of the nineteenth century geology and palaeontology had already achieved immense progress. But for archaeologists themselves to benefit, they had to overturn Buffon's proposition and transform medals into shells and inscriptions into fossils. To think of archaeology as natural

Excavation at Bürglstein near Salzburg carried out in 1825. In this picture the excavation has the air of a romantic country outing.

history meant that the observers of the earth had to draw on all the 'scraps', all the recoverable debris. This was – in contrast to the antiquarian tradition – to favour the whole in relation to its parts.

It was to fall to Boucher de Perthes to fulfil this pilot's role, even though there was nothing obvious about this customs official from Abbeville, this multi-talented man of letters, to lead him to the reconciliation of human and natural sciences. His debt to Doctor Casimir Picard, who initiated archaeological survey and excavation in the Somme Valley, is evident. But Boucher de Perthes succeeded in making the final part of his life (he began his work on the ground in 1837 at the age of forty-nine) a 'work of science' in the service of human history – this was the paradox of a man who seemed less equipped than many of his predecessors to become the founder of a discipline.

As president of a regional learned society, one of many at the time, he began by assisting his friend Picard's researches both materially and intellectually. He soon caught the fever for exploration and set out to continue the work of his friend, who died prematurely in 1841. But it was in 1837, below the town walls of Abbeville, that Boucher de Perthes began his work on the ground. Thus he came across – at a depth of over seven metres – an archaeological level characterised by quantities of animal remains, pottery and stone tools. Encouraged by these first discoveries, which were nothing spectacular (but accepted nonetheless by the Natural History Museum for their collection), he undertook work on the site of Menchecourt-lès-Abbeville, a site at which Cuvier had already identified bones of elephants and rhinoceros. It was there that he laid hands on his first 'antediluvian' tools. Further discoveries followed, but they were polished axes (Neolithic), the presence of which seemed intrusive to Boucher de Perthes's correspondents. Himself made suspicious by their scepticism, he insisted that objects be extracted *in situ*. In June 1842 he was able to retrieve an undeniably *in situ* Palaeolithic biface. From this time onwards he began to keep a systematic watch on works and quarries in the Abbeville region. Bolstered by increasingly numerous discoveries, he threw himself into the writing of a volume which was to become the first part of *Antiquités celtiques et antédiluviennes*. In 1846 a huge volume was finished and sent to the Académie des Sciences for approval. It was a failure. The appointed committee took exception to most of the author's conclusions, and the work appeared in 1847 without the much desired approval of this scientific body which Boucher de Perthes held in such high regard.

Determined but disorganised, Boucher de Perthes had made a rod for his own back. His geological explanations were often summary, his drawings of flints illegible, his functional interpretations naive and his theories ambitious. There is no doubt that some of his plates illustrate doubtful objects, if not fakes. It was all assembled to ruffle the feathers of a coterie which had shown itself hostile to researchers more qualified than he.

However, even if he deserved criticism, Boucher de Perthes's work had the merit of vantage point and originality. It made up the first synthesis on stratigraphy as applied to archaeology. This is how he established the age of a find:

On the material, on the workmanship, and above all on the subterranean position of the objects. From now on we admit a sort of ladder of life, a superposition of layers formed by the debris of generations and we seek in each layer indices of the history of these generations. Thus the deepest layers will offer us the oldest generations.[47]

Many others before him had had an intuitive idea of stratigraphy, but no one had insisted with such determination on the demonstrable value of stratigraphic observations provided that they were based on survey and identifiable conventions. In illustrating his type-sections and in

Simplified section made of the soil at Menchecourt near Abbeville, from *Antiquités celtiques et antédiluviennes* by Boucher de Perthes (1847). His originality lay in his application to archaeological layers of the stratigraphic methods of the geologists of the beginning of the nineteenth century.

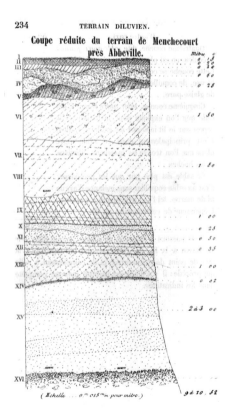

taking care to describe, like a geologist, the position and contents of the strata which he studied, Boucher de Perthes crossed the threshold into archaeological stratigraphy. He did not neglect the necessary typological study, but he made this subservient to stratigraphy, in contrast to the Scandinavian archaeologists. He did away with the suspicion which for at least half a century had impeded the association of human products with fauna, on the pretext of the ever-present possibility of the intrusion of implements into older layers. He called for a comparable treatment of fauna, flora and artefacts. Equally, he criticised the distaste of his predecessors for the lateral associations which alone could yield reliable dating:

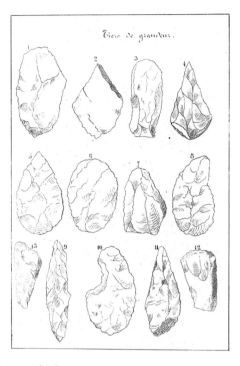

'Antediluvian stones' from Abbeville, from *Antiquités celtiques et antédiluviennes* by Boucher de Perthes (1847). Boucher de Perthes combined his stratigraphic approach with a typological description of the material found.

The study of the peat bogs, no more than that of the diluvial beds, was not pushed as far as it should have been [...]. One can still distinguish in the peat, especially at the time of extraction, part of the vegetation which composes it. The flora of the subterranean species, or the nomenclature of the peat plants, described layer by layer, as it rises towards the surface marking the succession of species in the same location over many centuries, could demonstrate the variations of soil and climate.[48]

Here was the clear expression of the programme of synthesis of natural and human sciences which distinguished archaeology in its desire to be freed from the antiquarian tradition. However sketchy, hasty and sometimes even credulous, Boucher de Perthes's book established the manifesto of a new archaeological science which dared to confront the prejudices of the discipline.

From then on, even if they were a minority in the learned world, good intellects (such as Isidore Geoffroy Saint-Hilaire, son of the man whom Goethe so much admired) accepted Boucher de Perthes's discoveries, whilst criticising his theories. Elsewhere, since the haughty condemnations of Buckland and Cuvier in denying the existence of human fossils, the situation had changed notably. William Pengelly had resumed MacEnery's excavations at Kent's Cavern and established that animal fossils and human industries were definitely contemporary. Hugh Falconer, a brilliant British naturalist, launched excavations at Brixham Cave, supported by the Royal

Society of London, which confirmed Pengelly's results. Buckland's geology was now replaced by that of Charles Lyell, which allowed more space for the principles of evolution and uniformitarianism, that is to say the process in terrestrial geology, and in 1857 a human fossil was discovered in Germany in the Neander Valley. Furthermore, when Falconer visited Abbeville in 1858, he was rapidly convinced of the interest of the discoveries and lost no time in inviting John Prestwich, a noted geologist and financer of the Brixham excavation, to join him there. Accompanied by the geologist and numismatist John Evans, Prestwich made the journey to Abbeville where he was soon followed by an entire committee of the Geological Society of London and by Lyell himself. The English scholars contributed to the international recognition of Boucher de Perthes, even if Charles Darwin, after reading the book, retained a more than sceptical attitude.[49] On 26 May 1859 Prestwich presented a report to the Royal Society of London which, based on his experience in Great Britain and France, upheld that 'flint implements were the product of the conception and work of man', and that they were associated with numerous extinct animals.[50] On 26 September and 3 October of that same year, a museum palaeontologist who had been at the Abbeville inquiry, Albert Gaudry, championed the value of Boucher de Perthes's findings before the Académie des Sciences. For the latter the year 1859 saw the 'time of recognition', but for archaeology this official recognition signified the learned world's abandonment of the age-old denial of the antiquity of man. The same year saw the publication of Darwin's *On the Origin of Species*.

Darwin's great work earned its author many caricatures.

1 Montfaucon 1719, V, 2, p. 194.
2 Legrand d'Aussy 1799, p. 3.
3 Ibid., p. 56.
4 Laming-Emperaire 1964, pp. 106–14.
5 Bercé 1986, p. 536.
6 Michelet 1959, p. 84.
7 Marsden 1983, pp. 8–9.
8 Daniel 1978, p. 31.
9 Marsden 1983, p. 18.
10 Chippendale 1983, p. 119, letter to Cunnington of 24 September 1802.
11 Colt Hoare 1810–12, I, p. 153.
12 See Piggott 1976, p. 138, and Daniel and Renfrew 1986, p. 30.
13 Grayson 1983, p. 7.
14 Laming-Emperaire 1964, p. 115; Grayson 1983, pp. 7–8.
15 Grayson 1983, pp. 57–8; Frere 1800, pp. 204–5.
16 Grayson 1983, pp. 87–9, Laming-Emperaire 1964, p. 141.
17 Esper 1774.
18 Cuvier 1801, p. 2.
19 Cuvier 1841, I, pp. 62–3.
20 Kühn 1976, p. 44; see also Biedermann 1890, p. 320.
21 See Goethe's own version of the Cuvier–Geoffroy Saint-Hilaire conflict, with his opinion on the story of contemporary anatomy in Goethe 1832.
22 Kühn 1976, p. 44; see also Biedermann 1890, p. 320.
23 Gummel 1938, p. 125.
24 Gummel 1938, p. 112.
25 Laming-Emperaire 1964, pp. 116–17.
26 Mongez 1812–17.
27 Laming-Emperaire 1964, pp. 121–2; Aufrère 1936.
28 Buckland 1823, pl. 69.
29 Grayson 1983, pp. 75–6. Grayson emphasises, however, that MacEnery was not in agreement with Buckland on the date of the flints, which he attributed to a post-diluvial age.
30 Laming-Emperaire 1964, pp. 144–6; Grayson 1983, pp. 99–108.
31 Tournal 1834.
32 'Uniformitarianism assumes the principle that the past history of the earth is uniform with the present in terms of the physical laws governing the natural order, the physical processes occurring both within the earth and on its surface, and the general scale and intensity of those processes. It asserts further that our only means of interpreting the history of the earth is to do so by analogy with events and processes in the present.' *Dictionary of the History of Ideas.*
33 Stoczkowski 1993. Stoczkowski drew attention to the anticipatory character of the idea of prehistory in Tournal.
34 Klindt-Jensen 1981, p. 15.
35 Ibid.
36 Cited by Rodden 1981, pp. 58–9.
37 Herbst 1848.
38 Gräslund 1987, p. 23; Thomsen 1836, pp. 32 and 58.
39 Klindt-Jensen 1975, p. 72.
40 Ibid., p. 73.
41 Boucher de Perthes 1847, I, p. 36, cited in Laming-Emperaire 1964, p. 162.
42 Gerhard 1850, p. 204.
43 Ibid.
44 Stark 1880, pp. 280–84.
45 Momigliano 1983, p. 283.
46 Weickert 1955, p. 143.
47 Boucher de Perthes 1847, I, p. 34.
48 Ibid., p. 547, note 24.
49 Darwin 1887, 3, pp. 15–16: 'The whole [Boucher de Perthes's book] was rubbish.'
50 Cohen-Hublin 1989, p. 186.

Congress of the Foremost Antiquaries in Rome, 1728. Caricature by the painter
and antiquary Pier Leone Ghezzi (1674–1755), one of the most active scholars in Rome
during the eighteenth century. In the foreground one can recognise Baron von Stosch,
among the most famous collectors of the time, sitting in an armchair. Behind him,
pen in hand, Ghezzi takes notes.

THE THREE CONTRADICTIONS OF THE ANTIQUARIES

Mankind has engaged with the past without always being aware of it; a past comprehended more as a continuum than a rupture in the steady flow of time. As far back in time as we can go we find antiquaries comparing remains with texts, monuments with their associated literature, mythological cycles with landscapes. We cannot capture antiquarianism at its roots – *archaiologia* at its birth – any more than we can observe the birth of religion or law, for despite all the ambitions of cognitive archaeology, we do not have access to the thoughts of prehistoric people. We simply know that to deny them any curiosity about the past is just as absurd as to deny them a sense of the divine, or the practice of language. To account for the human invention of culture we still depend upon a handful of scenarios which have been only marginally enriched by modern prehistory.[1] Life in the caves which served as a refuge to man, the building of light shelters and the use of worked stone as tools and weapons, are all part of a language common to antiquaries near and far, from China to the West. When we happen upon the notion of fossils among the philosophers of Ionia, or the principle of the stone–bronze–iron succession in ancient tradition, we are establishing not so much the reality of a Graeco-Roman prehistory as the vulnerability of our own representations of evolution.

The science of antiquities has had a chequered history. Despite the differences which distinguished the various antiquarian theories from one era or one region to the next, a relatively stable body of ideas was established. First, the antiquaries had to test their theses. Egyptian, Assyrian and Chinese scribes questioned the consistency of their sources, just as the Greeks did. The same question nagged at all those who collected antiquities, deciphered inscriptions, and sooner or later, dug the earth. Foundation texts contained much information about the origin of the arts and of techniques. Some of them seemed to be confirmed when the first antiquaries compared them with the objects discovered in the earth or preserved in the temples. Despite the profound differences between the Graeco-Roman and Chinese heritage, they had several things in common. Thus China became a kind of counterpoint to the 'wisdom of the Greeks' – a different way of conceptualising origins which was at once similar and dissimilar. Just when Lucretius resuscitated the idea (already an old one) of the three ages of humanity, Chinese tradition produced the following opinion, attributed to the philosopher Feng Huzi:

In the time of Xuanyuan, Shennong and Hexu, weapons were made of stone, to cut trees and build houses, and they were buried with the dead [...]. In the time of Huangdi, weapons were made of jade, to cut trees, build houses and dig the earth [...] and were buried with the dead. In the time of Yu, weapons were made of bronze to build canals [...] and houses. In our times, weapons are made of iron.[2]

As part of a process which is quite comprehensible given the Chinese context, jade was inserted between stone and bronze, but the idea is the same as that of Lucretius. The ages of man could be defined by technological stages which were subject to a development from the simple to the complex. Behind text or tradition the antiquary revealed objects which he could then classify and interpret, making of them a historical source; the remains of the past were no longer mere *sémiophores*, but instruments of knowledge.

Stones, bronzes, vessels, tools or monuments – the scope of antiquarian curiosity knew no bounds. These *sémiophores* had to be classified and given a place within an intelligible system. The Greeks believed the tripods of Hephaestus had the power to move by themselves. The ancient Chinese recounted fables about Ding bronze vessels which could cook food on their own without fire, put themselves away without being lifted and move about without being carried.[3] The idea of the supernatural was common to many antiquaries of the East and West. We have seen how, in seventeenth-century Europe, intelligent people enquired after the means of harvesting the vessels which sprang spontaneously from the bowels of the earth, or about

the role of dwarves and giants in the building of megaliths. The
notion of 'thunderbolts' was common to East and West from ancient
times. Lapidaries and encyclopaedists alike ascribed them special
properties up until the eighteenth century. Yet here and there
enquiring minds such as Mercati and later Jussieu and Mahudel
recognised them as stone tools. At the same time (the beginning of
the eighteenth century) the Chinese Emperor Kangxi explained:

> *The form and substance of thunderstones varies from place to place. The*
> *wandering Mongols use them instead of copper or steel [...]. A romance*
> *of the time of the T'ang says that there was at Yu-men-si a great temple*
> *dedicated to thunder, and that the people of the land would offer various*
> *materials to it in order to have these stones. This fable is ridiculous, the*
> *thunderstones are metals, stones and pebbles which fire from the thunder*
> *has metamorphosed, melting them quickly and fusing different substances*
> *irreversibly.*[4]

Without abandoning the old theory of the origin of thunder-
stones, the emperor–antiquary recognised their cultural importance
as tools which preceded the use of metals. In the same period the
Japanese historian, poet and statesman Arai Hakuseki (1657–1725)
believed that thunderstones in the shape of arrowheads had been left
behind by non-Japanese human groups whose existence was mentioned in the ancient chronicles.[5] Mankind's ideas about the past do
not spring from some unlikely circulation of theories, but from
unsystematic observations and inferences which are given expression
when societies are faced with putting into intellectual order the
vestiges of their past. Thus antiquarian studies seem to have developed
in the same way in the Far East and in the West. This impression may
stem in part from rather random encounters with a variety of
sources, but, without adopting too deterministic an approach to the
history of ideas, the disturbing coincidences must be explained.
At the heart of this mechanism for exploring time the antiquary
compares the text with the object. The presumed antiquities must
then be assigned their place within the natural or cultural order. It
follows that in widely differing circumstances, and given similar
assemblages, antiquaries may produce similar statements. A third
approach completes the strategy, in which local and universal history
are opposed. The amateur antiquary seeks devotedly and patiently to
collect, classify and interpret objects as historical evidence. But of
what kind of history? The local history of towns, or the history of
dynasties, nations or empires – or universal history? In the West

scholars since the Middle Ages had to struggle to impose national history upon a universal history itself divided between biblical and Graeco-Roman sources. In China their work had to be written into the history of dynasties of variable fortune. In a recent book Denis Twitchett gives an example of this effort to pass from the particular to the general in the Chinese historiography of the T'ang period (seventh to ninth centuries AD):

The record began with the Court Diaries (Ch'i-chü-chu) and the Administrative Record (Shih-cheng chi), the material which was successively compiled into a Daily Calendar (Jih-li) for each year, then into a Veritable Record (Shih-lu) for each reign, into a full-scale National History (Kuo shih) of the reigning dynasty, and finally after the dynasty had fallen and had been replaced by its successor into the Standard History (Cheng shih) of its period.[6]

At any event it was necessary to distinguish between a prehistory which could be universally applied, and a history dominated by political figures. The writing of ancient history was thus directly dependent upon the way in which the scholar dovetailed long-term history (the time of foundations and inventions) with short-term history (the time of politics, of observable and verifiable facts). In the West, recourse to the Varronian idea of *res divinae* and *res humanae* became a practical means of justifying the division of labour. The ordering of things human was sufficient unto itself. The historian left the business of things divine to the theologians. This division did not operate in China, but the collection and classification of antiquities were nevertheless useful in furnishing the emperor and scholars alike with the mass of historical information necessary for the coherence and understanding of imperial institutions. That is why Chinese scholars produced, well before their Western counterparts, the first manuals of antiquities, which owe their existence to the demands of court officials, connoisseurs and the curious. In China as in Greece local and universal were united without recourse to the philosophical contortions of scholars in an effort to bring together the remotest antiquity and the present. The most influential of the Jesuit missionaries in China, Matteo Ricci (1552–1610), who certainly did not lack a sense of history, expressed surprise at the behaviour of the Chinese in this matter:

In this realm they have much interest in antiquities: they have neither statues nor medals, but rather all kinds of bronze vessels which are highly valued and which they wish to be distinguished by a particular corrosion.

Without that they are worth nothing. Other antique vessels of pottery or of Japanese stone [jade] are appreciated. But much more than all these things they seek the paintings of famous artists, without colour, only in ink; or the writings of ancient authors on paper or material, with their seals to confirm that they are authentic.[7]

The interests of the Chinese differed from those of the European antiquaries because their vision of the past was based upon a different value system, one in which continuity prevailed over discontinuity. The Jesuit scholar was thus suggesting that for the Chinese, the radical gulf between antiquity and the present day scarcely existed: forms, traditions and institutions appeared immutable. This explains the value placed upon those details which gave an object temporal status: antiquities must justify their existence by means of formal traits which allow them to be assigned their proper place in time.

THE THREE TOOLS OF ARCHAEOLOGY

Confronted with the immense and disparate knowledge of the antiquaries, archaeology founded itself upon a unitary model, and aimed to affirm itself as a unified science which allowed the remains of the past to be organised into an ordered system by means of verifiable procedures of collection and classification. The scholars of the second half of the nineteenth century were staggered by the discovery of the great antiquity of man. Attracted by the progress made in the natural sciences, they wished to lay the foundations of a scientific archaeology free from the burden of antiquarian traditions. Typology freed archaeology from the tutelage of text; technology liberated it from the nature/culture dilemma; and stratigraphy from the local/universal paradox. Typology places the object in an identifiable time-frame and renders it useful as historical evidence. Attention to technological features, by establishing the 'natural' and 'cultural' components of each product, allows each object to be assigned its particular function. Stratigraphy adds another dimension: the object was buried by the action of depositional phenomena at the same time local and universal. Every object and every monument is destined to find its place in a general process of stratification which is linked to the history of the planet. These three principles were neither developed nor received in the same way. From Worm to de Mortillet or Montelius, via Winckelmann and Gerhard, the concept of 'type' in its different senses (stylistic or classificatory) formed the basis of the inevitable descriptive analysis of materials. Without typology there was no other route but the aesthetic one. Oscar Montelius in Sweden, Augustus Pitt-Rivers in Britain and Gabriel de Mortillet in France employed an evolutionist typology which was greatly influenced by Darwin.[8] The continuity of their theories with the older propositions of men such as Aubrey and Caylus is striking. At the Brussels International Conference of 1872 de Mortillet proposed the replacement of the nomenclature for prehistory based on fauna with a typological classification:

Following an excellent method used in geology, I have given each period the name of a typical locality which is well known and studied, only instead of saying Chelles period, Moustiers period, Solutré period and La Madeleine period I have changed the name of the locality into an adjective.[9]

De Mortillet's work did not just involve the replacement of a palaeontological nomenclature with a topographical one. He considered each prehistoric period as an assemblage of identifiable and definable types, and proceeded to establish a cultural chronology based on stratigraphic observation. This was a decisive step forward which gave prehistory a system of classification that was both homogeneous and flexible. De Mortillet's three laws sum up precisely the naturalist and evolutionist concept of prehistory in the nineteenth century. Montelius, in what was to become the bible of modern prehistory, came even closer to a formal typology:

The series may differ in their degree of sensitivity. They all have in common, however, that each link in the chain differs only slightly from the following link. The similarity of two links close to each other may be so great that an unaccustomed eye will find no difference. But the first and the last type in the series are often so different from each other that it seems at first glance that the one has no relationship with the other.[10]

Caylus expressed the variation of types using the metaphor of colours, while Montelius employed the more evolutionist metaphor of the chain to characterise the relationship between types; however, the common source of inspiration is clear. From Caylus to Montelius the typological method was defined as the display of particular properties: 'It must be said, however, that in general the enlightened eye […] notices considerable differences where the generality see only a perfect resemblance.'[11] The natural history paradigm did not only involve thinking of types as species, but led to a consideration of objects as beings:

It is after all extraordinary that man with all his works has been sub-
jected to the laws of evolution, and remains subjected to them. Is human
liberty thus fashioned that we may create no form to our liking? Are we
constrained, step by step, to pass from one form to another, however small
the difference? Development may be slow or fast, but man is always con-
strained in the creation of new forms to obey the same law of evolution
which is valid for the rest of nature.[12]

Where Caylus discerned a principle, Montelius was quick to perceive a fundamental law which determined the development of
types. Some years previously Pitt-Rivers had affirmed the evolutionary autonomy of types in a more direct way than Montelius:

Human ideas, as represented by the various products of human indus-
try, are capable of classification into genera, species, and varieties, in the
same manner as the products of the vegetable and animal kingdoms, and
in their development from the homogeneous to the heterogeneous they obey
the same laws.[13]

The typologist from Stockholm and the English general with a
passion for typology are in perfect agreement.[14] One attempts to
construct an analytical table of European prehistory by means of
combining type-series, and the other seeks to trace human culture to
its very origins through the detailed analysis of tools and their functions.[15] Admittedly there are slight differences to be detected
between Pitt-Rivers's principles of classification and Montelius's
typological method. Montelius's typology is based upon the attributes of objects, their grouping and their convergence. Pitt-Rivers's
takes more account of their use, function and technique of manufacture than of the semiology of form. But those differences apart, the
outline is the same: man was created not as the inventor of civilisation but as the unconscious instrument of its foundation.[16] Eventually this exclusive attention to objects was bound to end in a
palaeontology of types which neglected the social dimension of production, by minimising the environmental variables to the advantage
of formal analysis. In the name of a prehistory which paid greater
respect to context, Sophus Müller, Montelius's Danish counterpart,
severely criticised certain of his colleague's deductions:

One must, however, bear in mind that nothing can be compared by and
for itself, but only with other things, archaeological material, conditions of
discovery, and above all, place of discovery. To use conclusions derived from
pure analogy as a means of deducing the date and origin of material is bad
methodology except in rare cases.[17]

From then on the great archaeological debate was no longer the opposition of a philological model to one of natural history, but a consideration of the application, extension and consequences of the natural history model. Rather than thinking of the history of archaeology in terms of a confrontation between these two models, one can see two paths: one of formal typology, which leads from de Mortillet and Montelius to Henri Breuil for prehistory, Gero von Merhart for protohistory, and Adolph Furtwängler or John Beazley for classical archaeology; and a functionalist path which, from Pitt-Rivers and Müller to Vere Gordon Childe and André Leroi-Gourhan, pays more heed to technical processes, even to the social forms of production. As early as 1939 the visionary and underrated Finnish theoretician A.M. Tallgren wrote that archaeology must cease to be a natural science founded upon the study of objects and forms, and become an economic, social and historical science.[18] Contemporary archaeology has never ceased to debate the contradiction between human and natural sciences. In so doing it has detached itself from antiquarianism, but it has a long way to go in order to become a social science complete in itself. Modern prehistory, as part of a necessary critical movement, tends to deny the physiological and ecological determinisms in vogue since the beginning of the twentieth century, and discovers how close these often were to ideas known since antiquity.[19]

1 Stoczkowski 1993.

2 Yuan K'ang, Yueh chueh shu, cited in Chang 1986, pp. 4–5.

3 Mo Tzu (478–376 BC), cited in Chang 1986, p. 96.

4 *Mémoires* 1779, p. 86.

5 Bourdier 1993, p. 86.

6 Twitchett 1992, p. 33.

7 Clunas 1991, pp. 93–4.

8 Kunst 1982.

9 Mortillet 1872. See N. Richard's thesis of 1991, pp. 328–48, on this question.

10 Montelius 1903, p. 17.

11 Caylus 1752, VIII.

12 Montelius 1903, p. 20.

13 Pitt-Rivers 1874, p. 18.

14 Sigaut 1989.

15 Pitt-Rivers 1875, p. 92.

16 Pitt-Rivers 1868, p. 92.

17 Müller 1885, cited in Klindt-Jensen 1975, p. 93.

18 Tallgren 1936.

19 Stoczkowski 1993.

APPENDICES

ARCHAEOLOGICAL ANTHOLOGY

CHAPTER ONE

ANTIQUE AND MEDIEVAL SOURCES

•

Khaemwaset, restorer of Memphis

THE SON OF RAMESES II, KHAEMWASET
(1290–1224 BC), DISCOVERED AT MEMPHIS
A STATUE WITH A DEDICATORY
INSCRIPTION WHICH HE ATTRIBUTED TO
A SON OF THE PHARAOH KHUFU
(C. 2600 BC), PRINCE KAWAB.

the sublime chamber and according to his taste, a pond which should be used to purify (the) walking (?) and for water sacrifices in the [...] of Khafra so as to make him blessed with life.

(Farouk Gomaà (ed.), *Chaemwese, Sohn Ramses II und Hoher Priester von Memphis*, Wiesbaden, 1973, p. 68.)

The role of Khaemwaset was not restricted to that of priest, since he had the task of maintaining and restoring the lands of Memphis. His restoration activities are known to us from numerous inscriptions. The statue of Kawab and the inscription it bears attest to the historical knowledge of the priests, capable of deciphering and identifying an inscription more than a

Khaemwaset, king's son, sem-priest and the greatest of directors of craftsmen, was happy because this statue of Kawab, once doomed to turn into rubble (?) in the [...] of his father Khufu, had survived intact (?)[... in order to give him (or something similar)?] a place in the favour of the gods and to unite him with the transfigured members of the Ka-temple of Rosetau, because he so loved those sublime ancient ones, who came before, and the excellence of all their works — as a matter true a million times. This favour should be (consist of) every life, duration and happiness on earth for Khaemwaset [the king's son, sem-priest and greatest of directors of craftsmen], after having restored all the cults of them (i.e. his ancestors) in the temple and in the memory of the people, who had forgotten them and after having built, near

Statue of Kawab.

millennium old. But the story of Khaemwaset did not end in the thirteenth century BC. Several demotic manuscripts of the Roman period recount the history of a high priest (Satni) named Khaemwaset who was a magician and discoverer of ancient books: the story of the pious antiquary became the tale of the enchanter Satni-Khaemwaset (see G. Maspero, *Les Contes populaires de l'Egypt ancienne*, Paris, 1882).

The holy discovery of Nabu-apla-iddina

THE KING OF BABYLON NABU–APLA–
IDDINA (MID–NINTH CENTURY BC)
DISCOVERS AN ANCIENT STATUE OF THE
GOD SHAMASH AND RESTORES THE CULT.

Shamash, the great lord, who dwells in Ebab-bara, which is in Sippar, which during the troubles and disorders in Akkad the Sutû, the evil foe, had overthrown, and they had destroyed the sculptured reliefs – his law was forgotten, his figure and his insignia had disappeared, and none beheld them. Simmash-Shipak [1024–1007 BC], king of Babylon, sought for his figure, but he did not reveal himself to him. His image and his insignia he did not find, [...] he established his regular offerings [...]. During the distress and famine under Kashshû-nadin-akhi [1006–1004 BC], the king, those regular offerings were discontinued [...]. At a later time Nabû-aplu-iddina, the king of Babylon, [...] who overthrew the evil foe, the Sutû, [under his reign] Shamash, the great lord, who for many days with Akkad had been angry and had averted his neck, [...] had mercy and turned again his countenance. A model of his image, fashioned in clay, his figure and his insignia, on the opposite side of the Euphrates, on the western bank, were found, and Nabû-nadin-shum, the priest of Sippar, [...] that model of the image to Nabû-aplu-iddina, the king, his lord, showed, and Nabû-aplu-iddina, [...] who the fashioning of such an image had given him as a command and had entrusted to him, beheld that image and his countenance was glad and joyful was his spirit. To fashion that image he directed his attention, and through the wisdom of Ea, with the craft of Nin-igi-nangar-bu, Gushkin-bana, Ninkurra, and Nin-zadim with sumptuous gold and bright lapis-lazuli the image of Shamash, the great lord, he carefully prepared. With the rite of purification of Ea and Marduk before Shamash in Ekarzagina, which is on the bank of the Euphrates, he washed his mouth, and he took up his dwelling (there).

(L. W. King (ed.), *Babylonian Boundary Stones*, London, 1912, pp. 121–4.)

For the Mesopotamian sovereign an antiquary's knowledge was necessary for the re-establishment of a cult and for proper observance of its rites. The proper perpetuation of the ritual required an image of the divinity which had to be based on an ancient model. The archaeological discovery of the relief was thus an undoubted sign of the goodwill of the gods.

Prayer for the Obscure Masters

THE EXCAVATION OF AN ANCIENT TOMB,
DISCOVERED IN CHINA IN THE FIFTH
CENTURY AD BY BARON ZHU LIN AND
WRITTEN UP BY PRINCE XIE HUILIAN AT
THE START OF THE SIXTH CENTURY AD.

While excavating a moat north of the wall of the Eastern Precinct, we had gone down to a depth of several yards when we found an ancient tomb. There had been no marker of a burial ground above, and for the sarcophagus no tiles had been used, only wood. In the sarcophagus were two coffins, exactly square, with no headpieces. As for spirit vessels, we found twenty of so different kinds, of ceramic, bronze, and lacquer; most of these were of unusual form, and we were not able to identify them all. There were also more than twenty human figures made of wood, each of them three feet long. When the grave was first opened, we could see that these were all human figures, but when we tapped them or poked them with something, they disintegrated into dust under our hands. On top of the coffin were more than a hundred 'five-penny-weight' Han coins. In the water were joints of sugarcane, along with some plum pits and melon seeds, all of which floated up, none of them very rotten.

The grave inscription had not survived, so we were unable to ascertain the date or age of the tomb. My Lord commanded that those working on the wall rebury them on the eastern hill. And there, with pork and wine, we conducted a ceremony for the dead. Not knowing their names, whether they were near to us or far, we gave them the provisional title 'The Obscure Master and Mistress'.

In the seventh year of the Yung-chia Reign (AD 430) on the fourteenth day of the ninth month, Baron Chu Lin, Instructional Director and Clerk of the Censorate, charged as General Administrator of the Arsenal, General Registrar, Magistrate of Lin-chang, prepared ceremonial pork and wine and respectfully presented them to the spirits of the Obscure Master and Mistress:

I gathered this laboring multitude,
To build earthen ramparts was my charge,
I went to the depths of springs to make the
    moat,
Massed soil for the wall's base.
This single sarcophagus was opened,
Two coffins lay therein.
Hods were set aside in sorrow,
Spades cast down with streaming tears.
Straw spirit-figures were decayed,
The carts of clay were broken,
The banquet table had rotted,
Its vessels for service fallen in.
On the platter were still some plums,
In the crocks were still some pickles,
And of sugarcane, some joints were left,
Of melons there remained some rind.
Thinking back on you, good people,
What was the age in which you lived?
How long were you in the resplendent body?
At what date did the soul sink away?
Was it ripe old age or early death?
Were you eminent or obscure?
The tomb inscription has perished.
No part of your names comes down to us.
Who now are your descendants?
And who were your forebears long ago?
Were your name and deeds foul or fair?

How is it they have been utterly lost?
'A hundred-league wall made all at once',
Ten cubits high, even all around:
We could not turn the wallworks away,
We could not bend the moat around.
The cypress-core bindings had been destroyed,
The chambers of your tomb had fallen.
Touching coffin-heads stirred brooding,
Handling tomb figures strengthened lament.
As Ts`ao Pa once extended his kindness
    downward,
As generosity once flowed from Ch`en Ch`ung,
So we reverence these bones by the precinct folds,
And cover the skeletons by the wall's bend.
In emulation of ancient custom
Site another grave on your behalf.
Wheels move you from the northern fosse
To the 'long night' at the foot of eastern hills.
Joint burials are not of high antiquity,
But have continued since the Duke of Chou's
    day,
And respecting that past principle,
Again we inter your paired souls.
Of wine there are two jugs,
Of sacrificial beasts, the chosen pig.
Your spirits appear in a blur,
Tasting the bullock-shaped goblet.

(From S. Owen, *Remembrances, the Experiment of the Past in Classical Chinese Literature*, Harvard University Press, Cambridge, Mass., 1986, pp. 39–40.)

In Chinese experience the discovery of ancient tombs was a common occurrence. This text of Xie Huilian's, collated by Xiao Tong, son of Emperor Wu of Liang, is extraordinary because it brings together a rational description of the discovery with a prayer for the unknown dead which prefigures in a certain way the *Hydriotaphia* of Thomas Browne (see pp. 353–4). One notes the extreme precision of the archaeological description and the interest paid to the conditions of preservation, not just for objects but also for plant remains: the report of the excavation attests a naturalist's attention to solid details.

Hippias teaches 'History'

'ARCHAEOLOGIA' ACCORDING TO PLATO.

SOCRATES *Then the Spartans are breaking the law by not giving you money and entrusting their sons to you.*

HIPPIAS *I grant that. I think you said your say on my behalf, and there's no need for me to oppose it.*

SOCRATES *So we find the Spartans to be law-breakers, and that on the most important issue, though they appear to be most lawful. So when they applaud you, really Hippias, and enjoy your speech, what sort of things have they heard? Surely they're those things you know most finely, things about stars and movements in the sky?*

HIPPIAS *Not at all. They can't stand the subject.*

SOCRATES *Then do they enjoy hearing about geometry?*

HIPPIAS *No. Many of them can't even, well, count.*

SOCRATES *Then they're a long way from putting up with your displays of arithmetic.*

HIPPIAS *Good god, yes. A long way.*

SOCRATES *Well, do they like those things on which you know how to make the sharpest distinctions of anybody – the functions of letters, syllables, rhythms, and harmonies?*

HIPPIAS *Harmonies and letters, indeed!*

SOCRATES *Well, just what is it they love to hear about from you and applaud? Tell me yourself; I can't figure it out.*

HIPPIAS *The genealogies of heroes and men, Socrates, and the settlements (how cities were founded in ancient times), and in a word all ancient history – that's what they most love to hear about. So because of them I have been forced to learn up on all such things and to study them thoroughly.*

SOCRATES *Good lord, Hippias, you're lucky the Spartans don't enjoy it when someone lists our archons from the time of Solon. Otherwise, you'd have had a job learning them.*

HIPPIAS *How come, Socrates? Let me hear them once and I'll memorize fifty names.*

SOCRATES *That's right. I forgot you had the art of memory. So I understand: the Spartans enjoy you, predictably, because you know a lot of things, and they use you the way children use old ladies, to tell stories for pleasure.*

HIPPIAS *Yes – and, good lord, actually about fine activities, Socrates. Just now I made a great impression there speaking about the activities a young man should take up. I have a speech about that I put together really finely, and I put the words particularly well. My setting and the starting-point of the speech are something like this: After Troy was taken, the tale is told that Neoptolemus asked Nestor what sort of activities are fine – the sort of activities that would make someone famous if he adopted them while young. After that the speaker is Nestor, who teaches him a very great many very fine customs. I displayed that there and I expect to display it here the day after tomorrow, in Pheidostratus' schoolroom – with many other fine things worth hearing. Eudicus, Apēmantus' son, invited me. But why don't you come too, and bring some more people, if they are capable of hearing and judging what is said?*

(*Hippias Major*, 285b–286c, translated by Paul Woodruff, Basil Blackwell, Oxford, 1982.)

This is the first text in which the word *archaiologia* appears in the sense of knowledge and discourse on the past. It reveals how, at the end of the fifth and the start of the fourth century BC, historical genres had achieved a special place in Greece.

Lucretius

ON THE ORIGINS OF MANKIND.

1. The life of the first men
Yet the human race was hardier then by far –
No wonder, for the earth was hard that formed
*   them –*
Built upon bigger and tougher bones within,
Bowels and flesh sewn tight with well-strapped
*   muscles,*
Not easily overcome by heat or cold
Or by strange diet or bodily decay.
For many revolutions of the sun
They led the life of the pack, like beasts that roam.
There was no ruddy farmer to steady the plow;
Unknown were iron tools to till the fields,
How to plant out new shoots, or from tall trees
Prune away the old branches with the hook.
What the sun and the showers bestowed, what
*   the earth created*
Of its own doing, satisfied their hearts.
Often they met their bodies' needs by feeding
From the acorn-copious oak, and the berries you
*   see*
Ripen in winter, wild strawberries, purple-red,
Rose bigger and more plenteous from the earth.
Many other foods the flowering fresh earth bore,
Hard fare, but ample, for wretches born to die.
And springs and rivers called them to quench
*   their thirst,*
As now from the mountains clear cascades of
*   water*
Draw from afar the thirsty animals.
Those rovers found and dwelled in the sacred
*   groves*
Of the Nymphs, wherever the rush of a good
*   deep brook*
Spilled over to wash the wet and slippery stones,
The slippery stones, and trickled over the moss,
Or where streams sprung up bubbling from the
*   fields.*
They had no foundry skills, no use for fire;
They didn't know how to clothe themselves with
*   skins*

But lived in the wild woods and the mountain
*   caves,*
Stowing their dirt-rough limbs among the bushes
When driven to flee the wind's lash and the
*   downpour.*
They could not recognize the common good;
They knew no binding customs, used no laws.
Every man, wise in staying strong, surviving,
Kept for himself the spoils that fortune offered.

2. The origins of communal life
Huts they made then, and fire, and skins for
*   clothing,*
And a woman yielded to one man in wedlock …

… Common, to see the offspring they had
*   made;*
The human race began to mellow then.
Because of fire their shivering forms no longer
Could bear the cold beneath the covering sky;
Love sapped the strength of the men, and
*   children tamed*
Their parent's proud wills with their pleasing
*   ways.*
Then neighbours who wanted neither to harm
*   each other*
Nor to be harmed, began to join in friendship,
Setting aside as special the women and children,
Signaling with their hands and stammering
*   speech*
That the weak must be pitied, as was just.
Harmony wasn't always the result,
But the better part kept faithful to their vows;
If they had not, our race would have all
*   perished,*
Not kept its shoots alive unto this age.

3. The discovery of fire
Likewise – in case you're wondering to yourself –
Lightning brought fire to earth for mortal men,
It was the first; all flames have spread from there.
For we see many things dazzle like lightning
When the bolt from the sky laces them with fire.
Then too when a well-branched tree sways in the
*   wind,*

Sawing back and forth, weighing over another
    tree's branches,
Its great force crushes and grinds out seeds of fire
That sometimes flare up into heat and flame,
While the stocks and branches scratch against
    each other.
One or the other could have given men fire.
And how to use fire to soften and cook food
They learned from the sun – for they saw fruits
    in the fields
Grow mellow under hot rays beating down.

(Lucretius, *On the Nature of Things*, edited and
translated by Antony Esolen, Johns Hopkins
University Press, Baltimore and London, 1995.)

This text from the first half of the first century BC is the best-known passage from one of the ancient visualisations of the origins of man. Counter to the tradition of the Golden Age, it presents a primitive picture of the history of humanity which influenced an entire tradition from the Renaissance to our own times, and the echo of which can be found in certain modern representations of prehistory. The striking thing about this type of narrative is the role given to nature and material forces in the development of the primitive history of humanity.

The persistence of pagan cults

FASCINATED BY PAGANISM, THE FUTURE
EMPEROR JULIAN VISITS TROY.

I should never have favoured Pegasius unhesitatingly if I had not had clear proofs that even in former days, when he had the title of Bishop of the Galilaeans, he was wise enough to revere and honour the gods. This I do not report to you on hearsay from men whose words are always adapted to their personal dislikes and friendships, for much current gossip of this sort about him has reached me, and the gods know

that I once thought I ought to detest him above all other depraved persons. But when I was summoned to his headquarters by Constantius of blessed memory I was travelling by this route, and after rising at early dawn I came from Troas to Ilios about the middle of the morning. Pegasius came to meet me, as I wished to explore the city, – this was my excuse for visiting the temples, – and he was my guide and showed me all the sights. So now let me tell you what he did and said, and from it one may guess that he was not lacking in right sentiments towards the gods.

Hector has a hero's shrine there and his bronze statue stands in a tiny little temple. Opposite this they have set up a figure of the great Achilles in the unroofed court. If you have seen the spot you will certainly recognise my description of it. You can learn from the guides the story that accounts for the fact that great Achilles was set up opposite to him and takes up the whole of the unroofed court. Now I found that the altars were still alight, I might almost say still blazing, and that the statue of Hector had been annointed till it shone. So I looked at Pegasius and said: 'What does this mean? Do the people of Ilios offer sacrifices?' This was to test him cautiously to find out his own views. He replied: 'Is it not natural that they should worship a brave man who was their own citizen, just as we worship the martyrs?' Now the analogy was far from sound; but his point of view and intentions were those of a man of culture, if you consider the times in which we then lived. Observe what followed. 'Let us go,' said he, 'to the shrine of Athene of Ilios.' Thereupon with the greatest eagerness he led me there and opened the temple, and as though he were producing evidence he showed me all the statues in perfect preservation, nor did he behave at all as those impious men do usually, I mean when they make the sign on their impious foreheads, nor did he hiss to himself as they do. For these two things are the quintessence of their theology, to hiss at demons and make the sign of the cross on their foreheads.

These are the two things that I promised to tell you. But a third occurs to me which I think I must not fail to mention. This same Pegasius went with me to the temple of Achilles as well and showed me the tomb in good repair; yet I had been informed that this also had been pulled to pieces by him. But he approached it with great reverence; I saw this with my own eyes. And I have heard from those who are now his enemies that he also used to offer prayers to Helios and worship him in secret.

(*The Works of the Emperor Julian*, translated by Wilmer Cave Wright, Harvard University Press, Cambridge, Mass. and London, 1990.)

The personality of Julian (332–63), called the Apostate because he tried to renew the pagan tradition of the Empire (he became Emperor in 360), is one of the most fascinating in antiquity. This learned man, who had received a Christian education, was fascinated by paganism which he saw as one of the backbones of the Empire. This letter shows the degree to which fidelity to the old cults was maintained, despite the proclamation of Christianity as the state religion in 312. And with this there remained a knowledge of and attention to the most prestigious sites of antiquity, which were visited and, after a fashion, maintained.

The protection of heritage under the Emperor Augustus

THE BRONZE TABLETS OF HERCULANEUM
EXPRESS CONCERN FOR THE PROTECTION
OF MONUMENTS WITHIN THE EMPIRE
DURING THE FIRST CENTURY AD.

Since the foresight of the best of princes has enabled us to look as far as the roofs of our city and has considered the eternity of all Italy, which he looks after not only by his most

august precept, but also by his example, so he helps in the happiness of the century by preserving the works of private individuals as well as of public monuments, and as all should refrain from the most bloody of activities, that by the ruination of houses and towns, gives in peacetime the appearance of war, it is decreed: if anyone, for commercial reasons, should buy a building with the aim that by pulling it down he should acquire more than he paid for it, then he is to pay to the public treasury double the price that he paid for it and may nevertheless be brought before the Senate. And since selling should not be worse esteemed than buying, these vendors should also be punished who knowingly act wrongly against the Senate's wish, and it is decreed that such sales be annulled. Furthermore, the Senate asserts that it reserves its position as to those proprietors who have changed some aspect of their ownership with the intention that it should not be seen as a transaction (of sale).

(From T. Mommsen and O. Gradenwitz, *Fontes Juris Romani*, Freiburg, 1893.)

This senatorial decree proclaimed in AD 44–56 under the consulates of Gnaius Hosidius Geta and Lucius Vagellus, on the tenth day of the kalends of October, well expressed the emperor's concern for the protection of heritage sites: it was not a matter of archaeological anxiety but of the desire to prevent destruction of the urban centres by speculation.

Respect for the past

A BARBARIAN KING CONCERNS
HIMSELF WITH HERITAGE,
ACCORDING TO CASSIODORUS.

Our palace having been built, as is known, by skilled architects, wise men ought to look after it with care and prudence, for its wonderful beauty, if it is not kept in repair, will be spoilt by the onset of old age. In it are the delights of our power, the glorious face of the empire, the laudatory witness of the kingdoms; it, too, is shown for the admiration of ambassadors and of course any master is judged by the quality of his dwelling place. And so it is that the most prudent mind will find the greatest pleasure in being able simultaneously to enjoy the most beautiful dwelling and let his spirit that is fired by public cares be relaxed by the harmony of its fabric. It is said that it was the Cyclops who first built vast structures in Sicily, corresponding to the height of their caverns, after Polyphemus had been pitiably deprived of his one eye by Ulysses in the mountain caverns. Thence, it is said, the science of architecture was brought to Italy, so that posterity, in its desire to emulate the ancients might keep for its use what had been discovered by such founders. And so it is that we have decided that your eminence ought to undertake the charge of our palace, from the time of this decree, both maintaining in their pristine state the old monuments and making new ones that are similar to the old; for just as a fair body is appropriately dressed in clothes of a single colour, so the visual effect of a palace ought to be felt equally in each of its constituent parts. To do this, you will acquire the requisite ability by assiduous reading of the geometer Euclid and you will in your mind's eye construct his schemes set out in such admirable variety, so that when the need arises you will have abundant knowledge at your fingertips. Archimedes, too, that most subtle of minds, and Metrobius, too, should always be your companions so that you can give of your best for new schemes, you who will then be learned in the books of the ancients.

(From Cassiodorus, *Variae*, Monumenta Germaniae Historiae, XII, lib. VII, Berlin, 1894, p. 204.)

Theodoric, king of the Ostrogoths (AD 493–526), charged his representative to supervise the restoration of his palace having regard to continuity with the ancients. This text collected by Cassiodorus, one of the finest scholars of the period, strongly expresses the idea that the grandeur of the present reflects the majesty of the past, and thus respect for ancient monuments was part of the architect's profession.

The megaliths of Brittany in the year 1000

SURVEYORS AND LAWYERS SET TERRITORIAL BOUNDARIES IN BRITTANY AND REGARD THE MEGALITHS AS MERE HEAPS OF STONES.

Rudalt, son of Orscand the Great, Bishop of Vannes, gave to Saint-Cado, in perpetuity with all its revenues, a village within sight of the sea, where the river Etel flows, namely into the overflow, which runs into the aforesaid river Etel, between this village and that called Mellionuc. Half of the marsh also belongs to Saint-Cado [...]

At the far side of the marsh a ditch goes up across Mont Haelgoret and proceeds practically straight eastwards; just before reaching a pile of stones, it curves gently at three o'clock and immediately curves back again almost as far as the limits of the said village, towards a fallen stone, in a limestone area; shortly afterwards it curves in again to the left up to a little pond, which it leaves to its right to continue as far as the junction of two water-meadows; after leaving the water-meadow which goes down to the well, it follows, at three o'clock, the other water-meadow, together with a ditch, until it reaches the place where three ditches join; the Saint-Cado ditch then runs at nine o'clock and crosses rugged terrain until it reaches a water-meadow. Then the ditch runs straight to the sea, across the marsh.

Another charter concerning Saint-Cado

The aforesaid Orscand, after the death of his father Rudalt, granted to Saint-Cado a quarter of the bourg des Romains, *with a quarter of its gardens, as well as a quarter of Kerprat. Here are the limits of this land: from the standing stone situated on the road which leads from the abbey to Saint-Germain, it goes up to the meadow; it then follows the meadow, along with a ditch, as far as the* bourg. *From the* bourg *the ditch goes south, and, before reaching the Chauve well, the boundary follows the ditch and the road which runs from the abbey to a very tall standing stone, which is situated on the road where the boundary started, as already stated.*

(V. Mortet, *Recueil de textes relatifs à l'histoire de l'architecture et à la condition des architectes en France au Moyen Age*, A. Picard, Paris, 1911, pp. 53–5.)

Given the requirements of juridical acts of this type, land-surveyors and lawyers were very aware of all the characteristics of the ground and revealed the prominent features of the historic landscape. The vocabulary is descriptive and makes no allusion to the giants or magicians who, according to tradition, had erected the monuments.

The search for treasure

IN THE TWELFTH CENTURY, WILLIAM OF MALMESBURY RELATES HOW GERBERT D'AURILLAC, POPE IN THE YEAR 1000, DISCOVERED THE TREASURE OF OCTAVIAN.

Otto, succeeding his father to the empire of Italy, made Gerbert archbishop of Ravenna and, a little later, the Roman pontiff. On the instigation of the Devil, Gerbert pushed his luck in such a way that he never left anything unfinished, once he had thought of it. In the end, his desires fell on treasures, formerly concealed by the pagans and which he discovered by necromancy, simply clearing away what covered them.

HOW GERBERT DISCOVERED THE TREASURES OF OCTAVIAN

There was a statue in the Campus Martius near Rome, I know not whether of bronze or iron, having the forefinger of the right hand extended, and on the head was the inscription 'Strike here'. In the past, men had battered the harmless statue with many axe-blows, supposing that the inscription meant that they might find a treasure there. But Gerbert showed their error by solving the problem in a very different manner: noting where the shadow of the finger fell at midday, when the sun is at its height, he fixed a post there, and when night came, he went there, accompanied only by a servant carrying a lantern. The earth opened by means of his accustomed arts and revealed an entrance wide enough to enter. They saw before them a vast palace, with golden walls, golden roofs, everything of gold: golden soldiers apparently playing with golden dice; a king of the same metal, reclining with his queen; delicacies set before them, and servants standing by; and vessels of great weight and value, of an art that outshone nature. In the inmost part of the dwelling a carbuncle of the highest quality though of small size, dispelled the darkness of night. In the opposite corner stood a boy, holding a bow, bent and with its arrow pointed. But while the precious art of everything ravished the spectators' eyes, there was nothing that could be touched, even though it could be seen: for immediately as one stretched out his hand, all these images seemed to rush forward and assail such presumption. Held back by fear, Gerbert suppressed his inclination, but his servant could not refrain from seizing a knife of marvellous workmanship which he saw on a table; he no doubt thought that in the midst of so much booty, so small a theft might be undetected. But the images all started up with a clamour, and the boy let fly with his arrow at the carbuncle and plunged them into darkness; and if the servant had not, at his master's word, quickly thrown back the knife, they would both have paid dearly. And thus with their boundless greed unsatiated, they departed, the lantern guiding their steps.

(William of Malmesbury, *De Gestis Regum Anglorum*, II, 169, ed. W. Stubbs, London, 1887, pp. 196–7.)

William of Malmesbury, an English monk of the twelfth century, was not an admirer of Gerbert, son of farmers from Aurillac who became Pope in Rome from 999 to 1003 under the name of Sylvester II. Gerbert, one of the great minds of his time, had studied at Vich in Catalonia, then close to the border with the Caliphate of Cordoba. He knew law as well as mathematics and had finished his studies in Rome. Involved with the dramatic political and dynastic conflicts of his time, he had confirmed enemies who created the legend of the magician Pope in the twelfth century. One of the favourite themes of these stories is naturally the search for treasure: everything described here is in the order of marvels, the fantastic and the strange, just as in the adventures of the Abbot Lupicinus (see pp. 88–9).

The protection of antiquities in the fourteenth century

TREATISE ON THE CONSERVATION OF ANCIENT BUILDINGS IN ROME.

So that the city might not be disfigured by its ruins, and that the ancient buildings might bear public witness to the grace of our city, we forbid any man to destroy or to have destroyed any ancient building within the walls of Rome, on pain of a fine of one hundred livres de Provins, of which half is for the Treasury and the other half for the person who brought the charge. Further, it lies with the Senator to pursue such enquiries, and neither he nor any other may give permission contrary to these present dispositions; if he gives it, it carries a fine of one hundred gold florins, payable to the treasury, and any permission given has no validity.

(Roman statutes of 1363, from Rodocanachi, *Les monuments de Rome après la chute de l'Empire*, Hachette, Paris, 1914, pp. 62–3.)

In nine centuries, since the emperors of the Later Empire, the problem of the protection of the monuments of Rome had hardly changed, except that the fourteenth-century city was much poorer than the Imperial city.

CHAPTER TWO

THE EUROPE OF
THE ANTIQUARIES

·

Contemplation of the remains

THE ARCHAEOLOGICAL 'JUBILATIO'
OF FELICE FELICIANO.

On 24 September 1464 we started [from Toscolano] in order to enjoy ourselves, under the supreme command of the merry Sir Samuele da Tradate, while the worthy gentlemen Andrea Mantegna and Giovanni Antenoreo [Marcanova] acted as consuls, and I, Felice Feliciano, as proxy for the success of the undertaking. A noble band of participants followed us through the dark groves of laurel. Crowned with myrtle, evergreen ivy and other foliage, Samuele strode before us. And when we entered the old chapel of Saint Dominic, we discovered a very important inscription of the Emperor Marcus Antoninus Pius Germanicus Sarmaticus. Then we betook ourselves to the church of the Protomartyr, which is not far from the said chapel, and found in the atrium another fine inscription of the divine Antoninus Pius, the grandson of the divine Hadrian, who had once lived in this neighbourhood. When we betook ourselves thence to the church of the finest Pontifex, we discovered quite close to it a very important inscription of the Emperor Marcus Aurelius Claudius. All these we copied in the books we had brought with us. I will not omit one thing, which is worthy to be mentioned: we discovered a shrine of the quiver-bearing Diana and other nymphs. For many reasons we concluded that it could not be anything else.

After we had observed all these things, we embarked in a large boat, which was adorned with tapestries and all kinds of things and in which we scattered laurel leaves and other noble foliage, and sailed about on the Lake of Garda, that liquid field of Neptune, while the Emperor Samuele played all the time on the lute and sang thereto.

Lastly, when we had triumphantly crossed the lake, we reached the safe harbour and disembarked. At that very place we entered the church of the Holy Virgin in Garda, where we sang exultant hymns of praise to the supreme Thunderer and expressed our deepest reverence for his sublime Mother, above all because he had enlightened our hearts by uniting us and had led our minds to visit such important sites and to study them, and because he had allowed us to behold with such enthusiasm such worthy and various and edifying things and so many ancient monuments. And because he had vouchsafed us such a favourable day rich with flowers, with a fair passage and a safe harbour, and because he had allowed us to achieve our goal safe and sound and above all to see such wonders of antiquity. To see such things, every right-thinking man should betake himself at once to travel.

Extract from Felice Feliciano's manuscript, fifteenth century.

(Felice Feliciano, *Alphabetum Romanum*, ed. Giovanni Mardersteig, Editiones Officinae Bodoni, Verona, 1960.)

On 23 September 1464 the four friends who embarked on an excursion to Lake Garda together embodied the spirit of the Italian Renaissance. Andrea Mantegna as artist, Felice Feliciano as epigrapher and illustrator, Giovanni (Antenoreo) Marcanova and, the least known, Samuel de Tradate as collectors and antiquaries. These men, amateurs of epigraphy to the point of enthusing over what are today known to be patent forgeries, were also admirers, readers and successors of Cyriac of Ancona, whose biography is incorporated into one of the three manuscripts which Feliciano had composed for his three companions.

Description of the city of Rome

LEON BATTISTA ALBERTI,
CARTOGRAPHER OF ROME.

The course and alignments of the walls of the city of Rome, of the river, of the streets, and also the sites and positionings of the temples, public buildings and gates and trophies, the extents of the hills, and even the area roofed for habitation, all of this, to the best of our present knowledge, I have depicted in great detail with my mathematical instruments: I have devised these so that anyone, even if endowed with little talent, can draw beautifully and with great ease on whatever size of surface is desired. I have been persuaded to do this by learned friends, whose studies I have decided to assist.

From all of this I have gathered the following: no traces whatsoever of the old walls are to be seen: also very few roads survive intact: then, no gate is further than one hundred and forty-six cubits from the centre of the city, that is from the Capitol, and the circuit of the walls when reconstructed does not exceed seventy five stades. This can be seen both from the real dimensions of the various structures and from the drawing itself.

(R. Valentini and G. Zucchetti, *Codice topografico della città di Roma*, Rome, 1953, IV, p. 212.)

Leon Battista Alberti was one of the universal spirits of the fifteenth century, attracted as much to painting and sculpture as to architecture, and at the same time a philosopher and a mathematician. An associate of the Roman curia, he was the contemporary of Flavio Biondo, Poggio

Bracciolini and Cyriac of Ancona. It was at the instigation of the group of learned men from this circle that he drew up in 1432–4 a cartographic project for the monuments of Rome. The method which he displays in this passage forms the very first original document on the use of techniques of archaeological survey in the Renaissance. Sadly, we do not know whether Alberti was able to execute his plan and, if he did, this plan has not come down to us. The techniques which he presents were to serve, however, as the basis for most of the proper topographic surveys of the city.

The power of the past

IN 1462 POPE PIUS II REAFFIRMED THE
LAW ON THE ANTIQUITIES OF ROME.
LETTER TO PREVENT THE DESTRUCTION
OF ANCIENT BUILDINGS IN THE CITY
AND ITS ENVIRONS.

PIUS, BISHOP, SERVANT OF THE SERVANTS OF GOD, IN PERPETUAL MEMORY OF THE MATTER.

Since we desire that our Mother city remain in its dignity and splendour, we need to show all vigilant care that the basilicas and churches of the city and its holy and sacred places, in which are kept many relics of the saints, be maintained and preserved in their splendid buildings, but also that the antique and early buildings and their relics remain for future generations, for these buildings are an ornament to our city and give it its greatest dignity while they preserve in monumental form the ancient virtues that perpetuate its glory. And, furthermore, it is to be particularly borne in mind that these buildings and remains of buildings allow the fragility of human works to be better appreciated; and that they should not be mocked, for these buildings, with which our ancestors thought they rivalled eternity by their great power and enormous cost, are now seen to be ruined and even destroyed by the effect of age and other avatars. For these and other reasons [...] we follow certain of our predecessors, Pontiffs of the Romans, of happy memory, who expressly forbad the demolition or destruction of these buildings [...] and thus, under pain of excommunication and of financial penalties expressed in this statute, which those who contravene it may incur forthwith, by our aforesaid authority and capacity we formally forbid all and singular, ecclesiastical as well as secular, of whatever eminence, dignity rank, order or condition, even if of Pontifical eminence or of any other ecclesiastical or worldly dignity, to dare to demolish, destroy, reduce, break down or use as if a quarry, by any means, directly or indirectly, publicly or secretly, any ancient public building or the remains of any public building above ground in the said City or its district, even if on private property in the countryside or in a town. And if anyone shall dare to act against this prohibition, we grant to our dear sons the keepers for the time being of the chamber of the said City, recently established, who shall make search by their officials, with full and free authority and capacity to imprison and seize and confiscate the animals, tools and other goods of any artificers or labourers detected in the work of demolition or destruction, as well as constraining those in whose name they work to pay the full fine.

(J.B. Fenzonio, *Annotationes in Statuta sive Jus Municipalae Romanae Urbis ...*, Rome, 1636, p. 667.)

Aeneas Silvius (1405–64) became pope in 1458 under the name of Pius II. It was he who revealed to the Germans the rediscovery of Tacitus' text on Germania by Italian scholars. In 1454, after the fall of Constantinople, he delivered a famous speech before the assembly of German princes at Frankfurt, calling them to form a league against the Turks.

Where Mehmet II, following Kritoboulos of Imbros (see p. 115), invoked Homer, Piccolomini depended on the strength and valour of the Germans according to Tacitus. This learned man well expressed in this bull the wish of the papacy to subscribe to the patrimonial tradition of the Roman emperors, but he relied on a more historical concept of the evolution of the city. The repetition of this kind of regulation attests less to its efficiency in the protection of antiquities than to the permanent nature of destruction: the eastern colonnade of the portico of Octavius was destroyed by Pius II himself for use as the Vatican builders-yard.

Letter from Raphael to Pope Leo X

ON THE NEED TO PROTECT THE ANTIQUITIES OF ROME AND TO CREATE A PLAN OF THE CITY.

TO POPE LEO X

Many are those, most holy father, who taking the measure of mighty things with their own feeble judgement, when they write about the deeds of the Romans, or the marvellous construction, wealth, decoration, and architectural grandeur of the city of Rome, consider them things of fable rather than reality. But to me it has always been and will always be otherwise. Since, pondering the spirit of those ancient souls, the traces of which can still be seen today in the ruins of Rome, I do not think it beyond reason to believe that many of those things which to us seem impossible, were to them most easy. Therefore, as I have been very interested in the study of such antiquities as these, and having lavished no little effort in looking for them and meticulously recording them, and continuously reading good authorities and comparing the monuments with their accounts, I think I have managed to obtain a certain knowledge of that ancient architecture. This familiarity with something so wondrous gives me very great pleasure, yet also very great pain in seeing in effect the corpse of this revered and noble city, once mistress of the world, so horribly torn [...].

How many popes, Holy Father, who held the same office as Your Holiness, but did not possess the same wisdom nor the same strength nor magnanimity, how many of these Pontiffs have allowed the ruin and dismembering of ancient temples, statues, arches and other buildings, the pride of their ancestors. How many, just to grub up pozzolana, have caused foundations to be dug away, so that soon after the buildings come crushing to the ground? How much lime has been made from statues and other ancient decorations? I would be so bold as to say that all of this new Rome, which we see now, however great it may be, however beautiful, however embellished with palaces, churches and other buildings, all of this is built with mortar made from ancient marbles. With not a little emotion I am reminded how, in the short time I have been in Rome, not yet twelve years, many beautiful things have been destroyed, such as the Pyramid which stood in Via Alexandrina, the arch which was at the entrance to the Baths of Diocletan, and the Temple of Ceres on the Via Sacra, part of the Forum Transitorium, which a few days ago was burned and destroyed, its marbles made into lime, most of the basilica of the forum ruined [...] in addition so many columns broken and split in two, so many architraves and fine friezes shattered, that it has been the shame of our age to have permitted it, and of which it could genuinely be said that even Hannibal and others like him could not have done worse.

(V. Golzio, *Raffaello nei documenti, nelle testimonianze dei contemporanei e nella letteratura del suo secolo,* Vatican City, 1936, pp. 78–92.)

The text published here is that of Munich A, with the principal variations from version B. For certain modifications, the text established by V. Wanscher has been referred to. Only the first part of this letter to Pope Leo X, dating to 1519, is reproduced here. The second part deals with survey methods according to techniques close to those of Alberti (see p. 339). None of the surveys that Raphael would have made have survived.

Preface by François Rabelais

INTERESTED IN ROMAN ANTIQUITIES, RABELAIS PREFACED AND 'CORRECTED' THE *TOPOGRAPHIE DE LA VILLE DE ROME* BY MARLIANO, PUBLISHED IN LYONS IN 1534.

François Rabelais, physician, greets the most illustrious and learned nobleman Jean du Bellay, Bishop of Paris and counsellor to the King in the most holy confession

[...]. My dearest wish, from the moment that I knew anything of belles-lettres, was to be able to travel in Italy and to visit Rome, the capital of the world; in your extraordinary bounty you have fulfilled that wish and you have crowned it in permitting me not only to visit Italy (which was already enough in itself), but to visit it with you, the most learned and cultured man who ever saw day (and I have not yet fully measured the worth of that) [...].

Long before we were in Rome, in my thoughts and reflections I formed a certain idea of the things I desired which drew me to Italy. I had first planned to meet the learned men who would conduct debates in the places on our itinerary, and to converse with them in a familiar manner concerning some thorny questions which have been worrying me for a long time. Then I resolved to observe (since this was within the province of my art) certain plants, certain animals and certain medicines, said to be rare in Gaul but widespread in these parts. Finally, I planned to paint a picture of the city, with my writer's pen,

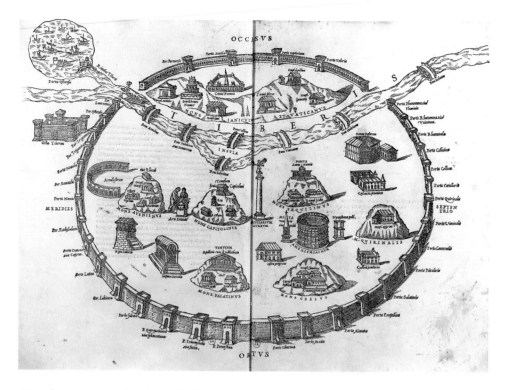

Map of Rome made by Bartolomeo Marliano
in 1534.

but also with the artist's brush, so that there
would be nothing which I could not find in my
notes once I was back among my compatriots. To
this end, I had taken with me a selection of
observations taken from various authors in both
languages. I was fairly successful in the first of
these three projects, though less than I had
hoped. As for the plants and animals, there are
none in Italy which we had not already observed
and described. We only saw a plane-tree, at the
lake of Diano Aricino. As far as the last project is
concerned, I brought it off with such zeal that no
one, I think, knows his house better than I know
Rome and all its quarters. And you yourself,
what leisure was left to you by this absorbing
and time-consuming embassy you devoted willingly to touring the monuments of the city. You
were not content to see the visible monuments,
you were also anxious about those yet to be
excavated, having bought to this end quite a fine
vineyard. Even though we had to stay there

longer than you thought in order to do this, and
even though, in order to obtain some sort of
product from my studies, I had undertaken a
topographical description of the city along with
Nicolas Leroy and Claude Chappuis, two most
honourable young people of your retinue, passionate about antiquities – there was Marliano,
beginning to write his book for you. The writing
of the book was certainly a relief to me, such
relief as Juno Lucina brings to women in difficult
childbirth. I had conceived the same child as
Marliano, but its birth was tormenting my spirit
and my heart itself. Even though the subject did
not call for arduous research, it did not however
seem easy to present an irregular and solid mass
according to a clear, ordered and well-constructed
plan. Inspired by Thales of Miletus, with the aid
of a sundial I divided the city into quarters
according to a circle split from east to west and
then from north to south, and I described it thus.
Marliano, on the other hand, chose to begin his
plan with the highest points. Far be it from me to
criticise this approach; on the contrary, I

congratulate him for being first to carry out what I was struggling to do. Alone, he has given us far more than we could expect from any of our contemporaries, however learned. In my opinion he has solved the problem so well, and dealt so well with the subject, that I cannot deny that I myself owe just as much as all those who study the liberal arts owe him together. It is just a pity that, called away from Rome by the ringing voice of your prince and your country, you had to leave before his book was finished. I did however make sure of its despatch to Lyons (the seat of my studies) immediately it was published. This was done thanks to the good offices and willingness of Jean Servin, a very industrious man; but, I do not know how, the book was sent without a dedication. To avoid its incomplete and, so to speak, headless appearance, it seemed fitting to place it under the auspices of your illustrious name. In your great benevolence, you will receive all favourably and extend to us (which you do already) your affection. Salutations. Lyons, the eve of the kalends of September, 1534.

(B. Marliano, *Topographia antiquae Romae libri septem*, ed. Rabelais, Lyons, S. Gryfius, 1534.)

Rabelais's interest in Roman antiquities is well known; Richard Cooper has even discovered the authorisation for export accorded by the Pope to the Cardinal of Bellay during a stay of two months in 1534 (Cooper 1988, pp. 168–9). His interest coincided with that of the Lyons printers who published in the first decades of the century several treatises on Roman antiquities by Italian scholars. The publication of Marliano's book at Lyons, in the same year as its impression in Rome by Bladus, is strange. We do not know whether it had the approval of the author. Rabelais's intervention is shown in several corrections, and that of Gryphe, the printer, by a more careful edition than that of the Italian original. The allusion by Rabelais to Marliano's survey method, which was distinctly less precise than the quartering procedure dear

to Alberti and Raphael, must be understood as a discreet criticism. Rabelais's interest in the antiquities of Rome is attested by another journey in 1548 in the company of the cardinal and the geographer André Thevet, who refers to it in his *Cosmographie universelle* published in Paris in 1575 (Cooper 1977). Rabelais was also interested in megaliths – he attributed to Pantagruel the construction of the *pierre levée* on the outskirts of Poitiers.

The plans of Bufalini

LEONARDO BUFALINI PRESENTS HIS TOPOGRAPHIC SURVEY OF ROME, MADE IN 1551.

TO THE READER

Whoever you are, Leonardo Bufalini of Friuli asks you not to judge harshly what he puts before you, which he esteems to be of the most beautiful of all things – that is, Rome and this representation of it. For he would not deem that he had done enough for you by putting before your eyes this resuscitation of it which is lived in today, if he had not also added to it, at the cost of a great deal of effort and money, and as though awakened from its grave, the ancient city too, once ruler of the whole world. Whether you are looking at the new or the old, bear in mind that it is of an accuracy attained not just by the square and compass but also by the nautical compass, taking account of the positions of the sky and the sun as well as of distances. Reflect that of this great benefaction the first author (after God) is Pope Julius III. He, with great liberality, has given up all save for the one city, and this he has laid open to all the world. Thus you may appreciate the happiness and good fortune of our own times, thanks to so good a Prince.

(Leonardo Bufalini, *Roma al tempo di Giulio III*, Rome, 1551, in A.P. Fruttaz, *Le piante di Roma*, Rome, 1962, pl. 189.)

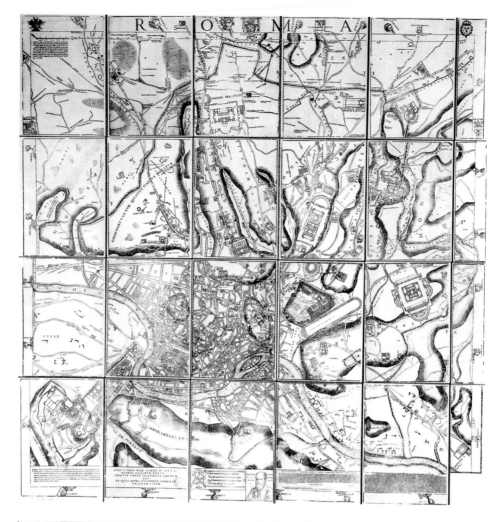

Topographical survey of Rome, undertaken by
Leonardo Bufalini in 1551. Detail (*above*).

Earlier plans of Rome were made by
painters and artists. Bufalini's plan was the
first topographic survey of the city by an
engineer, who made sure of the precision
of his measurements on the ground.
According to F. Ehrle (1911), he signalled
the progressive invasion of the engineers
into antiquarian knowledge.

The Viterbo forgeries

ANNIO OF VITERBO: THE PRINCE
OF FORGERS, ACCORDING TO
ANTONIO AGOSTINO.

Latino Latini of Viterbo, a learned and very reliable man, told me that Fra Giovanni Annio had had certain characters incised upon a slab which he had buried in a vineyard near Viterbo which was going to be dug soon afterwards. And when he knew that the workmen were in the vineyard, he arranged it so that they should enlarge their trench up to the place where the slab was hidden, telling them that he had discovered from his books that one of the most ancient temples in the world had stood there. Thus in digging in the direction of the slab, the first to find the stone ran to inform him and had him uncover it a little at a time, and he began to wonder as much at the stone as at the inscriptions. And with the authority of the text he went off to find those in charge of the town and told them that it was very important for the reputation of the town that this stone should be placed in some worthy and important place, because it told of the foundation of Viterbo, a town two thousand years older than Romulus, because its founders were Isis and Osiris. And he added other fables of his own such that he achieved his purpose, and so that one could see some more published examples of that [fable] which began thus: Ego sum Isis… *[I am Isis].*

It must be the same Annio of whose commentary Basso Floriano d'Ocampo said that had it not been dedicated to the Catholic kings of glorious memory, he would have taken it for a forgery.

(Antonio Agostino, *Dialogos de medallas, inscriciones y otras antiguedades*, Tarragona, 1587, pp. 447–8.)

Giovanni Nanni di Annio da Viterbo was the most famous forger of the Renaissance. He bequeathed to scholarship hundreds of pages of apocryphal texts. Agostino's criticism is interesting because it constitutes a reflection on the nature of forgery in archaeology. If Annio resorted to this kind of evidence at the end of the fifteenth century, it is because recourse to archaeological fact already occupied a place in the procedures of historical scholarship.

The birth of a town

THE ORIGINS OF AUGSBURG BY
SIGISMUND MEISTERLIN.

On the construction of the town of Augsburg/ How men lived at first and how the Swabians built this town/ and concerning the siting of the town the first chapter of the other book/ and here begins the other book.

When/ after the flood/ and the building of the tower of Babel and the confusion of the languages the lineages were separated/ each possessed its own area/ but the descendants of the son of Noah called Japhet were punished/ and they occupied a third of the world/ which was called Europe/ From this particular lineage was detached a people called the Senoni/ that is to say the 'sharp ones', who were called at that time the Schwenos/ in German Swabians/ these people were uncivilised in their ways/ but endowed with physical strength/ and great courage/ surpassing other races/ This population possessed a great part of the German lands/ and passed its time in hunting animals/ and lived on their meat/ and on plants and fruit/ and on acorns/ of that time the poet Juvenal speaks in the following manner/ at that time a cold cave gave a little shelter/ there, there was fire and safety/ there, a rough woman would make a crude bed with grasses/ and with the branches of trees/ On top she would throw an animal skin/ But the woman bore a great bosom to feed the children/

Often she was more horrific than the male/ who wore acorns on his head/ in these olden times no one feared thieves/ because men fed on the plants and apples/ which grew in open gardens/ Ovid, the renowned pagan, also speaks thus/ the houses were caves or of broad or small tree trunks joined with creepers/ thus men lived in peace/ although there were not yet a thousand ditches around the towns/ Boethius also speaks of those times/ Oh what happy times/ which were content with the faithful fertility of the sun/ some of the Swabians held the area/ situated between two rivers called the Lech and the Wertach/ and lived there/ when the time came that each people must protect itself against the others/ and as Ovid says/ they became hostile to strangers/ Also they came to model themselves/ on the other regions/ and attracted by the facilities/ offered by town life/ with the intention of protecting themselves and living together in another place/ for that reason they sought a suitable area/ where they could build a town/ and so the Swabians who lived between the Lech and the Wertach/ found a place which pleased them which was situated near a town/ this place was situated in the area where the two rivers met/ that is to say the Lech and the Wertach/ thanks to these rivers they could defend themselves even better/ They found also salubrious air/ and springs with fresh water/ So this place was well situated for all conveniences/ There they began to build houses to live in/ while before, naked and weaponless, they had shelter in neither castle nor in any house/ against the frost and heat/ and neither were they secure among themselves/ but then, with their natural ability, they built houses with crossed planks/ and reeds/ and they left the forests/ where they had lived before/ They would now live together/ so that they might defend themselves better/ and live peacefully/ they also surrounded the town with great ditches/ and behind them they heaped earth/ such that they had double advantage/ on one side they dug a ditch/ on the other they built

upwards surrounding the town with solid stones/ but not yet walling/ because they neither knew how nor could they do it/ although their ancestors had seen in Babylon gates made just of bricks which were bonded with pitch/ which probably they did not have in their region/ and perhaps because no one in that land knew how to burn limestone/ and the other techniques and arts of building/ For Isidore also says/ the ancients built their towns and their castles thus with stakes and rammed earth/ which was as good as a wall to them.

(Sigismund Meisterlin, *Eine Schöne Chronik*, Augsburg, 1522.)

This edition, published in Augsburg, consists of the same text as the 1457 manuscript (see p. 110), but the illustrations are completely different and demonstrate forcefully the impact of Humanism on the vision of history (see p. 111).

Pots that grow in the ground

IN THE FIELDS OF THE VILLAGE OF NUCHOW, THE EARTH PRODUCED POTS BY ITSELF, THROUGH AN EXTRAORDINARY NATURAL PROCESS.

AD 1416
The king left Wschowa for Srzem. A messenger came from his kinsman Ernest, Duke of Austria, to see with his own eyes the truth of a tale which he had learnt from a Polish soldier, John Warschewsky — that in a part of Poland, in one particular place, pots of many types were made by the action of nature alone and without any human intervention. Judging this tale hardly credible — or no more so than other tales that one hears — and thinking that it needed to be seen at first hand, Duke Ernest of Austria despatched a soldier, a man well able to judge of truth and natural virtue. And so King Wladislaus,

ready to dispel the doubts of his kinsman, Duke Ernest, went down to a field of the town of Nochow, between the Polish towns of Srzem and Kosten, and ordered the ground to be dug in his presence, in various places. He discovered many pots, of different shapes and sizes, created by the wondrous action and work of nature but just as if fashioned by a potter. He showed them to the messenger of Duke Ernest, who looked at each of the pots, marvels of the work of nature, such as are found not just in the one place (which we have mentioned at the start of this account) but in various parts of Poland. The king sent several pots of varying types to Duke Ernest, by means of the messenger, to bear witness to the truth of the matter. These very pots survive, soft and fragile when they emerged from the soil but then hardened by the power of the sun, and suitable for all kinds of human use.

(J. Dlugosz, *Historiae Polonicae*, Krakow, 1873.)

This is the oldest version to relate the fabulous birth of vases discovered in Poland (see p. 145).

The thunderbolts

MICHELE MERCATI DEMONSTRATES
THAT 'CERAUNITES' (THUNDERBOLTS)
ARE WORKED FLINTS.

The 'ceraunite' is common in Italy; it is often called an 'arrow' and is modelled from thin, hard flint into a triangular point. Opinion is divided on the subject. Many believe that they are cast down by lightning; yet those who study history judge that before the use of iron they were struck from very hard flint for the folly of war. Indeed, for the most ancient peoples, pieces of flint served as knives. We read in the holy scriptures of how Sephorah, the wife of Moses, circumcised her

son according to Israelite custom, with a well-sharpened stone; and Joshua, having entered Palestine, was ordered by God to prepare two stone knives for the same purpose, whence arose the practice in Israel of circumcising with stone. In the period that we are considering there was no worked iron in lands of the West; boats, houses, and all other works were fashioned with sharpened stones. In fact, flint or silex, as its name, so similar to sicilex, suggests, seems chosen for cutting. Sicilices are the things with which

'Thunderbolts', engraving from Michele Mercati's *Metallotheca*, 1719.

arrows and lances are pointed, as in the following verse of Festus, cited in Ennius: The veles, having thrown his javelins [sicilices], advanced into the open.

'Ceraunite' has the same shape as these, hence the opinion according to which the ancients, before the working of iron, cut sicilices from flint and that 'ceraunite' comes from this. It seems that among mortals, hate, from small beginnings grew to immense proportions, and the Africans made war on the Egyptians with clubs, which are called phalanges. *Before this, the Phoenicians (according to Pomponius Mela and Pliny) were the originators of war. Nor is what Lucretius describes true, that 'ancient weapons were hands, nails and teeth'.*

Since these are of little use to man as weapons, he used his intellect, and his hands provided him with weapons which were very suitable for killing so that someone who could not kill in a simple, savage way, could kill more nobly. First, his intellect showed him stones and sticks as weapons that he should master to attack and overcome an enemy from afar. Whereas originally fighting was restricted to individuals' disagreements, eventually whose peoples and nations took to war. Then ever more terrible weapons of war were occasioned by envy, greed and ambition, in their unquenchable thirst for human blood. They began to apply to spears and to every sort of weapon points of horn, bone and flint, as is maintained by those who believe that 'ceraunite' was fashioned to pierce the strongest cuirass. What is obvious from its crude form, its chipped surface, worked to a rough edge, was that it was not made by iron or a file, which then did not exist, but was fashioned by blows of a stone, into forms either triangular, rectangular or pointed. The small stump remains by which it was joined to the spear, by inserting it into the tip of the shaft. In spite of its rough appearance 'ceraunite' is shiny on account of its unusual hardness; in colour it is white, yellowish, reddish, dark red, green and black, and is sometimes even variegated. Of the same material are sometimes found narrow blades or plaques, a palm long and half an inch wide, some smaller, with pitted corners, polished surfaces, some flat and others slightly raised in a ridge down the centre. Those who think that the ancients used 'ceraunite' to tip their weapons say they used to adorn their bows with these plaques. But when were they in use, and in which period did the tyranny of iron, to which 'ceraunite' yielded, invade the world? The holy scriptures say that before the Floodwaters destroyed the race of men, iron had been made, and that its creator was Tubel-Cain, who was the seventh generation from the first father. Josephus writes in his Antiquities *that he was mighty in war, so much so that he seemed the creator of iron and war, and that he instigated hatred among a small group of blood relatives, and to absolve them had discovered how to make weapons of iron, so there were not any prior to this.*

(M. Mercati, *Metallotheca Vaticana, opus posthumum*, Rome, 1719.)

This text, published in 1719, had been drafted at the end of the sixteenth century by Michele Mercati (1541–93), the Vatican doctor. Here are all the elements that were to lead the antiquaries of the eighteenth century to accept definitively that the 'ceraunites' were made by men of the past.

Rubens writes to Peiresc

RUBENS RECEIVES AND COMMENTS ON PEIRESC'S INTERPRETATION AND DRAWINGS OF A TRIPOD.

I have finally received your much desired packet containing the very accurate drawings of your tripod and many other curiosities, for which I send to you the customary payment of a thousand thanks. I have given to M. Gevaerts the drawing of Jupiter Pluvius and showed him all the rest. I showed them also to the learned M. Wendelinus, who happened to be in Antwerp and came to see me yesterday with M. Gevaerts. But I have had no time these days, either yesterday or today, to read your discourse on the tripod, which doubtless touches on all that falls under human intellect, in this matter. Nevertheless, according to my accustomed temerity, I shall not fail to state my own views on this subject, which I am sure that you, with your usual candour, will take in good part.

In the first place, all utensils which rest on three feet were called 'tripods' by the Ancients, even though they served the most varied purposes, such as tables, stools, candelabra, pots, etc. And among other things they had a utensil to set on the fire under the lebes (chaudron in French) for cooking meat, and this is still used today in many parts of Europe. Then they made a combination of the lebes and tripod, much like our iron and bronze pots with three feet. But the Ancients gave it the most beautiful proportions and, in my opinion, this was the true tripod mentioned by Homer and other Greek

Letter from Rubens to Peiresc, 10 August 1630.

poets and historians, which was adopted in re culinaria *for cooking meats. And with regard to the use of entrails in their sacrifices, they began to have* inter sacram supellectilem ad eundem usum. *I do not believe, however, that the Delphic Tripod was of this type, but rather a kind of seat of three legs, as is still commonly used throughout Europe. [In margin: In ancient monuments we find seats with four feet, like the 'Sella Jovis', but also some stools, or seats with three feet, like our own stools.] This seat did not have a concave basin, or if it were concave to hold the skin of the Python, it was covered on top, and the Pytheness could sit on this cover, which had a hole underneath. It does not seem to me likely that she could sit with her thighs in the concavity, because of the discomfort of the depth of the basin and its cutting rim.*

It could also be that the skin of the Python was stretched over this hollow as over a drum,

and that because of this it was called the 'cortina', and that it was pierced, as well as the basin. It is true that in Rome one finds various tripods of marble, which have no concavity. And it was also often the custom, as you will see in several of the quotations below, to place on the same tripods statues dedicated to various gods; and this could not have been done except on a solid and level base. One must believe that the Delphic Tripod was copied and used for other gods, and that the word 'tripod' denoted every kind of oracle and sacred mystery, as we see it still used in pantomimes of Marcus Lepidus.

But the point which has more bearing on our subject I shall state with more care, and that is, that the Ancients used a certain kind of chafing-dish or réchaud (as they say in French) made of bronze, with a double coating in every part, to resist the fire. [In margin: In Paris there are two réchauds of this kind made in silver.] This was in the form of a tripod, and was used in their sacrifices and perhaps also in their banquets.

There is no doubt that this was the tripod of bronze so often mentioned in the Ecclesiastical History *of Eusebius, and by other authors – the tripod which served for burning incense to their idols – as you will see in the references below. And if I am not greatly mistaken, this bronze tripod of yours, considering its material, its small size, and the simplicity of workmanship, is one of those which was used to burn incense in the sacrifices. The hole in the middle served as an air-hole to make the coals burn better; just as all modern* réchauds *must still have one or many apertures for this purpose. And as far as one can see from the drawing, the bottom of the basin, or crater, is broken and consumed by the fire. [In margin: The capacity of your basin does not exceed that of the ordinary* réchaud *which we use today, and the shape is so appropriate to this purpose that if I should need such a utensil, I should want to have it made in this way]. That is all I can say at present on this subject, leaving to you freedom and authority to criticize. In any event, neither MM. Wendelinus nor Gevaerts advances sufficient arguments to the contrary. And so I rather think that, little by little, they will incline to this opinion.*

Rubens is responding to Peiresc's discourse and drawings of his newly acquired tripod. Gervaerts was preparing a book on Marcus Aurelius, and in 1628 Peiresc promised to obtain for him a drawing of the Rain God from the Antonine Column in Rome. Peiresc introduced new standards of precision in recording antiquities and Rubens rightly drew attention to the accuracy of Peiresc's tripod drawings. Rubens took a far more functional approach to the discussion of tripods, but his own views did not differ significantly from Peiresc's opinions. Peiresc was more inclined to see the orifice in the bowl as a source of mysterious winds than as a fire ventilator!

(David Jaffé, *Rubens' Self-portrait in Focus*, Australian National Gallery, Canberra.)

This commentary by David Jaffé has fundamentally reconstructed the intellectual relationship which united the two men, and makes them the most prestigious symbol of archaeology in the classical age.

CHAPTER THREE

FROM ANTIQUARY TO ARCHAEOLOGIST
·
On the childhood of man

THE YOUTH OF THE ANCIENT WORLD
AND THE ANTIQUITY OF THE MODERN,
ACCORDING TO
FRANCIS BACON AND PASCAL.

On the subject of antiquity, the idea that men have of it is utterly careless and hardly agrees with the meaning of the word. For the world's old age is its true antiquity and should apply to our own times, not to the world's youth, when the ancients lived. For their age, which from our own point of view is ancient and older, from the world's point of view is new and younger. And, in fact, just as we expect a greater knowledge of human life and a more mature judgement from an old man than from a young one, because of his experience and the range and wealth of matters which he has seen and heard and thought about; so we can likewise fairly expect much greater things from our own times, if only they knew their strength and had the will to exert it, than from former times, seeing that the age of the world is now more advanced and enriched with a multitude of experiments and observations.

(Francis Bacon, *Novum Organum,* translated by Peter Urbach and John Gibsch, Chicago and La Salle, 1994.)

Man is in ignorance during the first age of his life, but as he grows he educates himself constantly, for he takes advantage not only of his own experience, but also of that of his predecessors, because he keeps in his memory the knowledge that he has gained, and that of the ancients, which is ever present in the books which they have left behind them. And as he preserves this knowledge, he can also easily augment it, such that men are today in some way in

the same situation as these ancient philosophers would have been, had they lived up until the present, adding to the knowledge which they had that which their studies might have gained them with the advantage of so many centuries. It follows that, through a particular prerogative, not only does each man advance day by day in the sciences, but all men together make constant progress as the universe grows older, because the same thing happens in the succession of men as in the various ages of an individual. Such that the whole succession of men, during the course of so many centuries, must be considered as one individual who continues to live and learns all the time: and thus we see how unjustly we respect antiquity in its philosophers; for, since as old age is that age which is furthest from infancy, who cannot fail to see that great age in this universal man must not be sought in the times closest to his birth, but in those furthest away from it? Those whom we call the ancients were truly new in everything, and form, properly, the infancy of man; and as we have joined to their knowledge the experience of the following centuries, it is in ourselves that we can find that antiquity which we revere in the others.

(Blaise Pascal, Preface to the *Traité du vide, Complete Works,* Paris, 1954, pp. 533–4.)

The assessment of time initiated by Bacon and taken up by Pascal came as a reversal of the theories accepted since the first ancient historiographers. It made possible a history of mankind which would be in a particular way a history of human progress. It opened the way for a universal history which integrated man and nature.

The taste for travel

SPON, COLLECTOR OF INSCRIPTIONS,
VISITS GREECE.

It is to be expected that those who give accounts of their travels deal with their subject in their own way. Some speak only of palaces, churches and public squares. Others only address their readers on the subject of the layout of towns, their population, their fortification and their police. There are some who are more speculative, who like to describe the religion, customs and costumes of countries which they have only passed through.

Others describe to us the plants, minerals and trade of the places they have been to. I admit that a traveller should know how to reply to anything asked of him after his return; but it is a thing to be wished for rather than expected, short of finding a universal man with very good health, much income and leisure for his travels. For myself, I have not in truth neglected all these details, when I could learn them easily and at little cost: but it will not be hard to see, were I to own up to it, that my most important researches were towards knowledge of the ancient monuments of the countries which I saw on the voyage, and that this was my strongest inclination. I was never very eager to attend the famous Roman rituals, the concerts or the Italian operas, but as I had undertaken a work on ancient inscriptions to serve as a supplement to those of Gruterus (and made some progress with it before leaving), I passed the days, and whole months, in Rome, doing scarcely anything but look at the statues, bas-reliefs and ruins, and copying all the inscriptions – not only those which are not included in Gruterus, but also many of those which are, to see if they are exactly rendered: such that after having stayed there five months running, and assembled, through the agency of various intelligent people, all those bearing upon my subject from the kingdom of Naples and from other places in Italy where I did not intend to travel, I found myself in possession of more than two thousand which were unknown to that author, among which there are some very significant: and meditating upon the fine harvest which I could reap in Greece, where travellers up until now have merely brushed the surface of this curiosity, I was seized by a

strong desire at least to take a trip as far as Athens, which was once to Greece what Rome was to Italy. Perhaps I would not have carried out my design had I not found three English gentlemen who offered to join the party, and to share with me the risks of the journey: but as the passion for travel grows in the process, we had scarcely glimpsed the coast of Greece when we said to each other that it would not be right to leave it without seeing Constantinople, presently the foremost attraction there: and we had barely stayed there a month in that city when, seeing ourselves to be so close to Asia Minor, we thought ourselves obliged to pay it one of our visits before our return. All along that route I found things to satisfy my curiosity amply, having brought back a great number of Greek inscriptions which had never yet seen the light of day. I reproduce here the most interesting of them, of use in geography: but as this is not to everyone's taste I have relegated them to the end of the discourse, which will thus be less interrupted. I render them as exactly and as faithfully as possible: any infidelity committed by myself comes from not having always been able to put in the inscriptions according to the arrangement and the number of lines in the original, having been limited by the small size of the volume, which could be remedied in a Latin edition in a larger format, if this one is well received. Another infidelity of which I could be accused, however advantageous it may be to the reader, is that in the Greek inscriptions I separate the words which should be separated, when in truth most of the time there was no distinction on the stones and marbles I took them from, whether through the fault of the sculptors or for reasons unknown to us. This makes for such confusion, and gives so much difficulty in deciphering them, that for this reason in the book entitled Marmora Oxoniensa graeca incisa, for the relief of the reader, they were rendered first according to the original, and then in small letters with the words distinguished and marked with accents.

(J. Spon and G. Wheeler, *Voyage d'Italie, de Dalmatie, de Grèce et du Levant*, Lyons, 1678, preface.)

Spon and Wheeler were not the first visitors to Greece in the seventeenth century; they were preceded by more prestigious men, such as the Marquis of Nointel, Louis XIV's ambassador to the Sublime Porte [the Ottoman court at Constantinople], but their expertise and curiosity made their individual accounts of the journey, published separately, models of the genre. Spon linked his gifts as an antiquary to his experience as an epigrapher: he was the first to employ the concept of archaeology in the French language.

On immortality

MAN FACED BY REMEMBRANCE: *HYDRIOTAPHIA, URN-BURIALL, OR, A DISCOURSE OF THE SEPULCHRALL URNES LATELY FOUND IN NORFOLK. TOGETHER WITH THE GARDEN OF CYRUS... 1658 BY* THOMAS BROWNE.

TO MY WORTHY AND HONOURED FRIEND, THOMAS LE GROS OF CROSTWICK, ESQ.
When the Funerall pyre was out, and the last valediction over, men took a lasting adieu of their interred Friends, little expecting the curiosity of future ages should comment upon their ashes, and having no old experience of the duration of their Reliques, held no opinion of such after considerations.

But who knows the fate of his bones, or how often he is to be buried? Who hath the Oracle of his ashes, or whither they are to be scattered? The Reliques of many lie like the ruines of Pompeys, in all parts of the earth; And when they arrive at your hands, these may seem to have wandred far, who in a direct and Meridian Travell, have but a few miles of known Earth between your self and the Pole.

That the bones of Theseus should be seen again in Athens, was not beyond conjecture, and hopeful expectation; but that these should arise so opportunely to serve your self, was an hit of fate and honour beyond prediction.

We cannot but wish these Urnes might have the effect of Theatrical vessels, and great Hippodrome Urnes in Rome; to resound the acclamations and honour due unto you. But these are sad and sepulchral Pitchers, which have no joyful voices; silently expressing old mortality, the ruines of forgotten times, and can only speak with life, how long in this corruptible frame, some parts may be uncorrupted; yet able to out-last bones long unborn, and noblest pyle among us.

We present not these as any strange sight or spectacle unknown to your eyes, who have beheld the best of Urnes, and noblest variety of Ashes; Who are your self no slender master of Antiquities, and can daily command the view of so many Imperiall faces; Which raiseth your thoughts unto old things, and consideration of times before you, when even living men were Antiquities; when the living might exceed the dead, and to depart this world, could not be properly said, to go unto the greater number. And so run up your thoughts upon the ancient of dayes, the Antiquaries truest object, unto whom the eldest parcels are young, and earth it self an Infant; and without Ægyptian account makes but small noise in thousands.

We were hinted by the occasion, not catched the opportunity to write of old things, or intrude upon the Antiquary. We are coldly drawn unto discourses of Antiquities, who have scarce time before us to comprehend new things, or make out learned Novelties. But seeing they arose as they lay, almost in silence among us, at least in short account suddenly passed over; we were very unwilling lest they should die again, and be buried twice among us.

Beside, to preserve the living, and make the dead to live, to keep men out of their Urnes, and discourse of humane fragments in them, is not impertinent unto our profession; whose study is life and death, who daily behold examples of mortality, and of all men least need artificial *memento's, or coffins by our bed side, to minde us of our graves.*

'Tis time to observe Occurrences, and let nothing remarkable escape us; The Supinity of elder dayes hath left so much in silence, or time hath so martyred the Records, that the most industrious heads do finde no easie work to erect a new Britannia.

'Tis opportune to look back upon old times, and contemplate our Forefathers. Great examples grow thin, and to be fetched from the passed world. Simplicity flies away, and iniquity comes at long strides upon us. We have enough to do to make up our selves from present and passed times, and the whole stage of things scarce serveth for our instruction. A compleat peece of vertue must be made up from the Centos *of all ages, as all the beauties of Greece could make but one handsome* Venus.

When the bones of King Arthur were digged up, the old Race might think, they beheld therein some Originals of themselves; Unto these of our Urnes none here can pretend relation, and can only behold the Reliques of those persons, who in their life giving the Law unto their predecessors, after long obscurity, now lye at their mercies. But remembring the early civility they brought upon these Countreys, and forgetting long passed mischiefs; We mercifully preserve their bones, and pisse not upon their ashes.

In the offer of these Antiquities we drive not at ancient Families, so long out-lasted by them; We are farre from erecting your worth upon the pillars of your Fore-fathers, whose merits you illustrate. We honour your old Virtues, conformable unto times before you, which are the Noblest Armoury. And having long experience of your friendly conversation, void of empty Formality, full of freedome, constant and Generous Honesty, I look upon you as a Gemme of the Old Rock, and must professe my self even to Urne and Ashes,

> *Your ever faithfull Friend,*
> *and Servant,*
>
> *Thomas Browne.*

(Sir Thomas Browne, *Urne Buriall and the Garden of Cyrus*, ed. John Carter, Cambridge University Press, 1958, pp. 3–5.)

Browne combined the gifts of an observer with a writer's style. *Hydriotaphia* was undoubtedly the most thoroughly literary masterpiece of antiquarian learning before Winckelmann, and the style did not affect the precision of description or the originality of thought.

Archaeological stratigraphy

IN THE SEVENTEENTH CENTURY RUDBECK DESCRIBES AND DATES THE DIFFERENT STRATA OF THE SOIL.

§ IV. *Now, seeing that between Noah's Flood and today about 4000 years have passed, and that since that time all the humus, accumulated on the ground and derived from decomposed grass and leaves, that which the mists and rain have left, and from dust transported by the wind, amounts to no more that eight- or, at the most, nine-tenths of a* quart *[quarter], I made a measuring-stick divided into tenths and always carried it with me; and, according to this division, 1000 years correspond to a fifth of the stick and 500 years to a tenth, just as you can confirm by pl.31 fig. 104 [see p. 202].*

§ V. *To verify this idea, I sought to compare places where I know, on the one hand, it was bare of soil 10, 40, 80, 100, 200 or even 800 years ago, and, on the other, how much humus has piled up. Ten years ago I laid bare the ground around the fountains of the château, and I still find no visible traces of humus; to be precise, the grass had grown but its roots penetrated the sand, such as it was. Forty years ago, as M. Ingelbrecht Swensson told me, the road from Sandasen to Lagarden was remade; in the adjacent forest, sand was quarried to level the lowest parts of the road. In these holes and pits one could hardly discern the overlying humus,* as thin as a leaf with meagre ground cover. About one hundred years ago, in the reign of Jean, son of Gustav I, part of the castle was built on a sandy knoll, and the sand removed for the foundations was dumped a little to the west, and on this sand I found a layer of humus no thicker than a fifth of a doigt [inch] with vegetation above. When I had removed this, after the works for the new garden, there was − in the earth, at a depth of one, two, and sometimes three pieds [feet], depending of the slope of the former cutting − old humus, always resting on the knoll's sand and measuring about eight-tenths of a quart: according to my calculations, the humus reached in one hundred years a thickness no greater than the fifth of a doigt.

Everyone knows that Sweden was Christianised seven or eight hundred years ago, from which time there were no more cremations or barrow burials.

Looking at more recent mounds, of which I have examined 16,000, one finds no less than two-tenths of humus on them. In the largest royal tombs in ancient Uppsala, there were no burials later than 900 or 1000, when Christianity arrived. The humus of the highest mounds reached there a thickness of two tenths of a quart. All this proves the exactitude of the calculations for the humus, to know that a tenth of a quart corresponds to nearly five hundred years and a fifth of a doigt to one hundred years.

§ VIII. [...] On pl. 31 fig. 104, there is firstly the drawing of a measure of about half a foot or a quarter, divided into 10 parts, or 10 doigts. Alongside, there is a drawing of a layer of humus found at a great depth in the sediment (where neither human nor animal might have arrived without difficulty), a layer resting on small stones or pebbles around A; from thence, one measures its thickness to the level of vegetation, a thickness equivalent to nine-tenths but whose base is hard to determine, since the humus had begun to form in gaps between the stones. This humus was a little

paler; on the other hand, towards the middle (see B), slightly darker, and above a little paler; towards the vegetation, a little darker and striped, whilst the bark and pine-needles were sometimes intact, sometimes half or entirely decomposed; whatever, all is like a piece of burnt paper or cloth which, after combustion, gives the impression of being intact but which, when touched or breathed on, turns to dust. Just as I have learnt it in other locations, this differentiation is due to the fact that the forest has burnt, because it then becomes windswept dust and rain and snow affected: just as, in an open field, the humus is never as black as that in the forest. And, as a forest recovers after a fire, the humus becomes darker and darker. Here and there, one sees a few grains of sand, which seem to have been brought by birds or forest animals, on their paws or feet where the grains of sand might lodge and fall here and there.

In the second illustration C, there is only hard white sand, on which the humus lies cleanly, as if a black stripe had been painted over a white base. Thus, one can establish its beginning with an assured and precise means, and equally its thickness and depth. The colour of this humus is always less dark below, whilst increasingly dark towards the top, which shows that, at the outset, trees and vegetation were always smaller after Noah's Flood and that, in consequence, the dust found in the air, the rain and the snow was not over-thick, nourishing, fertile or redolent, which it later became, for the various reasons which I leave my distinguished reader to identify, to avoid my over-long excursions. The third drawing shows, near the letter D, gravel and, above that, the humus that is found in all places where flocks normally graze and which contains some grains of sand E, or small stones, which people or animals, for reasons to which I have already alluded, left or brought there. The final little drawing shows a burial mound with gravel on top, and inside it a sword fragment, c, amongst the bones and burnt remains of the corpse. The gravel in this *mound is located between* b *and* b, *and above, between* d *and* d, *one can see the humus, about 3* doigts *thick, which corresponds to about 1500 years.*

§ IX. The depth of humus found in grassland is about eight-tenths maximum, that in the wildest of forests, where no one can go without difficulty, about nine-tenths. This is always a little less compacted, to the extent that it compresses when we walk heavily on it, though still never surpassing much more than eight-tenths. The humus found on grassland, prominences, hills or mounds is always harder, however, so that it scarcely gives when walked over. Thus we understand that the age of the humus is calculated by slightly different means, depending on whether it is in open or forest land: the difference is, however, not important when one considers what is being compared: here, we do not search for dating by year, month or day, but for the distinction between several human generations in terms of the dating of a burial mound.

(From O. Rudbeck, *Atland eller Manheim*, 1697; ed. A. Nelson, Uppsala, 1937.)

Rudbeck was something of a genius, not only in his concept of stratigraphy but also in his daring intuition of a dating method derived from observation of superficial soil layers. Certainly his methods appear somewhat simplistic to us, but they mark a significant point in the establishment of conventions for observing strata based on survey and a precise description of soil composition. With Nicolas Bergier (see pp. 201–3), Rudbeck can be considered as a forerunner of the stratigraphic method. He only lacked recourse to the comparative analysis of finds, which would have enabled him to cross the boundary separating antiquarian practice from modern archaeological method. As later with Stukeley (see p. 360), the mixture of precise observation and religious fantasy which pervades his work is fascinating.

Treasure-hunting

THE DISCOVERY OF THE GRAVE OF CHILDERIC I AT TOURNAI, 1653.

Tournai, a fair-sized city with a circumference that exceeds four thousand paces, is divided in the middle by the river Scheldt, which separates the territory of the archbishopric of Cambrai from that of Artois and the Tournaisis. The part that is subject to the archdiocese of Cambrai has three well-known parishes: St John's, St Nicholas's, and, between them, St Brice's, which is the biggest and most favoured. Its incumbent, who is also Dean of Christianity, is the distinguished man, Giles Pattus; beside the churchyard and his own dwelling-place, he saw the house of St Brice's Treasurer, given over to the housing of the poor, decay through old age into ruin. He debated the matter with his churchwardens and decided to take off its roof and raze its walls so as to build a new house from the ground upwards, to rise higher than before.

Thus, in the year 1653, on 27 May, at the third hour after noon, while digging was in progress to the depth of seven feet or more, down to the rock, there was found first a gold clasp and soon a whole mass, round as if shaped by a disintegrated purse, in which were more than a hundred gold coins, disclosed by a blow of the pick of Adriaen Quinquin, mason of Tournai. He (being deaf and dumb from birth) began to make his ill-formed sounds and, so far as he could, alert the neighbourhood. There then ran up to him Dean Pattus and the two churchwardens, John de Berlo and Nicasius Rogers, brother of the abbot of Liessies, hastening (and with good cause) to claim whatever treasure there might be for their church and the dwelling-house of its paupers. In the same spot were found about two hundred Roman silver coins, but so worn and corroded that they could not be read; they mostly crumbled into dust. There were also excavated many objects of ironwork, rusted and consumed by age and the great wetness of the place, and two skulls, one larger than the other, with the bones of a human skeleton stretched out. And finally, within the space of about five feet, were found several remnants of a treasure: a sword of such fine steel that at the first touch it shattered into pieces; a hilt and sheath; a writing-case, ox's head, and many bees – more than three hundred – that constituted (so far as can be judged) the remnant of a yet more important whole that could not be seen clearly amidst such confusion; a needle, clasps, hooks, little hooks, studs, threads and buckles, all of gold, together with an infinite number of pyrope [gold-bronze] objects.

'The head of a warhorse dug out of the ground' [Silvius Italicus].

It would have been difficult, indeed impossible, to judge the period or the identity of the possessor of all these objects if there had not been found with them the gold ring of Childeric, king of the Franks, to indicate this.

The news of the discovery of the treasure became known through the whole city, and its authorities sent representatives to the Dean and churchwardens with the request to inspect what had been discovered. The Dean and churchwardens sent to them, not indeed everything (as was popularly believed during the five months before the return of his Highness), but just the royal ring, two ornaments from the bridle of the king's horse, the gold threads from his mantle, a gold needle, twently-seven gold bees, four clasps, studs and eighteen other buckles differently worked. All these the authorities of the city kept, so as to look at them more clearly. But the weight of these few objects was thirteen ounces of gold.

(From J.J. Chifflet, *Anastasis Childerici Francorum regis sive thesaurus sepulchralis Tornaci Neviorum effossus et commentario illustratus*, Antwerp, 1655.)

Chifflet's text communicates the atmosphere of excitement, wonder and greed which surrounded one of the most cele-

brated discoveries of seventeenth-century archaeology. The description of the discovery illustrates the lack of interest shown by the Tournai clerics in the circumstances of the find: it was a case not of excavation but of treasure-hunting.

The Cocherel discovery

ACCOUNT OF THE CIRCUMSTANCES OF THE DISCOVERY OF A MEGALITHIC GRAVE IN 1685 BY THE ABBOT OF COCHEREL IN NORMANDY.

It is very difficult to establish precisely the origin and antiquity of the ancient monuments which are found by chance when there are neither inscriptions, nor bas-reliefs, nor sculptures, nor engravings, nor decoration which might be used for chronology; or one finds nothing precise in History on which one might rest one's conjectures.

Thus one can only have the slightest comprehension of the tomb in question, all the things which have shed some light being missing, there only having been found there some stones of extraordinary size and shape, which had been placed under the heads of these bodies, either to preserve some mark of their status, or to satisfy established practices, or for some religious ceremony [...]. In the month of July 1685, the king having commanded that various works be undertaken on the River Eure to ease navigation, the lord of the parish of Cocherel had ordered work on the boat-passage for this river, for which he had need of three to four hundred feet of cut stone, requiring this gentleman to prospect the ground for all that it might provide him, not having the money to acquire from the local quarries, because no labourers could be found to work there, all the masons having been detailed to Maintenon for major works.

*He recalled having seen on a sizeable emi-
nence, catching the midday sun and hanging
above the river, two large stones set upright,
projecting no more than a foot out of the
ground, placed like the boundary markers used
to separate land-holdings. One of these stones
was six feet high, two-and-a-half feet wide and
one-and-a-half feet thick. The second was three
feet wide, the same thickness and six feet high.
These two stones had been found fifteen years
before by three unidentified men, who remain
unknown and who arrived in this place on a
feast day whilst all the inhabitants were in
church: they made a hole about three feet
square and rather deeper; they extracted the
bones of the two bodies from the head to
halfway down the spine; they left these bones
on the side of the hole which was not back-
filled, and left no indication that they intended
to search to left or right or above or below; they
went away without further ado leaving these
relics beside the hole. The lord of the place,
having been notified, made his first visit to the
site a few days later.*

*Seeing that the diggers had had so little rev-
erence for the bones, he was of the opinion that
the three strangers might have been English-
men with some memory of a fellow country-
man killed in the Battle of Cocherel, fought
close by in 1364, and that this memory
included a mention that something valuable
had been buried near these two marker stones,
and that having found and taken what they
most regarded, had no consideration for the
rest; and also he believed that it would be useless to bother with a longer investigation at
that time, whilst those who might know more
of the matter were long absent.*

(Le Brasseur, *Histoire civile et ecclésiastique du comté
d'Evreux*, Paris, 1722, pp. 172–3.)

The Cocherel discovery aroused massive
interest in Europe in the scholarly world.
The gentleman responsible gave a sworn
statement to a notary and had a number of
drawings made. By 1686 the Royal Society

of London had published a report on
Cocherel. The French version is fully pub-
lished by Le Brasseur in his *Histoire civile et
ecclésiastique du comté d'Evreux* (1722), and
Montfaucon devotes a chapter to it in his
Antiquité expliquée (volume V.2, chapter IX).

Barrows

HOW TO INTERPRET THE URNS
FOUND IN BARROWS.

*Ossa tamen facito parva referantur in urna
Sic ego etiam non mortuus exul ero.*
(Even if you put my ashes and bones into this
urn, my home will still be this grave.)

OVID

*Last week, in order to provide the kind reader
with a different topic, we presented two small
idols or graven images of our pagan ancestors;
now we shall continue with the promised six
remaining urns. Although we had a reasonable
number of urns, only six remain since some
were given as presents to connoisseurs of those
antiquities and others were broken and destroyed
during transportation.*

*Before I begin with the description of the
remaining urns, however, one or two general
statements concerning the urns must be briefly
made (for if this topic were to be elaborated upon
according to a connoisseur's taste, it would easily
fill several volumes).*

*I find quite ridiculous the opinion of those
who believe that the urns were generated by the
earth (as if they were earth-mushrooms), self-
growing, and that they sprouted in the spring,
and more precisely, in the month of May
(indeed, were they stewpots with a good chicken
or some other meat-stew, and did not emerge
from the earth only in May but throughout the
year, such that nothing was lacking and it was
only a case of: 'Help yourself and eat, because it's*

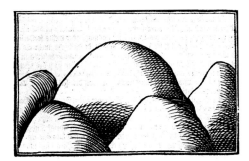

Tumuli, from Andreas Albert Rhode, Cimbrisch-Holsteinische Antiquitäten Remarques, 1719.

been kept for you', then it would be just the job for those who enjoy eating roast pidgeons but who want them to fly straight into their mouths.)

The incomparable geographer Münster (but, hush!, he is to be compared with Pliny, since both have the same reputation among the learned, i.e. none – Quis enim Plinio mendacior? *'Who tells more lies than Pliny?') is in favour of that kind of stupidity, saying in book IV, chapter 49: 'In Pohlandt' (meaning Poland) 'there are to be found pots shaped by Nature, which, once taken from the earth, are just like other pots.' Well shot, but wide of the mark! If Nature had taken pains to create these pots, she would certainly have created along with the pots the things inside, such as ashes, bones, pegs, brooches, hairpins, etc. And if she is able to do that, she can doubtless do more; so, instead of making pastry oneself, why not let Nature do the cooking? (I would really like to know what people understand by the word 'Nature'!)*

*Just as absurd as the opinions of Münster and his like are the views of those who believe that the pots were made by dwarfs or gnomes (*risum teneatis amici! *– restrain your laughter, my friends!), who still need them, and use them as offerings for their dead. It should be incredible to find among men the kind of stupidity that makes them believe in dwarfs or gnomes. Nonetheless it has to be confirmed that some who even want to be considered as the foremost scholars take the above-mentioned merely as an article of faith, having come to know of it* per

traditionem *(oh, what a fine thing tradition is!) through their parents and forefathers. And who wouldn't believe what their grandfather's mother, brother and wife had heard from their grandmother? I often have to laugh aloud when people, apparently not gullible at all, name their grandmother or grand-aunt as incontestible proof of those anecdotes and the like.*

[...] It is indeed inane to believe that the urns should belong to dwarfs and gnomes. An even greater stupidity, however, is the superstition of those who think that the seeds from the urns, when sown on fields or in gardens, should grow better than other grains; likewise the superstition of those who imagine that the milk contained in the urns should become richer and yield more butter, or that those who are convinced that chicken who drink from that milk won't get ill. This reveals sufficiently the prevailing simple-mindedness and superstition.

(A.A. Rhode, *Cimbrische-Holsteinische Antiquitäten Remarques,* ninth week, 28 February 1719, Hamburg, pp. 66–72.)

Andreas Albert Rhode had a sense of the absurd, a feeling for the landscape and the passion of a man of faith. His 'Remarks on Antiquities' was not only a manual of archaeology but, with its colourful expressions and vocabulary, a treatise on historical method which opened the way to the exploration of the soil and the stratigraphic and anthropological interpretation of remains. The most militant of eighteenth-century archaeologists was also the most lively voice of German protohistory.

Anatomy of the earth

STUKELEY OBSERVES AND DESCRIBES THE MEGALITHS OF GREAT BRITAIN.

A few years ago I spent some time every summer in viewing, measuring, and considering the works of the ancient Druids in our Island; I mean those remarkable circles of Stones which we find all over the kingdom, many of which I have seen, but of many more I have had accounts. Their greatness and number astonish'd me, nor need I be afraid to say, their beauty and design, as well as antiquity, drew my particular attention. I could not help carrying my inquiries about them as far as I was able. My studies this way have produced a vast quantity of drawings and writing, which consider'd as an intire work, may thus be intitled, Patriarchal Christianity or A Chronological HISTORY of the Origin and Progress of true Religion, and of Idolatory. [...]

In 1722, my late Lord Pembroke, Earl Thomas, who was pleas'd to favour my inquiries at this place, open'd a barrow, in order to find the position of the body observ'd in these early days. He pitched upon one of those south of Stonehenge, close upon the road thither from Wilton: and on the east side of the road. 'Tis one of the double barrows, or where two are inclos'd in one ditch: one of those, which I suppose the later kind, and of a fine turn'd bell-fashion. It may be seen in Plate IX. On the west side, he made a section from the top to the bottom, an intire segment, from center to circumference. The manner of composition of the barrow was good earth, quite thro', except a coat of chalk of about two foot thickness, covering it quite over, under the turf. Hence it appears, that the method of making these barrows was to dig up the turf for a great space round, till the barrow was brought to its intended bulk. Then with the chalk, dug out of the environing ditch, they powder'd it all over. So that for a considerable time, these barrows must have look'd white: even for some number of years. And the notion of sanctity annex'd to them, forbid people trampling on them, till perfectly settled and turf'd over. Hence the neatness of their form to this day. At the top or center of this barrow, not above three foot under the surface, my Lord found the skeleton of the interr'd; perfect, of a reasonable size, the head lying toward Stonehenge, or northward.

(William Stukeley, *Stonehenge, A temple restored to the British Druids*, Garland Publishing Inc., NY and London 1984.)

With Stukeley the passion for Druidism went easily with the observation of remains. One finds in him the same qualities as in Rudbeck: a doctor's passion for the anatomy of the earth, the privileged role assigned to survey and drawings, and the care devoted to the quality of excavations. Stukeley had the advantage of drawing on a strong tradition of landscape studies begun by Camden and developed by Aubrey. Nothing has come of his pandruidic theories but the quality of his surveys has remained unequalled until our times.

CHAPTER FOUR

ON THE REJECTION OF THE NATURAL HISTORY OF MAN

·

The long history of mankind

ASSESSMENT OF THE ORIGIN
OF THE PEOPLING OF AMERICA
BY ISAAC DE LAPEYRÈRE.

THEY ARE DECEIVED WHO DEDUCE THE ORIGINALS OF MEN FROM THE GRAND-CHILDREN OF NOAH, GROTIUS, CONCERNING THE ORIGINAL OF THE NATIONS IN AMERICA, CONFUTED.

It is the manner of all men, who search out the originals of nations, to derive them after the Flood from the grandchildren of Noah, who were the grandchildren of Adam. And great men are so earnest in this, (whom I very much prize, and have in continual respect for them) that they cut out all their originals out of this block; and either from some ancient record, or some old tradition, or the similitude of some old and obsolete name, or from any other conjecture; some they imagine that landed at such or such a place, to have been the authors or fathers of such a nation. As if Italus, who fled (for example) into Italy, and gave a name to that country, had been the father and author of all the Italians, and that nation had had no inhabitants before Italus. As if the Franks should be thought the authors and first founders of all the French Nation, and that there had been no Frenchmen before the Franks; because the Franks seized upon France, and changed the name of the province, and of Gallia made it Francia. Must needs Peru be thought to have had their original from the Chinensians,

because a piece of broken boat, like those of the Chinensians, was found on the banks of Peru? Those who guess so, seem to me to be like that two-penny Doctor, who told the sick man he had eaten an ass, because he saw the dorsers [panniers] standing under the bed.

Hugo Grotius sets out a discourse of the originals of the nations of America, whom he derives from the Norwegians, who eight hundred years ago were carried to Iceland, and went from thence to Greenland; and so from Greenland, through the lands adjoining, he conjectured, got to the south parts of America. Laetius did confute the conjecture of Grotius. Grotius vindicates himself from Laetius, and those things which in him Laetius had confuted, he by this absurdity resolved to restore. But, says he, if the Americans are not Germans (the Norwegians and Germans were with him all one) now they shall be the offspring of one nation; which is as much as to believe, with Aristotle, that they were from eternity, or born of the earth, as is reported of the Spartans; or of the ocean, according to Homer; or that there were some men before Adam, as one in France lately dreamed. If such things, says he, be believed, I see a great danger imminent to religion.

Grotius had a little before read a little discourse of the pre-Adamites, undigested, and about to be revised, which he under colour of friendship, by and acquaintance had required of me, which I friendly did communicate to him not that he should abuse me; nor do I desire to make return, or speak ill of the dead; let him keep with him his aspersion, and preserve it in his grave. Let this be enough, that the fame of the man, which now goes up and down the world with the creditable report of diverse and high endowments of learning, deceive not more with the allurements of his eloquence, and by his trappings of probable conjecture.

Grotius argues thus. The Norwegians landed in Greenland. They went forward from Greenland to America. Therefore the Norwegians were the authors of the nations in America. Let us grant, that Grotius took the right way of proving this, and that all were true he built upon this ground. Certainly, if America must needs be peopled by the Greenlanders, which were likewise Norwegians; he must prove first, according to his own ground, and first of all that the Norwegians, who first lighted upon it, found it empty, and only the winds blowing upon the leaves in those countries, whence he might gather this conclusion, that the Norwegians first planted Greenland, who afterwards straying about the world, strewed colonies over all America, and to the Americans and the Greenlanders should be indeed the posterity of the Norwegians, I say he ought first to have proved, that the Greenlanders were the offspring of the Norwegians, before he should guess that the Americans were sprung from the Greenlanders, and of the same stock of Norway.

It is most certain that the Norwegians first landed upon Greenland in the eastern parts of it, rough and wild, which the Norwegians called Ostreburg, going to find out the western parts better habitable, which they call Westreburg, found it full of all manner of herds and cattle as also full of the men of that climate, whom they called Schlegringians, who beat off the Norwegians, falling upon their quarters with a great slaughter. A true and faithful narrative of which is in the Greenland Chronicle written in Danish, which is in the hands of the most famous Gauminus, skilful in all languages, which I also knew in Denmark. The Norwegians were there strangers, not the founders of the Greenlanders, much less of the Americans.

[...] But what would Grotius say, if he were now alive, and should read that the Schlegringians were there, and inhabited Greenland before the Norwegians came? What manner of men would he say they were? Would he say they were from eternity, or sprung from Greenland itself, or cast out by the ocean upon land, or founded by another than Adam? If any such thing be believed says he, religion is in danger. The danger that he saw, was, that by this means he perceived the original sin of Adam was by this doctrine quite overthrown; because it is the common consent of all divines, that only by traduction it could pass upon all men.

This then I must prove, and this is only my task, to make it appear that we needed not Adam for our Father, nor traduction of Adam to make us partakers of his sin, as we needed not that Christ should be our Father, and his traduction should make us partakers of that grace which is by Christ, and all the following book shall be of this, which shall begin with the end of this.

(Isaac de Lapeyrère, *Men Before Adam*, 1656.)

It was apropos of the question of the peopling of America that Lapeyrère passed from the purely theological area of his thought to a geographical and archaeological discussion. José de Acosta had suggested in 1590 that America had been first settled by populations of Asiatic origin. The Dutch geographer Hugo Grotius, a few decades later, advocated a Nordic origin. In the course of his visit to Copenhagen Lapeyrère discovered Nordic antiquities and the work of Worm. He could thus attack the theories of the eminent geographer and pose the question of a human history longer than that of known history. The recourse to archaeological argument is one of the milestones of progress in the intellectual debate over scientific discussion based on proof.

The 'spy of the Grand Seigneur'

A 'SPY' WITH A GREAT TASTE
FOR ANTIQUITIES.

Letter to William Vospel, an Austrian monk, on the discovery of the tomb of Childeric accompanying the sending of a cabinet of antiquities.

As for what thou desirest to know, concerning the sepulchre of King Childeric, it is esteemed a piece of great antiquity, in regard he was a fourth monarch of France. He reigned over the Gauls or Franks in the year 458, Severus being Emperor of Rome, Severinus and Degalaiphus, Consuls. Yet in little more than three years, he was deposed, and banished by his subjects, whilst Ægidius, a Roman, was crowned in his stead. Neither did this man please the people so well, but that after some experience of his profession, avarice, and other vices, they expelled him also, and recalled their lawful sovreign. For Ægidius had vexed them with unreasonable taxes, fleecing them of many millions, which he privately sent out of the kingdom, disposing of this vast treasure at Rome, and among his friends in other parts, as a support against future contingencies: for he looked for some backblows of fate. Childeric therefore being restored to his crown, enjoyed it till his death, which was in the year 484. After whom succeeded in the kingdom, Clodovaus the Great, who was the first French king that embraced Christianity.

The time when Childeric's tomb was first discovered, was about two years ago, when the Cathedral of Tournay wanted reparation. For as the labourers were digging up the old charnel-house, they encountered a long stone; which giving them some fatigue, they broke in pieces, and found under it the entire skeleton of a man, lying at length, with abundance of Greek medals of gold and some other curiosities of the same metal, among which was a ring with this motto: SIGILLUM CHILDERICI REGIS. All of these relics were at first possessed by the canons of that church, where they were found; of whom they were begged by the Arch-Duke of Austria, who has them in his custody. Therefore, those who told them they are in the king of France's hands were misinformed themselves, or designed to abuse thee. For this cannot be supposed, during the present war between France and Spain, when they are more ready on both sides to plunder one another, than to grant civilities of this obliging nature.

I perceive thou art grown a great antiquary; and therefore in token of my esteem, I have sent thee a cabinet of such old things as I have scraped together in my travels, and during my residence in this city.

The agates which you will find in the uppermost drawer, may easily be dated by their figures, which are all after the fashion of Gentile Rome. As for the shells in the second, I leave them to thy own judgement; only this I will say, that they are not common. The third contains a miscellany of several antiques. The knives were used by the ancient Roman priests in their sacrifices. The weights are at least twelve hundred years old, by the parallels which I have seen in the king's library. The rings are also of the Parthian make, and the arrow to which they are fastened retains its oriental venom to this hour; as thou wilt find, by trying it on any animal that deserves it. But after all, the lowermost drawer contains nothing but counterfeits, for those medals are the work of Parmezan, the finest engraver in the world.

(Giovanni Paolo Marana, *The Eight Volumes of Letters Writ by a Turkish Spy, who Lived Five and Forty Years Undiscovered at Paris*, translated by William Bradshaw, London, 1748.)

The 'spy of the Grand Seigneur', protected by his status as a subject of the Sultan, could write things which could only be whispered in the privacy of free-thinking salons: he was both an antiquary fond of objects and 'shells' and a critic not deceived by biblical chronology.

On the origin of art

JOHANN JOACHIM WINCKELMANN
AND THE BIRTH OF ART HISTORY.

(a) In the infancy of art, its productions are, like the handsomest of human beings at birth, misshapen, and similar one to another, like the seeds of plants of entirely different kinds; but in its bloom and decay, they resemble those mighty streams, which at the point where they should be the broadest, either dwindle into small rivulets, or totally disappear.

The art of drawing among the Egyptians is to be compared to a tree which, though well cultivated, has been checked and arrested in its growth by a worm, or other casualties; for it remained unchanged, precisely the same, yet without attaining its perfection, until the period when Greek kings held sway over them; and the case appears to have been the same with Persian art. Etruscan art, when in its bloom, may be compared to a raging stream, rushing furiously along between crags and over rocks; for the characteristics of its drawing are hardness and exaggeration. But, among the Greeks, the art of drawing resembles a river whose clear waters flow in numerous windings through a fertile vale, and fill its channel, yet do not overflow.

As art has been devoted principally to the representation of man, we might say of him more correctly than Protagorus did, that 'he is the measure and rule of all things'. The most ancient records also teach us, that the earliest essays, especially in the drawing of figures, have represented, not the manner in which a man appears to us, but what he is; not a view of his body, but the outline of his shadow. From this simplicity of shape the artist next proceeded to examine proportions; this inquiry taught exactness; the exactness hereby acquired gave confidence, and afterwards success, to his endeavours after grandeur, and at last gradually raised art among the Greeks to the highest beauty. After all the parts constituting grandeur and beauty were united, the artist, in seeking to embellish them, fell into the error of profuseness; art consequently lost its grandeur; and the loss was finally followed by its utter downfall.

The following is, in a few words, the design of this treatise on the history of art. In the first place, I shall speak, generally, of the shape with which art commenced; next, of the different

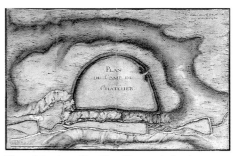

Plan of the site of Le Chatellier, made for the Comte de Caylus.

materials upon which it worked; and lastly, of the influence of climate upon it.

Art commenced with the simplest shape, and by working in clay, consequently, with a sort of statuary; for even a child can give a certain form to soft mass, though unable to draw anything on a surface, because merely an idea of an object is sufficient for the former, whereas for the latter much other knowledge is requisite; but painting was afterwards employed to embellish sculpture.

(b) I have already overstepped the boundaries of the history of art, and in meditating upon its downfall have felt almost like the historian who, in narrating the history of his native land, is compelled to allude to its destruction, of which he was a witness. Still, I could not refrain from searching into the fate of works of art as far as my eye could reach; just as a maiden, standing on the shore of the ocean, follows with tearful eyes her departing lover with no hope of ever seeing him again, and fancies that in the distant sail she sees the image of her beloved. Like that loving maiden we too have, as it were, nothing but a shadowy outline left of the object of our wishes, but that very indistinctness awakens only a more earnest longing for what we have lost, and we study the copies of the originals more attentively than we should have done the originals themselves if we had been in full possession of them. In this particular we are very much like those who wish to have an *interview with spirits, and who believe that they see them when there is nothing to be seen. In a similar manner the authority of antiquity predetermines our judgments yet, even this prepossession has been not without its advantages; for he who always proposes to himself to* find *much will by seeking for much perceive something. If the ancients had been poorer in art they would have written better of it. We are, compared to them, like poorly portioned heirs; but we look carefully about us, and by deductions from many particulars we arrive at least at a probable certainty capable of becoming a source of more instruction than the details bequeathed to us by the ancients, for, with the exception of a few critical observations, they are merely historical. We must not shrink from seeking after the truth, even though its discovery wounds our self-esteem; a few must go wrong that the many may go right.*

(J.J. Winckelmann, *The History of Ancient Art among the Greeks*, J.R. Osgood and Co., Boston, Mass., 1880.)

Winckelmann shared with Caylus a faith in a naturalistic and evolutionary vision of art, but added to his analysis an aesthetic for which Greece formed the unsurpassable horizon.

The excavations of Martin Mushard

USEFUL INSTRUCTIONS ABOUT
HOW TO AVOID MISSING URNS
WHILE DIGGING FOR THEM.

Since so little is known of the oldest times of this country, at all times a few amateurs in antiquity have endeavoured to deduce from graves the ways of life and customs of the pagans, and, after satisfying their curiosity to a certain degree, have filled thus the collections of antiquities with urns, shields, weapons and all kinds of utensils. These antiquities, however, are not always to be found, and since it is tedious to spend time and money in vain, the idea behind these pages is to provide the reader with sincerely useful instructions grounded on manifold experience.

The remarkable ruins used to be places of sacrifice, where, at special times, the inhabitants of whole villages or districts would congregate, sacrifice, feast and dance.

Their exploration is laborious and dangerous, they promise a lot, but keep little or nothing. Pro thesauro carbones *[coals instead of treasure]: accordingly, there aren't any graves. What can be found, however, above a layer of coal and topped up by ashes and earth, are flintstone wedges, the so-called sacrificial knives, fragments of sacrificial bowls and pots. Now, may any theory be derived from that?*

Nearby, the already mentioned hills, those forming a long square and being fenced with big stones (the biggest one usually lying eastwards), very seldom contain urns and used to be sites of public congregation, too. The circular hills have to be distinguished, though. Some of them are huge; excavating one of these is so laborious that the loss is extremely great when nothing can be found in it. They must hence be judged by their appearance. There are stone heaps somewhat higher and more peaked than the others; those, on account of the heavy stones they contain, are generally sunk two or three feet into the earth, and often inscribed in a circle of stones. Excavating those hills one will find only stones, sand and ashes between them; i.e. omnem move lapidem *[all stones have to be removed]. One always hopes to find the lintel above an urn, but in vain. Having found some flat stones which could perfectly well be lintels and after digging another four feet without any result, it is better to stop the excavation, since in that depth urns are unlikely to be found. That hill must hence be a sacrificial hill. Those hills have come to that height through frequently repeated sacrifices, implying each time a new layer of stones on top of which a new fireplace was to be built on untouched ground.* Religionis causa *[for religious reasons], they were raised by a con-spiration of people or, as it were, a community. Whoever comes across one of these will find all sweat and pain wasted on them. [...]*

Another type of burial site which bears no exterior sight of its contents must be pointed out; these are those in the open fields. Not far from them there usually stands a reminder for the living. The urns are to be found at the western or northern side of the monument, the closer to it, the more considerable, extremum occupat scabies *[the last gets scabies]. If the burial ground is in flat earth, the urns and utensils will be the best. As to where they are to be found, a shepherd or a plough-man may give the most valuable information. The iron rod, however, must not be forgotten, because from the noise it makes touching an object, it can be best told, whether it is a stone or an urn. Concerning the excavation of the urns, it has to be remarked that the lintel in the tumu-lus can be laid bare as elsewhere, but must not be hit hard with the spade and by no means trampled on. The urn should be dug out side-ways, then cleaned carefully and lifted with both hands. Afterwards it must be left to dry for an hour in the fresh air. If the pot is broken and you wish to restore it, then the fragments must be glued together and the cracks filled with the pulverized remains of another urn. The remains [...] may be simply covered with earth again. The fragments, when heated, are very useful for the removal of grease spots from clothing.*

(Martin Mushard, *Hannoverische Beiträge zum Nützen und Vergnügen*, 2, 1760–61.)

Martin Mushard (1669–1770) was a north German pastor like Andreas Albert Rhode. His passion for antiquities led him to undertake a number of cemetery exca-vations. This little text published in a pop-ular cultural review is a good summary of German theories of the time. It shows the expertise of the German antiquaries in cemetery excavation and the emergence of a stratigraphical technique which pro-gressively overturned the dilettantism of the treasure-hunters. This essay is one of the first excavation manuals published in Europe.

A letter from Voltaire

ON THE ORIGIN OF 'SHELLS'.

Sir,
I have the honour to send you, via Paris, the little book of Singularités de la Nature; *there are things in this little work which are closely analogous to what is happening in your château [Voltaire is alluding to the theory of the sponta-neous growth of shells developed in* La Sauvagère's *book]: I always resort to Nature, which is more creative than we, and I challenge all systems. I can see only people who put them-selves directly in the place of God, who want to create a world by words.*

The alleged shell-beds which cover the conti-nent, the coral formed by insects, the mountains raised by the sea; all of this seems to me made to be published as a sequel to A Thousand and One Nights.

You seem to me very wise, Sir, in only believ-ing what you see; others believe the opposite of what they see, or rather, they want to be taken in; half the world has always wanted to deceive the rest; happy is he who has sight and spirit as excellent as yours.

I have the honour to be, with the most respectful esteem,
Sir, your most humble and obedient servant,
Signed, VOLTAIRE

(M. F. de La Sauvagère, *Recueil de dissertations ou recherches historiques et critiques*, postscript by Voltaire, Paris, 1776.)

Voltaire's critical sense did not shield him from a certain scepticism. In an anonymous article which appeared in 1746 in the *Mer-cure de France* he maintained that the shells and petrified fish found in the mountains were the product of passing travellers who had discarded their leftover food. This attracted an ironic response from Buffon who suggested that it was monkeys who transported shells to the mountain heights and all the other 'uninhabitable places' (quoted by Gohau, 1990, p. 159). In relying on the works of the former director of the Engineer Corps, La Sauvagère, Voltaire conferred prestige on an author who saw the Breton megaliths as Caesar's camps.

Diderot's preface

DIDEROT'S PREFACE TO
L'ANTIQUITÉ DÉVOILÉE BY
NICOLAS ANTOINE BOULANGER.

If any man has ever in his life shown the true character of genius, it is this one. In the setting of a domestic persecution which began with life and only ended with it; in the setting of distraction after distraction and the most arduous of tasks, he pursued a great career. When one leafs through his works one might believe that he had lived for more than a century; however he saw, read, regarded, reflected, meditated, wrote and lived for but a moment: one could say of him what Homer said of the horses of the gods: the more space the eye discovers in the heavens, the more the celestial steeds can cross with one leap.

After poor, sketchy studies in the state schools, he was sent to work on the major roads: it was there that he spent his time, his health and his life, in canalising rivers, cutting through mountains and creating the great routes which make France a unique kingdom and will forever characterise the reign of Louis XV.

It was also there that he developed the precious seed within himself: he saw the multitude of diverse materials which the earth hides within its bosom and which attests to its antiquity and

its countless revolutions around the star which illuminates it; the changing climates, and the regions above which an overhead sun once blazed now touched by its oblique transient rays and covered with eternal ice; he gathered wood, stones, shells; he saw in our quarries the imprints of plants native to the coast of India; the plough turns up in our fields creatures whose relatives lie deep in the abyss of the seas; the man lying to the north on elephant bones and walking here on the home of the whales; he saw the food of a present world passing over the surface of a hundred past worlds; he considered the order which the layers of the earth maintained between themselves: an order now so regular, now so disturbed, that here the wholly new globe seems to have come from the hands of the great workman; there offering only an ancient chaos trying to sort itself out; elsewhere only the ruins of a vast fallen edifice, rebuilt and collapsed yet again, without so many successive overthrowings imagination itself might have retraced the first.

This is what gave rise to his first thoughts. Having considered in all aspects the catastrophes of the earth, he sought their effects on its former inhabitants; thence his conjectures on societies, governments and religions. But he acted to verify his conjectures by comparing them with tradition and stories; and he says 'I have seen, I have sought to interpret; let us now see what has been said and what is.' So he reached for the Latin authors and realised that he had no Latin; so he learnt it, but it lacked much where he could find the enlightenment he needed: he found the Latins too ignorant and too recent.

He turned to the Greeks. He learnt their language and had soon devoured the poets, philosophers and historians; but in the Greeks he found only fictions, lies and vanity, a people misrepresenting everything to appropriate all; children who wallowed in tales of marvels, where a small historical circumstance, a glimmer of truth would be lost in the prevailing deep gloom, which inspired the poet, painter and sculptor and which made the philosopher despair. He had no doubt that there had been earlier and simpler stories, and he bravely threw himself into the study of the Hebrew, Syriac, Chaldean and Arabic languages, both ancient and modern. What work! What perseverence! Such was the knowledge that he acquired when he committed himself to disentangle the mythology.

I have often heard him say that the methods of our scholars were correct and that had they only had more study and attention, they would have seen that they were in agreement and could have shaken hands. He saw priestly and theocratic government as the oldest: he was inclined to believe that savages were descended from wandering families that the terror of the first great events had exiled to the forests where they had lost their ideas of law, as we have seen in the Cenobites, who need only a little more solitude to be transformed into savages.

He said that if philosophy had found too many obstacles with us, it was because we had begun where we should have finished, by abstract maxims, general reasoning, subtle reflections which revolted by their unfamiliarity and boldness, and which might have been accepted painlessly had they been preceded by the factual story.

(N. A. Boulanger, *L'Antiquité dévoilée par ses usages ou Examen critique des principales opinions, cérémonies et institutions religieuses et politiques des différents peuples de la terre*, Amsterdam, 1756, pp. V–VII and pp. 23–7.)

Nicolas Antoine Boulanger (1722–59) was one of the most original minds of the eighteenth century. He belonged to the group of bridge-builders whose contribution to the understanding of French antiquities was decisive. Amongst them was Henri Gautier (1660–1737), successor of Bergier, author of a *Traité de la construction des chemins où il est parlé de ceux des Romains et de ceux des Modernes* (Paris, 1693), one of the most fervent advocates of a long chronology, discoverer of a tectonic which built on and surpassed the ideas of Steno and Legendre, brother of Sophie Volland, the friend of Diderot, tireless discoverer of monuments. Just as *L'Antiquité dévoilée* was proclaimed

by Diderot, *Le Despotisme oriental*, another work by Boulanger destined for a long life, was published by Holbach in 1761. Even if his ideas on the Flood were generally questioned by the Encyclopaedists, Boulanger, of whom Buffon was an avid reader, rapidly won their esteem. He conversed with de Jussieu and Rousseau and contributed to the 'Flood' and 'Duty' entries for the *Encyclopaedia*. His wide-ranging task envisaged in one way or another the elucidation, via the humanities, of the history of nature.

Jefferson's excavations

JEFFERSON DESCRIBES
THE EXCAVATION OF A BARROW
DISCOVERED IN VIRGINIA IN 1781.

I know of no such thing existing as an Indian monument; for I would not honor with that name arrow points, stone hatchets, stone pipes, and half-shapen images. Of labor on the large scale, I think there is no remain as respectable as would be a common ditch for the draining of lands; unless indeed it would be the barrows, of which many are to be found all over this country. These are of different sizes, some of them constructed of earth, and some of loose stones. That they were repositories of the dead, has been obvious to all; but on what particular occasion constructed, was a matter of doubt. Some have thought they covered the bones of those who have fallen in battles fought on the spot of interment. Some ascribed them to the custom, said to prevail among the Indians, of collecting, at certain periods, the bones of all of their dead, wheresoever deposited at the time of death. Others again supposed them the general sepulchres for towns, conjectured to have been on or near these grounds; and this opinion was supported by the quality of the lands in which they are found, (those constructed of earth being generally in the softest and most fertile meadow-grounds on river sides,) and by a tradition, said to be handed down from the aboriginal Indians, that, when they settled in a town, the first person who died was placed erect, and earth put about him, so as to cover and support him; that when another died, a narrow passage was dug to the first, the second reclined against him, and the cover of earth replaced, and so on. There being one of these in my neighborhood, I wished to satisfy myself whether any, and which of these opinions were just. For this purpose I determined to open and examine it thoroughly. It was situated on the low grounds of the Rivanna, about two miles above its principal fork, and opposite to some hills, on which had been an Indian town. It was of a spheroidical form, of about forty feet diameter at the base, and had been of about twelve feet altitude, though now reduced by the plough to seven and a half, having been under cultivation about a dozen years. Before this it was covered with trees of twelve inches diameter, and round the base was an excavation of five feet depth and width, from whence the earth had been taken of which the hillock was formed. I first dug superficially in several parts of it, and came to collections of human bones, at different depths, from six inches to three feet below the surface. These were lying in the utmost confusion, some vertical, some oblique, some horizontal, and directed to every point of the compass, entangled and held together in clusters by the earth. Bones of the most distant parts were found together, as, for instance, the small bones of the foot in the hollow of a scull; many sculls would sometimes be in contact, lying on the face, on the side, on the back, top or bottom, so as, on the whole, to give the idea of bones emptied promiscuously from a bag or a basket, and covered over with earth, without any attention to their order. The bones of which the greatest numbers remained, were sculls, jaw-bones, teeth, the bones of the arms, thighs, legs, feet and hands. A few ribs remained, some vertebrae of the neck and spine, without their processes, and one instance only of the bone which serves as a base to the vertebral column [the os-sacrum]. The sculls were so tender, that they generally fell to pieces on being touched. The other bones were stronger. There were some teeth which were judged to be smaller than those of an adult; a scull, which, on a slight view, appeared to be that of an infant, but it fell to pieces on being taken out, so as to prevent satisfactory examination; a rib, and a fragment of the under-jaw of a person about half grown; another rib of an infant; and a part of the jaw of a child, which had not cut its teeth. This last furnishing the most decisive proof of the burial of children here, I was particular in my attention to it. It was part of the right half of the under-jaw. The processes, by which it was attenuated to the temporal bones, were entire, and the bone itself firm to where it had been broken off, which, as nearly as I could judge, was about the place of the eye-tooth. Its upper edge, wherein would have been the sockets of the teeth, was perfectly smooth. Measuring it with that of an adult, by placing their hinder processes together, its broken end extended to the penultimate grinder of the adult. This bone was white, all the others of a sand color. The bones of infants being soft, they probably decay sooner, which might be the cause so few were found here. I proceeded then to make a perpendicular cut through the body of the barrow, that I might examine its internal structure. This passed about three feet from its centre, was opened to the former surface of the earth, and was wide enough for a man to walk through and examine its sides. At the bottom, that is, on the level of the circumjacent plain, I found bones; above these a few stones, brought from a cliff a quarter of a mile off, and from the river one-eighth of a mile off; then a large interval of earth, then a stratum of bones, and so on. At one end of the section were four strata of bones plainly distinguishable; at the other, three; the strata in one part not ranging with those in another. The bones nearest the surface were least decayed. No holes were discovered in any of them, as if made with bullets, arrows, or other *weapons. I conjectured that in this barrow might have been a thousand skeletons. Everyone will readily seize the circumstances above related, which militate against the opinion, that it covered the bones only of persons fallen in battle; and against the tradition also, which would make it the common sepulchre of a town, in which the bodies were placed upright, and touching each other. Appearances certainly indicate that it has derived both origin and growth from the accustomary collection of bones, and deposition of them together; that the first collection had been deposited on the common surface of the earth, a few stones put over it, and then a covering of earth, that the second had been laid on this, had covered more or less of it in proportion to the number of bones, and was then also covered with earth; and so on. The following are the particular circumstances which give it this aspect. 1. The number of bones. 2. Their confused position. 3. Their being in different strata. 4. The strata in one part having no correspondence with those in another. 5. The different states of decay in these strata, which seem to indicate a difference in the time of inhumation. 6. The existence of infant bones among them.*

(Thomas Jefferson, *Notes on the State of Virginia*, Harper and Row, New York and London, 1964.)

According to Mortimer Wheeler, the father of the modern stratigraphical method, this text by Jefferson (1743–1826) was one of the most astounding testaments of the birth of stratigraphical archaeology at the end of the eighteenth century. Jefferson's antiquarian interest was fostered in France between 1784 and 1789, when he was the United States' ambassador, by contact with David and reading Winckelmann. With the friend of the latter, the painter Clérisseau, who wrote *Les Antiquités de la France* (Paris, 1778), he visited Provence and admired the antique monuments, especially the Maison Carrée at Nîmes. Elected President of the United States in 1800, he was to become the most ardent advocate of the Neo-classical style in his country. In 1799, as president of the American Philosophical Association, he contacted all the Association's corresponding members, asking for reports on all the archaeological sites that they might know of (Willey and Sabloff, 1980, pp. 28–9). Sadly, his influence, like that of his European contemporaries, did not achieve a wide audience until the second half of the century.

CHAPTER FIVE

THE INVENTION OF ARCHAEOLOGY

·

The first inhabitants of Gaul

BOUCHER DE PERTHES MAKES A
GEOLOGICAL CHRONOLOGY POSSIBLE.

Before speaking of the work, it is worth saying a few words about the workers, because it is their age which serves us to determine that of their industry.

Received opinion is that this part of Europe in which we live is a new land and newly occupied. Its annals hardly extend to twenty centuries: its memories and traditions extend no further back than two thousand five hundred years.

The excellent works by Mm. de Caumont and Arnédée Thierry do not even take them so far back and the peoples who have occupied or merely passed through Gallic lands – the Gauls, the Celts, the Belgae, the Venetii, the Ligurians, the Aquitani or Iberians, the Kimris or Cymbri, the Scythians – have not left any remains to which this date might be assigned.

This system is perfectly based where the great monuments are concerned because tradition rests with them. These monuments would have struck the eyes of our ancestors, and their ruins would strike ours as they are still struck by those of the Asiatic cities and the structures called Pelagic and Cyclopean. Whilst one does not know the history of these nor even with real certainty that of their builders, what remains indicates, if not the precise instant of their construction, at least the period of civilisation to which they are attached; and, when they belong to that civilisation, they are part of what we would consider the antique period. We thus have nothing to say of present-day France or even of Roman or Gaulish France because,

according to us, our history did not commence there. It is in traversing the soil of civilisation, it is in penetrating to the Celtic soil, that we find the cradle of our fathers, or the earth trodden by the primordial population of Gauls.

In this study these beings who are no more, their superimposed traces, a sort of scale of passing days, will be our historical tablets, because the dust of ages can hardly be improvised and the colour of the centuries is inimitable.

If there were antediluvian men, their traces can exist.

Without leaving the place where we are, when digging down some feet, we encounter the debris of another epoch with other customs, other monuments, other weather, other men; when some feet lower we find another age and also other peoples, who can say if, in going even further down, if, in penetrating the entrails of an earth devastated by so many catastrophes, we should not acquire the proof that what was at the surface is today at the centre and that the intermediate landscapes, or the immense regions covered by the marine depths, do not hide from us the monuments and debris of unknown peoples.

The convulsions which have overturned our planet are proven; is it equally so that at each of these revolutions, it was without human creatures? From the first cataclysms, no trace of life. In those which followed one finds the remains of marine animals, then terrestrial vegetation, then saurians, then mammals, then nothing again: all have perished, the earth is deserted, it is only after an indefinite period that one sees the reappearance of new species which perish in their turn after the great destruction called the universal Flood.

Whether this traditional Flood corresponds to the geological flood, of the clysmian or diluvian epoch; whether they form one and the same catastrophe, whether they mark one and the same period, is a serious question that we shall not undertake to treat: we only wish to say that it was an immense and final cataclysm whose tradition has remained with most peoples.

So we all agree on it, men lived. But for how much time have they lived and how many similar upheavals have they experienced? Tradition does not say: how could it have said, if the destruction was total?

That in each of these terrible events, the surface of the globe had been swept clean and renewed is what geology shows us; but it shows equally that nothing is lost and that one retrieves in succession the remains of these diverse epochs.

These traces, have they all been perceived on the same day? No, it is only little by little and only in our own time that they have been reported in a positive way.

On this path of discovery we are only at the point of departure. So why say that we have reached the end of the voyage? Because we have lifted a corner of the veil, must we conclude that we have seen all that the veil conceals? We know today that at the moment of each of these revolutions there existed many animals: it is a truth demonstrated by the heaps of bones in the diluvial deposits. These deposits were unknown to us a hundred years ago; and at the beginning of this century we did not know a quarter of the antediluvian species that we know today. Perhaps in thirty years we shall know of more. [...]

To overturn all the acquired data, or those theories which rest far less on facts than on words and induction, then it is sufficient, as M. Alex. Brogniart says, for one fortunate incident, one of those unexpected encounters which are nonetheless convincing.

Who even knows if it is not here, under our feet and in these places, that there exists the evidence of this antiquity of the works of man and of an antiquity which surpasses all expectations! You have all, sirs, visited, at the gate of Abbeville, on the right of the Boulogne road and on that to Laviers, the Menchecourt sand-quarries. For some years, building sand has been extracted. It is more than thirty years ago

Antediluvian stones, Boucher de Perthes, 1847.

that M. Baillon and my father, who both figure among the founders of this Society, reported a deposit of diluvian bones in this quarry; and, in effect, a near-complete rhinoceros skeleton, and subsequently, numerous remains of elephants and other animals have been collected and sent to the museum in Paris and to that in this town where you can still see them. Oh well! Sirs, in these sands, at a depth of about eight metres amongst these same antediluvian bones have been found traces of the work of man, flint axes which I still submit for your examination with all the circumstances of discovery.

That the axes have the same age as the bones, I cannot confirm; their origin could be later just as they could be earlier. What I only maintain as probable is that they were there since the bones were, and that they were there by the same cause. It is now for geology to determine the epoch to which the deposit belongs.

This fact is not unique. Quite recently, in the month of last July, a hundred steps from here, in the bed of flint exposed behind the hospital garden, between the Champ-de Foire and the rue Millevoye, in a location recognised as diluvean by several geologists and notably by Mm. Ravin and Buteux, who have made an in-depth investigation of it, a location of which I will equally give you the analysis, I have found several other worked flints.

One could say that the pieces arrived there by some accident posterior to the formation of the bed.

For me, sirs, who has closely examined their position and probably for all those who will want to study it with me, this posteriority is an impossible thing. If the bed is diluvian, and I do not doubt it, these implements are diluvian; and it is necessary to believe in the existence of a people whose antiquity far exceeds those of whom tradition tell us. Now, this antiquity and this existence, we will demonstrate to you by the evidence. If I had some doubts about the Manchecourt axes and about their origin, the discovery of these has dissipated them.

I know that here again the evidence could be denied. It is impossible, one will say: human vestiges, utensils, worked flint axes cannot be found among diluvian debris. I can only reply: it is so, and it must be, because it would be stranger were it not so; and I will not cease to repeat: since there were men at that time, since tradition says so, since reflection proves it, since finally no one denies it, what then is surprising about their traces being recovered? One is the consequence of the other.

Let one admit even that these men were few in number; however small this number, it was sufficient to brush aside all absolute denial; and if there were only a single people, only a single family, only a single couple, one could not say with certainty; their remains will never be found.

We must then return to this conclusion; if men are older on earth than one had commonly believed, their monuments must also be so, or, in default of monuments, their utensils and weapons.

(Boucher de Perthes, *Antiquités celtiques et antédiluviennes*, 1847, 1, chap. 2, pp. 16–32.)

Boucher de Perthes was less cautious than Thomsen and remained convinced, following Cuvier, of the idea of a universal Flood. However, his cultural background as a man of the Enlightenment encouraged a rereading of the ancient authors and especially of Lucretius. He combined a philosophical approach to the human condition from the Greek inheritance to observation of the soil and the desire to construct a geological time-scale which overturned the idea of history as accepted at the start of the nineteenth century. In just referring to the idea of human evolution he won a greater public than his Scandinavian predecessors and became more the founder of a new discipline than the discoverer of a new technique of classifying the artefacts found in the earth.

BIBLIOGRAPHY

Carl Bernhard Stark's *Systematik und Geschichte der Archäologie der Kunst* was published in Leipzig in 1880 and was the most scholarly and comprehensive of the histories of archaeology, apart from the fact that it was limited to classical archaeology. More than a century later, such a biographical/bibliographical exercise would appear totally excessive. The bibliography presented here is thus limited: it only includes titles cited in the body of the text and some works of synthesis. At the time of writing the most complete general bibliographies are to be found in Hildebrandt 1937, Daniel 1978, Bouzek *et al.* 1983 and Trigger 1989. They need to be completed by the works of Willey and Sabloff 1980 for America and Chang 1986 for China. Glyn Daniel has provided a list of the main archaeological anthologies in his book of 1978. What I offer in this collection is restricted to some perhaps little-known texts and serves no other purpose than to emphasise certain aspects treated in the body of this volume. My information owes a lot to Stemmermann 1934, Gummel 1938, Abramowicz 1983, Settis 1984 and Pinon 1991. My debt to the works of Glyn Daniel and Stuart Piggott is also evident.

Abdessalam 1970
Chadi Abdessalam (director), *The Night of Counting the Years*, film better known as *The Mummy*, 1970.

Abel 1939
Othenio Abel, *Vorzeitliche Tierreste im Deutschen Mythus, Brauchtum und Volksglauben*, Fischer, Jena, 1939.

Abramowicz 1983
Andrzej Abramowicz, *Dzieje Zainteresowan starozytniczych w Polsce* (The History of Antiquarianism in Poland), 2 volumes, Polska akademia Nauk, Wrocław, 1983–7.

Adhémar 1937
Jean Adhémar, *Influences antiques dans l'art du Moyen Age français, recherche sur les sources et les thèmes d'inspiration*, The Warburg Institute, London, 1937.

Agostino 1587
Antonio Agostino, *Dialogos de Medallas, inscriciones y otras antiguedades*, Tarragona, 1587.

Armitage Robinson 1926
J. Armitage Robinson, *Two Glastonbury Legends, King Arthur and St Joseph of Arimathea*, Cambridge University Press, Cambridge, 1926.

Aubrey 1980–82
John Aubrey, *Monumenta Britannica*, ed. R. Legg and J. Fowles, Dorset Publishing Company, Kno-Na-Cre, Milborne Port, 1980–82.

Aufrère 1936
Louis Aufrère, *Essai sur les premières découvertes de Boucher de Perthes et les origines de l'archéologie primitive (1838–1844)*, L. Staude, Paris, 1936.

Aufrère 1990
Sydney H. Aufrère, *La Momie et la Tempête, Nicolas Claude Fabri de Peiresc et la mémoire égyptienne en Provence au début du XVIIème siècle*, Barthélemy, Avignon, 1990.

Bacon 1627
Francis Bacon, *Sylva Sylvarum or a Natural History in Ten Centuries*, London, 1627.

Bacon 1868
Francis Bacon, *Physical and Metaphysical Works including the Advancement of Learning and Novum Organum*, ed. Joseph Dewey, London 1868.

Beaune 1985
Colette Beaune, *Naissance de la nation France*, Gallimard, Paris, 1985.

Bercé 1986
Françoise Bercé, 'Arcisse de Caumont et les sociétés savantes', in P. Nora (ed.), *Les Lieux de mémoire*, II, 2, *La Nation*, Gallimard, Paris, 1986, pp. 533–94.

Berghaus 1983
Peter Berghaus (ed.), *Der Archäologe, Graphische Bildnisse aus dem Porträtarchiv Diepenbroick*, Landschaftsverband Westfalen-Lippe, Münster, 1983.

Bergier 1622
Nicolas Bergier, *Histoire des grands chemins de l'Empire romain*, Paris, 1622.

Bianchini 1697
Francesco Bianchini, *La istoria universale provata con monumenti e figurata con simboli*, Rome, 1697 (1747 edition).

Biedermann 1890
W. von Biedermann, *Goethes Gespräche, 7, 1829-1830*, Leipzig 1890.

Borges 1964
Jorge Luis Borges, 'The Wall and the Books', in *Other Inquisitions 1937-1952*, University of Texas Press, Austin, 1964.

Borges 1981
Jorge Luis Borges, 'Of Exactitude in Science', in *A Universal History of Infamy*, Penguin, Harmondsworth, 1981.

Borges 1985
Jorge Luis Borges, 'Tlön, Uqbar, Orbis Tertius', in *Fictions*, John Calder, London, 1985.

Boucher de Perthes 1847
Jacques Boucher de Perthes, *Antiquités celtiques et antédiluviennes, Mémoire sur l'industrie primitive et les arts à leur origine*, Treuttel et Würtz, Paris, 1847–64.

Boulanger 1756
Nicolas Antoine Boulanger, *L'Antiquité dévoilée par ses usages ou Examen critique des principales opinions, cérémonies et institutions religieuses et politiques des différents peuples de la terre*, Amsterdam, 1756.

Bourdier 1993
Marc Bourdier, 'Le Mythe et l'industrie ou la protection du patrimoine culturel au Japon', in *Genèses, Sciences sociales et Histoire*, no. 11, 1993, pp. 82–110.

Bouzek et al 1983
Jan Bouzek, Miroslav Buchvaldek, Philippos Kostomitsopoulos and Karel Sklenar, *Dejiny archeologie* (History of Archaeology), 2 volumes, Editions pédagogiques de l'Etat, Prague, 1983–4.

De Broglie 1891
Emmanuel de Broglie, *La Société de l'abbaye de Saint-Germain-des-Prés au XVIIIème siècle, Bernard de Montfaucon et les Bernardins*, Plon, Paris, 1891.

Browne 1658
Thomas Browne, *Hydriotaphia, Urn Buriall, or, A Discourse of the Sepulchrall Urnes lately found in Norfolk…*, London, 1658 (ed. F.L. Huntley Meredith, New York, 1966).

Bruno 1879
Giordano Bruno, *Opera Latina Conscripta*, F. Fiorentino *et al.*, Naples, 1879–91, I, 2.

Buckland 1823
William Buckland, *Reliquiae diluvianae*, John Murray, London, 1823.

Buffon 1776
G.L. Leclerc de Buffon, *Des époques de la nature*, vol. XXIX (1776) of *Histoire naturelle générale et particulière*, Paris, 1749–1804.

Cassin 1969
Elena Cassin, 'Cycles du temps et Cadres de l'espace en Mésopotamie ancienne', in *Revue de synthèse*, no. 56, 1969, pp. 242–7.

Caylus 1752
Anne Claude François de Caylus, *Recueil d'antiquités égyptiennes, étrusques, grecques et romaines*, 7 volumes, Paris, 1752–57.

Chang 1986
Kwang-chih Chang, *The Archaeology of Ancient China*, Yale University Press, New Haven and London, 1986 (4).

Chavannes 1967
Edouard Chavannes, *Les Mémoires historiques de Se-ma Ts'ien*, Librairie d'Amérique et d'Orient, Paris, 1967.

Cheng Yong and Li Tong 1983
Cheng Yong and Li Tong, 'Studies of the Mercury Interred in Qin Shi Huan's Tomb', in *KAOGU* (Archaeology), 7, 1983.

Cheynier 1936
André Cheynier, *Jouannet grand-père de la préhistoire*, Société archéologique du Périgord, Brive, 1936.

Chippindale 1983
Christopher Chippindale, *Stonehenge Complete*, Cornell University Press, Ithaca and London, 1983.

Clunas 1991
Craig Clunas, *Superfluous Things, Material Culture and Social Status in Early Modern China*, Polity Press, Cambridge, 1991.

Cohen and Hublin 1989
Claudine Cohen and Jean-Jacques Hublin, *Boucher de Perthes, 1788-1868 et les origines romantiques de la préhistoire*, Belin, Paris, 1989.

Colt Hoare 1810–12
Richard Colt Hoare, *The History of Ancient Wiltshire*, London, 1810–12.

Constantine 1984
David Constantine, *Early Greek Travellers and the Hellenic Ideal*, Cambridge University Press, Cambridge, 1984.

Cooper 1977
Richard Cooper, 'Rabelais and the *topographia antiquae Romae* of Marliano', in *Travaux d'humanisme et de Renaissance*, CLXII, Droz, Geneva, 1977, pp. 71–87.

Cooper 1988
Richard Cooper, 'Humanistes et antiquaires à Lyon', in *Il Rinascimento a Lione, Atti del Congresso internazionale*, Edizioni dell'Ateneo, Rome, 1988, pp. 161–74.

Cuvier 1801
Georges Cuvier, 'Extrait d'un ouvrage sur les espèces de quadrupèdes dont on a trouvé les ossements dans l'intérieur de la terre…', in *Journal de physique*, 1801, LII, pp. 253–7.

Cuvier 1841
Georges Cuvier, *Histoire des sciences naturelles, depuis leur origine jusqu'à nos jours, chez tous les peuples connus*, Fortin, Paris, 1841.

Daniel 1978
Glyn Daniel, *150 Years of Archaeology*, Duckworth, London, 1978.

Daniel 1981
Glyn Daniel, *Towards a History of Archaeology*, Thames and Hudson, London, 1981.

Daniel and Renfrew 1986
Glyn Daniel and Colin Renfrew, *The Idea of Prehistory*, Edinburgh University Press, 1986.

Darwin 1887
Francis Darwin (ed.), *The Life and Letters of Charles Darwin, Including an Autobiographical Chapter*, John Murray, London, 1887.

Dombrovski 1979
Yuri Dombrovski, *Le Conservateur des antiquités*, Julliard, Paris, 1979.

Dubois 1972
Claude Gilbert Dubois, *Celtes et Gaulois au XVIème siècle: le développement littéraire d'un mythe nationaliste*, Vrin, Paris, 1972.

Esper 1774
J.F. Esper, *Description des zoolithes nouvellement découverts d'animaux quadrupèdes inconnus et des cavernes qui les renferment dans le margraviat de Bayreuth au-delà des monts*, trans. J. F. Isenflamm, Nuremburg, 1774.

Etienne 1992
Roland and Françoise Etienne, *The Search for Ancient Greece*, Thames and Hudson, London and Abrams, New York, 1992.

Finley 1975
M.I. Finley, *The Use and Abuse of History*, Chatto and Windus, London, 1975.

Franz 1945
Leonhard Franz, *Goethe und die Urzeit*, Innsbruck
Universitätsverlag, Wagner, 1945.

Frere 1800
John Frere, 'Account of Flint Weapons Discovered at
Hoxne in Suffolk', in *Archaeologia 13*, 1800, pp. 204–5.

Gaehtgens 1986
Thomas W. Gaehtgens (ed.), *Johann Joachim
Winckelmann 1717-1768*, Meiner, Hamburg, 1986.

Garanger 1980
José Garanger, 'Tradition orale et Préhistoire en
Océanie', in A. Schnapp (ed.), *L'Archéologie
aujourd'hui*, Hachette, Paris, 1980, pp. 187–205.

Gassendi 1641
Pierre Gassendi, *Viri illustris Nicolai Claudii Fabricii de
Peiresc Senatoris Aquisextiensis Vita*, Paris, 1641.

Gayrard-Valy 1987
Yvette Gayrard-Valy, *Les Fossiles, empreintes d'un
monde disparu*, Gallimard, Paris, 1987.

Gerhard 1850
Eduard Gerhard, 'Archäologische Thesen', in
Archäologischer Anzeiger zur Archäologischen Zeitung,
VIII, 1850, pp. 203–6.

Glassner 1993
Jean-Jacques Glassner (ed. and trans.), *Chroniques
mésopotamiennes*, Les Belles Lettres, Paris, 1993.

Goethe 1832
Johann Wolfgang von Goethe, *Principes de philosophie
zoologique. Discutés en mars 1830 au sein de l'Académie
royale des sciences par Mr. Geoffroy Saint-Hilaire*, Paris
1832; 1868–79 in *Werke*, 34, Hempel, Berlin,
pp. 146–74.

Gohau 1990
Gabriel Gohau, *Les Sciences de la terre aux XVIIème et
XVIIIème siècles, naissance de la géologie*, Albin Michel,
Paris, 1990.

Golzio 1936
Vicenzo Golzio, *Raffaello nei documenti, nelle
testimonianze dei contemporanei e nella letteratura del suo
secolo*, Vatican City, 1936.

Gould 1990
Stephen Jay Gould, *Time's Arrow, Time's Cycle*,
Penguin, Harmondsworth, 1988.

Graevius 1694
Johann Georg Graevius, *Thesaurus antiquitatum
romanarum*, 12 volumes, Utrecht, 1694–9.

Grafton 1993
Anthony Grafton, *Rome Reborn, The Vatican Library
and Renaissance Culture*, Library of Congress,
Washington, 1993.

Gräslund 1987
Bo Gräslund, *The Birth of Prehistoric Chronology,
Dating Methods and Dating Systems in Nineteenth-
Century Scandinavian Archaeology*, Cambridge
University Press, Cambridge, 1987.

Grayson 1983
Donald K. Grayson, *The Establishment of Human
Antiquity*, Academic Press, New York, 1983.

Grignon 1774
Pierre Clément Grignon, *Bultin [sic] des fouilles faites
par ordre du roi, d'une ville romaine, sur la petite montagne
du chatelet, entre Saint Dizier et Joinville en Champagne*,
Bar-le-Duc, 1774.

Gronovius 1694–1703
Jacob Gronovius, *Thesaurus antiquitatum graecorum*,
13 volumes, Leiden, 1694–1703.

Guibert de Nogent 1981
Guibert de Nogent, *De vita sua*, ed. and trans.
E.R. Labande, Paris, 1981.

Gummel 1938
Hans Gummel, *Forschungsgeschichte in Deutschland, Die
Urgeschichtsforschung und Ihre Historische Entwicklung in
der Kulturstaaten der Erde, herausgegeben von Karl
Hermann Jacob-Friesen*, Walter de Gruyter, Berlin,
1938.

Guzzo 1993
Pier Giovanni Guzzo, *Antico e archeologia, scienza e
politica delle diverse antichità*, Nuova Alfa Editoriale,
Bologna, 1993.

Hamy 1906
Théodore Hamy, 'Matériaux pour servir à l'histoire
de l'archéologie préhistorique', in *Revue archéologique*,
1906, I, pp. 239–59 and II, pp. 37–48.

Hansen 1967
G.C. Hansen, 'Ausgrabungen im Altertum',
Das Altertum, 13, 1967, pp. 44–50.

Hazard 1961
Paul Hazard, *La Crise de la conscience européenne*,
Fayard, Paris, 1961.

Herbst 1848
C.F. Herbst, *Hvidegaards Fundet, Annaler for nordisk
Oldkyndighed*, 1848, p. 336.

Heeren-Diekhoff 1981
Elae Heeren-Diekhoff, *Das Hsi Ching Tsa Chi
(Vermischte Aufzeichnungen über die westliche
Hauptstadt)*, Munich, 1981.

Hildebrandt 1937
Bengt Hildebrandt, *C.J. Thomsen och hans lärda
förbindelser i Sverige 1816-1837, bidrag till den Nordiska
forn-och Hävdaforskningens Historia* [C.J. Thomsen and
his scholarly reports in Sweden, 1816–37.
Contribution to the history of archaeology and
research], 2 volumes, Stockholm 1937.

Hilprecht 1903
H.U. Hilprecht 1903, *Explorations in the Bible Lands*,
Philadelphia, 1903.

Hohenheim 1929
Theophrast von Hohenheim (Paracelsus), *Sämtliche
Werke*, I, 12, Karl Sudhoff, Berlin, 1929.

Holtzhauer 1969
Helmut Holzhauer, *J.W. Goethe, Winckelmann und sein
Jahrhundert (1805), Briefen und Aufsätzen*, Tübingen,
1969.

Hooke 1705
Robert Hooke, *The Posthumous Work of Thomas
Hooke*, ed. R. Waller, London, 1705.

Hotman 1583
François Hotman, *Franco-Gallia*, Paris, 1583.

Hunter 1975
Michael Hunter, *John Aubrey and the Realm of Learning*, Duckworth, London, 1975.

Huppert 1970
George Huppert, *The Idea of Perfect History: Historical Erudition and Historical Philosophy in Renaissance France*, University of Illinois Press, 1970.

Jacoby 1957
Felix Jacoby, *Die Fragmente der griechischer Historiker - erster Teil, Genealogie und Mythographie*, Brill, Leiden, 1957.

Jaffé 1988
David Jaffé, *Rubens' Self-portrait in Focus*, Australian National Gallery, Canberra, 1988.

Kendrick 1950
T.D. Kendrick, *British Antiquity*, Methuen, London, 1950.

King 1912
L.W. King (ed.), *Babylonian Boundary Stones*, London, 1912.

Klindt-Jensen 1975
Ole Klindt-Jensen, *A History of Scandinavian Archaeology*, Thames and Hudson, London, 1975

Klindt-Jensen 1981
Ole Klindt-Jensen, 'Archaeology and Ethnography in Denmark: early studies', in G. Daniel, 1981, pp. 14–19.

Kühn 1976
Herbert Kühn, *Geschichte der Vorgeschichtsforschung*, Walter de Gruyter, Berlin and New York, 1976.

Kunst 1982
Michael Kunst, 'Intellektuelle Information – genetische Information, zur Fragen der Typologie und typologischen Methode', in *Acta Praehistorica et archaeologica*, 13–14, 1982, pp. 1–26.

Lackenbacher 1990
Sylvie Lackenbacher, *Le Palais sans rival*, La Découverte, Paris, 1990.

Laming-Emperaire 1964
Annette Laming-Emperaire, *Origines de l'archéologie préhistorique en France*, Picard, Paris, 1964.

Lanciani 1902
Rodolfo Lanciani, *Storia degli scavi di Roma*, Rome, 1902.

Lapeyrère 1656
Isaac de Lapeyrère, *Men Before Adam*, London, 1656.

Lapeyrère 1732
Isaac de Lapeyrère, *An Account of Greenland*, London, 1732.

La Sauvagère 1758
Félix de La Sauvagère, *Dissertations militaires extraites du journal historique de la France*, Amsterdam, 1758.

Le Gall 1973
Joël Le Gall, Ernest de Saint-Denis and Raymond Weil, *Alésia, textes littéraires antiques*, Aubier, Paris, 1973.

Legrand 1897
P.E. Legrand, 'Biographie de C.F. Sebastien Fauvel', in *Revue archéologique*, 1897, pp. 41–66 and 185–201.

Legrand d'Aussy 1799
Pierre Legrand d'Aussy, *Mémoire sur les anciennes sépultures nationales*, Paris, 1799.

Leibniz 1717
G.W. Leibniz, *Collectanea Etymologica cum praefatione Jo. Georgi*, Eccardi, II, Hanover, 1717.

Lepenies 1976
Wolf Lepenies, *Das Ende der Naturgeschichte, Wandelkultureller Selbstverständlichkeiten in den Wissenschaften des 18. und 19. Jahrhunderts*, Hanser Verlag, Munich and Vienna, 1976.

Lepenies 1984
Wolf Lepenies, 'Der andere Fanatiker. Historisierung und Verwissenschaftlichung der Kunstauffassung bei J.J. Winckelmann', in *Ideal und Wirklichkeit der bildenden Kunst im späten 18. Jahrhundert*, ed. H. Beck, Gebrüder Mann Verlag, Berlin, 1984, pp. 19–29.

Lepenies 1986
Wolf Lepenies, 'Kunst und Naturgeschichte im 18. Jahrhundert', in Gaethgens, 1986, pp. 221–38.

Levy 1964
F.J. Levy, *The Making of Camden's Britannia*, Bibliothèque d'humanisme et de Renaissance, 26, 1964, pp. 70–97.

Long 1888
W.H. Long (ed.), *Oglander Memoirs*, London, 1888.

Lowenthal 1985
David Lowenthal, *The Past is a Foreign Country*, Cambridge University Press, Cambridge, 1985.

Magnus 1567
Olaus Magnus, *Historia de gentibus septentrionalitus*, Basle, 1567.

Maimonides 1970
Moïse ben Maimoun, called Maimonides, *Le Guide des égarés*, trans. S. Munk, Maisonneuve et Larose, Paris, 1970.

Mandowsky 1963
E. Mandowsky and C. Mitchell, *Pirro Ligorio's Roman Antiquities*, The Warburg Institute, London, 1963.

Marana 1748
Giovanni Paolo Marana, *The Eight Volumes of Letters Writ by a Turkish Spy, who Lived Five and Forty Years Undiscovered at Paris*, trans. William Bradshaw, London, 1748.

Marsden 1983
Barry M. Marsden, *Pioneers of Prehistory, Leaders and Landmarks in English Archaeology (1500-1900)*, Heskett, Ormskirk, 1983.

Martin 1727
Jacques Martin, *La Religion des Gaulois tirée des plus pures sources de l'Antiquité*, Paris, 1727.

Mazzarino 1989
Santo Mazzarino, *Fra oriente e occidente, Ricerche di storia greca arcaica*, Rizzoli, Milan, 1989.

Mémoires 1779
Mémoires concernant l'histoire, les sciences, les arts, les mœurs, les usages, etc. des Chinois par les missionnaires de Pékin, volume IV, Paris, 1779.

Ménage 1694
Gilles Ménage, *Gilles Ménage ou les bons mots, les pensées critiques de M. Ménage*, 2 volumes, Paris, 1694.

Mennung 1925
Albert Mennung, *Über die Vorstufen der prähistorischen Wissenschaft im Altertum und Mittelalter*, Schönebeck (Elbe), 1925.

Mercati 1719
Michele Mercati, *Metallotheca Vaticana, opus posthumum*, Rome, 1719.

Michelet 1959
Jules Michelet, *Journal*, volume I, 1828–48, year 1831, ed. P. Viallaneix, Paris, 1959.

Michell 1982
John Michell, *Megalithomania. Artists, Antiquarians and Archaeologists at the Old Stone Monuments*, Thames and Hudson, London, 1982.

Momigliano 1983
Arnaldo Momigliano, 'L'histoire ancienne et l'antiquaire', in *Problèmes d'historiographie ancienne et moderne*, Gallimard, Paris, 1983, pp. 244–93.

Mongez 1812–17
Antoine Mongez, *Mémoires sur les pierres tranchantes trouvées dans les sépultures anciennes*, Histoire et Mémoires de l'Académie royale de France, 5, 1812–17, pp. 70–1.

Montelius 1903
Oscar Montelius, *Die typologische Methode. Die älteren Kulturperioden im Orient und in Europa*, Stockholm, 1903.

Montfaucon 1719
Bernard de Montfaucon, *L'Antiquité expliquée et représentée en figures*, 15 volumes, Paris, 1719–24.

Morrisson 1981
Cécile Morrisson, 'La découverte des trésors à l'époque byzantine', in *Travaux et Mémoires*, no. 8, 1981, pp. 321–44.

Mortet 1911
Victor Mortet, *Recueil de textes relatifs à l'histoire de l'architecture et à la condition des architectes en France au Moyen Age*, A. Picard, Paris, 1911.

Mortillet 1872
Gabriel de Mortillet, 'Classification des diverses périodes de l'âge de la pierre', in *Revue d'anthropologie*, 1872, pp. 432–5.

Müller 1886
Sophus Müller, 'Mindre Bidrag til den forhistoriske Archaeologis Methode', in *Aarbøger*, 1886, p. 161.

Münster 1552
Sebastian Münster, *Cosmographiae universalis*, lib. VI, 1552.

Nisard 1878
C. Nisard, *Correspondance inédite du comte de Caylus avec le père Paciau, théatin, suivie de celle de l'abbé Barthélemy et de P. Mouette avec le même*, Paris, 1878.

Nora 1984
Pierre Nora, *Les Lieux de mémoire*, 7 volumes, Gallimard, Paris, 1984–92.

Olender 1989
Maurice Olender, *Les Langues du Paradis. Aryens et Sémites, un couple providentiel*, Gallimard-Le Seuil, Paris, 1989.

Owen 1986
Stephen Owen, *Remembrances, the Experience of the Past in Classical Chinese Literature*, Harvard University Press, Cambridge, Mass., 1986.

Petri 1917
Olaus Petri, 'En Swensk Crönecka', in *Samlade Skrifter af Olavus Petri IV*, ed. J. Sahlgren, Uppsala, 1917.

Piccolomini 1551
Aeneas Silvius Piccolomini, *Opera quae extant*, Basle, 1551.

Piggott 1976
Stuart Piggott, *Ruins in a Landscape, Essays in Antiquarianism*, Edinburgh University Press, Edinburgh, 1976.

Piggott 1985
Stuart Piggot, *William Stukeley*, Thames and Hudson, London, 1985.

Piggott 1989
Stuart Piggott, *Ancient Britons and the Antiquarian Imagination, Ideas from the Renaissance to the Regency*, Thames and Hudson, London, 1989.

Pinon 1991
Pierre Pinon, *La Gaule retrouvée*, Gallimard, Paris, 1991.

Pintard 1983
René Pintard, *Le Libertinage érudit dans la première moitié du XVIIème siècle*, Slatkine, Geneva, 1983.

Pitt-Rivers 1868
A.H.L. Fox Pitt-Rivers, 'Primitive Warfare Part II', in *Journal of the Ethnological Society of London*, new series, 1868, I, pp. 1–12.

Pitt-Rivers 1874
A.H.L. Fox Pitt-Rivers, 'On the Principles of Classification Adopted in the Arrangement of his Anthropological Collection, now Exhibited in the Bethnal Green Museum', in *Journal of the Anthropological Institute*, 1874, 4, pp. 293–308.

Pitt-Rivers 1875
A.H.L. Fox Pitt-Rivers, 'On the Evolution of Culture', in *Proceedings of the Royal Institute of Great Britain*, 1875, 7, pp. 496–514.

Plot 1677
Robert Plot, *The Natural History of Oxford-shire*, Oxford, 1677.

Plot 1686
Robert Plot, *The Natural History of Stafford-shire*, Oxford, 1686.

Pomian 1984
Krzysztof Pomian, *L'Ordre du temps*, Gallimard, Paris, 1984.

Pomian 1987
Krzysztof Pomian, *Collectionneurs, amateurs et curieux, Paris-Venise XVIème-XVIIIème siècle*, Gallimard, Paris, 1987.

Popkin 1987
R.H. Popkin, *Isaac de Lapeyrère*, Brill, Leiden, 1987.

Ramus 1587
Petrus Ramus, *Traité de l'art militaire ou usance de guerre chez J. César*, Paris, 1587.

Reiner 1985
Erica Reiner, *Your thwarts in pieces, Your moorin' rope cut, Poetry from Babylonia and Assyria*, University of Michigan, Ann Arbor, 1985.

Reinsch 1983
D.R. Reinsch, *Critobuli Imbriotae Historia*, Walter de Gruyter, Berlin, 1983.

Rhode 1719
Andreas Albert Rhode, *Cimbrisch-Holsteinische Antiquitæten Remarques*, Hamburg, 1719.

Richard 1991
Nathalie Richard, *La Préhistoire en France dans la seconde moitié du XIXème siècle*, thesis, Paris, 1991.

Richard 1992
Nathalie Richard, *L'Invention de la préhistoire, une anthologie*, Presses Pocket, Paris, 1992.

Ridé 1977
Jacques Ridé, *L'Image du Germain dans la pensée et la littérature allemande de la redécouverte de Tacite à la fin du XVIème siècle*, 3 volumes, Champion, Paris, 1977.

Rocheblave 1889
Samuel Rocheblave, *Essai sur le comte de Caylus*, Hachette, Paris, 1889.

Rodden 1981
Judith Rodden, 'The development of the Three Age System: Archaeology's first paradigm', in G. Daniel, 1981, pp. 51–68.

Rodocanachi 1914
Emmanuel Rodocanachi, *Les Monuments de Rome après la chute de l'Empire*, Hachette, Paris, 1914.

Rossi 1984
Paolo Rossi, *The Dark Abyss of Time. The History of the Earth and the History of Nations from Hooke to Vico*, The University of Chicago Press, Chicago-London, 1984.

Rudbeck 1937
Olof Rudbeck, *Atland eller Manheim*, ed. A. Nelson, Uppsala, 1937.

Rudolph 1962–3
R.C. Rudolph, 'Preliminary Notes on Sung Archaeology', in *Journal of Asian Studies* 22, 1962–3, fascicule 2, pp. 169–77.

Saxo Grammaticus 1911
Saxo Grammaticus, *Sakses Danesage*, Copenhagen, 1911.

Schlosser 1908
Julius von Schlosser, *Die Kunst und Wunderkammern der Spätrenaissance*, Leipzig, 1908.

Schnapper 1988
Antoine Schnapper, *Le Géant, la Licorne et la Tulipe, collections françaises au XVIIème siècle*, Flammarion, Paris, 1988.

Schück 1932
H. Schück, *Kgl Vitterhets, Historie och Antikvitets Akademien I-VIII*, Stockholm, 1932.

Settis 1984
Salvatore Settis (ed.), *Memoria dell'antico nell'arte italiana*, 3 volumes, Einaudi, Rome, 1984–6.

Shaugnessy 1991
Edward Shaugnessy, *Sources of Western Zhou History*, University of California Press, Berkeley, 1991.

Sigaut 1990
François Sigaut, 'De la technologie à l'évolutionnisme, l'œuvre de Pitt-Rivers', in *Gradhiva*, 8, 1990, pp. 20–37.

Sklenar 1983
Karel Sklenar, *Archaeology in Central Europe: the First 500 Years*, Leicester University Press, Leicester, New York, 1983.

Slotkin 1965
J.S. Slotkin, *Readings in Early Anthropology*, London, 1965.

Snodgrass 1987
Anthony Snodgrass, 'The Landscape of Ancient Greece', in *An Archeology of Greece*, University of California Press, Berkeley, 1987, pp. 67–92.

Sollberger 1967
E. Sollberger, *Lost Inscriptions from Mari - La civilisation de Mari, XVème rencontre assyriologique internationale*, Liège, 1967, pp. 103–8.

Soucek 1974
Priscilla Soucek, *Farhàd and Taq-Ibustan, the Growth of a Legend, Studies in Art and Literature of the Near East in Honor of Richard Ettinghausen*, The Middle East Center, 1974.

Spanheim 1664
Ezechiel Spanheim, *Dissertatio de praestantia et usu numismatum antiquorum*, Rome, 1664.

Spon 1673
Jacob Spon, *Recherche des Antiquités et Curiosités de la ville de Lyon*, Lyons, 1673.

Stark 1880
Carl Bernhard Stark, *Systematik und Geschichte der Archäologie der Kunst*, Leipzig, 1880 (Anastatique Fink, Munich, 1969).

Stemmermann 1934
P.H. Stemmermann, *Die Anfänge der deutschen Vorgeschichtsforschung. Deutschlands Bodenaltertümer in der Anschauung des 16ten und 17ten Jahrhundert*, dissertation, Heidelberg, 1934.

Stoczkowski 1993
Wiktor Stoczkowski, 'La préhistoire, les origines du

concept', *Bulletin de la Société Préhistorique Française*, 1993, 90, 1–2, pp. 13–21.

Stoczkowski 1993
Wiktor Stoczkowski, 'Origines de l'homme, quand la science répète le mythe', in *La Recherche*, 1992, 244, pp. 746–50.

Stubbs 1865
William Stubbs, *Gesta Henrici II et Ricardi I*, 1865.

Stukeley 1740
William Stukeley, *Stonehenge, A Temple Restored to the British Druids*, London, 1740.

Svenbro 1976
Jesper Svenbro, *La Parole et le Marbre, aux origines de la poétique grecque*, dissertation, Lund, 1976.

Svennung 1967
J. Svennung, *Zur Geschichte des Goticismus*, Almqvist and Wiksell, Stockholm, 1967.

Swozilek 1987
Helmut Swozilek, *Motiv Archäologie - Archäologische Motive in der Kunst (insbesondere Ur- und Frühgeschichte)*, Bregenz, 1987.

Taillepied 1585
Noël Taillepied, *Histoire de l'Etat et de la République des Druides*, Paris, 1585.

Tallgren 1936
A.M. Tallgren, 'Sur la méthode de l'archéologie préhistorique', in *Eurasia Septentrionalis Antiqua*, 1936, X, pp. 16–24.

Taylor 1948
F.H. Taylor, *The Taste of Angels, a History of Art Collecting from Rameses to Napoleon*, Boston, 1948.

Thierry 1993
François Thierry, 'Sur les monnaies sassanides trouvées en Chine', *Res orientales*, volume V, 1993, pp. 89–139.

Thomsen 1836
Ledetraad til Nordisk Oldkyndighed, Cophenhagen, 1836, (German trans., *Leitfaden für nordische Altertumskunde*, Hamburg, 1837).

Tournal 1834
P. Tournal, *Annales de Sciences naturelles*, 1834.

Trigger 1989
Bruce G. Trigger, *A History of Archaeological Thought*, Cambridge University Press, Cambridge, 1989.

Twitchett 1992
Denis Twitchett, *The Writing of Official History Under the T'ong*, Cambridge University Press, Cambridge, 1992.

Unger 1927
Eckard Unger, *Assyrische und Babylonische Kunst*, Breslau, 1927.

Unger 1931
Eckard Unger, *Babylon die Heilige Stadt nach der Beschreibung der Babylonier*, De Gruyter, Berlin, 1931.

Vacca 1704
Flaminio Vacca, *Memorie di varie antichità trovateci in diversi luoghi della città di Roma, scritti da Flaminio Vacca nell'anno 1594*, Rome, 1704.

Verelius 1664
O. Verelius, *Gothrici et Rolfi Westrogothicae regum*, Uppsala, 1664.

Wataghin 1984
Gisela Cantino Wataghin, 'Archeologia e "archeologie". Il rapporto con l'antico fra mito, arte e ricerca', in *Settis*, 1984, volume I, pp. 171–221.

Weickert 1955
Karl Weickert, 'Geschichte des D.A.I.', *Archäologischer Anzeiger*, 1955, pp. 127–56.

Weiss 1988
Roberto Weiss, *The Renaissance Discovery of Classical Antiquity*, Blackwell, Oxford, 1988, 2nd edn.

Willey and Sabloff 1980
Gordon R. Willey and Jeremy A. Sabloff, *A History of American Archaeology*, Thames and Hudson, London, 1980, 2nd edn.

Winckelmann 1880
Johann Joachim Winckelmann, *The History of Ancient Art Among the Greeks*, trans. G. Henry Lodge, James R. Osgood and Company, Boston, 1880.

Worm 1643
Ole Worm, *Danicorum Monumentorum libri sex*, Copenhagen, 1643.

Worm 1751
Ole Worm, *Olai Wormi et ad eum doctorum virorum epistolae*, Copenhagen, 1751.

Wright 1844
Thomas Wright, 'On Antiquarian Excavations and Researches in the Middle Ages', *Archaeologia*, XXX, 1844, pp. 438–57.

Zappert 1850
Georg Zappert, *Über Antiquitätenfunde im Mittelalter, Sitzungsberichte der Kaiserlichen Akademie der Wissenschaften, Philosophische-Historische Classe V*, Vienna, 1850, pp. 753–99.

Zevi 1987
Fausto Zevi, 'Gli scavi di Ercolano e le antichità', in *Le antichità di Ercolano*, Guida, Naples, pp. 9–38.

PHOTOGRAPHIC
ACKNOWLEDGEMENTS

Alinari–Anderson–Giraudon: 106
Alinari–Brogi–Giraudon: 107
Alinari–Giraudon: 103(t)
Antikvarisk-topografiska arkivet, Stockholm: 299
Archives Casterman, Paris: 14
Archivio di Stato, Turin: 127(b)
Artothek: 91, 292
Australian National Gallery, Canberra: 132
Bayerische Staatsbibliothek, Munich: 100, 262
Bérard C.: 52, 53
Biblioteca Apostolica Vaticana: 56(t), 58, 108, 115
Biblioteca Hertziana, Rome: 40
Biblioteca Nazionale Centrale, Florence: 26
Bibliothèque d'Art et d'Archéologie, Paris: 285
Bibliothèque du Muséum national d'histoire naturelle,
    Paris: 270, 271
Bibliothèque humaniste, Sélestat: 92
Bibliothèque municipale, Rennes: 254, 255
Bibliothèque nationale, Paris: 16, 28, 29, 35, 36, 42, 43, 55,
    60, 66, 67, 69, 72, 73, 75, 77, 81, 82, 88, 95–7, 111, 118,
    120, 127(t), 135, 137, 144–6, 154, 155, 157, 161(b), 164,
    169, 171–3, 175, 176, 180, 182–5, 189, 192, 195, 197,
    198, 200–203, 207(l), 220, 223, 231, 232, 239–44,
    247–53, 257, 258, 259(b), 261, 264, 265, 269, 280, 286–9,
    294–7, 300, 308, 312, 313, 341, 343, 346, 362, 370
Bibliothèque royale Albert-1er, Bruxelles: 38, 86, 87
Bibliothèque Sainte-Geneviève/Studio Ethel: 123
Bibliothèque universitaire, Basle: 148
Bildarchiv Preussischer Kulturbesitz, Berlin: 125
Bildarchiv Preussischer Kulturbesitz,
    Berlin/Jörg P. Anders: 264-5
Bodleian Library, Oxford: 114, 139, 178, 191, 193, 194,
    214–18
British Library, London: 12, 99, 112, 113, 150, 151, 213, 281
John Chadwick, *Linear B and Related Scripts*, British Museum
    Publications, 1987, fig.1
CNHMS/SPADEM, Paris: 102, 103(b)
Master and Fellows of Corpus Christi College,
    Cambridge: 94
Dagli Orti: 23, 44, 46, 50
Edimedia: 314
Frans Hals Museum, Haarlem: 131

Garanger J.: 24
J. Paul Getty Museum, Malibu: 136
Giraudon: 90, 93
Huot J-L.: 17
Istituto Archeologico Germanico, Rome: 59, 306, 307
Kunsthalle, Hamburg/Elke Walford: 278
Kunsthistorisches Museum, Vienna: 130
Landesmuseum, Oldenburg/H. R. Wacker: 274
Christian Larrieu/La Licorne: 305
Lauros-Giraudon: 290
Metropolitan Museum of Art, New York: 71
Museé Guimet 75(t)
Museum Carolino Augusteum, Salzburg: 311
Museum für Kunsthandwerk, Frankfurt: 147(l)
Museum für Kunst und Gewerbe, Hamburg: 147(r)
Narodni Galerie, Prague: 124
National Gallery of Canada, Ottawa: 10
Niedersächsische Staats- und Universitätsbibliothek,
    Göttingen: 207(r), 211(b)
Peale Museum, Baltimore: 272
Pierpont Morgan Library, New York: 348
Pix: 20, 21(t), 49
Private collections: 15, 21(b), 25, 31, 32, 34, 48, 57, 62, 63,
    75(b), 78, 109, 110(r), 126, 128, 129, 158, 159, 166, 167,
    186–8, 205, 206, 208, 209, 211, 236, 237, 257, 268, 301,
    316, 337, 357
Réunion des musées nationaux, Paris: 41, 56(b), 89, 133,
    227, 263
Royal Institute of British Architects, London: 259(t)
Royal Library, Copenhagen: 152, 153, 161t
Saint Louis Art Museum, Saint Louis: 276
Scala: 84, 101, 116, 117
Society of Antiquaries, London: 282
Staats- und Stadtbibliothek, Augsburg: 110(l)
Staats- und Universitätsbibliothek, Hamburg: 291
University Library, Cambridge: 142, 143
Vatican Museums and Galleries: 47
Wiltshire Archaeological and Natural History Society,
    Devizes: 283
Württembergische Landesbibliothek, Stuttgart: 149
Yorkshire Museum, York: 98